RULE BY SECRECY

ALSO BY JIM MARRS

Alien Agenda

Crossfire

RULE
BY
SECRECY

The Hidden History That Connects the Trilateral Commission,
the Freemasons, and the Great Pyramids

JIM MARRS

WILLIAM MORROW
An Imprint of HarperCollins*Publishers*

A hardcover edition of this book was published in 2000 by Harper-Collins Publishers.

HarperCollins books may be purchased for educational, business, or sales promotional use. For information please write: Special Markets Department, HarperCollins Publishers Inc., 10 East 53rd Street, New York, NY 10022.

First Perennial edition published 2001.

Designed by Carla Bolte

The Library of Congress has catalogued the hardcover edition as follows:
Marrs, Jim
    Rule by secrecy: the hidden history that connects the Trilateral Commission, the Freemasons, and the Great Pyramids/by Jim Marrs.
        p. cm.
    Includes bibliographical references and index.
    ISBN 0-06-019368-9
    1. United States—Foreign relations—1945–1989. 2. United States—Foreign relations—1989– . 3. Conspiracies—United States. 4. Secret societies—United States. 5. Trilateral Commission. 6. Council on Foreign Relations. I.Title
E 840 .M362000   99-056174
366'.0973—dc21

ISBN 0–06–093184–1 (pbk.)

12 13 ❖/RRD 40 39 38 37 36 35 34 33 32

CONTENTS

INTRODUCTION

*The world is governed by very different personages from
what is imagined by those who are not behind the scenes.*

—BENJAMIN DISRAELI

Be forewarned.

If you are perfectly comfortable and satisfied with your own particular view of humankind, religion, history, and the world, read no further.

If you truly believe that humanity has almost reached the peak of its scientific and spiritual fulfillment and that the corporate-owned mass media is keeping you well enough informed, stop here.

But if you are one of those millions who look at the daily news, scratch your head in wonder, and ask, "What in the world is going on?," or if you entertain questions of who we are, where we came from, and where we're all going, you are in for a joy ride.

This book deals with the secrets of government, hidden history, and clandestine religion; the secrets of wealth, power, and control; the secrets rarely recorded in the history books and never mentioned in the mass media. This material may be disturbing and unsettling to some. But no one has ever gained wisdom by studying material that only reinforced their own predetermined ideas.

Addressed here will be issues many would have us believe occupy only the fringe of knowledge. But how often have fringe issues suddenly become areas of major concern? Older readers might recall that irritating but seemingly inconsequential German radical who gained power in Europe in the 1930s. Then there was that small conflict halfway around the world in an obscure place called Vietnam. Or we might remember that little-noticed burglary of Democratic Party headquarters in 1972.

The book also deals with conspiracy, an activity long decried by the major media despite the fact that the American judicial system regularly convicts people for criminal conspiracy.

Do secret societies truly exist? Is there really a secret government? Is there a worldwide conspiracy bent on the subversion of freedom and democracy? Or is such talk just the irrational ramblings of "conspiracy theorists"?

The answer all depends to whom you choose to listen. And too many people writing about conspiracy—on both sides of the question—have their own particular agenda. It is time we step back and take the broader view of our world and its history.

As the new millennium begins, the American public is becoming more aware of one not-so-secret conspiracy: that for half the year they work for the government. About the first six months of any given year is spent making money which disappears into taxes before the worker even gets his or her check. Withholding this invisible tax money has, over the years, caused most citizens to forget just how much tax burden they really carry. And this is not to even mention the daily sales, state, city, and other taxes which openly burden us. The simple British tax on tea said to have precipitated the American Revolution was a pittance by comparison.

Despite assurances of a healthy economy by the skewed statistics of the mass media and politicians, polls indicate the public feel an increasing uneasiness about the direction of our national life.

This may be why more and more thoughtful people are taking a serious look at conspiracies and the secret groups that spawn them. The Internet is filled with Web sites and chat rooms where conspiracy is the watchword. More and more books and periodicals are being published filled with conspiracies ranging from the secrets of the Crusaders to the JFK assassination.

Yet despite the length and breadth of the Information Highway, the average American remains woefully ignorant. That is not to imply they are stupid or mentally challenged. They have simply not been exposed to the information now available. Many thoughtful, educated people in a variety of fields—physicians, lawyers, computer experts, stock brokers, accountants, bankers, merchants, scientists, teachers, etc.—are totally in the dark about a wide variety of issues and the connections between them concerning who *truly* rules the United States.

Primary causes for such ignorance are the lack of time to educate ourselves and our reliance on a corporate-owned mass media which does not present the information in all its broadest implications. As A. J. Liebling once said, freedom of the press is for those who own the presses . . . or the radio and TV stations.

So how does one know what is true and what is not? What is important and what is trivial? Who is really in charge? Are there ongoing conspiracies that affect us all? Are there plots that can be traced back through mankind's history? What are they and what is their purpose?

This book deals with these questions. But before there can be answers, the issue of conspiracy must be addressed.

A QUESTION OF CONSPIRACY

The concept of conspiracy has long been anathema to most Americans, who have been conditioned by the mass media to believe that conspiracies against the public only exist in banana republics or communist nations.

This simplistic view, encouraged by a media devoted to maintaining a squeaky-clean image of the status quo, fails to take into account human history or the subtleties of the word conspiracy.

The word is derived from the Latin *conspirare,* literally meaning to breathe together, to act or think in harmony. In modern times, conspiracy has taken on a sinister connotation. Most dictionaries now offer two definitions of the word: 1. To plan together secretly, especially to commit an illegal or evil act, or 2. To plan or plot secretly. One definition is vile, the other less so.

Secrecy is the connecting tissue found throughout man's past. There are secrets between individuals and groups as well as secrets to be kept by both church and government authorities. There are political secrets, even secrets of finance and commerce.

Obviously, a conspiracy among coworkers to buy the boss a present is not the same level of conspiracy as bank robbers scheming their next job. Likewise, the small merchant who keeps his business plan secret from his competitors is not participating in a conspiracy equal to corporate leaders plotting to fix prices.

The key to an evil conspiracy is the intent of the secrecy.

While some secrets may be benign—why spoil the surprise birthday party by telling?—other secrets, such as suppressing cures for cancer or AIDS or fomenting war, would be considered despicable by people of conscience. Those secrets that cost or ruin lives, that prevent people from living together in harmony, and are used for control or undue profit are unacceptable to most people. Therefore, whoever conspires to keep such secrets must be carefully scrutinized by everyone concerned with individual freedom.

Columnist Stewart Alsop once wrote, knowledge is power, and power is the most valuable commodity in government. So whoever knows the secrets controls the knowledge and therefore holds power. Many people today feel that a mere handful of persons and organizations control much of the global knowledge. This knowledge is jealously guarded by secrecy. It turns the old adage "What you don't know can't hurt you" right on its head. What you don't know *can* hurt you!

The issue of conspiracy also lies at the heart of how one views history. Here there are only two views: accidental or conspiratorial.

The former view is that history is simply a series of accidents, or acts of God, which world leaders are powerless to alter or prevent. One adherent of this view was President Jimmy Carter's national security adviser, Zbigniew Brzezinski. Brzezinski, today a member of the executive committee of the secretive Trilateral Commission, said in 1981, "History is much more the product of chaos than of conspiracy. . . . Increasingly, policy makers are overwhelmed by events and information."

Another supporter of the accidental view of history was journalist and self-described "secular humanist" George Johnson. He wrote that the notion of conspiracies has been "pushed by right-wing extremists since the beginning of the century," indicating "that the paranoid style of American politics didn't die with Senator Joseph McCarthy."

The conspiratorial view, on the other hand, could more accurately be called the "cause and effect" view. Obviously, accidents occur. Planes, trains, and cars crash. Ships sink. But in history, it is clear that human planning most often precipitates events.

So why haven't we heard more about such secret planning?

According to conspiracy researchers Jonathan Vankin and John Whalen the American public's attitudes are shaped by a sanitized "Disney" view of both history and current events. "The 'Disney version' of history could just as easily be called the '*New York Times* version' or the 'TV news version' or the 'college textbook version,'" they wrote. "The main resistance to conspiracy theories comes not from people on the street but from the media, academia, and government—people who manage the national and global economy of information."

Anthony C. Sutton, a London-born economics professor who was a research fellow at Stanford University's Hoover Institution, agreed that an "Establishment history" dominates textbooks, publishing, the media, and library shelves. "During the past one hundred years any theory of history or historical evidence that falls outside a pattern established by the American Historical Association and the major foundations with their grant-making power has been attacked or rejected—not on the basis of any evidence presented, but on the basis of the acceptability of the arguments to the so-called Eastern Liberal Establishment, and its official historical line," he commented. "Woe betide any book or author that falls outside the official guidelines. Foundation support is not there. Publishers get cold feet. Distribution is hit and miss, or non-existent."

This refrain was echoed by President Bill Clinton's academic mentor, Dr. Carroll Quigley. His 1966 book, *Tragedy and Hope: A History of the World in Our Time*, revealed his insider knowledge of modern secret societies. Quigley said it was withdrawn suddenly by a major New York publisher. "I am now quite sure that *Tragedy and Hope* was suppressed . . . ," Quigley wrote in the mid-1970s.

Researchers and writers—such as the late Gary Allen, A. Ralph Epperson, G. Edward Griffin, Dr. John Coleman, Jonathan Vankin, Anthony C. Sutton, and Eustace Mullins to name but a few—have written about conspiracies for many years. But these works are nearly always produced by small publishers with limited distribution. These authors charge that the mass media is controlled by corporate America, which has prevented any meaningful exposure of their material.

This concern is echoed even outside the U.S. A French publisher once was quoted as saying, "It would not be possible to trace ownership of corporations and the power structure in the United States. 'They' would not permit it. 'They' would find a way to hound and torture anyone who tried. 'They' seem to be a fairly small group of people who know each other, but many are not at all known to the public. 'They' move in and out of government jobs, but public service apparently serves to win private promotion rather than the other way around. The Government 'control' that practically everyone mentions cannot be traced through stock holdings, regulatory agencies, public decisions. It seems to function through a maze of personal contacts and tacit understandings." To this one might add their membership in secret societies.

Many conspiracy authors have written about dark plots to impose a "New World Order" from within modern secret societies such as the Trilateral Commission, the Council on Foreign Relations, the Illuminati, the Committee of 300, and others. Objective researchers point to the absence of libel suits against such writers as lending some credence to their views. Yet the mainstream news media rarely sees fit to discuss—much less investigate—such accusations.

Yet with the arrival of a new millennium, the theme of conspiracy has found its way into every aspect of American life—from books, TV, and film treatment to politics. Even the president of the United States is not immune to the lure of conspiracies.

In 1991, newly installed President Bill Clinton appointed his close friend and golfing buddy Webster Hubbell associate attorney general of the Department of Justice. In a recent memoir, *Friends in High Places,* Hubbell wrote that Clinton told him, "Webb . . . if I put you over at Justice, I want you to find the answers to two questions for me. One, who killed JFK? And two, are there UFOs?" "He was dead serious," added Hubbell. "I had looked into both but wasn't satisfied with the answers I was getting."

The president and his top appointee in the Justice Department can't get a straight answer? Who's in charge?

Following Hubbell's disclosure, Dr. Steven Greer, director of the Center for the Study of Extraterrestrial Intelligence (CSETI), revealed that in 1993 he gave a three-hour briefing on the reality of UFOs to then–CIA director Admiral James Woolsey. Greer said Woolsey was stymied in his attempts to verify Greer's information and was unable to obtain the relevant documents in CIA files.

When it comes to this nation's deepest, darkest secrets, it appears there are powers even higher than the president of the United States and the director of the Central Intelligence Agency.

Conspiracy writers and government officials are not alone in suspecting conspiracies.

A 1997 Scripps-Howard News Service poll in conjunction with Ohio University resulted in these remarkable statistics:

—51 percent of those polled believe it is likely that some federal officials were directly responsible for the assassination of President John F. Kennedy.

—More than a third suspect that the U.S. Navy shot down TWA Flight 800, either intentionally or unintentionally.

—A majority believe that it is possible that CIA officials intentionally allowed Central American drug dealers to sell cocaine to inner-city black children.

—60 percent felt the government is withholding information regarding Agent Orange and the causes of Gulf War Syndrome.

—Almost half suspect FBI agents set the fire which killed eighty-one Branch Davidians near Waco, Texas, in 1993. (This number undoubtedly grew much larger in 1999 with revelations about government deceit regarding pyrotechnic devices being used prior to the fire.)

—After the U.S. Air Force released a report that "aliens" reported at Roswell, New Mexico, in 1947, were actually crash dummies from tests first begun in 1954, more people now believe that the government is covering up both information and technology from extraterrestrials than before.

Reacting to this poll, the executive director of the Washington Committee for the Study of the American Electorate, Curtis Gans, lamented, "Paranoia is killing this country."

But is it truly paranoia? Is there really no one out there conspiring to gain wealth and power? An old wheeze reminds us, "Just because you're paranoid doesn't mean they're not out to get you!"

It is a growing belief that certain individuals with vast wealth and power, not generally known to the public, are the real masters in the United States and the world. "Power is a fact of life in America, but most Americans are far removed from it. Secrecy is power's chief tool. Government seems distant, yet somehow domineering. We are increasingly isolated from one another—stuck in front of computer and television screens, prisoners behind windshields. There is a frustrating feeling of disconnection to modern American life. . . . Conspiracy theories try to put the pieces back together," wrote Jonathan Vankin, a journalist who has studied a wide variety of conspiracy theories involving the U.S. government.

Conspiracy theories are an attempt to grasp the "big picture" of history. "We believe that many of the major world events that are shaping destinies occur because somebody or somebodies have planned them that way," mused conservative author Gary Allen. "If we were merely dealing with the law of averages, half of the events affecting our nation's well-being should be good for America. If we were dealing with mere incompetence, our leaders should occasionally make a mistake in our favor. . . . We are not really dealing with coincidence or stupidity, but with planning and brilliance."

Less reflective in his thinking was author Johnson, who set the tone for the Reagan years with the 1983 publication of his book *Architects of Fear: Conspiracy Theories and Paranoia in American Politics,* an outgrowth of a series of articles he wrote as a reporter for the *Minneapolis Star.* Johnson stated that a large number of Americans simply cannot accept the idea that "there are a number of ways to interpret events," adding confidently, "there is not a single all-embracing system." Johnson said paranoid Americans "build elaborate systems explaining all the world's troubles as part of a conspiracy" to rationalize their fear and hatred rather than accept what he described as a "pluralistic" view of history, economics, and politics.

"There is a difference between those who occasionally succumb to the attraction of pat, conspiratorial explanations and the conspiracy theorists . . . who believe everything bad that has ever happened is part of an all-engulfing, centuries-old plot," he offered.

Having said that, Johnson was forced to admit that "neither the historical nor the sociological analysis explains why so many conspiracy theorists construct such strikingly similar worldviews." Furthermore, he failed to note that those who sincerely believe that conspiracies don't exist only benefit those who may be conspiring.

RULE BY THE FEW

"Elites, not masses, govern America," concluded academics Thomas R. Dye and L. Harmon Zeigler in their book *The Irony of Democracy.* "In an industrial, scientific, and nuclear age, life in a democracy, just as in a totalitarian society, is shaped by a handful of men. In spite of differences in their approach to the study of power in America, scholars—political scientists and sociologists alike—agree that 'the key political, economic, and social decisions are made by tiny minorities.'"

The idea that a small, wealthy ruling elite—an oligarchy—controls America appears to be well supported by the facts. A disproportionate amount of America's resources is controlled by a handful of its 265 million population. According to a 1983 study by the Federal Reserve Board, a mere 2 percent of U.S. families control 54 percent of the nation's wealth, and only 10 percent of the people own 86 percent of the net financial assets. The majority of American families—55 percent—have zero or negative net worth. This study excluded the net worth of institutions, most of which are owned or controlled by the above-mentioned 2 percent.

This cycle of the rich getting richer while the poor get poorer has been accelerating since the 1960s through both Republican and Democratic administrations. It gained more momentum in the 1990s, according to the U.S. Census Bureau. From 1992 to 1994, the wealthiest 5 percent's share of the national income rose 14 percent, nearly twice that of everyone else's gain during the previous twenty-five years.

Current figures are even more gruesome. The average worker's median pay in 1998—adjusted for inflation—is one full dollar below the 1973 hourly rate. During the past twenty years, the income gap between males with a college education and those with none has grown from 42 percent to 89 percent. Union jobs have borne the brunt of this "downsizing." In 1970, the unions representing steel and auto workers counted nearly three million members. Today, membership is below one million.

"We have evolved into a two-tier society where people in the knowledge industries prosper, and those without a college education or technical skills fall by the wayside," noted *U.S. News & World Report*'s editor-in-chief Mortimer B. Zuckerman. Many are now questioning if this winnowing of the American middle class is truly natural evolution or conscious planning for a "New World Order."

It is widely reported that the United States uses the world's natural resources far out of proportion to its percentage of the planet's population. It is also an uncontested fact that as the new millennium dawns, the United States stands alone as the world's preeminent power.

So who really controls the United States and, hence, the world?

Everyone's heard how "they" own the vast majority of resources, manipulate stocks, control prices, and avoid taxes. "They" also maintain monopolies over energy, medicine, armaments, and manufacturing by suppressing new technologies.

And "they" wield undue influence over the news media and world governments with their control of multinational corporations as well as private organizations such as England's Royal Institute of International Affairs, the Council on Foreign Relations, and the Trilateral Commission.

"They" also belong to secret societies such as the Illuminati, Skull and Bones, Knights of Malta, and the inner circles of Freemasonry.

But who exactly are "they"? Who are the men—few women seem to be included—that may well control the destiny of planet Earth? Why do they act in secrecy and why are they attracted to secret organizations? What secrets do they possess that allow them to assume the role of a ruling elite? More important, what are their goals and agendas?

Many people have heard of the modern secret societies named above. But few have had the opportunity to learn of the details of their origins, intentions, and connections. Therefore it is natural to question just how much influence or control these groups may have over real events.

This book is a study of these secret societies—both modern and ancient—and their role in world history, an attempt to uncover their secrets, to search for the true meaning of their mysteries.

What becomes clear to even the most casual researcher is that secret societies not only do exist but have played key roles in world affairs over the centuries. What is unclear is exactly who they are and how many are involved. And what are the connections between these groups? After all, they are *secret* societies.

In 1909, Walter Rathenau of General Electric in Germany, said, "Three hundred men, all of whom know one another, direct the economic destiny of Europe and choose their successors from among themselves." Rathenau's figure may have provided the basis for conspiracy author Dr. John Coleman's claim that a "Committee of 300" controls a "secret, upper-level parallel government that runs Britain and the U.S."

Joseph P. Kennedy, sire of the famed Kennedy family, once remarked, "Fifty men have run America and that's a high figure."

In describing who rules the United States today, David Wallechinsky and Irving Wallace, authors of the popular *The People's Almanac,* echoed high school civics classes by listing the president, two-house legislature, and the nine-member Supreme Court. They also mentioned state, county, and city governments but correctly noted that "most of their laws can be voided by the federal government."

But what about hidden power and control? In a section entitled "Who REALLY rules?" these authors stated, "There are many forces at work in U.S. society, but the most powerful by far are the interlocking directorates of the major banks, corporations, and insurance companies, with the backing of the leaders of the military: In the words of former president Dwight Eisenhower, 'the military-industrial complex.'" Okay, but who controls this "military-industrial complex"?

A VIEW FROM THE FEW

It has not only been fringe conspiracy theorists who have spoken out about hidden control in the world.

British prime minister Benjamin Disraeli as far back as 1856 told the House of Commons, "It is useless to deny, because it is impossible to conceal, that a great part of Europe—the whole of Italy and France and a great portion of [then fragmented] Germany, to say nothing of other countries—is covered with a network of these secret societies. . . . And what are their objects? They do not attempt to conceal them. They do not want constitutional government . . . they want to change the tenure of land, to drive out the present owners of the soil and to put an end to ecclesiastical establishments [churches]."

President Woodrow Wilson, who, as will be seen, was intimately connected with conspiratorial power, wrote, "Some of the biggest men in the United States, in the field of commerce and manufacture, are afraid of somebody, are afraid of something. They know there is a power somewhere so organized, so subtle, so watchful, so interlocked, so complete, so pervasive that they had better not speak above their breath when they speak in condemnation of it."

U.S. Supreme Court justice Felix Frankfurter once revealed, "The real rulers in Washington are invisible, and exercise power from behind the scenes."

In a letter dated November 23, 1933, newly elected President Franklin D. Roosevelt wrote to President Woodrow Wilson's top adviser, Colonel Edward House, "The real truth of the matter is, as you and I know, that a financial element in the large centers has owned the government ever since the days of Andrew Jackson."

Roosevelt's son Elliot wrote, "There are within our world perhaps only a dozen organizations which shape the courses of our various destinies as rigidly as the regularly constituted governments."

Warnings about a secret government in the United States have been voiced by many people over the years.

Former New York mayor John F. Hylan stated in 1922, "The real menace of our Republic is the invisible government which like a giant octopus sprawls its slimy length over our city, state and nation. . . . At the head of this octopus are the Rockefeller-Standard Oil interests and a small group of powerful banking houses generally referred to as the international bankers [who] virtually run the U.S. government for their own selfish purposes."

Colonel L. Fletcher Prouty (retired) served as a Focal Point liaison officer between the Pentagon and the CIA from 1955 to 1963. From his vantage point, Prouty was able to witness the control mechanisms over both intelligence and the military.

Writing in 1973, Prouty said the United States is run by a "Secret Team," an "inner sanctum of a new religious order" answerable only to themselves. "The power of the Team derives from its vast intra-governmental undercover infrastructure and its direct relationship with great private industries, mutual funds and investment houses, universities, and the news media, including foreign and domestic publishing houses.

". . . All true members of the Team remain in the power center whether in office with the incumbent administration or out of office with the hardcore set. They simply rotate to and from official jobs and the business world or the pleasant haven of academe."

Prouty wrote, "This great machine has been constructed by such able men as 'Wild Bill' Donovan, Clark Clifford, Walter Bedell Smith, Allen Dulles, Maxwell Taylor, McGeorge Bundy and many others, who have guided and molded it into the runaway giant that it is today. It is big business, big government, big money, big pressure . . . all operating in self-centered, utterly self-serving security and secrecy."

The skeptic should note how these same names will continually crop up in connection with modern secret societies.

The great innovative thinker R. Buckminster Fuller also came to understand that the United States is ruled by powerful men behind the scenes. "The USA is not run by its would-be 'democratic' government," he wrote shortly before his death in 1983. "Nothing could be more pathetic than the role that has to be played by the President of the United States, whose power is approximately zero. Nevertheless, the news media and most over-thirty-years-of-age USA citizens carry on as if the President has supreme power."

President Franklin D. Roosevelt, himself closely connected to many of the prominent members of the secret societies, once remarked, "In politics, nothing happens by accident. If it happens, you can bet it was planned that way."

Another insider who confirmed that a plot was afoot was America's first secretary of defense, James Forrestal, who may have paid with his life for his forthrightness. Beginning in 1947, Forrestal voiced his concern that government leaders were consistently making concessions to the Soviets. He had amassed more than three thousand pages of notes, which he told a friend would be turned into a book to expose the real motives of his superiors.

"These men are not incompetent or stupid. They are crafty and brilliant. Consistency has never been a mark of stupidity. If they were merely stupid, they would occasionally make a mistake in our favor," he noted.

Forrestal, who was privy to many secrets—he was listed as an original member of a supersecret group in charge of the UFO issue according to the controversial MJ–12 documents—resigned his office at the request of President Truman on March 2, 1949. Two months later, again at the request of Truman, Forrestal entered Bethesda Naval Hospital for a routine examination. A doctor assured his brother that Forrestal was well but refused to allow either the brother or the family priest to see him. On the day that his brother came to take him from the hospital, Forrestal's body was found on a lower floor of the hospital with a rope around his neck. Officials claimed Forrestal had committed suicide, but many people—both then and now—disbelieved this verdict. His notes and diaries were taken and held by the government for more than a year before a sanitized version was finally released to the public.

Although various officials claimed Forrestal was insane at the time, his unbalanced state must have provoked an ability to see into the future. Just before leaving for Bethesda, Forrestal told a friend that American soldiers would soon be dying in Korea. This statement came fifteen months before the North Koreans launched a "surprise" attack on the South.

Another crazy man who voiced a prophetic vision of war was Senator Joseph McCarthy, who mistook evidence of a worldwide conspiracy as support for his own prejudice against Communism.

McCarthy, who caused such misery in his misguided and zealous attack on Communism, nevertheless was on track in his assessment of the conspiracy to promote war for profit. He charged that the Yalta agreements of 1945 between Roosevelt, Churchill, and Stalin were behind the conflicts of the postwar world. The secret agreements between these world leaders—among them the ceding of Eastern Europe to Stalin, the Middle East to Britain, and the Pacific and Southeast Asian region to America—

were confirmed in the mid-1970s by the release of some of Churchill's papers and correspondence.

On September 23, 1950, McCarthy stated, "Here [at Yalta] was signed the death warrant of the young men who are dying today in the hills and valleys of Korea. Here was signed the death warrant of the young men who will die tomorrow in the jungles of Indochina [later called Vietnam].

"How can we account for our present situation unless we believe that men high in Government are concerting [sic] to deliver us to disaster? This must be the product of a great conspiracy, a conspiracy on a scale so immense as to dwarf any previous such venture in the history of man," McCarthy warned. "What can be made of this unbroken series of decisions and acts contributing to the strategy of defeat? They cannot be attributed to incompetence."

McCarthy moved on to an inglorious end because he could not—or would not—look past the specter of a worldwide "communist" conspiracy. Fortunately, over time it became possible to discredit his reckless and inflated accusations. Unfortunately, the demise of "McCarthyism" left the secrets intact.

Were all these people deluded conspiracy theorists? Or did they all, in their own incomplete and limited way, try to reveal the secret agendas behind the facile history fed to the public?

Commentators like Noam Chomsky and Gore Vidal have spoken out against the "national security state" from the Left. The late Senator Barry Goldwater and evangelist Pat Robertson have spoken out from the Right. Even mainstream centrists like commentator Bill Moyers and attorney Gerry Spence have warned of a "secret government." When historical figures along with concerned citizens from opposite ends of the political spectrum all say the same thing, it is time to start paying close attention to what's going on in the nation today.

Authors David Wise and Thomas B. Ross wrote of such matters in the early 1960s in their book *The Invisible Government,* which the CIA attempted to suppress. They warned that secret government agencies had financial connections to foundations and universities and that they used American businesses as cover for their operations, in direct violation of their charters. More recently these authors wrote, "Nothing has happened . . . to persuade us that the danger of an invisible government in an open society has in any way diminished."

In *Rule By Secrecy* will be found new information and new ways to view history. An attempt will be made to tie together the loose ends of our collective knowledge, to make sense of a long trail of conspiratorial leads and evidence.

There is no guarantee that all of the information presented here is absolute ground truth. But to get a grasp on truth requires as much data as possible. Nothing should be dismissed out of hand. All information, no matter how seemingly outlandish or inconsequential, should be considered and evaluated.

While there seems to be any number of secret societies—both political and religious—operating in the world, only those that appear to have the greatest impact upon the public are considered here. Splinter sects and odd cults—such as the Avengers, Beati Paoli, the Order of the Peacock Angel, Heaven's Gate, etc.—only distract from researching the truly effective organizations.

At this point permit me to make one thing very clear: Nothing presented here is intended to intrude on anyone's religious beliefs. Freedom of religion is one of the greatest aspects of American life. Every person should be permitted the comfort of their own beliefs as long as those beliefs don't adversely impact on another person.

But in researching history and the secret societies, one finds that religion and politics, particularly in the past, have been inextricably intertwined. To exclude religious matters would be a failure to tell half the story. This material must be intellectually considered. How it may fit into one's worldview should be determined by each reader, depending upon their own religious views and level of intellectual sophistication.

The immense wealth of information on secret societies, most of it written long ago, is filled with names, dates, and events that are meaningless to the modern reader. Therefore, judicious editing and space limitations make this study somewhat cursory by necessity. It is my hope that just enough detail has been retained to support this account of secret society activity while still providing ease of reading over a very complex and controversial subject.

The secretive nature of these groups makes any attempt to discover absolute proof of their methods and ultimate objectives very nearly impossible. Just like law enforcement agencies investigating organized crime, researchers often must look for patterns of behavior and personal links between people and organizations. While the evidence usually speaks for itself, guilt by association must be considered and avoided. All secret society members are not conspirators. The entire scope of the various issues must be examined thoroughly with a watchful eye for subterfuge and deceit. Much historical information is incomplete or distorted by conventional chroniclers.

What then are the secrets that link the Council on Foreign Relations and Freemasonry back to Egypt's Great Pyramid and beyond?

Set preconceptions and conditioning aside and join the attempt to uncover the history and goals of those who rule by secrecy.

PART I

MODERN SECRET SOCIETIES

Secrecy is the freedom zealots dream of: no watchman to check the door, no accountant to check the books, no judge to check the law. The secret government has no constitution. The rules it follows are the rules it makes up.

—BILL MOYERS

ecret societies not only exist, they have played an important role in national and international events right up to this day.

In considering the reach of modern secret societies, it is instructive to first look at America's immediate past presidents and the people and events surrounding them.

While many Americans popularly viewed President Bill Clinton as a youthful saxophone player with an eye for the ladies, most were unaware of his connection to three of the most notorious of modern secret societies: the Trilateral Commission, the Council on Foreign Relations (take particular notice of the initials CFR as they crop up incessantly in the study of U.S. policy decisions and world conflicts), and the Bilderbergers.

The Trilateral Commission publishes its membership as well as position papers, but its inner workings are secret. The CFR also publishes a membership roll, but members are pledged to secrecy regarding its goals and operations. The Bilderberg group keeps both its agenda and membership a secret.

Prominent members of the Clinton administration who belonged to the council included former CFR president Peter Tarnoff, Anthony Lake, Al Gore, Warren Christopher, Colin Powell, Les Aspin, James Woolsey, William Cohen, Samuel Lewis, Joan Edelman Spero, Timothy Wirth, Winston Lord, Lloyd Bentsen, Laura Tyson, and George Stephenopoulos. Former Trilateral members included Bruce Babbitt, Stephen W. Bosworth, William Cohen, Thomas Foley, Alan Greenspan, Donna Shalala, and Strobe Talbott.

Publisher John F. McManus noted that in the fall of 1998, as impeachment loomed over him, Clinton hurried to New York to seek support from his CFR friends. "Bill Clinton knows well that he serves as president because the members of the 'secret society' to which he belongs chose him and expect him to carry out its plans," wrote McManus.

Clinton was not the only recent president with connections to these groups.

President George Bush was a Trilateralist, a CFR member, and a brother in the mysterious Order of Skull and Bones. President Ronald Reagan, a former spokesman for General Electric, did not officially belong to these groups, but his administrations were packed with both current and former members as will be detailed later.

President Jimmy Carter's administration was so filled with members of the Trilateral Commission that conspiracy researchers had a field day. Even the Establishment media began to talk.

THE TRILATERAL COMMISSION

By the early 1970s, thanks to burgeoning communications technology, many Americans were becoming more aware of secretive organizations such as the Council on Foreign Relations. Former CFR chairman David Rockefeller, apparently in an effort to deflect public attention from CFR activities, instigated the creation of a more public offshoot organization: the Trilateral Commission.

Both the commission and its predecessor, the CFR, are held out by conspiracy researchers as the epitome of covert organizations which may be guiding public policy in directions opposite to those either in the best interest of or desired by the public.

The concept of the Trilateral Commission was originally brought to Rockefeller by Zbigniew Brzezinski, then head of the Russian Studies Department at Columbia University. While at the Brookings Institution, Brzezinski had been researching the need for closer cooperation between the trilateral nations of Europe, North America, and Asia.

In 1970, Brzezinski wrote in *Foreign Affairs,* a CFR publication, "A new and broader approach is needed—creation of a community of the developed nations which can effectively address itself to the larger concerns confronting mankind. . . . A council representing the United States, Western Europe, and Japan, with regular meetings of the heads of governments as well as some small standing machinery, would be a good start."

Later that year, he published a book entitled *Between Two Ages: America's Role in the Technetronic Era.* Within those pages, Brzezinski spelled out his vision for the future.

He prophetically foresaw a society ". . . that is shaped culturally, psychologically, socially, and economically by the impact of technology and electronics—particularly in the area of computers and communication."

Brzezinski's visions would raise the suspicions of those opposed to the consolidation of world political and economic power. Declaring "National sovereignty is no longer a viable concept," he predicted "movement toward a larger community by the developing nations . . . through a variety of indirect ties and already developing limitations on national sovereignty." He foresaw this larger community being funded by "a global taxation system."

In explaining that a cooperative hub, such as the Trilateral Commission, might set the stage for future consolidation, he reasoned, "Though the objective of shaping a community of developed nations is less ambitious than the goal of world government, it is more attainable."

Brzezinski's hope for a global society did not exclude nations then under the rule of Marxism, which he described as "a further vital and creative stage in the maturing of man's universal vision" and "a victory of the external man over the inner, passive man, and a victory of reason over belief."

Brzezinski's plan for a commission of trilateral nations was first presented during a meeting of the ultrasecret Bilderberg group in April 1972, in the small Belgian town of Knokke-Heist. Reception to Brzezinski's proposal reportedly was enthusiastic. At that time international financiers were concerned over Nixon's devaluation of the dollar, surcharges on imports, and budding détente with China, all of which were causing relations with Japan to deteriorate. In addition, energy problems were growing in response to price increases by the Organization of Petroleum Exporting Countries (OPEC).

With the blessing of the Bilderbergers and the CFR, the Trilateral Commission began organizing on July 23–24, 1972, at the 3,500-acre Rockefeller estate at Pocantico Hills, a subdivision of Tarrytown, New York. Participants in this private meeting included Rockefeller, Brzezinski, Brookings Institution director of foreign policy studies Henry Owen, McGeorge Bundy, Robert Bowie, C. Fred Bergsten, Bayless Manning, Karl Carstens, Guido Colonna di Paliano, Francois Duchene, Rene Foch, Max Kohnstamm, Kiichi Miyazawa, Saburo Ikita, and Tadashi Yamamoto. Apparently these founders were selected by Rockefeller and Brzezinski.

The Trilateral Commission officially was founded on July 1, 1973, with David Rockefeller as chairman. Brzezinski was named founding

North American director. North American members included Georgia governor Jimmy Carter, congressman John B. Anderson (another presidential candidate), and Time, Inc. editor-in-chief Hedley Donovan. Foreign founding members included the late Reginald Maudling, Lord Eric Roll, *Economist* editor Alistair Burnet, FIAT president Giovanni Agnelli, and French vice president of the Commission of European Communities Raymond Barre. The total exclusive membership remains about three hundred persons.

According to the commission's official yearly publication, *Trialogue,* "The Trilateral Commission was formed in 1973 by private citizens of Western Europe, Japan, and North America to foster closer cooperation among these three regions on common problems." Skeptical conspiracy authors saw "closer cooperation" as more like "collusion" of the multinational bankers and corporate elite with an eye toward one-world government.

The Trilateral Commission has headquarters in New York, Paris, and Tokyo. An executive committee of thirty-five members administers the commission, which meets roughly every nine months rotating between the three regions.

It is not surprising that the question of who funds this group has arisen. Commission spokesmen stress that the group does not receive any government funding. A report in 1978 showed that commission funding from mid-1976 to mid-1979 was $1,180,000, much of which came from tax-exempt foundations such as the Rockefeller Brothers Fund, which in 1977 alone put up $120,000. Donations also came from the Ford Foundation, the Lilly Endowment, the German Marshall Fund and corporations such as Time, Bechtel, Exxon, General Motors, Wells-Fargo, and Texas Instruments.

In addition to its newsletter, *Trialogue,* the commission has regularly issued a number of "Task Force Reports" or "Triangle Papers" which are publicly available. "For years, conspiracy-oriented newsletters of the Right and Left have been peddling Trilateral 'secrets' which were obtained directly from the Commission!" snickered journalist and Trilateral Commission researcher Robert Eringer. It is obvious to most researchers that, as these papers are available to the public, they don't contain any true inner "secrets."

One such paper, entitled *The Crisis of Democracy,* was published by the commission in 1975. One of its authors, Harvard political scientist

Samuel P. Huntington, avowed that America needed "a greater degree of moderation in democracy." He argued that democratic institutions were incapable of responding to crises such as the Three Mile Island nuclear accident or the Cuban refugee boatlift operation. The paper suggested that leaders with "expertise, seniority, experience and special talents" were needed to "override the claims of democracy."

Just a few examples indicate that those espousing Trilateralist policies often end up implementing those same policies in the government. Three years after his paper was published, Huntington was named coordinator of security planning for Carter's National Security Council. In this capacity, Huntington prepared Presidential Review Memorandum 32, which led to the 1979 presidential order creating the Federal Emergency Management Agency, a civilian organization with the power to take totalitarian control of government functions in the event of a national "emergency."

Yale University economist Richard Cooper headed the commission's task force on monetary policy, which recommended selling official gold reserves to private markets. Cooper became undersecretary of state for economic affairs, presiding as the International Monetary Fund sold a portion of its gold.

Trilateralist John Sawhill authored an early commission report, *Energy: Managing the Transition,* which made recommendations on how to manage a movement to higher-cost energy. Carter appointed Sawhill deputy secretary of the Department of Energy. C. Fred Bergsten aided in the preparation of a commission report called *The Reform of International Institutions,* then went on to become assistant secretary of the treasury for international affairs.

"Many of the original members of the Trilateral Commission are now in positions of power where they are able to implement policy recommendations of the Commission; recommendations that they, themselves, prepared on behalf of the Commission," noted journalist Eringer. "It is for this reason that the Commission has acquired a reputation for being the Shadow Government of the West."

"The Trilateral Commission's tentacles have reached so far afield in the political and economic sphere that it has been described by some as a cabal of powerful men out to control the world by creating a supernational community dominated by the multinational corporations," wrote researcher Laurie K. Strand in a piece entitled "Who's in charge—Six Possible Contenders" for the *People's Almanac #3.*

Even *U.S. News & World Report* took note of the commission's globalist agenda, reporting, "The Trilateralists make no bones about this: They recruit only people interested in promoting closer international cooperation. . . ."

Researchers Anthony C. Sutton and Patrick M. Wood in their book *Trilaterals Over Washington* voiced suspicions of the group and offered this view of its inception. "The Trilateral Commission was founded by the persistent maneuvering of David Rockefeller and Zbigniew Brzezinski. Rockefeller, [then] chairman of the ultrapowerful Chase Manhattan Bank, a director of many major multinational corporations and 'endowment funds' has long been a central figure in the mysterious Council on Foreign Relations. Brzezinski, a brilliant prognosticator of one-world idealism, has been a professor at Columbia University and the author of several books that have served as 'policy guidelines' for the CFR. Brzezinski served as the (Trilateral) commission's executive director from its inception in 1973 until late 1976 when he was appointed by President Carter as assistant to the president for national security affairs."

It was Brzezinski who recruited Carter for the Trilateral Commission in 1973. In fact, during President Jimmy Carter's administration, so much Trilateral material was made public that considerable debate ensued within the news media.

Even the Establishment-oriented *Washington Post* pondered in early 1977, "But here is the unsettling thing about the Trilateral Commission. The President-elect (Carter) is a member. So is Vice-President-elect Walter F. Mondale. So are the new secretaries of State, Defense and Treasury, Cyrus R. Vance, Harold Brown and W. Michael Blumenthal. So is Zbigniew Brzezinski, who is a former Trilateral director and Carter's national security advisor, also a bunch of others who will make foreign policy for America in the next four years."

Sutton and Wood commented, "If you are trying to calculate the odds of three virtually unknown men (Carter, Mondale, and Brzezinski), out of over 60 (Trilateral) commissioners from the U.S., capturing the three most powerful positions in the land, don't bother. Your calculations will be meaningless."

Carter administration Trilaterals also included Ambassadors Andrew Young, Gerard Smith, Richard Gardner, and Elliot Richardson, White House economic aide Henry Owen, Deputy Secretary of State Warren Christopher, Director Paul Warnke of the Arms Control and Disarmament Agency, Undersecretaries of State Richard Cooper for economic affairs and Lucy Benson for security assistance, Undersecretary of the Treasury Anthony Solomon, Robert Bowie of the CIA, and Assistant Secretary of State Richard Holbrooke.

Lest anyone think that the Trilateral Commission was simply some organ of the Democratic Party, *U.S. News & World Report* in 1978 listed prominent Republicans who were members. These included former Secretaries Henry Kissinger of State, William Coleman of Transportation, Carla Hills of Housing and Urban Development, Peter Peterson of Commerce, and Casper Weinberger of Health, Education, and Welfare.

Also listed were ex-Energy administrator John Sawhill, ex-CIA Director and future President George Bush, ex-Deputy Secretaries of State Robert Ingersoll and Charles Robinson, ex-Deputy Defense Secretary David Packard, former Environmental Protection Agency administrator Russell E. Train, Ambassadors William Scanton to the United Nations and Anne Armstrong to Britain, and members of Congress John Anderson, William Brock, William Cohen, Barber Conable, John Danforth, and Robert Taft, Jr., and Marina Whitman, former member of the Council of Economic Advisors.

Provoking additional concern among conspiracy researchers was President Carter's selection of banker Paul Volcker to head America's powerful central bank, the Federal Reserve. Reportedly appointed on instructions from David Rockefeller, Volcker had been the North American chairman of the Trilateral Commission as well as a member of those other secret groups, the Council on Foreign Relations and the Bilderbergers. He was replaced as chairman of the Federal Reserve during the Reagan administration by current chairman Alan Greenspan, also a member of the Trilateral Commission, the CFR, and the Bilderbergers.

It is easy to see why so many people believed that U.S. Government policy was being directed from these Rockefeller-dominated organizations.

Despite having been written nearly twenty years ago, the words of Sutton and Wood ring true today for many average Americans concerned over the state of the nation and suspicious of a superelite trying to gain world control. They wrote, "By Biblical standards, the United States most certainly deserves judgment—perversion runs amok, child abuse is common, greed and avarice are the passwords to success and morals have rotted. If we are about to be thrown into the pits of the dark ages, the most logical catalyst, or motivator on the horizon is the Trilateral Commission."

Former senator and presidential candidate Barry Goldwater echoed the fears of many when he wrote, "What the Trilaterals truly intend is the creation of a worldwide economic power superior to the political government of the nation-states involved. As managers and creators of the system they will rule the world."

Such criticism prompted David Rockefeller to defend the commission in a 1980 edition of the *Wall Street Journal*. "Far from being a coterie of international conspirators with designs on covertly ruling the world, the Trilateral Commission is, in reality, a group of concerned citizens interested in fostering greater understanding and cooperation among international allies. . . ."

But some criticism came from within the Carter administration itself. Secretary of State Edmund Muskie charged that Brzezinski was making foreign policy rather than coordinating it. William Sullivan, who had been U.S. ambassador to Iran, accused Brzezinski of sabotaging U.S. efforts to ease relations with Iran following the departure of the Shah. "By November 1978, Brzezinski began to make his own policy and establish his own embassy in Iran," complained Sullivan.

It was accusations such as these that prompted sudden concern in Washington over secret and semisecret organizations. Columnist Nicholas von Hoffman noted, "Brzezinski has long spooked those who worry about the Trilateral Commission, that Rockefeller-inspired group of globally minded big shots from the major industrial powers. For countless Americans of both a rightward and a leftward persuasion, the commission, which tried to influence governments' trade and diplomatic policies, is a worrisome conspiracy."

Concern spilled over into veterans organizations. In 1980, the American Legion national convention passed Resolution 773, which called for a congressional investigation of the Trilateral Commission and its predecessor, the Council on Foreign Relations. The following year a similar resolution was approved by the Veterans of Foreign Wars (VFW).

Congressman Larry McDonald introduced these resolutions in the House of Representatives but nothing came of it. McDonald, who as national chairman of the John Birch Society was a vocal critic of these secret societies, died in the still-controversial downing of Korean Airlines 007 on September 1, 1983.

During the 1980 presidential campaigns, Republican candidate Ronald Reagan went on the record blasting the nineteen Trilaterals in the Carter administration—including Carter himself, who wrote that his association with the commission was "a splendid learning opportunity"—and vowed to investigate the group if elected. While competing with George Bush for the nomination, Reagan lambasted Bush's membership in both the Trilateral Commission and the CFR and pledged not to allow Bush a position in a Reagan government.

Yet during the Republican national convention a strange series of events took place.

While Reagan was a shoe-in as the presidential candidate, the vice presidency was the object of a contentious fight. In midweek, national media commentators suddenly began talking about a "dream ticket" to be composed of President Reagan and Vice President (and former president) Gerald Ford. Pressure began building for this concept, which would have created a shared presidency and, hence, divided power. It was even suggested that since Ford had been president he should choose half of the Reagan cabinet.

Faced with the prospect of presiding over half a government, Reagan rushed to the convention floor late at night and announced, "I know that I am breaking with precedent to come here tonight, and I assure you at this late hour I'm not going to give you my acceptance address tonight. . . . But in watching the television at the hotel and seeing the rumors that were going around and the gossip that was taking place here . . . let me as simply as I can straighten out and bring this to a conclusion. It is true that a number of Republican leaders . . . felt that a proper ticket would have included the former president of the United States, Gerald Ford, as second place on the ticket. . . . I then believed that because of all the talk and how something might be growing through the night that it was time for me to advance the schedule a little bit. . . . I have asked and I am recommending to this convention that tomorrow when the session reconvenes that George Bush be nominated for vice president."

Reagan never again uttered a word against the commission or the CFR. Following his election, Reagan's fifty-nine-member transition team was composed of twenty-eight CFR members, ten members of the elite Bilderberg group, and at least ten Trilaterals. He even appointed prominent CFR members to three of the nation's most sensitive offices: Secretary of State Alexander Haig, Secretary of Defense Casper Weinberger, and Secretary of the Treasury Donald Regan. Additionally, he named Bush's campaign manager, James A. Baker III, who then served as chairman of the Reagan-Bush campaign committee, as his chief of staff. Baker is a fourth-generation member of a family long connected to Rockefeller oil interests.

Then little more than two months after taking office, President Reagan was struck by an assassin's bullet which, but for a quarter of an inch, would have propelled Bush into the Oval Office seven years before his time. Oddly enough, the brother of the would-be assassin, John W. Hinckley, had scheduled dinner with Bush's son Neil the very night Reagan was shot. Hinckley's Texas oilman father and George Bush were longtime friends. It should also be noted that Bush's name—including his then little-publicized nickname "Poppy"—along with his address and phone number were found in the personal notebook of oil geologist George DeMohrenschildt, the last known close friend of Lee Harvey Oswald. The existence of a 1963 FBI report mentioning a "George Bush of the CIA" in connection with reactions of the U.S. Cuban community to the JFK assassination drew media attention during the 1992 election. Many researchers view these seemingly small, unconnected, and little-reported details as collectively pushing the notion of coincidence to the breaking point.

The undeniable ties connecting America's leadership to the CFR and the Trilateral Commission—along with the fact that globalist banker David Rockefeller was a leading luminary in both groups—has prompted much anxiety among conspiracy writers on both the Left and Right.

"If the Council on Foreign Relations can be said to be a spawning ground for the concepts of one-world idealism, the Trilateral Commission is the 'task force' assembled to assault the beachheads," wrote authors Sutton and Wood in 1979. "Already the commission has placed its members . . . in the top posts the U.S. has to offer."

Texe Marrs (no known relation to this author), president of Living Truth Publishers in Austin, Texas, has warned, "The Trilateral Commission is a group with the goal of hastening the era of World Government and promoting an international economy controlled behind the scenes by the Secret Brotherhood (the Illuminati)." The late senator Barry Goldwater was just as cautionary. In his 1979 book, *With No Apologies,* Goldwater warned, "David Rockefeller's newest international cabal [the Trilateral Commission] . . . is intended to be the vehicle for multinational consolidation of the commercial and banking interests by seizing control of the political government of the United States."

Such allegations resulted in a 1981 commentary by *Washington Post* writers normally disinterested in any conspiracy theory. They at last acknowledged the Trilateral presence by sarcastically writing, "Remember those dreaded three-sided Trilateralists, the international conspirators headed by David Rockefeller who were going to take over the world? Jimmy Carter was one. George Bush used to be one too and it cost him dearly in his campaign last year against Ronald Reagan.

"Well, guess who's coming to the White House. Guess who invited them. Guess who will lead the delegation. Right. The Trilateralists are coming. President Reagan has asked them to come. They will be led by David Rockefeller. The Trilateralists have landed and the conspiracy theorists no doubt will be close behind," they sneered.

Despite public denials, the Trilateral Commission certainly counts as a secret society as its meetings are not open to public scrutiny. And it most certainly represents an extension of the even more secretive Council on Foreign Relations, as all eight North American representatives to the founding meeting of the Trilateral Commission were CFR members.

COUNCIL ON FOREIGN RELATIONS

Globalism did not begin with the Trilateral Commission. The concept of a one-world community stretches back far beyond the twentieth century, but became concentrated in the granddaddy of the modern American secret societies—the Council on Foreign Relations (CFR).

The council began as an outgrowth of a series of meetings conducted during World War I. In 1917 New York, Colonel Edward Mandell House, President Woodrow Wilson's confidential adviser, had gathered about one hundred prominent men to discuss the postwar world. Dubbing themselves "the Inquiry," they made plans for a peace settlement which eventually evolved into Wilson's famous "fourteen points," which he first presented to Congress on January 8, 1918. They were globalist in nature, calling for the removal of "all economic barriers" between nations, "equality of trade conditions," and the formation of "a general association of nations."

Colonel House, who once described himself as a Marxist socialist but whose actions more reflected Fabian socialism, was the author of a 1912 book entitled *Philip Dru: Administrator*. In this work, House described a "conspiracy" within the United States with the goals of establishing a central bank, a graduated income tax, and the control of both political parties. Two years after the publication of his book, two, if not all three, of his literary goals had been met in reality.

By late 1918, stalemate on the Western Front and the entry of America into the war forced Germany and the Central Powers to accept Wilson's terms for peace. The subsequent Paris Peace Conference of 1919 resulted in the harsh Treaty of Versailles, which forced Germany to pay heavy reparations to the Allies. This ruined the German economy, leading to depression and the eventual rise of Adolf Hitler and his Nazis.

Attending the Paris peace conference were President Woodrow Wilson and his closest advisors, Colonel House, bankers Paul Warburg and Bernard Baruch, and almost two dozen members of "the Inquiry." The conference attendees embraced Wilson's plan for peace, including the formation of a League of Nations. However, under American law, the covenant had to be ratified by the U.S. Senate, which failed to do so, apparently distrusting any supernational organization.

Undaunted, Colonel House, along with both British and American peace conference delegates, met in Paris's Majestic Hotel on May 30, 1919, and resolved to form an "Institute of International Affairs," with one branch in the United States and one in England. The English branch became the Royal Institute of International Affairs. This institute was to guide public opinion toward acceptance of one-world government or globalism.

The U.S. branch was incorporated on July 21, 1921, as the Council on Foreign Relations (CFR). It was built upon an existing, but lackluster, New York dinner club of the same name, which had been created in 1918 by prominent bankers and lawyers for discussions on trade and international finance. Article II of the new CFR's bylaws stated that anyone revealing details of CFR meetings in contravention of the CFR's rules could be dropped from membership, thus qualifying the CFR as a secret society.

This secrecy has been assiduously protected by America's major media. "Analysts of the Soviet press say the Council crops up more regularly in *Pravda* and *Izvestia* than it does in the *New York Times*," noted journalist J. Anthony Lucas in 1971.

Since 1945, the CFR has been headquartered in the elegant Harold Pratt House in New York City. The building was donated by the Pratt family of Rockefeller's Standard Oil. The mansion, with its painted French doors, elegant tapestries, and fireplaces, presents a clublike atmosphere.

Characterization of the CFR as an "old boys' club" is enhanced by the fact that many members belong to other upper-crust Social Register groups such as the Century Association, the Links Club, the University Club, and Washington's Metropolitan Club.

In the CFR's 1997 annual report, Board Chairman Peter G. Peterson acknowledged that there was a "kernel of truth" to the charge that the council was an organization of "New York liberal elite," but stated the CFR today is "reaching further into America" with an increasing number of members now living outside New York and Washington.

The CFR's invitation-only membership, originally limited to 1,600 participants, today numbers more than 3,300, representing the most influential leaders in finance, commerce, communications, and academia. Admission is a very discriminating and painful process: candidates have to be proposed by a member, seconded by another member, approved by a membership committee, screened by the professional staff, and finally approved by the board of directors.

In an effort to adjust to the modern world, the Council extended its membership by the early 1970s to include a few blacks and more than a dozen women. To broaden its influence beyond the eastern seaboard, the CFR created Committees on Foreign Relations composed of local leaders in cities across the nation. More than thirty-seven such committees comprising about four thousand members existed by the early 1980s.

Original CFR members included Colonel House, former New York senator and Secretary of State Elihu Root, syndicated columnist Walter Lippmann, John Foster Dulles and Christian Herter, who both later served a secretaries of state, and Dulles's brother Allen, who later served as director of the CIA.

Founding CFR president, millionaire John W. Davis, was financier J. P. Morgan's personal attorney, while Vice President Paul Cravath also represented Morgan properties. The council's first chairman was Russell Leffingwell, one of Morgan's partners. Since most of the earliest CFR members had connections to Morgan in one way or another, it could be said that the council was heavily influenced by Morgan interests.

Funding for the CFR came from bankers and financiers such as Morgan, John D. Rockefeller, Bernard Baruch, Jacob Schiff, Otto Kahn, and

Paul Warburg. Today, funding for the CFR comes from major corporations such as Xerox, General Motors, Bristol-Meyers Squibb, Texaco, and others as well as the German Marshall Fund, McKnight Foundation, Dillion Fund, Ford Foundation, Andrew W. Mellon Foundation, Rockefeller Brothers Fund, Starr Foundation, and the Pew Charitable Trusts.

According to the Capital Research Center's *Guide to Nonprofit Advocacy and Policy Groups,* CFR board members are associated with such influential organizations as the Committee for Economic Development, Institute for International Economics, Committee for a Responsible Federal Budget, the Business Enterprise Trust, the Urban Institute, the Business Roundtable, Council on Competitiveness, U.S. Chamber of Commerce, National Alliance for Business, Brookings Institution, Business-Higher Education Forum, Washington Institute for Near East Policy, Ethics and Public Policy Center, Hoover Institution, Center for Strategic and International Studies, Wilderness Society, and the American Council for Capital Formation.

The CFR played a key role in American policy during World War II, and journalist J. Anthony Lucas noted, "From 1945 well into the sixties, Council members were in the forefront of America's globalist activism."

In a 1997 mission statement, CFR officials, whose "ranks include nearly all past and present senior U.S. government officials who deal with international matters," stated the council is merely "a unique membership organization and think tank that educates members and staff to serve the nation with ideas for a better and safer world."

Critics dispute this goal, noting that the CFR has had its hand in every major twentieth century conflict. Many writers view the CFR as a group of men set on world domination through multinational business, international treaties, and world government.

Even insiders seem to have a hard time convincing their fellows that there is no attempt at conspiratorial control. Admiral Chester Ward, retired judge advocate general of the U.S. Navy and a longtime CFR member was quoted as saying, "CFR, as such, does not write the platforms of both political parties or select their respective presidential candidates, or control U.S. defense and foreign policies. But CFR members, as individuals, acting in concert with other individual CFR members, do."

Journalist Lucas agreed, commenting that even if one rejects a "simple-minded" dictatorial view of the CFR, "one must also recognize that influence flows as well through more intricate channels: the personal ties forged among men whose paths have crossed time and again in locker rooms, officers' messes, faculty clubs, embassy conference rooms, garden parties, squash courts, and board rooms. If the Council has influence—and the evidence suggests that it does—then it is the influence its members bring to bear through such channels."

Admiral Ward went on to explain that the one common objective of CFR members is "to bring about the surrender of the sovereignty and the national independence of the United States. . . . Primarily, they want the world banking monopoly from whatever power ends up in the control of global government," Ward added.

He detailed CFR methods in a 1975 book coauthored with Phyllis Schlafly titled *Kissinger on the Couch*. "Once the ruling members of the CFR have decided that the U.S. Government should adopt a particular policy, the very substantial research facilities of CFR are put to work to develop arguments, intellectual and emotional, to support the new policy, and to confound and discredit, intellectually and politically, any opposition," he explained.

The public manifestation of the CFR is its publication *Foreign Affairs,* termed "informally, the voice of the U.S. foreign-policy establishment." Although council supporters claim "articles in *Foreign Affairs* do not reflect any consensus of beliefs. . . ," critics counter that the CFR signals members to its desired policies through such articles.

Even the stodgy *Encyclopaedia Britannica* admitted, "Ideas put forward tentatively in this journal often, if well received by the *Foreign Affairs* community, appear later as U.S. government policy or legislation; prospective policies that fail this test usually disappear."

Alvin Moscow, a sympathetic biographer of the Rockefeller family, wrote more to the point stating, "So august has been the membership of the Council that it has been seen in some quarters as the heart of the eastern Establishment. When it comes to foreign affairs, it *is* the eastern Establishment. In fact, it is difficult to point to a single major policy in U.S. foreign affairs that has been established since [President] Wilson which was diametrically opposed to then current thinking in the Council on Foreign Relations." (emphasis in the original)

The Council has two methods of communicating the thoughts and desires of its inner circle of leadership: regular luncheon or dinner meetings where prominent thinkers and leaders from around the world address council members and council study groups that periodically present position papers on subjects of interest.

The Council also offers a Corporation Service, through which subscribing companies are provided twice-a-year dinner briefings by government officials such as the treasury secretary or CIA director. Noted author John Kenneth Galbraith, who resigned from the CFR in 1970 "out of boredom," called such off-the-record talks a "scandal." "Why should businessmen be briefed by Government officials on information not available to the public, especially since it can be financially advantageous?" he reasoned.

Author G. Edward Griffin agreed that initially the CFR, as a front for the British Round Table group, was dominated by the J. P. Morgan family. "The Morgan group gradually has been replaced by the Rockefeller consortium, and the roll call of participating businesses now reads like the Fortune 500," he wrote in 1994.

One example of Rockefeller domination of the CFR came in the early 1970s when David Rockefeller went over the heads of a nominating committee and offered the editorship of *Foreign Affairs* to William Bundy, a former CIA official instrumental in prosecuting the Vietnam War.

Demonstrating how every U.S. government administration since the Council's inception has been packed with CFR members, conservative journalist and CFR researcher James Perloff noted, "The historical record speaks even more loudly. . . . Through 1988, 14 secretaries of state, 14 treasury secretaries, 11 defense secretaries and scores of other federal department heads have been CFR members."

Nearly every CIA director since Allen Dulles has been a CFR member, including Richard Helms, William Colby, George Bush, William Webster, James Woolsey, John Deutsch, and William Casey. "Many of the council's members have a personal financial interest in foreign relations," noted researcher Laurie Strand, "because it is their property and investments that are guarded by the State Department and the military [and the CIA]."

Many researchers have alleged that the CIA, in fact, serves as a security force, not only for corporate America, but for friends, relatives, and fraternity brothers of the CFR. This may be a two-way street. According to a former executive assistant to the deputy director of the CIA Victor Marchetti along with former State Department analyst John D. Marks, "The influential but private Council, composed of several hundred of the country's top political, military, business, and academic leaders, has long been the CIA's principal 'constituency' in the American public. When the agency has needed prominent citizens to front for its proprietary companies or for other special assistance, it has often turned to Council members."

CFR members who take government positions tend to bring in fellow members. When CFR member Henry Stimson came to Washington as secretary of war in 1940, he brought with him fellow member John J. McCloy as assistant secretary for personnel. McCloy, in turn, did his part over the years to bring more CFR members to government. "Whenever we needed a new man [for a government position], we just thumbed through the roll of council members and put through a call to New York," once commented McCloy, a former CFR chairman, chairman of Chase Manhattan Bank, mentor to David Rockefeller, and himself foreign policy adviser to six U.S. presidents.

Another example of the influence of the CFR can be seen in the meteoric rise of Henry Kissinger. In 1955, Kissinger was merely another unknown academic who attended a meeting at the Marine Corps School at Quantico, Virginia, hosted by then presidential foreign affairs assistant Nelson Rockefeller. This meeting was the start of a lengthy friendship between the two culminating in a $50,000 outright gift to Kissinger from Rockefeller. Kissinger soon was introduced to David Rockefeller and other prominent CFR members. Through the CFR, Kissinger obtained funding and entree to ranking officials of the Atomic Energy Commission, the three branches of the military, the CIA, and the State Department. He used this access to produce a best-selling book entitled *Nuclear Weapons and Foreign Policy,* in which he argued that a nuclear war might be "winnable." By the time of Nixon's administration, Kissinger was secretary of state, and he remains a formidable force in world affairs.

According to published reports, the Clinton administration was topheavy with more than one hundred CFR members helping to begin the Clinton years. CFR members were named ambassadors to Spain, Great Britain, Australia, Chile, Syria, South Africa, Russia, Romania, Japan, Korea, Mexico, Italy, India, France, Czech Republic, Poland, Nigeria, and the Philippines. Currently, more than a dozen members of both the House and Senate are CFR members.

Author Robert Anton Wilson commented, "If the CFR had millions of members like, say, the Presbyterian Church, this list might not mean much. But the CFR only has 3,200 members."

Because of its Wall Street/banking origins and its inherent secrecy, the Council on Foreign Relations came under strident attack by conservative writers. This public attention led to the creation of the less secretive Trilateral Commission.

Public awareness of the pervasive CFR presence in government became so widespread that the late Gary Allen, whose book on globalist organizations, *None Dare Call It Conspiracy,* sold more than five million copies despite being ignored by the Establishment media, commented just before the 1972 national elections, "There really was not a dime's worth of difference [between presidential candidates]. Voters were given the choice between CFR world government advocate Nixon and CFR world government advocate Humphrey. Only the rhetoric was changed to fool the public."

In a call to action, Allen echoed the admonition of many researchers who are suspicious of the CFR's motives when he wrote, "Democrats and Republicans must break the Insider control of their respective parties. The CFR-types and their flunkies and social climbing opportunist supporters must be invited to leave or else the Patriots must leave." Many conspiracy researchers today see a parallel situation in the 2000 election, shaping up to be a contest between Democrat Al Gore and Republican George W. Bush, both of whom have long-standing business and family ties to Wall Street and CFR members.

Author Perloff warned from a Christian perspective that a monumental battle is shaping up between the Kingdom of Christ and "an evil, one-world government: the kingdom of the Antichrist. . . . Many notables of the American Establishment have given themselves over to one side in this conflict, and it is not the side the ancient scriptures recommend. . . . Whether or not they are conspirators, whether they are conscious or not of the ultimate consequences of their actions, their powerful influence has helped move the world toward apocalyptic events."

Clearly the CFR has exerted a powerful influence, if not outright control, over U.S. policies for nearly the past century. But for almost fifty years, this influence has been shared with another closely connected secretive group—the Bilderbergers.

BILDERBERGERS

The Bilderbergers are a group of powerful men and women—many of them European royalty—who meet in secret each year to discuss the issues of the day. Many suspicious researchers claim they conspire to manufacture and manage world events.

Despite the fact that many highly regarded American media members meet with the Bilderbergers, little or nothing gets reported on the group or its activities, leading writers to claim censorship and news management.

As with the Trilateral Commission and the Council on Foreign Relations, Bilderbergers often carry cross-membership in two or more of these three groups.

British author David Icke presented a story from Dr. Kitty Little which gives fascinating insight into the long-range planning of one secret group. Dr. Little, who worked for Britain's Ministry of Aircraft Production during World War II and later the Atomic Energy Research Establishment, recounted how she attended the meeting of a Labour Party "study group" at Oxford University in 1940.

The speaker that evening was a young man who claimed to be part of a "Marxist takeover" plot. The speaker said he was a member of a nameless group (it had no name to make it harder to prove its existence) that aimed to engineer Marxist control in Britain, Europe, and parts of Africa. He explained that since Britons distrusted extremists, group members would pose as moderates, which would allow them to dismiss critics as right-wingers. The speaker added that he had been selected to head the group's political section and that he expected to be named prime minister of the United Kingdom some day.

The speaker was Harold Wilson, who indeed became prime minister during the 1960s and '70s.

Wilson was referring to the group which has come to be known as the Bilderbergers. It still has no official name, but it has been identified with the Bilderberg Hotel in Oosterbeek, Holland, where it was first discovered by the public in 1954. Its meeting in February 1957 on Saint Simons Island near Jekyll Island, Georgia, was the first on U.S. soil.

Wilson has not been the only head of state to mingle with the Bilderbergers. In 1991, then Arkansas governor Bill Clinton was honored as a Bilderberg guest. The next year he ran for and won the presidency of the United States. After his election, Clinton made no mention of the Bilderberg meetings, but, according to *The Spotlight* (a Washington tabloid that has covered Bilderberg conferences for years), Hillary Clinton attended in 1997, becoming the first American first lady to do so. Thereafter, talk steadily grew concerning her future role in politics.

The official creation of this highly secret organization came about in the early 1950s following unofficial meetings between members of Europe's elite in the 1940s. They included European foreign ministers, Holland's Prince Bernhard, and Polish socialist Dr. Joseph Hieronim Retinger, a founder of the European Movement after World War II. Retinger became known as the "father of the Bilderbergers."

Retinger was brought to America by Averell Harriman (CFR), then U.S. ambassador to England, where he visited prominent citizens such as David and Nelson Rockefeller, John Foster Dulles, and then CIA Director Walter Bedell Smith. Previously, Retinger had formed the American Committee on a United Europe along with future CIA Director and CFR member Allen Dulles, then CFR Director George Franklin, CIA official Thomas Braden, and William Donovan, former chief of the Office of Strategic Services (OSS), forerunner of the CIA. Donovan began his intelligence career as an operative of J. P. Morgan Jr., and was known as an "Anglophile," a supporter of close British-American relations. Retinger continued his participation in Bilderberg meetings until his death in 1960. Another CIA-connected person who helped create the Bilderbergers was *Life* magazine publisher C. D. Jackson, who served under President Eisenhower as "special consultant for psychological warfare."

From these associations came the idea of holding regular meetings of prominent businessmen, politicians, bankers, educators, media owners and managers, and military leaders from around the world. The Bilderbergers also are closely tied to Europe's nobility, including the British royal family. According to several sources, meetings are often attended by royalty from Sweden, Holland, and Spain.

The primary impetus for the Bilderberger meetings came from Dutch Prince Bernhard, whose full name and title was Bernhard Julius Coert Karel Godfried Pieter, Prince of the Netherlands and Prince of Lippe-Biesterfeld.

Bernhard was a former member of the Nazi *Schutzstaffel* (SS) and an employee of Germany's I.G. Farben in Paris. In 1937 he married Princess

Juliana of the Netherlands and became a major shareholder and officer in Dutch Shell Oil, along with Britain's Lord Victor Rothschild.

After the Germans invaded Holland, the royal couple moved to London. It was here, after the war, that Rothschild and Retinger encouraged Prince Bernhard to create the Bilderberger group. The prince personally chaired the group until 1976, when he resigned following revelations that he had accepted large payoffs from Lockheed to promote the sale of its aircraft in Holland.

Since 1991 the Bilderberg chairmanship has been held by Britain's Lord Peter Carrington, former cabinet minister, secretary-general of NATO, and president of the Royal Institute of International Affairs, a sister organization to the CFR. Carrington has been linked to the Rothschild banking empire by both business connections and marriage.

Americans with famous names who have attended Bilderberger meetings include CFR members George Ball, Dean Acheson, Dean Rusk, McGeorge Bundy, Christian Herter, Zbigniew Brzezinski, Douglas Dillon, J. Robert Oppenheimer, Walter Reuther, Jacob Javits, Robert McNamara, Walter Bedell Smith, and General Lyman Leminitzer. Other noteworthy attendees have included J. William Fulbright, Henry Ford II, Georges-Jean Pompidou, Giscard d'Estaing, Helmut Schmidt, and France's Baron Edmond de Rothschild.

"In fact, the Bilderbergers are a sort of unofficial CFR, expanded to an international scale," stated author Neal Wilgus.

Author and former intelligence officer Dr. John Coleman claimed "The Bilderberger Conference is a creation of [Britain's] MI6 under the direction of the Royal Institute of International Affairs." Considering the U.S. intelligence connections, it also can be legitimately argued that the Bilderberg conferences have been at least partially organized and sponsored by the CIA.

According to "Strictly Confidential" minutes of the first Bilderberg conference, "Insufficient attention has so far been paid to long-term planning, and to evolving an international order which would look beyond the present-day crisis [the Cold War]. When the time is ripe our present concepts of world affairs should be extended to the whole world."

Investigative reporter James P. Tucker, who has doggedly tracked the Bilderbergers for years, wrote, "The Bilderberg agenda is much the same as that of its brother group, The Trilateral Commission. . . . The two groups have an interlocking leadership and a common vision of the world. David Rockefeller founded the Trilaterals but shares power in the older Bilderberg group with the Rothschilds of Britain and Europe."

The Bilderbergers usually meet once a year at plush resorts around the globe, and their activities are cloaked in total secrecy despite the attendance by top-level American media members. Although the group claims to merely hold informal discussions on world affairs, there is evidence that its recommendations often become official policy.

The concept of a unified Europe under centralized control—a goal of the medieval Knights Templar—appears well along the way to becoming a reality thanks to the Bilderbergers. George McGhee, a Bilderberger and former U.S. ambassador to West Germany, acknowledged that "the Treaty of Rome, which brought the [European] Common Market into being, was nurtured at Bilderberg meetings."

Jack Sheinkman, chairman of Amalgamated Bank and a Bilderberger member, stated in 1996, "In some cases discussions do have an impact and become policy. The idea of a common European currency was discussed several years back before it became policy. We had a discussion about the U.S. establishing formal relations with China before Nixon actually did it."

Sheinkman may be one of those Bilderberger members who do not understand the true goals of the group's elite leadership. According to Icke, "The Bilderberg Elite, like Carrington and those on the steering committee, coordinate the regular attenders of Bilderberg meetings—who know the real game plan—and those invited on a rare or one-time basis—who may not know the true agenda of the organization, but can be fed the party line that world institutions are the way to peace and prosperity."

And what is this "true agenda"? It may have been revealed when Prince Bernhard stated, "It is difficult to reeducate the people who have been brought up on nationalism to the idea of relinquishing part of their sovereignty to a supernational body. . . ."

The 1998 meeting of the Bilderbergers was conducted on May 14–18 in the palatial Turnberry Hotel near Glasgow, Scotland. As usual, there was little or no reporting on this event by America's mainstream media.

Unlike their American counterparts, some members of Scotland's news media found their voice. Under the headline "Whole world in their hands," Jim McBeth of *The Scotsman* described the tight security surrounding the meeting, commenting, "Anyone approaching the hotel who did not have a stake in controlling the planet was turned back."

McBeth described the Bilderberg guest list as "an international who's who of the wealthy, influential and powerful. . . Once a year, the 120 men and women credited with putting Bill Clinton into the Oval Office and ousting Lady [Margaret] Thatcher from No. 10 [Downing Street], meet to discuss world events and, some claim, manipulate them," he added. At least one reporter, Campbell Thomas with the *Scottish Daily Mail,* was arrested by security officers, handcuffed, and held for eight hours for daring to approach the Bilderberg meeting.

It was reported that one of the decisions of the 1998 Bilderberg meeting was to encourage British prime minister Tony Blair to press harder for Britain's entry into the growing European union, a step viewed with suspicion by his predecessor Margaret Thatcher. Blair may have gone further in this plan to reduce Britain's independence, as his plan to dissolve the House of Lords was successful later in 1998. While the Lords were viewed by many as unenlightened idlers, others saw the wealthy, but patriotic, Lords as a bulwark against the erosion of English sovereignty by supporters of the "New World Order."

Unlike their American brethren, the Canadian media actually reported news of the 1996 Bilderberg meeting near Toronto with such headlines as "[Canadian prime minister Jean] Chretien to Speak at Secret World Meeting," "[Canadian publisher Conrad] Black Plays Host to World Leaders," and "World Domination or a Round of Golf?"

When asked to comment about the lack of reporting by journalist William F. Buckley who attended the Bilderberg meeting in Canada, a secretary commented, "I don't think that is the nature of the meeting, is it?" Paul Gigot of the *Wall Street Journal,* another attendee, explained, "The rules of the conference, which we all adhere to, are that we don't talk about what is said. It is all off the record. The fact that I attended is no secret."

Perhaps these reporters don't talk about what they learn at these secret meetings, but it is clear that their association shapes their editorial positions. Media critics have long charged that the differences in editorial positions of America's major news outlets are negligible.

"If the Bilderberg Group is not a conspiracy of some sort, it is conducted in such a way as to give a remarkably good imitation of one," wrote journalist C. Gordon Tether of London's *Financial Times* in

1975. About a year later, following ongoing arguments over censorship, Tether was fired by *Financial Times* editor Max Henry "Fredy" Fisher, a member of the Trilateral Commission.

An obvious connecting link between the CFR, Trilateral Commission, and the Bilderbergers is the Rockefeller family, particularly the youngest son, David.

Several wealthy and well-known businessmen constituted what amounted to an "American royalty" in the early part of the twentieth century: steel magnate Andrew Carnegie, banker Andrew Mellon, and transportation moguls Cornelius Vanderbilt and Edward Harriman.

But none approached the lasting power or international ties of the Rockefellers and Morgans.

ROCKEFELLERS

John Davison Rockefeller continues to be the most recognized (and perhaps most despised) rich man in the world even though he's been dead since 1937. During the past century, no one family in America has assembled such power and influence as the Rockefellers, thanks to their wealth and close ties to England.

Years ago the Rockefeller name continually cropped up in any discussion of secret societies, but today's mass media rarely speak of the Rockefeller role in world events. But at one time the name of John D. Rockefeller was on everyone's lips and his finances were known to all.

An 1897 edition of a rural Texas newspaper reported, "John D. Rockefeller sleeps eight and one-half hours every night, retiring at 10:30 and rising at 7. Every morning when he gets up he is $17,705 richer than he was when he went to bed. He sits down to breakfast at 8 o'clock and leaves the table at 8:30, and in that short half hour his wealth has grown $1,041.50. On Sunday he goes to church, and in the two hours he is away from home his riches have grown $4,166. His nightly amusement is playing the violin. Every evening when he picks up the instrument he is $50,000 richer than he was when he laid it down the previous night. These little facts give some idea of the relentless growth of this man's fortune."

One insight into the forging of John D.'s business philosophy might be gained by an anecdote told by Nelson Rockefeller. It seems when John D. was a small child his father, William "Big Bill" Rockefeller, who sold cancer "cures" from a medicine wagon, taught him to leap into his arms from a tall chair. One time his father held his arms out to catch him but pulled them away as little John jumped. The fallen son was told sternly, "Remember, never trust anyone completely, not even me."

At the start of the American Civil War, Rockefeller was a young agricultural commodities broker in Cleveland, Ohio. He quickly recognized the potential of the fledgling petroleum industry there, and in 1863 he and some associates built a refinery. In 1870 he incorporated Standard Oil Company of Ohio.

"The National City Bank of Cleveland, which was identified in congressional hearings as one of three Rothschild [the dominant European banking family] banks in the United States, provided John D. Rockefeller with the money to begin his monopolization of the oil refinery business, resulting in the formation of Standard Oil," noted a recent investigative video entitled, "The Money Masters."

Rockefeller, who was quoted as saying "Competition is a sin," ruthlessly eliminated competitors by either mergering or buying them out. Failing that, he cut prices until his competitors were forced to sell. He also managed lucrative railroad rebate agreements, which ensured him a near monopoly on the transportation of oil. Standard Oil—the direct ancestor of Exxon—prospered enormously, and by 1880 Rockefeller owned or controlled 95 percent of all oil produced in the United States.

Trouble for Rockefeller began in 1902 with the publication of a series of articles by Ida Tarbell, the daughter of a Pennsylvania oil producer run out of business by Rockefeller. Based on five years of research, Tarbell's series was published in *McClure's Magazine* and entitled "The History of Standard Oil Company." One reviewer proclaimed her work a "fearless unmasking of moral criminality masquerading under the robes of respectability and Christianity."

Tarbell's expose resulted in government and court actions, which appeared to break up Standard's oil monopoly. However, as early as 1882 Rockefeller had moved to mask his business dealings by creating the first great American corporation: Standard Oil Trust. "The trust embraced a maze of legal structures, making its workings virtually impervious to public investigation and understanding," explained *The New Encyclopaedia Britannica*.

Such maneuvering continued in 1892 when the Ohio Supreme Court ordered the trust dissolved. Instead, Rockefeller simply moved Standard's headquarters to New York City. In 1899 all assets and interests were transferred to a new creation, Standard Oil Company of New Jersey.

In 1906 the U.S. government charged Standard Oil with violating the Sherman Anti-Trust Act. Although apologists argued that Standard was simply caught in an emotional tidal wave of public discontent over the excesses of big business, the U.S. Supreme Court on May 15, 1911, couched its decision in these clear terms: "Seven men and a corporate machine have conspired against their fellow citizens. For the safety of the Republic we now decree that this dangerous conspiracy must be ended by November 15th."

Eight of the companies formed after the dissolution retained "Standard Oil" in their names, but even these were soon altered to present the image of diversity. Standard Oil Company of New York first merged with the trust company Vacuum Oil to form Socony-Vacuum, which in 1966 became Mobil Oil Corporation. Standard Oil of Indiana joined with Standard Oil of Nebraska and Standard Oil of Kansas and by 1985 had become Amoco Corporation. In 1984 the combination of Standard Oil of California and Standard Oil of Kentucky had become Chevron Corporation, while the old Standard Oil of New Jersey in 1972 became Exxon Corporation. Other former Standard companies include Atlantic Richfield, Buck-eye Pipe Line, Pennzoil, and Union Tank Car Company.

Ironically, the breakup of Standard only increased the wealth of Rockefeller, who now owned one fourth share of the thirty-three different oil companies created by the breakup of Standard. Shortly after the turn of the century, Rockefeller became America's first billionaire.

Continued Rockefeller control was confirmed in the late 1930s by the only study of true ownership in America's largest corporations ever made by the Securities and Exchange Commission. The study, *The Distribution of Ownership in the 200 Largest Nonfinancial Corporations*, was published in 1940. It concluded that Rockefeller holdings, while seemingly small—most were under 20 percent of outstanding stocks—nevertheless when compared to the remaining widely dispersed ownership were considered sufficient "to give the Rockefeller family control over the corporations."

Once again, interlocking directorships allowed the Rockefellers and others to maintain control over the oil industry. "All of the eight largest oil companies were interlocked in 1972 through large commercial banks with at least one other member of the top group," wrote Dr. John M.

Blair, former assistant chief economist for the Federal Trade Commission. "Exxon had four such interlocks—with Mobil, Standard of Ind., Texaco, and ARCO. Mobil had three—with Exxon, Shell, and Texaco—as did Standard of Indiana—with Exxon, Texaco, and ARCO—as well as Texaco—with Exxon, Mobil, and Standard of Ind.—and Shell with Mobil. Whenever all of the six [largest] commercial banks—exclusive of Bank of America and Western Bancorporation—hold their board meetings, directors of the top eight—excluding Gulf and SoCal—meet with directors of, on the average, 3.2 of their largest competitors."

Ironically, by the turn of the new century, the old Standard monopoly was being reformed by the anticipated merging of two of the world's oil giants: Exxon and Mobil. This $75 billion "megadeal" was quickly called "Rockefeller's revenge." At this writing the consolidation of oil companies has continued with announced plans for British Petroleum PLC to acquire Amoco.

By the time of his death in 1937, Rockefeller and his only son, John D. Rockefeller Jr., had not only built up an amazing oil empire but had established such institutions as the Rockefeller Institute for Medical Research (established 1901), the General Education Board (1903), the University of Chicago (1889), the Rockefeller Foundation (1913), the Lincoln School (1917), where the Rockefeller children began their educations, and Rockefeller University in New York City.

The Rockefellers also were greatly interested in the eugenics movement, a program of scientifically applied genetic selection to maintain and improve "ideal" human characteristics, including birth and population control. This idea grew from the writings of the Victorian scientist Sir Francis Galton, who after study reached the conclusion that prominent members of British society were such because they had "eminent" parents, thus combining Darwin's concepts of "survival of the fittest" with the class-conscious question "who's your daddy?"

If this sounds like a Nazi experiment run wild, consider that in the late nineteenth century, the United States joined fourteen other nations in passing some type of eugenics legislation. Thirty states had laws providing for the sterilization of mental patients and imbeciles. At least sixty thousand such "defectives" were legally sterilized.

Of course, to determine who was dirtying the gene pool requires extensive population statistics. So in 1910 the Eugenics Records Office was established as a branch of the Galton National Laboratory in London, endowed by Mrs. E. H. Harriman, wife of railroad magnate Edward Harriman and mother of diplomat Averell Harriman. Mrs. Harriman in 1912 sold her substantial shares of New York's Guaranty Trust bank to J. P. Morgan, thus assuring his control over that institution.

After 1900, the Harrimans—the family that gave the Prescott Bush family its start—along with the Rockefellers funded more than $11 million to create a eugenics research laboratory at Cold Spring Harbor, New York, as well as eugenics studies at Harvard, Columbia, and Cornell. The first International Congress of Eugenics was convened in London in 1912, with Winston Churchill as a director. Obviously, the concept of "bloodlines" was highly significant to these people.

In 1932 when the Congress met in New York, it was the Hamburg-Amerika Shipping Line, controlled by Harriman associates George Walker and Prescott Bush, that brought prominent Germans to the meeting. One was Dr. Ernst Rudin of the Kaiser Wilhelm Institute for Genealogy and Demography in Berlin. Rudin was unanimously elected president of the International Federation of Eugenics Societies for his work in founding the German Society for Race Hygiene, a forerunner of Hitler's racial institutes.

Eugenics work, under more politically correct names, continues right up to today. General William H. Draper Jr. was a "Supporting Member" of the International Eugenics Congress in 1932 and, despite or because of his ties to the Harriman and Bush families, was named head of the Economic Division of the U.S. Control Commission in Germany at the end of hostilities. According to authors Tarpley and Chaikin, "General Draper (in later years) founded 'Population Crisis Committee' and the 'Draper Fund,' joining with the Rockefeller and Du Pont families to promote eugenics as 'population control.' The administration of President Lyndon Johnson, advised by General Draper on the subject, began financing birth control in the tropical countries through the U.S. Agency for International Development (USAID).

"General Draper was George Bush's guru on the population question. . . . Draper's son and heir, William H. Draper III, was co-chairman for finance—chief of fundraising—of the Bush-for-President national campaign organization in 1980." The younger Draper went on to work with population control activities of the United Nations.

Rudin's eugenics work was to a large part funded by Rockefeller money. "These wealthy American families, like their counterparts in

Britain, feel themselves to be racially superior and they wish to protect their racial superiority," commented author Icke.

Nepotism proved a connecting link in these family chains. According to biographer Alvin Moscow, "Starting in the year 1917 and continuing over the next five years, the elder Rockefeller handed over his fortune to his only son and heir with no strings attached."

John Jr., while dealing primarily with philanthropic activities, nevertheless followed his father's mode of business practices, particularly in his opposition to unions. This stance softened, at least publicly, following the Ludlow Massacre of 1914 in which Colorado militia members fired on strikers at the Rockefeller-owned Colorado Fuel and Iron Company, killing forty persons.

Rockefeller Jr. helped create the United Service Organization (USO) for soldiers during World War II and supervised the building of Rockefeller Center in Manhattan. After the war, it was Rockefeller who donated land in Manhattan for the headquarters of the United Nations.

Rockefeller Jr. sired one daughter, Abby, who died of cancer in 1976 at age seventy-two, and five sons—John III, Nelson, Laurance, Winthrop, and David.

The eldest, John III, became chairman of the Rockefeller Foundation and guided millions of dollars to international agencies such as the India International Centre and the International House of Japan. His personal money went to his fabulous Oriental art collection and the creation of the Population Council, a center concerned with overpopulation and family planning. He died in 1978, but his son, John "Jay" Davison Rockefeller, carried on the family's political interest by serving as governor of West Virginia.

Nelson Aldrich Rockefeller also carved out a career in politics. Prior to World War II he journeyed to Venezuela, where he discovered the culture of South America, as well as the lucrative oil business. Because of his knowledge of the area, President and fellow New Yorker Franklin D. Roosevelt set Rockefeller on his government vocation by appointing him coordinator for inter-American affairs. Rockefeller also served as a four-term governor of New York state following various posts in the family oil and banking businesses.

In 1953 the Department of Health, Education and Welfare (HEW) was established, and Rockefeller was named undersecretary upon the recommendation of Secretary Oveta Culp Hobby. Here Rockefeller was able to push through many social programs as detailed by author Alvin Moscow, who wrote, "Oveta Culp Hobby was out front as the Secretary; Nelson worked behind the scenes, finding key personnel to head various programs, promulgating research and studies, putting together new programs and then trying to steer those new programs through the Eisenhower administration and through a sometimes skeptical Congress." Eisenhower even appointed Rockefeller special assistant for foreign affairs, the same office his close friend Henry Kissinger held under President Nixon.

He continually sought the Republican presidential nomination, but his plans were thwarted by Nixon in both 1960 and 1968 and by Senator Barry Goldwater in 1964. Rockefeller eventually was appointed vice president of the United States in 1974 by President Gerald R. Ford, himself an appointee of President Richard Nixon, who was forced to resign over the Watergate scandal. Rockefeller died at age seventy in 1979 under controversial circumstances involving a young female staff assistant.

Laurance Spelman Rockefeller became the most business-oriented of the brothers and enjoyed a successful career as a venture capitalist. Developing an early interest in aviation, he invested in Eastern Airlines in 1938 along with famed aviator Captain Eddie Rickenbacker and turned the airline into one of the world's largest. Rockefeller also invested heavily in the dreams of a young Scotsman named James McDonnell Jr., who went on to launch what became McDonnell-Douglas Aircraft Corp. He entered the realm of environmentalism and became chairman of the Citizens Advisory Committee on Environmental Quality, president of the American Conservation Association, and chairman of the New York Zoological Society.

Winthrop Rockefeller was considered the maverick of the Rockefeller clan. Dropping out of Yale in 1934, he made his way to Texas where he worked as an oil field roustabout. During World War II, he served as a combat infantryman in the Pacific theater earning a Purple Heart and Bronze Star with two Oak Leaf Clusters. Returning home, he developed a taste for drinking, women, and New York café society. But in 1953, tiring of this lifestyle, he suddenly moved to Arkansas where he was voted "Arkansas Man of the Year" in 1956. His famous name allowed him to gain the office of governor in 1967. It was then that a young Arkansas Democrat, Rhodes scholar, and DeMoley member named Bill Clinton may have gained the attention of Rockefeller. Winthrop, too, died of cancer in 1973, just two months before his sixty-first birthday.

David Rockefeller was the youngest of the five Rockefeller brothers and the one who became the most powerful, if not the most prominent. After earning a B.S. degree from Harvard, he entered the London School of Economics, a school largely funded by the Rockefeller Foundation, the Carnegie United Kingdom Trust Fund, and the widow of J. P. Morgan partner Williard Straight. Here he came into contact with the teachings of Ruskin and other socialists, including Harold Laski. Educated at Oxford, Laski early on advocated political pluralism but later turned to Marxism and became a luminary in Britain's Socialist Party. He once wrote that the state is "the fundamental instrument of society."

Returning to the States, David Rockefeller exhibited his deep feelings for England in a letter to the *New York Times* in April 1941 in which he stated, "We should stand by the British Empire to the limit and at any cost. . . ." Just before the outbreak of war, he obtained a doctorate degree from the University of Chicago. His doctoral thesis was entitled "Unused Resources and Economic Waste." Perhaps articulating the driving ambition of the Rockefeller brothers, he wrote, "Of all forms of waste, however, that which is most abhorrent is idleness. There is a moral stigma attached to unnecessary and involuntary idleness which is deeply imbedded in our conscience."

During the war, he entered the U.S. Army as a private but was soon working in North Africa and France with the Office of Strategic Services (OSS), forerunner to the CIA. This experience, along with his schooling in England, strengthened a lifelong concern with foreign affairs. It was most probably during this time that Rockefeller developed high-level intelligence contacts which later brought him insider knowledge of many top-secret operations.

By 1948 David Rockefeller was chairman of the board of trustees of the Rockefeller Institute. The president of the institute was Dr. Detlev Wulf Bronk, a biophysicist specializing in the human nervous system. According to the controversial MJ–12 documents, Bronk not only was a member of MJ–12—reportedly a supersecret group in charge of the UFO issue—but leader of the team that autopsied "extraterrestrial biological entities" recovered from a crashed disk near Roswell, New Mexico, in July 1947.

After the war, Rockefeller joined the staff of Chase National Bank of New York, where his uncle, Winthrop Aldrich, was chairman of the board and president. Chase traced its history back to central bank advocate Alexander Hamilton's Bank of the Manhattan Company begun in 1799, and by 1921 it had become the second largest national bank in the United States. In 1955 Rockefeller played a major role in the merger of Chase with the Bank of Manhattan Company, which resulted in Chase Manhattan Bank. In 1969 the bank became part of Chase Manhattan Corp. in line with the trend of establishing holding companies to avoid banking laws prohibiting certain activities, such as the acquisition of finance companies. That same year David Rockefeller became the company's board chairman and chief executive officer, thanks primarily to his preeminence in international banking.

His connections to the world of international politics as well as intelligence were improved when his uncle Aldrich retired as chairman of the bank in 1953 to become U.S. Ambassador to the Court of Saint James (England). Aldrich was succeeded by John J. McCloy, a former chairman of the Council on Foreign Relations. McCloy, who has been called the "architect of the postwar American intelligence establishment," served as assistant secretary of war from April 1941 to November 1945, president of the World Bank from 1947 to 1949, and U.S. Governor and High Commissioner for Germany from 1949 to 1952. McCloy also served on the Warren Commission, helping mediate disagreements with members who were troubled by the controversial "single bullet" theory of JFK's assassination. According to author Alvin Moscow, David Rockefeller soon became "the undisputed protégé of McCloy."

David Rockefeller had already joined the Council on Foreign Relations in 1941 before war came, and by 1950 had been elected vice president.

His interest in foreign affairs could not have been entirely altruistic, since it has been estimated that the multinational banks, with Chase leading the way, loaned more than $50 billion to developing nations between 1957 and 1977. Even sympathetic biographer Moscow admitted, "David's fascination with international relations, necessitating intricate knowledge of the governmental, social and economic policies of nations throughout the world, on both sides of the Iron Curtain, dovetailed uniquely with his interest and concern in expanding Chase Manhattan's business in the international banking market."

To say that David Rockefeller may be one of the most important men in America would be an understatement. According to Gary Allen, in the year 1973 alone, "David Rockefeller met with 27 heads of state, including the rulers of Russia and Red China." In 1976 when Australian president Malcolm Fraser visited the United States, he conferred with David Rockefeller before meeting President Gerald Ford. "This is truly incredible," wrote author Ralph Epperson, "because David Rockefeller has neither been elected or appointed to any governmental position where he could officially represent the United States government."

But the Rockefeller influence—if not control—extends far beyond their banking and oil interests. The Rockefeller Brothers Fund, for example, in 1997 listed nearly $500 million in assets. It was incorporated in 1940 by the five brothers. Since that time, the Fund has dispersed more than $461 million in grants to a wide range of activities and institutions including various universities, numerous arts programs, the Smithsonian Institution, Buddhist Zen Center, Aspen Institute, Asian Cultural Council, Brookings Institution, National Audubon Society, National Park Foundation, Planned Parenthood of New York City, NAACP, German Marshall Fund of the U.S., Yale University, Center for Strategic and International Studies, National Academy of Sciences, and the Society for International Development.

In 1977 the Fund contributed $1 million to the Council on Foreign Relations. Perhaps due to the adverse publicity of conspiracy writers, this amount had dropped to a mere $45,000 in 1997, $25,000 of which went to study the "economic and political implications of Korean unification." The Trilateral Commission, which received $120,000 from the Fund in 1977, was not mentioned in their 1997 annual report.

In 1997 the Fund also spent more than $1.2 million in grants for various projects in New York City, an area of special and long-term interest by the Fund.

The Fund is especially involved in environmental issues, as evidenced by its donations to National Environmental Trust, Greenpeace Environmental Trust, National Wildlife Federation, American Conservation Association, Environmental Defense Fund, among others. Conspiracy authors have noted that if someone owned an interest in companies which might be adversely affecting the environment, what better way to gain some measure of control over activists than by heavy contributions?

Abby M. O'Neill, niece of the five Rockefeller brothers, in 1998 ended her term as chairwoman of the Fund. The position was assumed by Nelson's son, Steven C. Rockefeller. The one-world outlook of the Rockefellers was still evident in the Fund's 1997 annual report. Mrs. O'Neill wrote that the Fund had "a refocused 'One World' strategy, with an explicitly global perspective and an emphasis on the convergence of national and international frameworks."

Fund president and CFR member Colin G. Campbell wrote that Rockefeller money was being used to help create "a number of cross-sectoral partnerships . . . that involve such sometimes unlikely partners as nonprofit and for-profit entities, government agencies and nongovernment organizations, research universities and grassroots activist groups."

"In fact much of the U.S. government's involvement in health, education and welfare in the latter half of the twentieth century seems to have been pioneered by the Rockefeller Foundation in the first half of the century," commented author Moscow.

Rockefeller activities always seem to involve or produce world leaders. Henry Kissinger already has been mentioned. Prior to World War II, a Rockefeller Foundation division on economic research was headed by Canadian W. L. Mackenzie King. A mentor to John D. Jr., Mackenzie later became prime minister of Canada.

Contributing to the power of their name was the fact that Rockefeller projects were nearly always successful. According to biographer Alvin Moscow, the brothers "moved warily before lending the Rockefeller name or finances to any new endeavor or enterprise. But once committed, they stayed with their commitments for the long haul, giving generously of their money, their time and their efforts. It became known in various civic and social circles that if a Rockefeller was involved, the project most likely had merit and was expected to succeed."

Despite their close ties and commitments to Britain, the Rockefellers gave the appearance of being a purely American phenomenon. Another American banking empire actually began in Britain.

MORGANS

If John D. Rockefeller had an equal in the halcyon days of the robber barons it was John Pierpont Morgan, a man even more demonstrably connected with an "Anglophile network."

The Morgan banking empire continues to hold sway over both business and political decisions being made today, and many Morgan employees and agents can be counted among the membership of the secret societies.

Morgan's mother was Juliet Pierpont Morgan, whose father, the Reverand John Pierpont, was vocally pro-British and the son of a Yale University founder. J. P. Morgan's father, Junius Spencer Morgan, was an American financier who traveled to England in the 1850s where he was befriended by another expatriate American named George Peabody, a man already doing business with the British Rothschilds. Joining with Peabody under the name Peabody, Morgan & Company, Junius's wealth grew as the result of obtaining loans for the North during the American Civil War. His son, John Pierpont Morgan, was born in 1837.

Junius and son took charge of the business upon the retirement of Peabody in 1864 and promptly changed the name to Morgan and Company.

The Morgans, too, became closely connected to the British Rothschilds, even staying in their home on occasion. Many authors have written that the Morgans eventually became a covert agent for the Rothschilds. "Morgan's activities in 1895–1896 in selling U.S. gold bonds in Europe were based on his alliance with the House of Rothschild," noted author Gabriel Kolko.

The idea that the Morgans were the American front for Britain's Baron Nathan Mayer Rothschild's interests also was advanced by Eustace Mullins, the author who in 1952 first revealed the maneuvering which resulted in the creation of the Federal Reserve System. Regarding the Rothschilds, Mullins wrote, "Even though they had a registered agent in the United States . . . it was extremely advantageous to them to have an American representative who was not known as a Rothschild agent." Mullins said the Rothschilds "preferred to operate anonymously in the United States behind the facade of J. P. Morgan and Company."

"Part of the reality of the day was an ugly resurgence of anti-Semitism," wrote George Wheeler, author of *Pierpont Morgan and Friends: Anatomy of a Myth*. "Someone was needed as a cover. Who better than J. Pierpont Morgan, a solid, Protestant exemplar of capitalism able to trace his family back to pre-Revolutionary times?"

"The possibilities are obvious that a major portion of the wealth and power of the Morgan firm was, and always had been, merely the wealth and power of the Rothschilds who had raised it up in the beginning and who sustained it through its entire existence," agreed author Griffin.

Although J. P. Morgan was born in America and educated in Boston, in 1856 he traveled to Germany where he studied at the University of Gottingen, founded by England's George II in 1737 who then was serving as Elector of Hanover. Notorious for its expulsion of dissident professors called the "Gottingen Seven,"—which included the brothers Grimm and other adherents of Georg Hegel including Karl Marx—the university continued to be a hotbed of antiestablishment and secret society activity.

Returning to the United States, Morgan joined the New York banking firm of Duncan, Sherman and Company, the American representatives of their London company. "Thereafter, Morgan appears to have served as a Rothschild financial agent and went to great length to appear totally American," Griffin wrote.

At the outbreak of the American Civil War, young Morgan demonstrated that legalities and honesty played little part in his business practices. In May 1861 twenty-four-year-old Morgan offered to sell five thousand military rifles to the commander of the federal army stationed at St. Louis for twenty-two dollars apiece. The commander, desperate for rifles, agreed, but when the rifles arrived he refused payment, claiming the weapons were obsolete and defective. Morgan sued the army and won a court judgment ordering that he be paid the $109,912.

A congressional investigating committee in 1862 concluded that Morgan had defrauded the government. The committee found that the rifles, considered "thoroughly unserviceable, obsolete and dangerous," had been bought for $3.50 each from a New York arsenal by a Simon Stevens, who was employed by Morgan. When the St. Louis commander agreed to buy the weapons sight unseen, Morgan had used the agreement as collateral to borrow money to pay for the weapons. So the U.S. Army had bought its own defective rifles from Morgan, who, at no financial risk to himself, realized about 500 percent profit on each gun.

In 1871 he became a partner in one of his father's firms, Drexel, Morgan and Company, which later became simply J. P. Morgan and Company. This firm soon became the predominant source of U.S. government financing.

"Because of his links with the Peabody firm, Morgan had intimate and highly useful connections with the London financial world, and during the 1870s he was thereby able to provide the rapidly growing industrial corporations of the United States with much-needed capital from British bankers," noted *The New Encyclopaedia Britannica*.

Next to the European Rothschild family, the Morgan Company became one of the most powerful banking houses in the world. But that wasn't enough for John P. Morgan, who inherited the family interests in 1890 following his father's death in a carriage accident on the French Riviera. Five years earlier he began the reorganization of America's largest railroads and by 1902 was the world's most powerful railroad magnate, controlling about five thousand miles of track.

Morgan even helped bail out the U.S. government following a bank panic in 1893. Forming a syndicate, Morgan propped up the government's depleted reserves with $62 million in Rothschild gold. In the 1890s he oversaw the merger of Edison General Electric and Thomson-Houston Electric Company to form General Electric, which quickly dominated electrical equipment manufacturing. Next, Morgan merged several steel firms to form United States Steel Corporation, and in 1902 he created International Harvester Company out of several competing agricultural equipment manufacturers.

This diversified Morgan empire has never been equaled and continues to dominate the American financial industry to this day. "Through a system of interlocking memberships on the boards of companies he had reorganized or influenced, Morgan and his banking house achieved a top-heavy concentration of control over some of the nation's leading corporations and financial institutions," explained *The New Encyclopaedia Britannica*. This empire was extended to include tax-exempt foundations, trusts, pension funds, and even government positions. Such manipulation can explain how control over the commercial and economic life of the United States was achieved and maintained for those with the knowledge, willpower, and wealth.

Although J. P. Morgan and John D. Rockefeller competed with each other in many areas, "in the end, they worked together to create a national banking cartel called the Federal Reserve System," wrote Griffin.

The initial plan for the Federal Reserve System was conceived at a secret meeting in 1910 at Morgan's private resort on Jekyll Island off the coast of Georgia.

Morgan, connected to the Rockefellers through his investment associate Nelson Aldrich, remained the dominant American capitalist until his death in 1913, the same year the Fed was created.

Morgan's son, John Pierpont Jr., known as Jack, continued to increase the family's fortune following his father's death. Groomed to his place as head of the Morgan empire, the younger Morgan spent eight years working in the firm's London office developing close ties to Britain's elite banking circles. During World War I, Morgan organized more than two thousand banks for the underwriting of more than $1 billion in Allied bonds. He became the only banker to purchase supplies, both military and otherwise, for both the British and French governments during the war. This indicates considerable leverage and clout within those governments, again suggesting the involvement of the Rothschilds.

ROTHSCHILDS

Although largely unknown to modern Americans, the name of Rothschild is synonymous with international banking and can be found behind the scene of many major world events.

This secretive banking dynasty was begun by Mayer Amschel Bauer, a German Jew born on February 23, 1744, in Frankfurt, then a hotbed of anti-Semitism stemming from the widely publicized philosophies of Immanuel Kant and Johann Fichte. His father dealt in fine silk cloth despite ordinances prohibiting Jews from the practice.

Young Mayer studied to become a Rabbi. He was particularly schooled in *Hashkalah,* a blending of religion, Hebrew law, and reason, which had become popular during the Age of Enlightenment. The death of his parents forced Mayer to leave Rabbinical school and become an apprentice at a banking house.

Quickly learning the trade, he became court financial agent to William IX, royal administrator of the Hesse-Kassel region, and a prominent Freemason. He ingratiated himself to William, who was only one year older than himself, by joining his interest in Freemasonry and antiquities. Mayer would search out ancient coins and sell them to his benefactor at greatly reduced prices. Considering his Rabbinical training coupled with his serious searches for antiquities, he surely developed a deep understanding of the ancient mysteries, particularly those of the Jewish Cabala. It was during this same period that the metaphysics of the Cabala began to fuse with the traditions of Freemasonry as will be described later.

Young Mayer also added to his client list the royal German family of Thurn und Taxis, a descendant of which would be executed as a member of the secret society which created Adolf Hitler. The prominent Thurn and Taxis family administered a courier service throughout the Holy Roman Empire. "They prospered because they received before their rivals news of market trends, commodity prices and major political events," noted Rothschild biographer Derek Wilson. Mayer saw firsthand that information, especially obtained quickly, often meant great wealth. Today, the axiom has become "time equals money." To prevent prying eyes from reading their mail, the family wrote all correspondence in *Judendeutsch,* German written in Hebrew characters. This code has prevented most researchers from any clear understanding of their methods and intentions.

During this time, according to *The New Encyclopaedia Britannica,* "Mayer set the pattern that his family was to follow so successfully—to do business with reigning houses by preference and to father as many sons as possible who could take care of the family's many business affairs abroad."

According to several authors, the family fortune was built upon money embezzled from William IX, who was paid an enormous sum by the British government to provide Hessian soldiers to fight American colonists during the Revolutionary War. William handed over this money to Mayer for investment, but instead it reportedly was used to establish his son Nathan as head of the London branch of the family banking house. Mayer eventually repaid the money but "Nathan manipulated the situation in such a way that this became the origin of the enormous Rothschild fortune," Icke wrote.

Biographer Derek Wilson acknowledged this by writing, "It was the temporary diversion of the immense sums of money originating in Hesse-Kassel which enabled N. M. [as Nathan liked to be called] to launch his banking operation, providing him with both liquidity and prestige."

"From the earliest days, the Rothschilds appreciated the importance of proximity to politicians, the men who determined not only the extent of budget deficits but also the domestic and foreign policies. . . ." wrote biographer Niall Ferguson. "Rothschild influence extended to royalty as well. Nathan first came into contact with British royalty thanks to his father's purchase of outstanding debts owed by George, Prince Regent—later King George IV—and his brothers."

Ferguson traced Rothschild influence on through the British royalty to Queen Victoria's prince consort, Albert, and his son. The British Rothschilds also were quite close to most prominent Victorian politicians such as Lord John Russell, Lord William Gladstone, Benjamin Disraeli, Arthur Balfour, Joseph Chamberlain, and Lord Randolph Churchill, Winston's father.

It was also about the time of Nathan's arrival in London that Mayer Bauer changed his name to Rothschild (literally "red shield") taken from a red shield emblem on the ghetto home of his ancestors. This name change undoubtedly was an attempt to separate his family from the raging anti-Semitism prevalent in Germany at the time. To further insulate the family from such racism, the Rothschilds used a stable of registered agents and front men to operate their far-flung business dealings.

This may be a good point to dismiss claims that the modern secret societies, either wittingly or otherwise, are furthering the aims of an international Jewish conspiracy. While it is undoubtedly true that many of the world's wealthy elite have a Jewish heritage, one should not be sidetracked by the issue of race or religion. There is no evidence of substance to prove that Jews or Hebrews—or any other racial or religious group—are any more greedy or ambitious than anyone else.

Furthermore, any discussion of anti-Semitism is frequently lost in a misunderstanding of the distinction between Hebrews, Jews, and Zionists.

The American Heritage Dictionary of the English Language describes a Hebrew as a member of the Semitic people, a race descended from Abraham of the Old Testament which, ironically enough, also includes most Arabs. A Jew, on the other hand, is a adherent of Judaism, a religion handed down by the Israelites. A Zionist is a member of a political movement concerned with preserving and furthering the aims of the state of Israel. These constitute three separate issues: race, religion, and politics.

To lump these singular issues into one single conspiracy is both wrong headed and contrary to the historical evidence. Most people in modern America realize that it is wrong to judge a person on race, an attribute over which that person has no control. Likewise, it is considered bad manners by most to publicly attack another person's religion. Only one's politics are considered fair game for dissension and argument.

It is here, in the realm of politics, that much confusion has been sown. Supporters of Zionism for years have skillfully attacked their opponents as "anti-Semites" to the extent that many Americans, Jews and gentiles alike and especially the media, are loath to even question the policies of Israel no matter how odious.

Furthermore, the broad brush of anti-Semitism frequently has been used to besmirch anyone offering a conspiratorial view of history.

While it may be true that secret organizations in the past were built along both racial and religious grounds, attempting to bring race or religion into a discussion of modern secret societies and conspiracies only serves to confuse the issue and repel conscientious researchers. Although many international financiers are of Jewish descent, it is no more fair to accuse the Hebrew race of an international conspiracy than it would be to blame all Caucasians for the acts of Hitler's Nazis.

W. Cleon Skousen, a former FBI agent who served as police chief of Salt Lake City in the late 1950s, wrote about international conspiracies in several books, including *The Naked Communist*. He, too, came to understand that racial identification was "an oversimplified explanation for the rise of the global power structure which has snared mankind." He explained, "In studying the global conspiracy it is important to keep in mind that it was not any particular race or religion but the 'passion for money and power' which has drawn the tycoons of world finance into a tightly knit, mutual-aid society."

But such considered and reasoned understanding of anti-Semitism was not in vogue during Mayer Rothschild's time. So he built his financial empire while studiously attempting to avoid the racism of his day.

This is not to imply that the Rothschilds were not proud of their Jewish ancestry. By all accounts, family leaders have been most devout in their observance of Jewish traditions and customs. Over the years, the family has donated liberally to Jewish causes and may have even played a vital role in establishing the state of Israel, although some conspiracy writers claim that Rothschild interest in Israel more concerns the control of oil than love of a homeland.

One method utilized to avoid racism was the enlistment of non-Jewish operatives as fronts for the Rothschild organization. At the time of the American Civil War, J. P. Morgan publicly made anti-Semitic remarks, yet he furthered the goals of the Rothschilds. "How much of Morgan's apparent anti-Semitism was real and how much may have been a pragmatic guise is, in the final analysis, of little importance. . . . Regardless of one's interpretation of the nature of the relationship between the Houses of Morgan and Rothschild, the fact remains that it was close, it was ongoing, and it was profitable to both. If Morgan truly did harbor feelings of anti-Semitism, neither he nor the Rothschilds ever allowed them to get in the way of their business," noted author Griffin.

According to author Icke, Morgan and Rockefeller were wealthy "gofers" who used Rothschild financing to "build vast empires which controlled banking, business, oil, steel, etc., and ran the United States economy in the way the Oppenheimers do in South Africa."

Another expediency was the use of Mayer Rothschild's sons, known as the "Frankfurt Five," who were carefully schooled and groomed to loyally further the family banking business.

While Mayer and his eldest son, Amschel Mayer, supervised from their Frankfurt bank, son Nathan Mayer established the London branch in 1804. Meanwhile, the youngest son, Jakob (who preferred to be called James), joined Paris banking circles in 1811 while Salomon Mayer began operating in Vienna and Karl Mayer in Naples.

Mayer also worked with neighbors. "The Warburgs began lobbying for Rothschild business in Hamburg as early as 1814, though regular dealings were not established until the 1830s. . . ." wrote biographer Niall Ferguson.

In 1785 the Rothschilds shared quarters with a family named Schiff. A grandson, Jacob Henry Schiff, immigrated to America in 1865 after meeting Abraham Kuhn, who invited him to join his New York investment firm. In 1875 young Schiff married the daughter of Solomon Loeb, then head of the powerful investment banking firm of Kuhn, Loeb & Company of New York City. Schiff became head of the firm in 1885 with the death of Loeb. It was Schiff who financed the purchase of the Union Pacific for railroad magnate Edward H. Harriman, father of later world statesman W. Averell Harriman. Both Schiff and Averell Harriman were to play important roles in the rise of Communism in Russia.

The elder Harriman's two sons attended Yale and were inducted into the Order of the Skull and Bones—William Averell (The Order, 1913) and Edward Roland Noel (The Order, 1917). During the 1930s W. Averell's banking firm of W. A. Harriman & Company merged with the private international banking firm of Brown Brothers creating Brown Brothers, Harriman & Company, a longtime partner of which was Prescott Bush (The Order, 1917), father of George Bush (The Order, 1949).

Intermarriages between the prominent Jewish immigrant families were common around the turn of the century. "As they set about protecting their vast estates, moreover, these Jewish dynasts often found it useful in the United States as in western Europe to marry among each other," wrote history professor Howard M. Sachar. "Solomon Loeb and Abraham Kuhn, it is recalled, married each other's sisters, and Jacob Schiff became an instant partner by marrying Loeb's daughter. In turn, Felix Warburg, scion of a distinguished Hamburg banking family, assured himself a senior partnership in Kuhn, Loeb by marrying Schiff's daughter Frieda. Felix's brother Paul married Solomon Loeb's daughter Nina—from Loeb's second wife—and thus became his own brother's uncle. Another partner, Otto Kahn, married Adelaide Wolff, daughter of one of the firm's original investors. At Goldman, Sachs & Co., two Sachs boys married two Goldman daughters."

Another more recent example of these upper-level connections was the much publicized 1950s love affair between Elie de Rothschild and Winston Churchill's former daughter-in-law, Pamela Churchill. After the affair broke up, she moved to New York where, after a short-lived marriage to a Broadway producer, she wed financier and CFR member Averell Harriman. In 1993 Pamela Harriman was named U.S. Ambassador to France by President Clinton.

Unrelenting attention to business, coupled with intermarriages and the use of front men, built a gigantic and secretive Rothschild banking empire. This empire exerted considerable influence on the economic and hence the political history of Europe as well as the United States, although here in a more covert and indirect manner.

In 1806 Nathan had become an English citizen and wed Hannah Cohen, the oldest daughter of Levi Barent Cohen, then London's leading financier. The marriage cemented his acceptance by the British banking establishment.

"Nathan Rothschild was able to brag later that in the 17 years he had been in England he had increased his original 20,000 pounds stake given to him by his father by 2,500 times, i.e. to 50,000,000—a truly vast sum at that time, comparable in purchasing power to billions of U.S. dollars today," stated one Rothschild investigator.

Derek Wilson, a sympathetic biographer of the Rothschilds, noted that in 1810 Nathan was merely one of several financiers operating in London. But by 1815 he had become the principal financier to the British government and its Bank of England. "This remarkable coup could only have been achieved by a complex series of dealings, many of which were encased in a secrecy which cannot now be penetrated," remarked Wilson.

Author Icke saw this connection as proof of conspiratorial control by the Rothschilds. "They had the crown heads of Europe in debt to them and this included the Black Nobility dynasty, the Hapsburgs, who ruled the Holy Roman Empire for 600 years," he wrote. "The Rothschilds also took control of the Bank of England. If there was a war, the Rothschilds were behind the scenes, creating the conflict and funding both sides."

"They may have held citizenship in the country of their residence, but patriotism was beyond their comprehension," wrote Griffin. "They were also very bright, if not cunning, and these combined traits made them the role model of the cool pragmatists who dominate the political and financial world of today."

The Rothschild financial empire arose from loans to Europe's rulers and from the family's successful use of fractional banking. To understand fractional banking requires a brief look at the nomenclature and history of money; to understand its application requires a look at one of the most powerful financial institutions on the planet.

SECRETS OF MONEY AND THE FEDERAL RESERVE SYSTEM

Money—whether a piece of paper or a figure on a computer screen—is intrinsically worthless, yet it fuels the modern world. The trappings of money and banking have been compared to those of a religion, yet only those who profit from it understand the inner workings of the money cult. And they work hard to keep it that way.

In America the ultimate control of money rests with the bankers of the Federal Reserve System (the Fed), "the crucial anomaly at the very core of representative democracy, an uncomfortable contradiction with the civic mythology of self-government," as described by author William Greider, a former assistant managing editor of the *Washington Post*. His 1987 book *Secrets of the Temple: How the Federal Reserve Runs the Country* disparages "nativist conspiracy theories" yet presents an eloquent argument demonstrating conspiratorial control by the Fed.

Early man had no need for money. He hunted when he was hungry and farmed to stockpile food for the winter. If he needed a commodity which belonged to his neighbor, bartering was the order of the day.

But as work became more specialized, the limits to barter became apparent. The sheepherder could not always take his entire herd to market. So humans turned to coins as a measure of wealth. Precious metal, particularly gold, was limited in supply, always desirable, and easily transported as small coins imprinted with words or pictures to assure authenticity and purity—plus there was some ancient, almost holy, reverence attached to it. But heavy, bulging sacks of gold coins were burdensome, not to mention a tempting target for thieves and robbers.

Thus was born paper money. A paper bill was simply a promissory note. As such, paper was considered as valuable as real goods or services. This procedure worked well for a time, but then certain individuals realized that paper money, if loaned for a fee, could be used to generate more money.

The early goldsmiths who warehoused gold coins used this stockpiled wealth as the basis for issuing paper money. Since it was highly unlikely that everyone would demand their gold back at the same time, the smiths became bankers. They would loan out a portion of their stockpile for interest or profit. This practice—loaning the greater portion of wealth while retaining only a small fraction for emergencies—became known as fractional-reserve, or fractional banking. This system worked well enough unless everyone suddenly wanted their deposits back and started a "run" on the bank.

Added to fractional banking was the concept of "fiat" money—intrinsically worthless paper money made acceptable by law or decree of government. An early example of this system was recorded by Marco Polo during his visit to China in 1275. Polo noted the emperor forced his people to accept black pieces of paper with an official seal on them as legal money under pain of imprisonment or death. The emperor then used this fiat money to pay all his own debts.

"One is tempted to marvel at the [emperor's] audacious power and the subservience of his subjects who endured such an outrage," wrote author Griffin, "but our smugness rapidly vanishes when we consider the similarity of our own Federal Reserve Notes. They are adorned with signatures and seals; counterfeiters are severely punished; the government pays its expenses with them; the population is forced to accept them; they— and the 'invisible' checkbook money into which they can be converted— are made in such vast quantity that it must be equal in amount to all the treasures of the world. And yet they cost nothing to make. In truth, our present monetary system is an almost exact replica of that which supported the warlords of seven centuries ago."

But today it is the bankers, not warlords, who profit from money and they have created an incredible mechanism for doing so: the Federal Reserve System.

Anyone seeking to prove the existence of conspiracies in America need look no further than the origin of our present central bank. Here is a well-documented conspiracy involving the very names tied to modern secret societies.

The early American colonists had printed small quantities of paper money and were prospering. Benjamin Franklin explained, "In the colonies we issue our own money. It is called Colonial Script. We issue it in proper proportion to the demands of trade and industry to make the products pass easily from the producers to the consumers. . . . In this manner, creating for ourselves our own paper money, we control its purchasing power, and we have no interest to pay to no one."

The English parliament, at the urging of the Bank of England, put a stop to this colonial prosperity with passage of the Currency Act of 1764, which prohibited the printing of currency. The colonists were forced to accept notes from the Bank of England. Franklin and others claimed it was this outlawing of debt-free money which caused economic depression and widespread unemployment precipitating the American Revolution.

The very idea of a central bank run by professional bankers has been a contentious issue since the founding of the United States. The arguments for and against a central bank can be seen in the debates of Founding Fathers Thomas Jefferson and Alexander Hamilton.

Hamilton believed in strong central government and a central bank overseen by a wealthy elite. "No society could succeed which did not unite the interest and credit of rich individuals with those of the state," he wrote. Supporters of Hamilton's elitist ideals formed America's first political party, the Federalists. Hamilton, once described as a "tool of the international bankers," argued that "a national debt, if it is not excessive, will be to us a national blessing."

The Bank of North America was created in 1781, even before the drafting of the Constitution, by Continental Congressman Robert Morris, who tried to craft it into a central bank copying the Bank of England. It lasted just three years before being discontinued due to rampant fraud and the inflation caused by the creation of baseless "fiat" currency.

Hamilton, a former aide to Morris, became secretary of the Treasury and in 1791 headed the next attempt at a central bank by establishing the First Bank of the United States, a move strongly opposed by Jefferson and his followers.

Jefferson knew from European history that a central bank could quickly become the master of a nation. He pointed to the British experience and noted that "The other nations of Europe have tried and trodden every path of force or folly in fruitless quest of the same object, yet we still expect to find in juggling tricks and banking dreams, that money can be made out of nothing. . . ."

"I sincerely believe . . . that banking establishments are more dangerous than standing armies; and that the principle of spending money to be paid by posterity, under the name of funding, is but swindling futurity on a large scale," he wrote to John Taylor in 1816, adding, "Already they have raised up a money aristocracy. . . . The issuing power should be taken from the banks and restored to the people to whom it properly belongs."

Jefferson further believed a central bank to be unconstitutional. "I consider the foundation of the Constitution as laid on this ground: That 'all powers not delegated to the United States, by the Constitution, nor prohibited by it to the States, are reserved to the States or to the people.' To take a single step beyond the boundaries thus specially drawn around the powers of Congress, is to take possession of a boundless field of power, no longer susceptible of any definition. The incorporation of a bank, and the powers assumed by this bill, have not, in my opinion, been delegated to the United States, by the Constitution."

Ironically, Jefferson's supporters, considered liberal in their time, formed what was to become the Republican Party.

Jefferson was not alone among the Founding Fathers to express distaste over the profit of banking. "Our whole banking system I ever abhorred, I continue to Abhor, and I shall die abhorring. . . ." wrote John Adams in 1811. "Every bank of discount, every bank by which interest is to be paid or profit of any kind made by the [lender], is downright corruption. It is taxation for the public for the benefit and profit of individuals. . . ."

The First Bank of the United States also was closely modeled after the Bank of England and created a partnership between the government and banking interests. Twenty percent of the bank's capital was obtained through the federal government with the remaining 80 percent pledged by private investors, including foreigners such as the Rothschilds. "The law records show that they [the Rothschilds] were the power in the old Bank of the United States," wrote author Gustavus Myers. It is clear that conspiring European bankers and their New World associates were trying to gain control over America's money supply.

This bank also caused inflation by the creation of fractional-reserve notes. Money merchants prospered but the average citizen suffered. In 1811, when the bank's twenty-year charter came up for renewal, it was defeated by one vote in both the Senate and the House.

But the costs of the War of 1812, along with chaotic financial conditions, prompted Congress to issue a twenty-year charter to the Second Bank of the United States in 1816. This central bank ended in 1836, after President Andrew Jackson in 1832 vetoed a congressional bill to extend its charter, precipitating what became known as the Bank War. Jackson, the first president from west of the Appalachian Mountains and the hero of the Battle of New Orleans, denounced the central bank as unconstitutional as well as "a curse to a republic; inasmuch as it is calculated to raise around the administration a moneyed aristocracy dangerous to the liberties of the country."

It was probably no coincidence that America's first assassination attempt was made on Jackson in 1835 by a man named Richard Lawrence, who claimed to be "in touch with the powers in Europe." Lawrence's pistols misfired, and the unharmed but infuriated Jackson withdrew government funds from the "den of vipers" and Second Bank president Nicholas Biddle retaliated by curtailing credit nationally, causing widespread economic panic. According to author Eustace Mullins, Biddle was an agent of Jacob Rothschild in Paris.

Next, Jackson was censured by Biddle's friends in the Senate by a vote of 26–20 for failure to obtain Congressional authorization to withdraw the funds. The political motivation behind this action was confirmed in 1837, when the Senate annulled Jackson's censure by a 24–19 vote. Biddle disappeared from the scene, and by the end of his two terms "Old Hickory" had managed to totally eliminate the national debt.

Jackson saw Biddle's maneuverings as a bald-faced attempt to blackmail the government into renewing the bank's charter. He warned, "The bold effort the present bank had made to control the Government, the distress it had wantonly produced . . . are but premonitions of the fate that awaits the American people should they be deluded into a perpetuation of this institution, or the establishment of another like it."

There were other attempts to resurrect a central bank, but none succeeded until the creation of the Federal Reserve System in 1913.

The effort to resurrect a central bank actually began three years earlier. "There was an occasion near the close of 1910, when I was as secretive, indeed, as furtive as any conspirator. . . . I do not feel it is any exaggeration to speak of our secret expedition to Jekyll Island as the occasion of the actual conception of what eventually became the Federal Reserve System. . . ." wrote Frank A. Vanderlip, one of the men who created the Fed. He went on to become president of New York's National City Bank.

Vanderlip was referring to a secretive trip on the night of November 22, 1910, by seven men representing perhaps as much as one fourth of the wealth of the world, to Jekyll Island, J. P. Morgan's island retreat off the coast of Georgia. This mission was so secret that only first names were used and the regular servants on the island had been relieved by new employees who did not know any of the participants.

The secretive seven were Vanderlip, who represented William Rockefeller and Jacob Schiff's investment firm of Kuhn, Loeb & Company; Assistant Secretary of the United States Treasury Abraham Piatt Andrew; senior partner of J. P. Morgan Company Henry P. Davison; First National Bank of New York (a Morgan dominated institution) president Charles D. Norton; Morgan lieutenant Benjamin Strong; Kuhn, Loeb & Company partner Paul Mortiz Warburg; and Rhode Island Republican Senate "Whip" Nelson W. Aldrich, chairman of the National Monetary Commission, the only nonbanker in the group. But Aldrich was an associate of banker J. P. Morgan and father-in-law of John D. Rockefeller Jr. Warburg, a representative of the European Rothschilds, was brother to Max Warburg, chief of the M. M. Warburg Company banking consortium in Germany and the Netherlands.

The group secluded themselves for a week on Jekyll Island and prepared plans for banking reform which the government deemed necessary due to a series of financial panics. Today, many researchers believe these panics were artificially created with a view toward forcing public acceptance of these very "reforms."

Author Ralph Epperson noted that Morgan returned to the States after visiting Europe in early 1907 and began rumors that the Knickerbocker Bank of New York was insolvent. Frightened depositors started a run on the bank, which sparked runs on other banks and the Panic of 1907 began. "A study of the panics of 1873, 1893 and 1907 indicates that these panics were the result of the international bankers' operations in London," concluded author Eustace Mullins, the authorized biographer of poet Ezra Pound, who encouraged Mullins to research the Fed in 1948.

Princeton University president (soon to be U.S. president) Woodrow Wilson proclaimed his solution to the financial panic, "All this trouble could be averted if we appointed a committee of six or seven public-spirited men like J. P. Morgan to handle the affairs of our country." Cries for a stable national banking system rose.

"So the American people, who had suffered through the American Revolution, the War of 1812, the battles between Andrew Jackson and the Second Bank of the United States, the Civil War, the previous panics of 1873 and 1893, and now the Panic of 1907, were finally conditioned to the point of accepting the solution offered by those who had caused all of these events: the international bankers. That solution was a central bank," wrote Epperson.

Under pressure from constituents, Congress passed the Aldrich-Vreeland Act of 1908 which authorized national banks to issue emergency currency called "script" and created the National Monetary Commission—chaired by Senator Aldrich—to recommend ways of stabilizing the U.S. monetary system.

"From the start, it was obvious that the Commission was a sham," wrote author Griffin. "The so-called fact-finding body held no official meetings for almost two years while Aldrich toured Europe consulting with the top central bankers of England, France and Germany. Three-hundred thousand tax dollars were spent on these junkets, and the only tangible product of the Commission's work was 38 massive volumes of the history of European banking." These volumes focused on the German *Reichsbank* whose principal stockholders were the Rothschilds and Warburg's family firm, M.M. Warburg Company.

The Commission's final report was prepared by the seven prominent men who secretly journeyed to Morgan's Jekyll Island Hunt Club ostensibly to hunt ducks. These men concluded not to have one central bank in the United States, but several and they agreed that no one was to utter the words "central" or "bank." Most important, they decided that this creation would be made to look like an official agency of the U.S. government.

Speaking before an appreciative audience of the American Bankers' Association, Aldrich stated, "The organization proposed is not a bank, but a cooperative union of all the banks of the country for definite purposes." Warburg had conceived of the idea of constructing this cooperative union in a manner palatable to both the bankers and the public. Any restrictions on the bankers could be—and were—removed later.

But this proposal, which came to be known as the Aldrich Plan after its Senate sponsor, was ill-fated from the start. Too many people saw that it was a transparent attempt to create a system of the bankers, by the bankers, and for the bankers. "The Aldrich Plan is the Wall Street plan," warned congressman Charles A. Lindbergh, father of the famed aviator. When Aldrich proposed his plan as a bill, it never got out of committee.

Author Greider sneered that "conspiracy-minded critics exaggerated the importance of the Jeykll Island meeting" but conceded that "their suspicions were poetically accurate" as the bankers knew "any proposal identified as Wall Street's bill would be doomed in the Democratic House of Representatives."

A new tactic was needed and it came in the form of House Banking and Currency Committee chairman, congressman Carter Glass of Virginia, who attacked the Aldrich Plan by openly stating it lacked government control and created a banking monopoly. Glass drafted an alternative, the Federal Reserve Act, and expressed anti–Wall Street sentiments.

Jekyll Island planners Vanderlip and Aldrich spoke out venomously against Glass's bill, even though entire sections were identical to the Aldrich Plan. It was clearly an effort to garner public support for the Glass bill by the appearance of banker opposition.

These efforts were underscored by a banking reform organization called the National Citizens' League, "entirely financed and controlled by the banks under the guidance of Paul Warburg," according to Griffin.

"The function of the organization was to disseminate hundreds of thousands of 'educational' pamphlets, to organize letter-writing campaigns to Congressmen, to supply quotable material to the news media, and in other ways to create the illusion of grass-roots support for the Jekyll Island plan," he added.

Heading the league was economics professor J. Laurence Laughlin of the University of Chicago, a school heavily endowed by John D. Rockefeller.

While popular support for a new banking system was garnered, another often-used tactic was played out in the political arena. President William Howard Taft was already on the record pledging to veto any legislation creating a central bank. A more compliant leader was needed by the bankers.

This leader was Woodrow Wilson, the academic who had been retained as president of Princeton University by his former classmates Cleveland H. Dodge and Cyrus McCormick, both directors of Rockefeller's National City Bank of New York. "For nearly 20 years before his nomination Woodrow Wilson had moved in the shadow of Wall Street," wrote author Ferdinand Lundberg. Wilson, who had praised J. P. Morgan in 1907, had been made governor of New Jersey. He now became the bankers' choice for president. Wilson's nomination was secured by the man who would from that point onward be his constant companion and adviser, Colonel Edward Mandell House, a close associate of Warburg and Morgan. "The Schiffs, the Warburgs, the Kahns, the Rockefellers and the Morgans [all] had faith in House," noted Professor Charles Seymour, who edited House's papers.

But there was a problem. Early polling indicated that Democrat Wilson could not defeat Republican Taft. In a maneuver that has been used successfully several times since, former president Theodore "Teddy" Roosevelt, also a Republican, was encouraged to run as a third-party candidate with large sums of money provided to his Progressive Party by two major contributors closely connected to Morgan. The scheme worked well. Roosevelt pulled votes from Taft so that Wilson, who already had pledged to sign the Federal Reserve Act, was elected by a narrow margin.

The appearance of opposition by Wall Street was necessary. William McAdoo, Wilson's son-in-law who was appointed secretary of the Treasury, later revealed, "Bankers fought the . . . Federal Reserve Act with the tireless energy of men fighting a forest fire. They said it was populistic, socialistic, half-baked, destructive, infantile, badly conceived and unworkable." However, McAdoo said in interviews with these bankers, "I perceived gradually, through all the haze and smoke of controversy, that the banking world was not really as much opposed to the bill as it pretended to be. . . ."

Wilson signed the Federal Reserve Act on December 23, 1913, just two days before Christmas with some Congressmen already home for the holidays and with the average citizen's attention clearly elsewhere.

"Congress was outflanked, outfoxed and outclassed by a deceptive, but brilliant, psycho-political attack," commented Griffin.

The Federal Reserve System today is composed of twelve Federal Reserve banks, each serving a section of the country, but dominated by the New York Federal Reserve Bank. These banks are administered by a board of governors appointed by the president and confirmed by the Senate, usually a rubber-stamp procedure.

The Fed is such a pivotal force in the world economy that financial experts in every nation play close attention to any action it takes. "The attention is warranted," wrote Kim Clark of U.S. News & World Report, "since even the slightest interest-rate tick can roil markets and create or destroy millions of jobs."

But the real story of the Fed is who controls it and why. "Using a central bank to create alternate periods of inflation and deflation, and thus whipsawing the public for vast profits, had been worked out by the international bankers to an exact science," noted Allen.

Congressman Lindbergh in 1913 said that the Federal Reserve System "establishes the most gigantic trust on earth. . . . When the President signs this act, the invisible government by the money power . . . will be legitimized. The new law will create inflation whenever the trusts want inflation. From now on, depressions will be scientifically created," he warned.

The Fed was quickly filled with the very people who had masterminded its creation. Morgan banker Benjamin Strong became the first governor of the New York Federal Reserve Bank while the first governor of the Fed's board of directors was none other than Paul Warburg, the man most credited with planning the details of the system, who later went on to become chairman of the Federal Reserve System.

Despite the word "Federal" in its name, the Fed is not part of the U.S.

government. It is a private organization owned by its member banks which, in turn, are owned by private stockholders. And who are these stockholders?

"An examination of the major stockholders of the New York City banks shows clearly that a few families, related by blood, marriage, or business interests, still control the New York City banks which, in turn, hold the controlling stock of the Federal Reserve Bank of New York," reported researcher Eustace Mullins in his 1983 book, *The Secrets of the Federal Reserve*. Mullins presented charts connecting the Fed and its member banks to the families of the Rothschilds, Morgans, Rockefellers, Warburgs, and others.

This private bank control of the Fed continues today. "The Federal Reserve Bank of New York—which completely dominates the other 11 branches through stock ownership, control and influence, having the only permanent voting seat on the Federal Open Market Committee and handling all open market bond transactions—has 19,752,655 shares outstanding and is majority-owned by two banks: Chase Manhattan Bank (now merged with Chemical Bank), with 6,389,445 shares or 32.35 percent; and Citibank, NA, with 4,051,851 shares or 20.51 percent. Together, those two banks own 10,441,295 shares or 52.86 percent—which is majority control," stated a 1997 report by researcher Eric Samuelson.

It would appear that the warnings of Jefferson and Lindbergh about private control over a central bank have proven correct.

Griffin pointed out that with the creation of the Federal Reserve, the major bankers finally obtained a long-standing goal—taxpayer liability for the losses of private banks. He quoted Paul Warburg, who admitted, "While technically and legally the Federal Reserve note is an obligation of the United States Government, in reality it is an obligation, the sole actual responsibility for which rests on the reserve banks. . . . The government could only be called upon to take them up after the reserve banks had failed."

"The man who masterminded the Federal Reserve System is telling us that *Federal Reserve notes constitute privately issued money with the taxpayers standing by to cover the potential losses of those banks which issue it,*" Griffin explained (emphasis in the original).

The money to cover government overspending comes from a mechanism instigated by these same men at this same time period—a national income tax and the means to collect it.

In fact, the banker globalists behind Wilson had a field day. Sounding eerily like today's politicians, Wilson proclaimed his government was "more concerned about human rights than about property rights." Masked by this rhetoric, Wilson pushed through more "progressive" legislation than any previous American administration, adding to the Federal Reserve System enforcement of the graduated income tax (with the Internal Revenue Service of the Treasury Department to enforce it), the Federal Farm Loan Act (which created twelve banks for farmers), the Federal Trade Commission to regulate business, among other bills.

To many people at the time, all of this legislation appeared necessary. Some still would argue that perhaps it is better that knowledgeable bankers be in charge of our nation's money supply. After all, a 1963 Federal Reserve publication states, "The function of the Federal Reserve is to foster a flow of money and credit that will facilitate orderly economic growth, a stable dollar, and long-run balance in our international payments."

But has the Fed accomplished it's stated goals? Everyone over the age of forty has experienced the alternating periods of inflation and recession. In 1972 President Nixon devalued the dollar after Europeans refused to accept it. "Since 1976 the United States has had a negative trade balance, and, in 1985, for the first time since 1914, U.S. debts owed to foreign creditors exceeded foreign debts owed to U.S. creditors," noted *The New Encyclopaedia Britannica*.

If the true functions of the Fed are as claimed, then it has failed miserably. "It would seem that such a system with such a dismal record . . . would be abolished without delay," mused author Epperson, who suggested that perhaps the "system was created to do exactly the opposite of what it tells the American people."

Another secret aspect of the money game is demand deposits, money placed in a bank which can be withdrawn any time on demand. We know this system as checking accounts. Today they are rapidly being replaced by plastic "debit" cards. Depositors today pay ever-increasing "service charges" for the privilege of allowing their money to be used for profit by their bank.

Consider that when a person deposits $50 in a bank, this is in effect a loan to the bank since it must be repaid on demand. Therefore, on the books the $50 is considered a liability. However, the bank then loans the $50 to someone else who must repay it with interest. Now the $50 is considered an asset. The same $50 is both an asset and a liability, thus counteracting each other, proving that money is essentially worthless.

But then there's the matter of interest. When the $50 is put into a savings account, there is some small amount of interest accrued, often on the condition that the money can't be withdrawn quickly. When the $50 is placed in a checking account, the depositor draws no interest at all. But when the bank loans $50, they charge healthy interest based on current rates and reap the profit. It is clear then that in banking debt equals profit.

This is a primary secret of money.

It is not too difficult to see that it is much more profitable to open a bank than a checking account. It may also explain why the once mighty United States has become a debtor nation.

Usury is a term that has all but disappeared from our language. Younger people today have no concept of the word. Once usury was defined as any interest charged for a loan, but modern dictionaries softened this to merely "excessive" interest. The Texas constitution once defined usury as any interest in excess of 6 percent. This ceiling was increased over the years until the whole concept was deleted. Banking critics have noted that even the Bible only required 10 percent for God.

"Charging interest on pretended loans is usury, and that has become institutionalized under the Federal Reserve System," argued author Griffin. This has been accomplished by masking the operations of the Fed in secrecy and arcane economic terms. "The . . . mechanism by which the Fed converts debt into money may seem complicated at first, but it is simple if one remembers that the process is not intended to be logical but to confuse and deceive," Griffin added.

Greider agreed, writing, "The details of [the Fed's] actions were presumed to be too esoteric for ordinary citizens to understand." Some believe this ignorance may be a blessing. Henry Ford was quoted as saying, "It is well enough that the people of the nation do not understand our banking and monetary system for, if they did, I believe there would be a revolution before tomorrow morning."

"Most Americans have no real understanding of the operation of the international moneylenders," concurred the late senator Barry Goldwater. "The bankers want it that way. We recognize in a hazy sort of way that the Rothschilds and the Warburgs of Europe and the houses of J. P. Morgan, Kuhn, Loeb and Company, Schiff, Lehman and Rockefeller possess and control vast wealth. How they acquire this vast financial power and employ it is a mystery to most of us.

"International bankers make money by extending credit to governments. The greater the debt of the political state, the larger the interest returned to the lenders. The national banks of Europe are actually owned and controlled by private interests." These same private interests can be demonstrated to own and control the Federal Reserve System.

According to author Greider, today's money managers have designed such intricate and esoteric details surrounding their financial transactions that the Fed has assumed the proportions of a cult.

"To modern minds, it seemed bizarre to think of the Federal Reserve as a religious institution," he wrote. "Yet the conspiracy theorists, in their own demented way, were on to something real and significant. . . . [The Fed] did also function in the realm of religion. Its mysterious powers of money creation, inherited from priestly forebears, shielded a complex bundle of social and psychological meanings. With its own form of secret incantation, the Federal Reserve presided over awesome social ritual, transactions so powerful and frightening they seemed to lie beyond common understanding. . . .

"Above all, money was a function of faith. It required implicit and universal social consent that was indeed mysterious. To create money and use it, each one must believe and everyone must believe. Only then did worthless pieces of paper take on value."

Many researchers and writers see the profit of debt, couched in ancient and mystical jargon, and coupled with the documented connections of bankers dominating government decisions, as the cause for increasing debt, both public and private.

"Thanks to the Federal Reserve's decision to tolerate an enormous increase in the money supply, and to the flood of foreign capital seeking safe haven in the United States, American consumers and businesses still have a surfeit of credit available to them," wrote Phillip J. Langman and Jack Egan in the business-oriented *U.S. News & World Report* in January

1999. They also noted, "The economy continues to create new jobs, but Americans are going into debt faster than their incomes are rising."

Prior to the 1930s paper bills could be redeemed for gold, since Section 10 of the Constitution specified gold and silver as the only lawful tender. Older Federal Reserve notes bore the inscription, "Redeemable in lawful money at the United States Treasury, or any Federal Reserve bank." But no more.

"A new dimension of trust had added to the illusion [of real worth]," explained Greider. "Finally, the last prop for the money illusion was kicked away in this century: the gold standard was abandoned." The original purpose of money—to represent tangible goods and services—has been forgotten.

The simple secrets of money have been carefully hidden by the priesthood of the money cult. "The American public, not unlike its political leaders, depended on familiar clichés for its limited understanding of money," commented Greider. "Average citizens simply could not understand the language, and most economists made no effort to translate for them."

Money today is increasingly mere electronic blips in a computer accessed by plastic cards at ATMs. There is nothing to back it up. Yet this illusory money is loaned at interest by great institutions. As the total amount of money grows, its worth decreases. This is called inflation, in effect a built-in tax on the use of money. And inflation can be manipulated upward or downward by those who control the flow of paper money or the electronic blips.

"The result of this whole system is massive debt at every level of society today," wrote author William Bramley. "The banks are in debt to the depositors, and the depositors' money is loaned out and creates indebtedness to the banks. Making this system even more akin to something out of a maniac's delirium is the fact that banks, like other lenders, often have the right to seize physical property if its paper money is not repaid."

In the Great Depression of the 1930s, money retained its value. It was simply hard to come by and prices were depressed to reflect its scarcity. Today, America is experiencing an inflationary depression—prices continue to rise because of an inflated money supply. The more money that's in circulation, the less it is worth.

EMPIRE BUILDING

Bankers such as the Rothschilds quickly learned that they could manipulate the worth of money by controlling the amount in circulation. Fractional banking allowed them to issue or withhold money at their discretion.

They multiplied their profits and power many times over by making loans to entire nations rather than mere individuals. "As they matured and learned the magic of converting debt into money, they moved beyond the confines of Frankfurt," noted Griffin. As documented by several authors, the Rothschilds also added efficient intelligence networks and quasi-official smuggling to enhance their empire.

For example, when Napoléon refused to take loans from the Rothschilds, creating his own Bank of France instead, he made vengeful enemies. After his return from exile in 1815, Napoléon was forced by circumstances to borrow heavily to defend France from the British Duke of Wellington and his cobbled-together European army. London's Nathan Rothschild accommodated Napoléon with a loan of five million pounds. At the same time, Nathan, with the aid of other Rothschild family members, smuggled a vast amount of gold through France to equip Wellington. Again, the Rothschilds played both ends against the middle.

When Wellington's revitalized army defeated Napoléon at Waterloo in June 1815, news of the victory was rushed to England by Rothschild couriers bearing their well-known and untouchable red pouches. The Rothschild messenger arrived a full day ahead of Wellington's own courier. Knowing of his capacity for early intelligence, all eyes on the London Stock Exchange turned to Nathan Rothschild, who, appearing despondent, ordered the sale of his stocks. Certain that Wellington had been defeated, a selling frenzy began, with the end result that Nathan Rothschild's agents soon were able to buy up a hefty majority of Britain's debts for only a small portion of their true value.

Much later, Nathan Rothschild commented on his act by saying, "It was the best business I have ever done."

By the early nineteenth century the Rothschilds had managed to acquire nobility titles. The French line affixed the "de" in front of their names in 1816 while the Austrian branch became barons in 1882. In 1885 a reluctant Queen Victoria finally baronized Nathaniel Rothschild, Nathan's grandson.

"Throughout the first half of the nineteenth century, the brothers conducted important transactions on behalf of the governments of England, France, Prussia, Austria, Belgium, Spain, Naples, Portugal, Brazil, various German states and smaller countries. They were the personal bankers of many of the crowned heads of Europe. They made large investments, through agents, in markets as distant as the United States, India, Cuba and Australia," noted Griffin.

Of course, to protect such high-level investments, the Rothschilds needed to control to some extent the activities of the nations in which they operated. They also financed various countries and then played them against each other as a means of coercing compliance to their will. This ploy became known as the "balance of power" game and it required great secrecy.

"By remaining behind the scenes, they were able to avoid the brunt of public anger which was directed, instead, at the political figures which they largely controlled," explained Griffin, adding, "This is a technique which has been practiced by financial manipulators ever since, and it is fully utilized by those who operate the Federal Reserve System today."

The Rothschilds have remained clannish through the twentieth century as evidenced by biographer Wilson's description of how Lionel de Rothschild "once went through with me a list of every living family member—dozens of them. And he was able to provide a quick verbal sketch of each one."

By the late 1990s the patriarchs of the Rothschild empire were Barons Guy and Elie de Rothschild in France and Lord Jacob Rothschild and Sir Evelyn de Rothschild in Britain.

Despite today's openness in the media, the Rothschilds still hold their secrets. In 1998 Oxford Fellow and history tutor Niall Ferguson was allowed to publish a detailed biography of the Rothschilds—but only covering the years up to 1848. He referred to "the lunatic fringe" of conspiracy writers who saw worldwide control in Rothschild activities and purported to present a "scholarly history" of the family.

However, Ferguson's protestations of Rothschild innocence stumbled under his own admission that even as an official biographer his research was curtailed. "From the outset, it was formally agreed that I would be entitled to quote freely from any material in the Rothschild Archive in London predating March 1915 . . . and . . . from any other archives and private collections of papers as far as their curators gave me permission to do so," he explained.

Even then, Ferguson discovered significant gaps and omissions in the archives, particularly for the years preceding the American Civil War. As a self-styled "atheist from a Calvinist background," he paid no attention whatsoever to the metaphysical aspects of the Rothschild background, their knowledge of Cabalistic tradition, or their connection to Freemasonry and other secret societies.

The Rothschilds cannot escape all media scrutiny, however, and occasionally there is a brief view afforded by news events, such as the July 8, 1996, "mysterious suicide" of forty-one-year-old Amshel Rothschild, chairman of the family financial empire.

Amshel, as an eldest son, had become chief executive officer of Rothschild Asset Management in 1990 and ascended to the chairmanship in 1993. He reportedly was "uncomfortable" with his role in the banking empire having been coerced into it by his father, Lord Victor Rothschild. Rumors circulated that family members were dissatisfied with his business policies. According to journalist Sally Bedell Smith, the Rothschild firm had suffered about $9 million in losses in the year preceding Amshel's death. This came at a time when Evelyn Rothschild had just concluded a joint venture with the second largest bank in China. In an effort to absorb this loss, Amshel planned to consolidate the family's far-flung operations into one $28 billion global concern.

Amshel Rothschild was found dead in the marble bathroom of his Paris hotel room. He was lying at the base of the towel rack which was only five feet off the floor, prompting one reporter to comment, "Hanging himself could not have been easy for a man six feet one." He was wearing only a terry cloth robe and one end of the robe's belt was wrapped around his neck. The other end was attached to the towel hanger rail which reportedly was accidentally pulled from the wall by one of the investigators.

Cause of death was initially reported as a heart attack but was later changed to apparent suicide by strangulation. There was no suicide note nor evidence of foul play, though the police report was sent directly to the French minister of the interior, bypassing normal channels. This maneuvering was apparently done at the request of the publicity-shy family, a good indication of its power over government.

With no apparent personal problems and no note, suicide was the least likely theory of Amshel's death.

Despite the curious circumstances of his death and his position in world banking, there was hardly a word of Amshel mentioned in the news media and the verdict that he had hanged himself was noted without question or comment. The *1997 Britannica Book of the Year* mentioned his death in only one sentence. It was buried in a section entitled "Economic Affairs: Banking," and stated, "The British banking industry was shaken in July by the apparent suicide of Amshel Rothschild, chief executive of asset management and investment for the London branch of the Rothschild dynasty and heir apparent to the family's global banking operations." The lack of coverage of the questionable death of so prominent a person argues well for those who see hidden control over the media.

Rothschild biographer Wilson was awed by the staying power of the family. "Genetics, mythology, deliberate training, the opportunities provided by wealth and connections—all have played their part in producing one of the most remarkable—perhaps *the* most remarkable—family of recent history," he concluded with admiration. "Few dynasties, with the exception of hereditary monarchies preserved from oblivion by the right of primogenitude, have maintained their influence in the world for seven generations."

Primogenitude refers to a primary condition of Mayer Amschel's original will instructing that only the eldest son in each generation could control the family wealth. By this method, not only has the Rothschild family been held tightly together but, as in the secret societies, those family members not privy to the innermost control have little knowledge of its financial dealings. Former top executives of the Rothschild businesses complained they often were kept "out of the loop" on important decisions.

This family togetherness and secrecy coupled with the incredible power of their wealth may explain patriarch Mayer Rothschild's oft-repeated quote, "Permit me to control the money of a nation, and I care not who makes its laws."

Rothschild influence spread worldwide. Rothschild influence over Japan's dominant banking house of Nomura came through the friendship of Edmund Rothschild with Tsunao Okumura, the man most responsible for creating that financial giant.

It was a Rothschild who helped create the state of Israel. In 1917, after serving as a member of the British Parliment, Zionist 2nd Lord Lionel Walter Rothschild—the eldest son who inherited Nathan's money and title after his death in 1915—received a letter from British Foreign Secretary Arthur Balfour expressing approval for the establishment of a homeland for Jews in Palestine. This letter later became known as the Balfour

Declaration. In 1922 the League of Nations approved the Balfour mandate in Palestine, thus paving the way for the later creation of Israel. Baron Edmond de Rothschild, who built the first pipeline from the Red Sea to the Mediterranean to bring Iranian oil to Israel and founded the Israel General Bank, was called "the father of modern Israel."

In the United States, journalist William T. Still said the family's creation of American wealth was "profound." "Working through the Wall Street firms of Kuhn, Loeb & Co., and J. P. Morgan Co., the Rothschilds financed John D. Rockefeller so that he could create the Standard Oil empire," Still wrote. "They also financed the activities of Edward Harriman [railroads] and Andrew Carnegie [steel].

Whether or not the Rothschilds truly dominate or influence the economy of the United States, the close connections between America's wealthy families and secret societies with those of Britain provide a solid and demonstrable link to Europe.

One such link is a sister organization to the Trilateral Commission, CFR, and Bilderbergers: the Royal Institute of International Affairs.

THE ROYAL INSTITUTE OF INTERNATIONAL AFFAIRS—ROUND TABLES

The agendas and methods of the modern American secret societies did not originate in America, but were imports from the secret societies that had dominated Europe for centuries.

Returning to the 1919 meeting in Paris which led to the creation of the Council on Foreign Relations, it must be noted that the council was merely the American branch of a proposed "Institute of International Affairs." The English branch retained the original name, being known as the Royal Institute of International Affairs (RIIA).

Like the CFR, creation of the institute was initiated by Woodrow Wilson's adviser Colonel House, bankers Warburg and Baruch, and other member's of House's "Inquiry" group of internationalists. The RIIA was built upon an existing secret society, the Round Table Groups, established around 1910 by the trust of English diamond magnate Cecil Rhodes.

Author Donald Gibson explained these creations thusly, "The Royal Institute had been created in 1919 to perpetuate British power in the world, and it helped to create the Council on Foreign Relations as part of an effort to link England's upper class and its foreign policy interests to those of the United States."

This view is echoed by author Icke, who wrote, "The so-called 'special relationship' between Britain and America is, in fact, the relationship between the RIIA and the Council on Foreign Relations."

The RIIA settled in Chatham House, located in London's Saint James's Square just across from the home of the wealthy Astor family. British foreign policy is frequently said to emanate from Chatham House.

Leading the creation of the RIIA was Lionel Curtis, a veteran of South Africa's Boer War who became secretary to Sir Alfred Milner, Britain's high commissioner in South Africa. Curtis had been one of the bright young protégées of Milner known as "Milner's Kindergarten." He has been described as a "British public administrator and author, advocate of British imperial federalism and of a world state, who had considerable influence on the development of the Commonwealth of Nations. . . . He was chiefly responsible for replacing the term [British] 'empire' with 'commonwealth.'"

Milner, an "ardent imperialist" educated at Oxford and New College, provoked the Boer War of 1899–1902 by his rigid attitudes and in victory gained British control over South Africa's diamond mines and a good portion of its gold supply. It was no coincidence that Milner became a principal trustee of the estate of Cecil Rhodes, the diamond tycoon of South Africa.

Cecil Rhodes, more than any other one person, provided the impetus to form several secret societies including the RIIA and the CFR, beginning with his Round Table groups.

Professor Carroll Quigley, a prominent historian and professor of history at the Foreign Service School of Georgetown University and President Clinton's academic mentor, explained, "The Rhodes Scholarships [Clinton received one] . . . are known to everyone. What is not so widely known is that Rhodes in five previous wills left his fortune to form a secret society, which was to devote itself to the preservation and expansion of the British Empire. And what does not seem to be known to anyone is that this secret society . . . continues to exist to this day."

Since Quigley and many others identify the Round Table Groups as the ancestor of the modern secret societies, it would indicate a closer look be given to Cecil Rhodes, his trustee Lord Milner, and their viewpoints.

RHODES AND RUSKIN

Cecil Rhodes, the progenitor of the modern secret societies, and his academic mentor, John Ruskin, carried on a philosophical tradition which can be traced to ancient Greece and beyond. Others who followed this tradition included Socialist pioneers Karl Marx and Friedrich Engels.

Born in 1853, Rhodes, son of the vicar of Bishop's Stortford, was steeped in religious concepts from an early age. In 1879 he joined a brother who was operating a South African cotton farm. Both brothers soon succumbed to the lure of diamond prospecting.

After some initial success finding diamonds, Rhodes formed de Beers Consolidated Mines, Ltd., named after the Nicolaas de Beers family mining claims he acquired.

For eight years Rhodes divided his time between mining in Kimberley, South Africa, and studies at Oxford, where he fell under the spell of fine arts professor John Ruskin.

The son of a prosperous wine merchant, Ruskin had departed from mainstream thinking to the extent that one biographer described his as "an inwardly difficult, lonely life, often pursued and struck at by madness." Given to frequent masturbation and nympholepsy (a frenetic fondness for underage girls), Ruskin nevertheless failed to consummate his marriage to nineteen-year-old Effie Gray in 1848. Six years later, still a virgin, she had the marriage annulled, a shocking development in those times.

Ruskin was an ardent student of the King James Version of the Bible but eventually gave up his belief in God. "John Ruskin, the man who inspired Cecil Rhodes, Alfred Milner, and those who formed the Round Table secret society, was himself influenced by the esoteric writings of [Greek philosopher] Plato and by Madame Blavatsky [founder of the occult Theosophy Society], the books of Lord Edward Bulwer-Lytton and secret societies in the mold of the Order of the Golden Dawn," wrote author Icke.

Ruskin, who reportedly read Plato's *Republic* every day, embraced Plato's concept of the perfect society being one that had structure imposed from centralized leadership—a ruling class—downward. Marx and Engels, the founders of modern Communism, also were students of Plato and echoed Ruskin's views. Advocating tight central control over the state, either by a dictator or a special ruling class, Ruskin proclaimed, "My continual aim has been to show the eternal superiority of some men to others, sometimes even of one man to all others."

According to Quigley, Rhodes was so stirred by Ruskin's philosophies that he copied one of his Oxford lectures in long-hand and kept it with him for thirty years.

Michael Baigent and Richard Leigh, authors of *The Temple and the Lodge,* showed that Rhodes was active in British Freemasonry, which involved him with other prominent nineteenth century persons such as the royals George IV and William IV, as well as Lord Randolph Churchill (Winston's father), Marquis of Salisbury, Arthur Conan Doyle, Rudyard Kipling, and Oscar Wilde. This group's preoccupation with the philosophies of Plato, Ruskin, and the Theosophist Madame Blavatsky coincided with the ideals of Freemasonry.

With the aid of a close friend, German diamond merchant Alfred Beit, Rhodes expanded his diamond company until, by 1891, de Beers owned 90 percent of the world's diamond production. In the mid-1890s Rhodes founded the Diamond Syndicate, forerunner of today's Central Selling Organization which controls almost 80 percent of the worldwide diamond trade.

He also gained large control over the rapidly developing Transvaal gold mines. With ever-expanding wealth, Rhodes's dreams also grew to include plans for a railroad from South Africa to Cairo and expanding the British Empire to include that century-long dream of reclaiming the American colonies.

As with the Morgans and Rockefellers, behind Rhodes we find the vast power of the Rothschild family.

"They were financiers to Cecil Rhodes, making it possible for him to establish a monopoly over the diamond fields of South Africa," wrote author Griffin. "They are still connected with the de Beers." In November 1997, when Baron Edmond Adolphe Maurice Jules Jacques de Rothschild died at age seventy-one from emphysema in Geneva, it was reported that he left substantial holdings in de Beers Consolidated Mines, Ltd. of South Africa.

Lending support for a relationship between Rhodes and the Rothschilds was author and former British Intelligence Officer Dr. John Coleman, who wrote, "Rhodes was the principal agent for the Rothschilds . . . [who] dispossessed the South African Boers of their birthright, the gold and diamonds that lay beneath their soil." According to Coleman, Rhodes's first Round Table group was established in South Africa with funding from the British Rothschild family to train business leaders loyal to Britain in ways to maintain control over that country's wealth. The idea of Rothschild funding behind Rhodes also was supported by author Frank Aydelotte, who wrote in *American Rhodes Scholarships,* "In 1888 Rhodes made his third will . . . leaving everything to Lord Rothschild. . . ."

The Round Tables started out as a collection of semisecret groups formed along the lines of the Illuminati and Freemasonry with "inner" and "outer" circles and a pyramid hierarchy. The inner circle was called the Circle of Initiates (or the Elect) while the outer circle was called the Association of Helpers. Two members of Rhodes's inner Circle of Initiates were British financiers Lord Victor Rothschild and Lord Milner. Rhodes called his secret society the Round Table after the legendary meeting place of King Arthur. It should be noted that the Arthurian legend concerning the Holy Grail is closely connected to the controversial notion of a continuing bloodline from Jesus—the *Sangreal* or royal blood which shall be discussed later.

Coleman wrote that, armed with immense wealth gained from control of gold, diamonds and drugs, "Round Tablers fanned out throughout the world to take control of fiscal and monetary policies and political leadership in all countries where they operated."

Setting an example for today's interlocking corporate directorships and tax-exempt foundations, "The Round Table itself consists of a maze of companies, institutions, banks and educational establishments, which in itself would take qualified insurance actuaries a year to sort out," according to Coleman.

While some might dismiss Coleman as a conspiracy theorist, they could not say the same of Dr. Quigley.

"There does exist, and has existed for a generation, an international Anglophile network which operates, to some extent, in the way the radical Right believes the Communists act," confirmed Quigley. "I know of the operations of this network because I have studied it for 20 years and was permitted for two years, in the early 1960s, to examine its papers and secret records. I have no aversion to it or to most of its aims and have, for much of my life, been close to it and to many of its instruments. . . . In general my chief difference of opinion is that it wishes to remain unknown, and I believe its role in history is significant enough to be known."

Quigley's words were echoed by authors Wallechinsky and Wallace who quoted from Rhodes's will. It called for "the establishment, promotion and development of a Secret Society, the true aim and object whereof shall be the extension of British rule throughout the world . . . [to include] the ultimate recovery of the United States of America."

In 1890 Queen Victoria, impressed with his imperialistic views, named Rhodes prime minister of Africa's Cape Colony. Upon his death from heart disease in 1902, Rhodes's reputation as an inflexible businessman and politician was softened by the news of his generous scheme to provide scholarships to Oxford for promising young men. Though Rhodes was praised for prohibiting the disqualification of applicants on the basis of race, it is clear he remained a product of his time since he once affirmed his desire for "equal rights for every white man."

Rhodes himself was thought to have been a member of a covert group known as the "Olympians" after the Greek gods. According to author Coleman, this was merely another name for the globalists he termed the Committee of 300. Additionally, Rhodes was thought to have been connected to the secretive and mysterious Illuminati as well, most probably through his Masonic connections.

Quigley identified Rhodes's secret society in the plural as the Round Table Groups, which had added branches in seven nations by 1915. Though created by Curtis and others, funding for the society came principally from Rhodes's followers and Lord Milner. "Since 1925 there have been substantial contributions from wealthy individuals and from foundations and firms associated with the international banking fraternity, especially the Carnegie United Kingdom Trust, and other organizations associated with J. P. Morgan, the Rockefeller and Whitney families . . ." Quigley added, not mentioning the Rothschilds by name.

With Rhodes's death, Milner, Rothschild, and their international banker associates gained complete control over the Round Tables, which began expanding far beyond the British Empire. Professor Quigley explained, "At the end of the war of 1914, it became clear that the organization of this [Round Table] system had to be greatly extended." Lionel Curtis was called upon to establish the Royal Institute of International Affairs as an umbrella organization for the Round Table Groups.

Quigley saw the goals of these groups—the chief aim of which apparently was to form the world's nations into one English-speaking entity so as to maintain peace and bring both stability and prosperity to underdeveloped areas—as "largely commendable."

In a great irony, the Round Table organization—which professed world peace as a primary goal—may have directly led to the development of the atomic bomb. During its expansion period, the Round Tables established many splinter organizations, one of which was the Institute for Advanced Study (IAS) in Princeton, New Jersey. This was the "American copy of All Souls College at Oxford," according to Quigley. The IAS was funded liberally by the Rockefeller General Education Board. It was here that the scientists working on the atom bomb were assisted by IAS members Robert Oppenheimer, Niels Bohr, and Albert Einstein.

For all that, Quigley wrote admiringly, "They were gracious and cultured gentlemen of somewhat limited social experience who were much concerned with the freedom of expression of minorities and the rule of law for all. . . ."

Other writers have not been so complimentary. Journalist William T. Still in his book *New World Order: The Ancient Plan of Secret Societies* wrote of "the centuries-old plans of secret societies to wrench the Constitution from the citizens of the United States."

"Rhodes committed the same error made by so many humanitarians before him," wrote author William Bramley, "he thought that he could accomplish his goals through the channels of the corrupted Brotherhood network. Rhodes therefore ended up creating institutions which promptly fell into the hands of those who would effectively use those institutions to oppress the human race."

But it was not only Round Table organizations which allowed America's wealthy and powerful to mingle and converse. In certain circles, there were fraternal connections through much more secret groups, such as the ominous Order of Skull and Bones.

SKULL AND BONES

Skull and Bones, a highly secret fraternal order apparently only found at Yale University, has been the source of an unprecedented number of government officials who have furthered the globalist aims of their brethren in other covert groups, according to researchers.

"Members of the CFR when accused of being involved in a conspiracy, have protested to the contrary. And by and large they are right," wrote conspiracy researcher and author Anthony C. Sutton. "Most CFR members are not involved in a conspiracy and have no knowledge of any conspiracy. . . . However, there is a group WITHIN the Council on Foreign Relations which belongs to a secret society, sworn to secrecy, and which more or less controls the CFR." (emphasis in original)

Members have included extremely powerful men such as Henry Stimson, Secretary of War under President Franklin D. Roosevelt, and described as "a man at the heart of the heart of the American ruling class"; U.S. Ambassador to Russia Averell Harriman; publisher Henry Luce, and J. Richardson Dilworth, longtime manager of the Rockefeller fortune.

According to Sutton and others, this secret society is the American chapter of an earlier German secret organization. Known variously as Chapter 322, the "Brotherhood of Death," or "The Order," this group is most popularly known as "Skull and Bones" or simply "Bones."

The American chapter of The Order was founded at Yale University in 1832 by General William Huntington Russell and Alphonso Taft.

Taft, who would become Secretary of War in 1876 and U.S. Attorney General and an ambassador to Russia, was the father of William Howard Taft, the only person to serve as both president and chief justice of the United States.

Russell would go on to become a member of the Connecticut Legislature. His family was at the center of Russell and Company, a firm controlled by some of Boston's finest "blue blood" families that were enriched first by the slave trade and then by opium smuggling in the early nineteenth century. Some researchers believed this unsavory background explained the pirate symbol of skull and crossed bones adopted as The Order's insignia, an emblem originally used as the flag of the old Knights Templar.

According to Sutton, The Order was brought from Germany to Yale by Russell, whose cousin, Samuel Russell, was an integral part of the British-inspired Opium Wars in China. A pamphlet detailing an 1876 investigation by a rival secret society of Skull and Bones headquarters at Yale (known as the "Tomb") stated, "Its founder [Russell] was in Germany before Senior Year and formed a warm friendship with a leading member of a German society. He brought back with him to college authority to found a chapter here. Thus was Bones founded."

The secret German society may have been none other than the mysterious and infamous Illuminati. Ron Rosenbaum—one of the few journalists to take a serious look at Skull and Bones—took note that the official skull and crossbones emblem of The Order was also the official crest of the Illuminati. In an investigative piece for *Esquire* magazine Rosenbaum wrote, "I do seem to have come across definite, if skeletal, links between the origins of Bones rituals and those of the notorious Bavarian Illuminists . . . [who] did have a real historical existence . . . from 1776 to 1785 they were an esoteric secret society with the more mystical freethinking lodges of German Freemasonry."

Author Ecke agreed, writing that The Order was merely the "Illuminati in disguise. . . . The symbolism of [its] initiation ceremony would appear to indicate at least close links with Freemasonry," he added. Masonic emblems, symbols, a German slogan, even the layout of their initiation room—all are identical to those found in Masonic lodges in Germany associated with the Illuminati.

Considering the nefarious background of its founders and their families, authors Webster Griffin Tarpley and Anton Chaitkin warned, "The background to Skull and Bones is a story of opium and Empire, and a bitter struggle for political control over the new U.S. republic."

Whatever its inception, Skull and Bones was officially incorporated as the Russell Trust in 1856. The Order conducts annual meetings at a club site on New York's Saint Lawrence River named Deer Iland (sic). The misspelling was at the request of its donor, Bones member George D. Miller.

While undoubtedly the preeminent secret club, Skull and Bones is not the only one. According to Tarpley and Chaitkin, "Princeton has its 'eating clubs,' especially Ivy Club and Cottage Club, whose oligarchical tradition runs from Jonathan Edwards and Aaron Burr through the Dulles brothers. At Harvard there is the ultra-blue-blooded Porcelian (known also as the Porc or Pig Club); Theodore Roosevelt bragged to the German Kaiser of his membership there; Franklin D. Roosevelt was a member of the slightly 'lower' Fly Club."

Other secret clubs exist at Yale—Wolf's Head and Scroll & Key to name two—and, as stated by Rosenbaum, anyone in the Eastern Establishment who does not belong to Skull and Bones almost assuredly belongs to one of these other groups. But no other group has the demonstrable blood and wealth connections of the Skull and Bones.

Each year, only fifteen Yale juniors are selected to participate in Skull and Bones during their senior year.

In addition to extraordinary secrecy—Bones members are required to leave the room if anyone should mention the group—The Order has its own membership designations. Neophyte members are called Knights, after the fashion of earlier secret societies such as the Knights Templar, Knights of Malta, or Knights of Saint John. Once a full member, he is known as a Patriarch, one honored as a founding father.

Outsiders are derogatorily referred to as "Gentiles" or "vandals."

Author Sutton noted that active membership in Skull and Bones comes from a "core group of perhaps 20–30 families. . . . First we find old line American families who arrived on the East coast in the seventeenth century, e.g. Whitney, Lord, Phelps, Wadsworth, Allen, Bundy, Adams and so on," he wrote. "Second, we find families who acquired wealth in the last 100 years, sent their sons to Yale and in time became almost old line families, e.g. Harriman, Rockefeller, Payne, Davison."

Ecke wrote that these families exhibited an Old World concern over their heritage and bloodlines. He said they utilize arranged marriages "to protect or 'advance' the genetic lines of the pseudo-blue bloods who owe the origins of their inherited wealth and influence to drug running, slavery and carefully chosen marriage partners. These intermingled families help and support each other in their quest for financial, political and genetic dominance."

"You . . . get the feeling there's a lot of intermarriage among these Bones families," Rosenbaum agreed. "Year after year there will be a Whitney Townsend Phelps in the same Bones class as a Phelps Townsend Whitney. . . . In fact, one could make a half-serious case that functionally Bones serves as a kind of ongoing informal Establishment eugenics project bringing vigorous new genes into the bloodlines of the Stimsonian elite."

Nepotism runs deep in The Order as seen in the fact that modern finances of the Russell Trust were handled by John B. Madden Jr., a partner in Brown Brothers Harriman, formed by the merger of Brown Bros. & Company and W. A. Harriman & Company in 1933. Madden started there in the 1940s working under Senior Partner Prescott Bush, father of former president George Bush, all of them members of Skull and Bones.

A more recent example of members' fierce loyalty was shown in the 1980s scandal of President Bush's connection with the criminal activity in the Bank of Credit and Commerce International (BCCI). As the bank's illegal activities came to light—involving many prominent names— attempts were made by the Bush administration to block or blunt any meaningful investigation. Finally a formal investigation of the BCCI was launched by the Senate Foreign Relations Subcommittee on Terrorism, Narcotics, and International Operations headed by Massachusetts senator John Kerry. Kerry was chairman of the Democratic Senate Campaign Committee, which had received significant BCCI contributions, and he was also a member of Skull and Bones. The Kerry-led investigation foundered. Jack Blum, a special counsel to Kerry's subcommittee, stated, "I proposed a serious investigation of BCCI and was brushed aside. . . . A high-level cover-up of everything concerning BCCI was set into place after Customs stumbled across their money-laundering operation in Miami, and it's still in place."

The interests of both the Morgans and Rockefellers were well represented in The Order. Member Percy Rockefeller tied The Order to Standard Oil properties, while a number of Morgan men show up on the rolls of Skull and Bones.

While J. P. Morgan was not a Bonesman, Harold Stanley (The Order, 1908) joined Morgan's Guaranty Trust banking firm in 1915 and eventually became a Morgan partner and president of the combined Morgan, Stanley & Company. W. Averell Harriman (The Order, 1913) was a board member of Guaranty Trust. H. P. Whitney (The Order, 1894) and his father, W. C. Whitney (The Order, 1863) were both directors of Guaranty Trust.

The flow of financial power was not always channeled through direct membership in Skull and Bones. "The Order controls the substantial wealth of Andrew Carnegie, but no Carnegie has ever been a member of The Order," wrote author Sutton. "The Order used the Ford wealth so flagrantly against the wishes of the Ford family that two Fords resigned from the board of the Ford Foundation. No Ford has been a member of The Order. The name Morgan never appeared on the membership lists, although some of Morgan partners are with the inner core, for example, [partner Harold] Stanley [of Morgan, Stanley & Co.], [the son of Henry P.] Davison and [John] Perkins."

McGeorge Bundy (The Order, 1940) was president of the Ford

Foundation from 1966 to 1979. During the early to mid-1960s, Bundy served as a national security adviser to both Presidents John F. Kennedy and Lyndon Johnson. At the same time, his brother William Bundy (The Order, 1939) who had been with the CIA, served as Assistant Secretary of State for East Asian and Pacific Affairs.

Many other illustrious names can be connected to Skull and Bones, such as Low, Forbes, Coolidge, Delano, Taft, Stimson, and others. Prominent recent Bonesmen include President George Bush (The Order, 1949); William Bissell (The Order, 1925) whose brother, Richard Bissell, became Deputy Director of Plans for the CIA; Amory Howe Bradford (The Order, 1943), who married Carol Warburg Rothschild in 1941 and soon became general manager of the *New York Times;* Henry Luce (The Order, 1919) who became head of the powerful and influential Luce publishing empire which included *Time* and *Life* magazines; and William F. Buckley (The Order, 1950) a nationally syndicated conservative columnist.

Authors Tarpley and Chaitkin did not see all this as a harmless college fraternity. "The present century owes much of its record of horrors to the influential Anglophile American families which came to dominate and employ the Skull and Bones Society as a political recruiting agency, particularly the Harrimans, Whitneys, Vanderbilts, Rockefellers and their lawyers, the Lords and Tafts and Bundys," they commented.

Other researchers see Skull and Bones as the epicenter of New World Order control. The Order has been called a "stepping stone" to the Council on Foreign Relations, Bilderbergers, and the Trilateral Commission.

After examining The Order's influence and control in the areas of foreign policy, finance, education, and religion, Christian author and publisher Texe Marrs urged, "The Order of Skull and Bones must be unmasked for what it is—a great and present danger to our freedoms and to our constitutional rights."

Rosenbaum, in a possible explanation of The Order's sinister trappings, wrote that it was simply due to an "impressionable young Russell [who] just stumbled on the same mother lode of pseudo-Masonic mummery as the Illuminists." Although, perhaps with some sarcasm, he also voiced the possibility that "the Eastern Establishment is the demonic creation of a clandestine elite manipulating history, and Skull and Bones is one of its recruiting centers."

Rosenbaum also wrote he saw Skull and Bones in "headlong

decline" and in recent years it has become "a more lackadaisical, hedonistic, comfortable, even, said some, decadent group."

Controversy concerning The Order surfaced during the 1980 presidential election. Former U.S. Labor Party National Chairman Lyndon H. LaRouche began an independent bid for the presidency. In the New Hampshire primary elections, LaRouche attacked Republican candidate George Bush for his affiliation with The Order, stating, "Skull and Bones is no mere fraternity, no special alumni association and added mumbo-jumbo. It is a very serious, very dedicated cult-conspiracy against the U.S. Constitution. Like the Cambridge Apostles, the initiate to the Skull and Bones is a dedicated agent of British secret intelligence for life." Many observers believed that the revelations of Bush's connection to Skull and Bones, the CFR, and the Trilateral Commission cost him the New Hampshire primary and eventually the presidency in 1980.

"The Order has either set up or penetrated just about every significant research, policy, and opinion-making organization in the United States," declared Sutton.

There are indications Sutton may be correct. One of the most thorough investigations of institutional stockholders ever conducted was a 1980 study by the Senate Committee on Governmental Affairs entitled *Structure of Corporate Concentration*. Its conclusion, as reported by author Donald Gibson, was to the point: "Financial institutions, part of or extensively interrelated with the Morgan-Rockefeller complex, are the dominant force in the economy."

After studying this report, Gibson wrote, "The board of directors of Morgan included individuals serving on the boards of 31 of the top 100 firms. Citicorp was tied to 49 top companies, and Chase Manhattan, Chemical Bank, and Metropolitan Life each had 24 other top companies represented on their boards. These and a multitude of other overlaps among the top 100 firms provide a dense network of relationships reinforced by frequent ties through private clubs, educational background, marriages, and membership in organizations such as the Council on Foreign Relations [Skull and Bones, The Trilateral Commission] and the Business Council."

Gibson also noted that at least two Morgan-Rockefeller institutions were among the top six stockholders in AT&T, General Motors, Du Pont, Exxon, General Electric, IBM, United Technologies, and Union Pacific.

As with other secret societies, many telltale connections between Skull and Bones and the CIA are discernible. In addition to the afore-mentioned Bush, Bundy, and Bissell, other Bonesmen who became CIA officials included Director of Personnel F. Trubee Davison (The Order, 1918); Beirut CIA Station Chief James Buckley (The Order, 1944); Rhodes scholar and Deputy Director for Plans Hugh Cunningham (The Order, 1934); and poet Archibald MacLeish (The Order, 1915) who helped Office of Strategic Services (OSS) William Donovan form the CIA in the late 1940s.

"Yale has influenced the Central Intelligence Agency more than any other university, giving the CIA the atmosphere of a class reunion," stated Yale history professor Gaddis Smith. Rosenbaum made a point of mentioning that Yale slang for a secret society member is "spook," the same term used in the CIA for an undercover operative.

Yet the CIA is only one of numerous U.S. government "alphabet" offices which many charge are used as agents of change and control along with dozens and dozens of front organizations, foundations, think tanks, and study groups created and/or financed by the secret societies. Many researchers claim such private organizations were actually created by leading secret society members.

TAX-EXEMPT FOUNDATIONS AND ALPHABET AGENCIES

Today, there are more than forty thousand tax-exempt foundations operating within the United States alone, most professing the most laudable of intentions. Yet many can be seen as furthering the secret societies' agenda of globalization and centralized government.

Norman Dodd, director of research for the House Select Committee to Investigate Foundations and Comparable Organizations, in 1952 reported that the president of the Ford Foundation told him bluntly that "operating under directive from the White House" his foundation was to "use our grant-making power so as to alter our life in the United States that we can be comfortably merged with the Soviet Union." With the collapse of Communism, the advent of the United Nations and NATO along with various economic treaties now in place, it would appear that this goal is close to becoming realized.

A superficial glance at some of the past and current organizations and foundations linked to Skull and Bones, the CFR, the Trilateral Commission, the Illuminati, and other secret societies by several writers reveals some surprises. To name just a few, these include the Agency of International Development, American Civil Liberties Union, American Council of Race Relations, American Press Institute, Anti-Defamation League, Arab Bureau, Aspen Institute, Association of Humanistic Psychology, Battelle Memorial Institute, Center for Advanced Studies in the Behavioral Sciences, Center for Constitutional Rights, Center for Cuban Studies, Center for Democratic Institutions, Christian Socialist League, Communist League, Environmental Fund, Fabian Society, Ford Foundation, Foundation for National Progress, German Marshall Fund, Hudson Institute, Institute for Pacific Relations, Institute on Drugs, Crime and Justice, International Institute for Strategic Studies, Mellon Institute, Metaphysical Society, Milner Group, Mont Pelerin Society, National Association for the Advancement of Colored People, National Council of Churches, New World Foundation, Rand Institute, Stanford Research Institute, Tavistock Institute of Human Relations, Union of Concerned Scientists, International Red Cross, and the YMCA.

The Aspen Institute, for example, is a "global concern with considerable diplomatic influence" with nearly $60 million in net assets that "regularly hosts presidents, prime ministers, philosophers, statesmen, advisers, educators, journalists, artists, activists and a roster of corporate representatives to rival the Fortune 500 list," noted Paul Anderson, writing in the *Aspen Times Weekly*. "Yet, despite its national—indeed, international—prominence, the Institute remains an enigma to the majority of local residents and visitors."

The Institute was founded in the 1940s as the Aspen Institute for Humanistic Studies—the appellation regarding humanism was dropped in the 1970s. Founders included Walter Paepcke, a Chicago industrialist; Robert Maynard Hutchins, president of the Rockefeller-dominated University of Chicago; Mortimer Adler, a philosopher; and CFR and Bones member Henry Luce, the powerful head of Time-Life publications. All of these men were closely connected to the University of Chicago-affiliated Encyclopaedia Britannica, Inc.

Despite a series of fierce disagreements with the town of Aspen over expansion and land use, the Institute continues to utilize the restful Rocky Mountain atmosphere to soothe attendees at its many influential seminars and conferences.

The Institute for Policy Studies (IPS), an umbrella organization encompassing hundreds of diverse groups representing both the Left and the Right of the political spectrum, is still active in Washington. It is another example of an organization linked to the secret societies. Author Coleman wrote, "IPS has shaped and reshaped United States policies, foreign and domestic, since it was founded by James P. Warburg and the Rothschild entities in the United States, bolstered by Bertrand Russell and the British socialists through its networks in America. . . . The objectives of IPS came from an agenda laid down for it by the British Round Table . . . one of the most notable being to create the 'New Left' as a grassroots movement in the U.S. IPS was to engender strife and unrest and spread chaos like a wildfire out of control, proliferate the 'ideals' of left-wing nihilistic socialism, support unrestricted use of drugs of all types, and be the 'big stick' with which to beat the United States political establishment."

According to Coleman, IPS founders Richard Barnett and Marcus Raskin have controlled such diverse elements as the Black Panthers, Daniel Ellsberg, National Security Council staff member Morton Halperin, the Weathermen, the Venceramos and the campaign staff of candidate George McGovern.

Author S. Steven Powell noted that a stated IPS goal was "the dismantling of all economic, political, social, and cultural institutions in the United States." Following an extensive investigation just prior to the collapse of Communism, he concluded, "An ordered accounting of [IPS activities] reveals that much of what the institute does, for all intents and purposes, also serves the interests of the Soviet Union. . . . [The] IPS has been remarkably successful in promoting a sweeping radical agenda by maintaining the facade of a liberal scholarly research center."

According to researchers, much of IPS funding comes from CFR-connected organizations, including the Rubin Foundation, represented by the New York law firm of Lord, Day & Lord. The Lord family has counted members on the rolls of Skull and Bones since 1898. Winston Lord (The Order, 1959), a former aide to Henry Kissinger, in 1983 was chairman of the Council on Foreign Relations and later President Reagan's ambassador to China.

A long-time president of the Ford Foundation was the ubiquitous McGeorge Bundy, CFR member, Bonesman, and the National Security Advisor who presided over the Gulf of Tonkin incident precipitating the Vietnam War.

In the mid-1980s a movement toward rewriting the U.S. Constitution gained momentum in part due to the work of the Center of the Study of Democratic Institutions, which was established with Ford Foundation money. It foundered in the face of widespread opposition.

The worldviews of the wealthy are impressed on their fellows by underwriting great centers of education such as the London School of Economics and Political Science. Funding for the creation of this school came from the Rockefeller Foundation, the Carnegie United Kingdom Trust Fund, and others connected to J. P. Morgan & Company. This prestigious school was established by Sidney James Webb, an founding member of the Fabian Society.

Founded in London in 1883, the Fabian Society was a group of evolutionary socialists who took their name from the Roman general Fabius Cunctator, who managed to defeat Hannibal's larger army through a series of hit-and-run attacks. By avoiding head-on pitched battles, Fabius managed to conquer in the long run. The Fabian socialists, whose aim was "the reorganization of society by the emancipation of land and Industrial Capital from individual and class ownership," took note of Fabius's tactics.

In fact, the question of tactics was about the only difference between Fabian socialists and communists. Where communists desired to establish socialist governments through revolution, the Fabians were content to slowly move toward socialism through propaganda and legislation.

The Fabians once were chastised for their methods by one of their most prominent members, author H. G. Wells. In 1906 Wells said, "I find in our society . . . a curious conceit of cunning, something like a belief that the world may be maneuvered into socialism without knowing it." Rather than accept this call for more openness, the Fabians ignored Wells and continued their tactics of stealth and subterfuge.

Other notable Fabians included George Bernard Shaw and English economist John Maynard Keynes, whose "new economics" of greater debt and tighter economic control by government was the mainstay of American economics until the arrival of "Reaganomics" and a "counterreformation" instigated by University of Chicago economist Milton Friedman and his monetarist theories.

After failing to achieve their socialist ideals within Britain's Liberal and Conservative parties, the Fabians in 1906 formed the powerful British Labour Party.

Early in the twentieth century, Fabian Society founder Webb reorganized the University of London into a federation of teaching institutions, crafted Britain's Education Acts of 1902 and 1903, and founded the London School of Economics.

Famous students from the London School of Economics include David Rockefeller, Joseph Kennedy Jr. and his younger brother, the future President John F. Kennedy, Robert Kennedy Jr., future senator Daniel Moynihan, author Zecharia Sitchin, and newscaster Eric Sevareid.

Government "alphabet" agencies susceptible to secret society control include not only the Central Intelligence Agency (CIA) but the National Security Council (NSC), Federal Bureau of Investigation (FBI), National Security Agency (NSA), Defense Intelligence Agency (DIA), National Reconnaissance Office (NRO), Drug Enforcement Agency (DEA), Bureau of Alcohol, Tobacco and Firearms (BATF), Internal Revenue Service (IRS), Federal Emergency Management Agency (FEMA), and many others. These agencies are themselves secretive, citing reasons of national security, executive privilege, or the need to protect informants or criminal case files.

One prime example of tight inner government control by secret society members may be found in the National Security Council, which, since its creation by the National Security Act of 1947, has come to dominate U.S. policy decisions including those involving the use of armed force. Most Americans have no idea who exactly comprises the powerful NSC. They might be surprised to learn that council principals are the president, vice president, and secretaries of State and Defense, positions predominately held by members of the CFR or the Trilateral Commission throughout the twentieth century.

If the top leadership of government and business is controlled by the secret societies, as alleged by most writers on the subject, then the activities of subservient agencies and divisions must be of little consequence. Government bureaucrats—honest and well-intentioned workers for the most part—simply follow orders and policies set by superiors. Many government employees have lost their jobs or resigned in the face of directives that bewilder and perplex those not privy to the inner secrets.

Many people today believe that this same small group of men and women along with friends and associates not only manipulate many of the major world issues but also control the tax-exempt foundations. These people connect with each other through a variety of means—

international business and politics, conferences, social gatherings, foundations, etc.—and therefore constitute a cohesive group. This group has been called by many names: the New World Order, the Committee of 300, the Illuminati, the Secret Brotherhood, or often simply "they." More than one author even suggest that these persons are themselves guided or controlled by non-human intelligences, described as "prison wardens" or "Custodians."

"Until the dawn of the twentieth century, this plan for a New World Order was centered in Masonry, then Illuminated Masonry, but with the advent of the Round Table Groups—which still exist today—and their American brethren, the Council on Foreign Relations, the torch has been passed from century to century," wrote journalist William T. Still.

By mid-1999 it appeared that the same old torch was still being passed as election year 2000 began to shape up. Advocating "compassionate conservatism," George W. Bush, the eldest son of the former President and CIA director who belonged to of all of the aforementioned secret societies, was the leading Republican candidate. Clinton's Vice President and CFR member Al Gore led a contentious gang of Democrats. Early on, Gore sought guidance from the leading lights of Wall Street.

Once again, the American electorate was to choose between a globalist-supported Bush or a globalist-supported Gore. Obviously, the globalists will be the winner, regardless of the election outcome.

In late 1999 globalism suffered a slight setback when more than sixty thousand demonstrators, representing an odd mixture of unionists, environmentalists, and strict constitutionalists, protested the loss of United States sovereignty and jobs during a meeting of the World Trade Organization (WTO) in Seattle. Predictably, the corporate-controlled news media styled the protest as unruly rioters although other accounts claimed that trouble began only after heavily armed police began clubbing and gassing participants.

Simply, the controversial General Agreement on Tariffs and Trade (GATT) renamed in 1995, the WTO was widely seen as nothing more than a vehicle to further the Bilderberger goal of removing all trade barriers. Noting that free trade "breaks up old nationalities" and "hastens the social revolution," Karl Marx in 1848 proclaimed, "I am in favor of free trade."

As the goal of a New World Order moves closer to reality today, authors and researchers who are suspicious of the role of secret societies and their financial backers in government, business, and foundations feel they face a disheartening maze of obstructions in trying to bring the story to the public. Major publishers won't publish and news agencies won't accept or distribute the stories and often ridicule such writers as "alarmists" and "conspiracy theorists." Occasionally, there is even the threat of violence against investigators who dig too deep.

The eyes of the average citizen—conditioned to consider only the issues presented in their daily media—glaze over at any discussion of secret societies or hidden history. After all, they ask, if any of this were real, wouldn't it be covered on *Sixty Minutes* or the nightly news?

IT'S NEWS TO US

While the mass news media does not operate in secret, its internal structure and operation remain a mystery to most of the public. And its influence cannot be understated.

Throughout 1998, no one could long consider the Clinton Administration's transfer of nuclear technology to China or the president's signing of questionable Executive Orders such as an extension of the international zone along the southern U.S. border more than 150 miles. The mass media had everyone's attention focused solely on Clinton's sexcapades.

"The media may not always be able to tell us what to think, but they are strikingly successful in telling us what to think about," stated media critic Michael Parenti.

Many people complain that the major media are superficial, conformist, and subjective in their selection of news. A recent Pew Research Center poll showed respondents who thought news reporting unfair and inaccurate ranged into the 60 percentiles. A survey by the news industry publication *Editor & Publisher* showed that journalists themselves do not disagree. Nearly half of its members indicated their belief that news coverage is shallow and inadequate.

The purpose of the mass media is not to tell it like it is, according to media critics, but rather to tell it like the media owners want it to be. Parenti wrote that the major role of the press is "to continually recreate a view of reality supportive of existing social and economic class power." This skewed perspective can clearly be seen in the terms used in stories concerning "labor disputes"—it's never "management disputes." He pointed out that management always makes "offers" while labor issues "demands."

"Much of what is reported as 'news' is little more than the uncritical transmission of official opinions to an unsuspecting public," wrote Parenti. "What [reporters] pass off as objectivity, is just a mindless kind of neutrality," said journalist Britt Hume, who added reporters "shouldn't try to be objective, they should try to be honest."

Yet the power of the combined media is overwhelming. A 1994 study by Veronis, Suhler & Associates revealed that the typical American spends more than four hours a day watching TV, three hours listening to radio, forty-eight minutes listening to recorded music, twenty-eight minutes reading newspapers, seventeen minutes reading books, and fourteen minutes reading magazines.

The consolidation of the corporate media power which produces these time-consuming products has accelerated tremendously in the 1990s, turning formerly prestigious news organs into little more than advertising distribution systems. And even those are dwindling in number. Ben Bagdikian, former dean of the School of Journalism at the University of California in Berkeley, reported that in 1982, fifty corporations controlled most of the mass media in the United States. By January 1990 that number had shrunk to a mere twenty-three. By the end of 1997 this number was down to ten.

According to Standard and Poor's Industry Surveys—Publishing the top ten media corporations (moving from the largest on down) were Time-Warner (magazines, radio/TV, cable); Walt Disney Co. (newspapers, magazines, radio/TV, cable); Tele-Communications Inc. (cable); News Corp. (newspapers, magazines, radio/TV, cable, other); CBS Corp. (radio/TV, cable, other); General Electric (radio/TV, cable); Gannett Co. (newspapers, radio/TV, cable); Advance Publications (newspapers, magazines); Cox Enterprises (newspapers, radio/TV, cable); and New York Times Co. (newspapers, magazines, radio/TV).

These ten companies take in a yearly gross revenue greater than the next fifteen largest media companies combined.

During the 1990s "Telecommunication firms were engaged in the most visible and dramatic drive for corporate alliance and consolidation," wrote author Greider in *One World, Ready or Not.* "AT&T, Time Warner, TCI, MCI, Ameritech and Nynex, CBS, ABC, Disney and many others—the overlapping deals were stunning as U.S. firms rushed to unite market power and technological assets in cable and telephone systems, broadcasting, filmmaking, publishing and other media, while simultaneously forging telecom partnerships abroad. U.S. consumers would provide the capital for these huge new conglomerates through the deregulated rates they paid to cable and telephone companies. The winners, it was clear, would be a handful of broad and powerful media combines, as dominant as the railroad and oil trusts were in the 1890s."

World War II veterans might wince to learn that with the July 1998 acquisition of Random House publishers, the German firm of Bertelsmann A.G. became the largest trade publisher in the English-speaking world. This one company now controls more than twenty top publishers, including Ballantine, Bantam, Crown, Del Ray, Delacorte Press, Broadway Books, Dell, Dial, Doubleday, Fawcett, Harmony, Laurel, Pantheon, Princeton Review, and Times Books. Adding to this publishing clout, in October 1998 Bertelsmann, headquartered in Mayer Rothschild's hometown of Frankfurt, purchased a 50 percent interest in barnesandnoble.com, the bookseller's Internet site.

Over and above ownership consolidation, there is a decreasing number of distribution companies, which are critical to the widespread dissemination of information. *Standard & Poor's* editors noted that in 1996, distribution problems caused by the consolidation of formerly independent distributors "disrupted deliveries and relationships with retail clients . . . canceled, missed and late deliveries were common occurrences." Authors have complained for years that books on controversial subjects always seem to encounter distribution or publicity problems. With an estimated eight hundred new magazines added each year to the existing eighteen thousand or so (most fail within the first year), it is easy to understand the importance of distribution.

Major banks own significant amounts of stock in the ever-decreasing number of media corporations, which in turn are controlled by secret society members. "Through elite policy-shaping groups like the Council on Foreign Relations and the Business Roundtable, they steer the ship of state in what they deem to be a financially advantageous direction," noted authors Martin A. Lee and Norman Solomon in 1990. "GE, CapCities, CBS, the *New York Times* and the *Washington Post* all have board members who sit on the Council on Foreign Relations." Little has changed today. A cursory glance at the 1998 edition of *Stan-*

dard & Poor's Corporation Records showed several CFR and Trilateral members sit on the boards of the major media corporations.

Corporate ownership intermingled with secret society members, many of whom are employed in the media, may explain why Bilderberg, Trilateral, and CFR meetings are not reported by America's "watchdog" media. In fact, the membership lists of these societies read like a who's who of the mass media.

These members include many past and present media corporate leaders such as Laurence A. Tisch and William Paley of CBS; John F. Welch Jr., of NBC; Thomas S. Murphy of ABC; Robert McNeil, Jim Lehrer, Hodding Carter III, and Daniel Schorr of Public Broadcast Service; Katherine Graham, Harold Anderson, and Stanley Swinton of Associated Press; Michael Posner of Reuters; Joan Ganz-Cooney of Children's TV Workshop (*Sesame Street*); W. Thomas Johnson of CNN; David Gergen of *U.S. News & World Report;* Richard Gelb, William Scranton, Cyrus Vance, A. M. Rosenthal, and Harrison Salisbury of the *New York Times;* Ralph Davidson, Henry Grunwald, Sol Linowitz, and Strobe Talbott of *Time;* Robert Christopher and Phillip Geyelin of *Newsweek;* Katherine Graham, Leonard Downie Jr., and Stephen S. Rosenfeld of the *Washington Post;* Arnaud de Borchgrave of the *Washington Times;* Richard Wood, Robert Bartley, and Karen House of the *Wall Street Journal;* William F. Buckley Jr. of *National Review;* and George V. Grune and William G. Bowen of *Reader's Digest.* Furthermore, sitting on the boards of directors of the corporations which own the media are secret society members.

Some of the well-known reporters, anchors, and columnists who are members of the CFR and/or the Trilateral Commission include Dan Rather, Bill Moyers, C. C. Collinwood, Diane Sawyer, David Brinkley, Ted Koppel, Barbara Walters, John Chancellor, Marvin Kalb, Daniel Schorr, Joseph Kraft, James Reston, Max Frankel, David Halberstram, Harrison Salisbury, A. Ochs Sulzberger, Sol Linowitz, Nicholas Katzenbach, George Will, Tom Brokaw, Robert McNeil, David Gergen, Mortimer Zuckerman, Georgie Ann Geyer, Ben J. Wattenberg, and many others. Small wonder so many researchers see a conspiracy of silence among these media peers.

Then there are "media watchdog" organizations such as Accuracy in Media (AIM). Many persons assume such groups are watching out for the public's interests.

Not according to writer Michael Collins Piper, who in 1990 made public that AIM founder Reed Irvine was paid $37,000 a year as an "advisor for the division of international finance" of the Federal Reserve System. Noting that many Fed members also belong to the secret societies, Piper wrote, "To this day, Irvine and AIM never touch on any subject which is sensitive to the interests of the international Establishment: whether it be the Bilderberger group, the Trilateral Commission, the Council on Foreign Relations or the truth about the privately owned Federal Reserve."

There are also choke points within the flow of information, such as the international desk at Associated Press headquarters in New York, where one person decides what news from outside the United States makes it onto the wire service. It is important to understand that the real control over the mass media is not direct control over the thousands of hardworking editors, reporters, and news directors throughout the nation, but rather the control over the distribution of the information.

Then there is the tremendous pressure created by fear of job security and loss of sources. Many national columnists must rely on insider sources to provide juicy information. Much of this information comes from government sources which would dry up if they published the wrong story. Even the more hard-hitting national reporters still must pull their punches if they want to maintain their insider sources.

The ever-concentrated corporate ownership of the media has meant that objectivity in news, long viewed as a public service, flies out the window in favor of bottom-line profits based on ratings. At the time of the JFK assassination, the three major TV networks—ABC, CBS, and NBC—supported their news departments with public service funds. Today, these same news departments are funded as programming with a resultant concern over ratings. News today is "a kind of commodity in the marketplace, no longer a holy profession," commented former CBS correspondent Daniel Schorr. "Today, it doesn't matter anymore. You just make your money and to hell with public service."

Veteran newsman Walter Cronkite agreed. Quoted in a professional journal, he said the current state of television journalism is "disastrous and dangerous" and decried "unreasonable profits . . . to satisfy shareholders. In demanding a profit similar to that of the entertainment area, they're dragging us all down."

"I challenge any viewer to make the distinction between [TV talk show host] Jerry Springer and the three evening newses and CNN," commented *60 Minutes* correspondent Morley Safer.

The watchdog media in America, as they like to portray themselves, appear to be more like lapdogs to their corporate owners. This may explain why six of the top ten "censored stories" of 1995, as determined by Alternet news service, involved business stories such as the monopolization of telecommunications, the worsening child labor situation, increased government spending on nuclear arms, medical industry fraud, the chemical industry's battle to subvert environmental laws and the broken promises of the North American Free Trade Agreement (NAFTA).

Such stories failed to reach a wide audience because, as Greider accurately pointed out, "any who question the reigning mantra of economic orthodoxy will be harshly disciplined by the press and multinational interests."

It is especially intriguing that none of America's major "watchdog" media show much interest in determining who owns the corporations which control the media and the nation. One explanation for this lack of investigative zeal may be found in the story of an NBC-TV news researcher who in 1990 contacted Todd Putnam, editor of *National Boycott News*. The news staffer was interested in "the biggest boycott going on right now." Putnam replied, "The biggest boycott in the country is against General Electric." To which the NBC staffer immediately responded, "We can't do that one. . . . Well, we could do that one, but we won't." In 1986 NBC was bought by General Electric.

COMMENTARY

There can be no argument regarding the reality of secret societies today. The existence of groups like the Trilateral Commission, Council on Foreign Relations, and the Bilderbergers is well documented. The only question is the extent of their control and manipulation of major world events.

Likewise, there is no question that members of these societies exert inordinate control over many of the largest corporations and banks in the world. These corporations, in turn, control essential minerals, energy, transportation, pharmaceuticals, agriculture, telecommunications, and entertainment—in other words, the basics of modern life.

They also provide an inner core of ranking government officials on a revolving door basis. These officials often implement the very policies conceived and desired by the societies.

These societies hold considerable sway over national elections and policy, yet seem strangely immune to any investigation, whether by government or the mass media. Since its inception in 1913, there has never been an outside, objective audit of the Federal Reserve System despite periodic calls for such. The same can be said for the powerful private foundations which direct so much of modern science and culture.

Taken together the facts suggest that the overall goal of these modern societies is to bring about one world government with attendant centralized social control and loss of national sovereignty. This objective is coming ever closer to reality, largely through the increasing corporate and financial control over both governments and economies.

Samuel Berger, Clinton's national security adviser and a regular attendee of the Bilderberger meetings, revealed that group's outlook in a recent talk at the Brookings Institution when he stated, "Globalization—the process of accelerating economic, technological, cultural and political integration—is not a choice. It is a growing fact. It is a fact that will proceed inexorably, with or without our approval. It is a fact that we ignore at our peril."

No one is suggesting that this issue be ignored. Quite the contrary. Conspiracy writers seek a more open dialogue on this matter. It's the major media that shies away from the subject.

It may be that global government is desirable. It certainly appears inevitable. And it's nothing new. World domination has been the focus of men since before Alexander the Great. Why then is there so much secrecy about this issue today?

The question of whether or not the plan for one world government is a sinister conspiracy to subjugate the population or simply an attempt to facilitate a natural evolutionary step is a matter still to be decided, apparently with little or no help from the mass media.

But one thing is absolutely clear. It is apparent that globalization or one world government or the New World Order is not simply the imaginings of conspiracy theorists or paranoids but the articulated goal of the secret brotherhoods, organizations, and groups, all of which carry the imprint of the old orders of Freemasonry, the Round Tables, and the Illuminati, which will be examined more closely later.

The recognition of a ruling elite by knowledgeable experts like Quigley and the others quoted, coupled with the suspicions of many more regarding secret control, has created a climate in which the average person feels less and less control over both the nation's destiny and his or her own.

It is not necessary to believe in such widespread conspiracies. What is necessary is to know that others do believe and act accordingly. To comprehend the world around us, we must study the full range of evidence if we are to avoid either destructive paranoia or baseless and naive faith.

The evidence points clearly to a commonality of purpose on the part of secret society members and that these members, their relatives, associates, and hirelings are closely interrelated.

That luminaries of the modern secret societies—people connected by blood, marriage, social and business associations—are at the controls of the international corporations which dominate much of modern life through their power over business, advertising, government, and the mass media is beyond dispute. They have dominated the scene since the days of Mayer and Nathan Rothschild, Cecil Rhodes and Alfred Milner, J. P. Morgan and John D. Rockefeller.

And their societies can be traced directly to earlier secret organizations, forming a conspiratorial chain throughout history. They appear to be following a plan formulated and articulated many years ago. This plan, an outgrowth of the objectives of the Illuminati and Freemasonry, found expression in the Round Tables of Mason Cecil Rhodes. It was carried forward by the "illuminized" members of the Royal Institute of International Affairs, Council on Foreign Relations, the Trilateral Commission, and their numerous foundations and trusts. This incestuous brotherhood also made ample use of secret intelligence agencies in both Britain and America to further their plans.

All this prompts several questions. If the CFR, the Trilateral Commission, and the Bilderbergers are simply innocent well-intentioned people working to bring about a peaceful and prosperous world, as they claim, then why all the secrecy? Why all the front organizations, some of which are the antithesis of others? Why do they obviously distrust public attention?

Which leads to the single most important question: If they do create a centralized one-world government, what's to prevent some Hitler-like tyrant from taking control?

Secrecy is the key. Any activity that is justified and honorable should be able to withstand the light of public scrutiny. When the secrets of these societies are laid bare before the public, everyone will be able to judge for themselves the merit of their goals and purposes.

Until that time, the diligent researcher must sift through the historical record, piecing together the clues which will prove or disprove secret society involvement in world events, searching for the telltale fingerprints of conspiracy.

PART II

THE FINGERPRINTS OF CONSPIRACY

War is a racket. . . . War is largely a matter of money. Bankers lend money to foreign countries and when they cannot pay, the President sends Marines to get it.

—MARINE MAJ. GEN. SMEDLEY D. BUTLER (1881–1940)

Conspiracy writers have long accused members of the secret societies of using their torch of power and influence to light the fires of war. They have been charged with fomenting the Cold War, two world wars, the American, French, and Russian Revolutions, along with countless other conflicts and revolts. It is also claimed that these hidden hands can be traced directly to the secret organizations of the past.

And a careful study of history indeed reveals the telltale fingerprints of the secret societies throughout the history of warfare.

Of all human activities, war alone offers the greatest potential for profit—both from war materials and from the loans to produce them. And there are deeper rationales, such as the need to distract the public from their domestic troubles as well as the hidden agendas of their rulers.

"American capitalism needed international rivalry—and periodic war—to create an artificial community of interest between rich and poor, supplanting the genuine community of interest among the poor that showed itself in sporadic movements," wrote history professor Howard Zinn.

This view was addressed in detail in a controversial 1966 study of war and peace called the "Report from Iron Mountain."

REPORT FROM IRON MOUNTAIN

The study that led to the Report from Iron Mountain began in 1961 with Kennedy administration officials such as McGeorge Bundy (CFR, Bilderberger, and Skull and Bones), Robert McNamara (Trilateralist, CFR, and Bilderberger) and Dean Rusk (CFR and Bilderberger). Knowing of Kennedy's goal of ending the Cold War, these men were concerned that there had been no serious planning for long-term peace.

In early 1963 a special study group was selected to study the hypothetical problems of peace just as government think tanks such as the Rand and Hudson Institutes studied war. The fifteen members of this group have never been publicly identified, but it reportedly included highly regarded historians, economists, sociologists, psychologists, scientists, and even an astronomer and industrialist. The group met about once a month at various locations around the nation.

But its principal meetings were at Iron Mountain, a huge underground corporate "nuclear hideout" near Hudson, New York, site of the Hudson Institution, widely regarded as a CFR think tank. Here, in case of nuclear attack, were housed redundant corporate offices of Rockefeller-controlled Standard Oil of New Jersey, the Morgan bank, Manufacturers Hanover Trust, and Dutch Shell Oil, then headed by Bilderberger founder Prince Bernhard.

A copy of the Report from Iron Mountain was leaked by a man identified only as "John Doe," a Midwestern university professor who claimed to have been a participant. It was published by Dial Press in 1967. John Doe told the publisher that, while he agreed with the findings of the study, he disagreed with the group's decision to conceal their work from a public "unexposed to the exigencies of higher political or military responsibility." He said he believed the American public, whose tax money paid for the report, had a right to know its disturbing conclusions, while his fellow authors feared "the clear and predictable danger of a crisis in public confidence which untimely publication of the Report might be expected to provoke."

Over the years, the Report from Iron Mountain has received little or no publicity, and certain members of the government and media have attempted to brush it off as a joke or satire. But Dial Press published this work with no such disclaimers, and the serious and erudite tone of this footnoted study along with its global and macro-analytical approach belies the charge of fiction. It is an amazing document, written at the onset of our national experience in Vietnam, and most certainly reflects the elitist views of those who are said to have solicited the study.

John Doe said the "Iron Mountain Boys," as they called themselves, conducted an informal, off-the-books secret study uninhibited by normal government restraints. They submitted their report in March 1966.

According to the report, "War itself is the basic social system, within which other secondary modes of social organization conflict or conspire. It is the system which has governed most human societies of record, as it is today." The report's authors saw war as both necessary and desirable as "the principal organizing force" as well as "the essential economic stabilizer of modern societies."

They expressed concern that through "ambiguous leadership" the "ruling administrative class" might lose its ability to "rationalize a desired war," leading to the "actual disestablishment of military institutions," an eventuality they viewed as "catastrophic."

Therefore the report writers concluded, "We must first reply, as strongly as we can, that the war system cannot responsibly be allowed to disappear until (1.) we know exactly what [forms of social control] we plan to put in its place and (2.) we are certain, beyond reasonable doubt, that these substitute institutions will serve their purposes. . . ."

Most significantly, the report states, "The elimination of war implies the inevitable elimination of national sovereignty and the traditional nation-state." It added, "The possibility of war provides the sense of external necessity without which no government can long remain in power. . . . The basic authority of a modern state over its people resides in its war powers."

The report goes on to say that war "has served as the last great safeguard against the elimination of necessary social classes . . . hewers of wood and drawers of water" and that war functions to control "essential class relationships."

Its authors credited military institutions with providing "antisocial elements with an acceptable role in the social structure. . . . It is not hard to visualize, for example, the degree of social disruption that might have taken place in the United States during the last two decades if the problem of the socially disaffected of the post–World War II period had not been foreseen and effectively met," noted the report. "The younger, and more dangerous, of these hostile social groupings have been kept under control by the Selective Service System." In the past, juvenile delinquents often were given the choice of going to jail or into the Army.

The report suggests what should be done with the "economically or culturally deprived" among us. "A . . . possible surrogate for the control of potential enemies of society is the reintroduction, in some form consistent with modern technology and political process, of slavery. . . . The development of a sophisticated form of slavery may be an absolute prerequisite for social control in a world at peace." Perhaps this refers to the current growing practice of private businesses utilizing prison labor or to "wage slaves," those so mired in credit that they have lost any option but to continue working for wages in an unfulfilling job.

It is highly intriguing to compare the recommendations of this report with life in the United States today. The Iron Mountain "boys" listed these possible substitutes for the "functions of war":

—a comprehensive social-welfare program
—a giant, open-ended space research program aimed at unreachable targets (missions to Jupiter, etc.)
—a permanent, ritualized, ultraelaborate disarmament inspection system (as in Iraq and Bosnia)
—an omnipresent, virtually omnipotent international police force (a UN peacekeeping force as in the Persian Gulf War or the Balkans)
—an established and recognized extraterrestrial menace (UFOs and alien abductions)
—massive global environmental pollution
—fictitious alternate enemies (Saddam Hussein, Muammar Quaddafi, Slobodan Milosevic, and whoever follows them)
—programs generally derived from the Peace Corps model (the Job Corps, Volunteers in Service to America)
—a modern, sophisticated form of slavery (addressed above)
—new religions or other mythologies (New Age theologies, cults, etc.)
—socially oriented blood games (the National Football League, World Wrestling Federation)
—a comprehensive program of applied eugenics (abortion and birth control)

The authors admitted that "alternative enemies" might prove unlikely, but stressed that "one *must* be found" (emphasis in the original) or, more probably, that "such a threat will have to be invented."

Finally, the Iron Mountain Special Study Group proposed the establishment by presidential order of a permanent and top-secret "War/Peace Research Agency," organized "along the lines of the National Security Council (outside the purview of Congress, the media and the public)," provided with "non-accountable funds" and "responsible solely to the President." The purpose of this agency would be "Peace Research," to include creating the above listed substitutes for the functions of war and the "unlimited right to withhold information on its activities and its decisions from anyone except the President, whenever it deems such secrecy to be in the public interest."

No one seems to know—or is willing to tell—if such a secret agency was ever considered or created. Regardless if it was or not, the tone of this proposal is certainly conspiratorial and it was hatched by men connected to the secret societies whose class-conscious objectives are reflected in this report. These same men were responsible for the involvement of America in Vietnam in the 1960s and 1970s, and their mindset was behind the attempt to foment war in Nicaragua in the 1980s as well as the conflicts of the 1990s in the Middle East and Balkans.

"In human terms, it is an outrageous document," commented Leonard C. Lewin, who arranged for the report's publication. "And it explains, or certainly appears to explain, aspects of American policy otherwise incomprehensible by the ordinary standards of common sense."

Despite this study of "peace," as the Cold War drew to a close in the early 1990s, there was one more large scale, seemingly "incomprehensible" modern war to further the aims of those secret society men who seek profit from hostilities: war in the Persian Gulf.

PERSIAN GULF

The Allied victory in the Persian Gulf war of 1991 was loudly trumpeted by the American mass media, but the actions leading to this conflict were sparsely reported throughout the coverage. These machinations involved people in secret societies and indicated a very different rationale for the war than the one presented to the public.

No one can argue that the United States military, with some assistance from British, French, and Arab forces, did not perform magnificently during this brief conflict. It took only between January 17 and February 28, 1991, for the coalition of Operation Desert Storm to soundly defeat the Iraqi forces of Saddam Hussein, then representing the fifth largest army in the world. This astounding military success was due primarily to the Allied forces' superiority in both weaponry and training as opposed to Saddam's conscripts who, though veterans of combat against Iran, had limited training and low morale.

This disparity created a lopsided war which resulted in more than 300,000 Iraqi casualties, both military and civilian, and 65,000 prisoners, compared to the extraordinary low Allied losses of 234 killed, 470 wounded, and 57 missing.

Primary leader of the war was U.S. President George Bush, a former CFR member, Trilateralist, and Skull and Bonesman.

As with most Middle East conflicts, the primary issue was oil. Both Bush and then Secretary of State James Baker were deeply involved in the oil business. Any Bush policy which increased the price of oil meant more profit to his companies, those of his oilmen supporters and, of course, to the Rockefeller-dominated oil cartel.

An added bonus was that any conflict which divided the Arab world would only strengthen the power of the U.S., Britain, and Israel in the region. A coalition of countries fighting for the United Nations could only advance the globalists' plan for a one-world military force.

This "battle of the New World Order was some kind of manufactured crisis with a hidden agenda," wrote conspiracy researchers Jonathan Vankin and John Whalen after careful study of the events leading to this conflict.

Bush and Saddam Hussein had had a close relationship for many years. In his role as CIA director, and later as vice president, George Bush had supported Saddam through his eight-year war against Iran following the ouster of the Shah in 1979.

By 1990 Saddam's Iraq was a primary threat to the balance of power between Israel and its Arab neighbors, but Saddam was strapped for cash due to the Iraq-Iran War and couldn't pay his bills. Under pressure from the international bankers for slow repayment of loans and from the Organization of Petroleum Producing Countries (OPEC), which refused to allow him to raise oil prices, Saddam turned his eyes to Kuwait as a source of income. At the time it was the third largest producer of oil next to Iraq and Saudi Arabia.

Kuwait had been carved out of Iraq by Britain, who in 1899 took control of Kuwait's foreign policy under an agreement with the dictatorial Sabah family. The Sabahs had produced a series of ruling sheikhs since assuming control of the area's nomad tribes in 1756. Kuwait became a British Protectorate in 1914 when German interest suddenly gave the area strategic importance. British dominance was solidified by sending British troops to the area in 1961 after Iraq sought to reclaim it.

The Pentagon had known that Iraqi troops were massing along the Kuwait border since mid-July 1990. On July 25 Saddam sought advice from the United States on his intentions to reclaim Kuwait. He met with U.S. Ambassador April Glaspie, who told him, "I have direct instructions from President Bush to improve our relations with Iraq. We have considerable sympathy for your quest for higher oil prices, the immediate cause of your confrontation with Kuwait. . . .

"I have received an instruction to ask you, in the spirit of friendship not confrontation, regarding your intentions: Why are your troops massed so very close to Kuwait's borders?"

According to transcripts released long after the war, Hussein explained that, while he was ready to negotiate his border dispute with Kuwait, his design was to "keep the whole of Iraq in the shape we wish it to be." This shape, of course, included Kuwait, which Saddam considered still a part of Iraq. "What is the United States' opinion on this?" he asked.

"We have no opinion on your Arab-Arab conflicts, like your dispute with Kuwait," replied Glaspie. "Secretary Baker has directed me to emphasize the instruction, first given to Iraq in the 1960s, that the Kuwaiti issue is not associated with America."

"Shortly after this, April Glaspie left Kuwait to take her summer vacation, another signal of elaborate American disinterest in the Kuwait-Iraq crisis," noted authors Tarpley and Chaitkin in *George Bush: The Unauthorized Biography*. On July 31 Bush met with GOP congressional leaders but said nothing about the Gulf situation.

The crisis escalated on August 2, when Iraqi troops moved into Kuwait. Bush froze all Iraqi assets in the United States, adding to Saddam's money woes, which had worsened in 1990 after international bankers refused him further loans. Glaspie was prohibited from speaking out by the State Department, so the American public could not learn of Bush's duplicity.

In later testimony before the Senate Foreign Relations Committee, Glaspie pointed out that the July 25 conference was her first and only meeting with Saddam, who had not met with any foreign ambassador since 1984, the midpoint of his war with Iran.

But if Saddam had not met with U.S. diplomats, the same could not be said of American businessmen. Economist Paul Adler noted, "It was known that David Rockefeller met with the Iraqi leader on at least three known occasions after the Chase Manhattan consortium became the lead banker in a number of major Iraqi credit syndications." It was also reported that Alan Stoga, a vice president of (Henry) Kissinger

Associates met with Iraqi leaders during a two-year period preceding the Gulf conflict.

"Saddam began to realize that he could not get what he wanted from the striped-pants set. He began doing business with the people who mattered to him—foreign businessmen, defense contractors, technologists and scientists, occasionally even visiting newsmen," reported the Washington newspaper, *The Spotlight*.

Following the money trail of such nondiplomatic contacts which led to the Gulf War, Congressman Henry Gonzalez, chairman of the House Committee on Banking, Finance and Urban Affairs, discovered that almost $5 billion in loans had been passed to Saddam Hussein in the 1980s through the Atlanta, Georgia, branch of Italy's government-owned bank, Banca Nazional del Lavoro (BNL). The branch manager, Christopher Drogoul, was finally brought into federal court, where he pleaded guilty to approving this huge cash transfer without the approval of BNL's head office in Italy. However, the whole investigation was put on hold during the Gulf War.

Most observers disbelieved that Drogoul could have conducted such a massive transaction without the knowledge of his superiors. Bobby Lee Cook, one of Drogoul's several defense attorneys, argued that his client had been made the patsy in "a scheme orchestrated at the highest levels of the U.S. Government."

In court, BNL official Franz von Wedel testified that his boss Drogoul had acted on the advice of the bank's consultants, Kissinger Associates.

In both 1989 and 1990 the Bush Justice Department had quashed indictments against the BNL by the Atlanta Attorney General's office following an FBI raid on the bank on August 4, 1989. Action against the bank managers was held up for more than a year. Indictments were finally handed down one day after Bush declared a cease-fire in the Gulf War.

This scandal—dubbed "Iraqgate"—prompted Gonzalez to prepare a House resolution calling for the impeachment of Bush Attorney General William Barr for "obstruction of justice in the BNL scandal." House Judiciary Committee Chairman Jack Brooks called on Barr to appoint a special prosecutor in the case. In a classic case of who-will-watch-the-watchers?, Barr said he could find no evidence of wrongdoing on his part and refused to appoint a special prosecutor. It was one of the only times that an attorney general had failed to appoint a special prosecutor when asked to do so by Congress.

WHO PAYS THE TAB?

The clincher of this sordid story of financial scheming and official malfeasance was that not only had most of the $5 billion been used by Saddam to buy weaponry to be used against American servicemen, but the U.S. taxpayers picked up the tab!

Gonzalez said $500 million of the loans to Saddam came through the government-backed Commodity Credit Corporation (CCC) and had been intended to purchase grain from U.S. farmers. However, grain shipped through the port of Houston had gone to then-Soviet bloc nations in exchange for weapons, while the remainder of the grain purchase had freed Saddam's limited cash reserves to buy more military materials. The Bush administration had pledged taxpayer guarantees should Saddam default on the loans, which he did after sending troops to Kuwait. According to at least one public source, more than $360 million in American tax money was paid to the Gulf International Bank in Bahrain which was owned by seven Gulf nations including Iraq. This amount was only the first of an estimated $1 billion to be paid to ten banks by the CCC to cover the $5 billion of Saddam's defaulted loans.

"The $1 billion commitment, in the form of loan guarantees for the purchase of U.S. farm commodities, enabled Saddam to buy needed food on credit and to spend his scarce hard currency on the arms buildup that brought war to the Persian Gulf," wrote author Russell S. Bowen.

Even after the Iraqi invasion began on August 2, Bush publicly appeared strangely noncommittal. Asked by reporters if he intended any intervention in the Gulf crisis, Bush said, "I'm not contemplating such action. . . ."

His attitude apparently changed drastically that same day after meeting with British prime minister Margaret Thatcher, a regular attendee of Bilderberg meetings who had been implicated with Bush in both the Iran-Contra and October Surprise scandals.

After meeting with Thatcher, Bush began to describe Saddam as a "new Hitler" and said "the status quo is unacceptable and further expansion [by Iraq] would be even more unacceptable."

Despite assurances from Saddam that Kuwait was his only objective and with no concrete evidence to the contrary, Bush nevertheless personally telephoned the leaders of Saudi Arabia and warned that they would be the next target of the "new Hitler." Panicked, the Saudis handed over as much as $4 billion to Bush and other world leaders as secret payoffs to protect their kingdom, according to Sabah family member Sheik Fahd Mohammed al-Sabah, chairman of the Kuwait Investment Office.

Long after the Persian Gulf War, when audits found this money had been diverted into a London slush fund, anti-Sabah elements in Saudi Arabia criticized the payoff. They were told by al-Sabah, "That money was used to buy Kuwait's liberation. It paid for political support in the West and among Arab leaders—support for Desert Storm, the international force we urgently needed."

Whether this money played any role or not, Bush soon drew a "line in the sand" to block further Iraqi intrusion. It is interesting to note that this line was located between the Iraqi forces and oil interests owned by his son, soon-to-be Texas governor George W. Bush.

Bush, the president's eldest son, was a $50,000-a-year "consultant" to and a board member of Harken Energy Corp. of Grand Prairie, Texas, near the home of the Texas Rangers baseball team of which the younger Bush was a managing general partner.

In January 1991, just days before Desert Storm was launched, Harken shocked the business world by announcing an oil-production agreement with the small island nation of Bahrain, a former British protectorate and a haven for international bankers just off the coast of Saudi Arabia in the Persian Gulf. Bahrain was listed among the top forty countries of the world with the highest per capita Gross Domestic Product in 1996.

Veteran oilmen wondered aloud how unknown Harken, with no previous drilling experience, obtained such a potentially lucrative deal. Furthermore, it was reported that "Harken's investments in the area will be protected by a 1990 agreement Bahrain signed with the U.S. allowing American and 'multi-national' forces to set up permanent bases in that country."

The younger Bush, in October 1990, told *Houston Post* reporter Peter Brewton that accusations that his father ordered troops to the area to protect Harken drilling rights were "a little far-fetched." He further claimed he sold his Harken stock before the Iraqi invasion, but Brewton could find no record of the sale in the files of the Securities and Exchange Commission (SEC).

Records of Bush's Harken stock sale finally turned up in March 1991, eight months after the July 10, 1990, SEC deadline for filing such disclosures. One week after Saddam's troops entered Kuwait, Harken stock had dropped to $3.03 a share. The tardy SEC records revealed that by some good fortune, Bush had sold 66 percent of his Harken stock on June 22, 1990—just weeks prior to Iraq's invasion—for the top-dollar price of $4.00 a share, netting him $848,560. Despite locating productive wells in South America, the drop in oil prices in early 1999 caused Harken stock to remain about $4.00 per share.

Stock purchases, oil and grain deals, arms sales, loans and guarantees, the weakening of the Arabs to benefit Israel, the movement toward a global army and government created a mind-numbing entanglement. "It is doubtful whether the 'real' reasons why the United States went to war in the Persian Gulf will ever emerge," wrote Vankin and Whaley. "Unlike in Vietnam, where the ambiguous outcome elicited natural suspicions, in the Gulf the decisiveness of victory has buried the reality deeper than any Iraqi or American soldier who went to a sandy grave."

The duplicity didn't end with the fighting. Throughout the Clinton administration there have been periodic air forays into Iraq, ostensibly to punish Saddam for preventing UN inspection of his development centers for biological and nuclear weaponry. However, this time there was a big difference—probing questions were raised by both a suspicious public and a few less timid members of the news media.

Following missile and bombing strikes in late 1998, a letter writer to a national news magazine asked, "By using weapons of mass destruction to deter Iraq from manufacturing weapons of mass destruction, would America not be doing the very thing we're warning Iraq not to do?" Others raised the question of why we attacked Iraq for refusing UN inspection of its sensitive military installations when President Clinton also had refused to allow such inspections in the United States—a refusal greeted with general approval by the public.

Scott Ritter, a member of the United Nations Special Commission (UNSCOM) created to locate and eliminate Saddam Hussein's secret weapons caches, resigned in August of 1998 and accused the U.S. government of using the commission to justify an attack on Iraq. Ritter said that before his resignation he disbelieved Baghdad's minister of defense when he told him the UNSCOM team was being used to "provoke a crisis," but he slowly came to agree with the charge. Ritter's superiors scoffed at the allegation, claiming Ritter's knowledge of the situation was "limited."

However, in early 1999 it was reported that Washington had used UNSCOM to plant electronic bugs in the Ministry of Defense (Iraq's Pentagon) and other U.S. officials confirmed much of Ritter's accusations.

"The relationship between the United States and the inspection commission . . . has long been a subject of debate," wrote *U.S. News* reporter Bruce B. Auster. "The issue is sensitive because UNSCOM is an arm of the UN Security Council, not an agency of the United States, although it does rely on the United States for intelligence and personnel."

On December 15, 1998, after stockpiling cruise missiles in the Persian Gulf during the fall, the U.S. launched a much-delayed air strike against Baghdad.

But with Christmas nearing, most Americans couldn't get too worked up over civilian casualties halfway around the word. And any doubts about U.S. involvement in the Persian Gulf—except among those unfortunates having to deal with Gulf War Syndrome caused by a lethal combination of oil fires, biological agents, and radioactive uranium-tipped artillery and tank shells—had been thrown away, along with the yellow ribbons which had proudly displayed the total support of the uninformed.

VIETNAM

While human connivance to actually create war may seem unbelievable to those unaware of the secret societies' methods, there is much evidence indicating that the Vietnam War was largely contrived by men of the "Iron Mountain" mindset.

Many conspiracy writers saw the Vietnam War as a classic example of the Hegelian dialectic in action—create a problem (the Viet Cong supported by North Vietnam), offer the solution (ever-increasing aid and troops to South Vietnam) to create synthesis (U.S. hegemony over Southeast Asia).

United States involvement in Vietnam began with the secret agreements of Yalta during World War II. America's "sphere of influence" in the postwar world was to be the Pacific—we still have a presence in the Philippines and the South Pacific islands—and Southeast Asia. However, after hostilities ended in Europe, France was quick to resume its military control of French Indochina and U.S. plans for the region were put on hold.

The history of the Vietnam War can be personified in Nguyen That Thanh, the son of a lowly Vietnamese rural educator. This man later changed his name to Ho Chi Minh (He Who Enlightens) and became the driving force behind Indochinese nationalism for three decades. He also can be connected to the same forces which produced the communist movement during the twentieth century.

As a young man during World War I, Ho lived in France where he came into contact with French socialists and their philosophies derived from Illuminati and Freemasonry roots. In 1919 he spoke before the Warburg brothers and the other attendees of the Versailles Peace Conference, calling for expanded rights in Indochina.

In 1930 Ho founded the Vietnamese Communist Party, which later was changed at the urging of Soviet leaders to the Indochinese Communist Party to avoid being perceived as simply a national movement. However, the nationalism of Ho's party was reaffirmed in 1941, when he and others entered Vietnam and created the League for the Independence of Vietnam, or the Viet Minh.

When the Japanese overran Indochina in 1945, Ho and General Vo Nguyen Giap began working with the American Office of Strategic Services to oust the occupation forces.

Ho continued to receive American aid after the Japanese withdrew from Vietnam following their surrender on August 14, 1945. "We had a trusted agent whom we regularly supplied with weapons, radio equipment, operators and medicine. All of it served to reinforce his position and status," wrote journalist Lloyd Shearer.

France's Charles de Gaulle realized that Ho intended to create an independent Vietnam which would give his American handlers entrée to the area. So in October 1945 de Gaulle ordered French troops into Saigon. Hoping to reclaim Vietnam as a French possession, de Gaulle even promised to return Vietnamese emperor Bao Dai to power, but Ho would settle for nothing less than independence.

After years of fighting, Ho's Viet Minh, led by his able general Giap, had gained control of most of the countryside and, in May 1954 the French Army was defeated at Dien Bien Phu and forced to leave.

In a subsequent Geneva conference in July to determine Vietnam's future, Ho's delegation was met by a rival delegation representing the French-backed emperor Bao Dai. The resulting conflict was reconciled by dividing Vietnam along the Seventeenth Parallel with Ho given control of the north. Ho accepted this division chiefly because the Geneva Accords promised a vote on reunification by both sides and he was confident both would join together under his leadership. The accords were not signed by the United States.

South Vietnam, which contained most of Vietnam's resources and wealth, ended up in the hands of Ngo Dinh Diem, a Catholic in a land that was 95 percent Buddhist. Diem had lived in the United States following the French defeat and had met with high-ranking officials and CFR members. A veteran of twenty years of civil service, Diem was supported by Colonel Edward Lansdale, head of the newly arrived U.S. Military Advisory and Assistance Group. Lansdale's group was there to aid the 234,000-man Vietnamese National Army, created and financed by the United States.

The Diem government, with the agreement of the United States, postponed indefinitely any reunification elections. "All this suggests that the U.S. conspired against the Geneva terms. . . ." wrote journalist Michael McClear. This also virtually guaranteed civil war in Vietnam.

Vietnamese nationalists, largely anti-Catholic Buddhists and veterans of the Viet Minh, aided by a growing number of expatriates returning from the North, began reclaiming areas in the South under the name Viet Cong San or just Viet Cong.

Increasing violence prompted the arrival of American military "advisers" in South Vietnam, a move not totally supported by Congress. "No amount of American military assistance in Indochina can conquer an enemy which is everywhere and at the same time nowhere, an 'enemy of the people' which has the sympathy and covert support of the people," warned Senator John F. Kennedy in 1954.

Aid to communist North Vietnam came from Russia and China while South Vietnam grew more and more dependent on American support. The balance of power steadied. The stage was set for war.

JFK OPPOSED GLOBALISTS

By 1963 the biggest obstacle to a wider war in Southeast Asia was President John F. Kennedy, who had already voiced his reservations about U.S. involvement.

Democrat John F. Kennedy upset Eisenhower's vice president, Republican Richard Nixon, in the 1960 election and his top advisers came from the secret societies. Special Advisor John Kenneth Galbraith noted, "Those of us who had worked for the Kennedy election were tolerated in the government for that reason and had a say, but foreign policy was still with the Council on Foreign Relations people." The overabundance of CFR members in government even caught the attention of President Kennedy, who remarked, "I'd like to have some new faces here, but all I get is the same old ones."

Immediately after his election, Kennedy was faced with a confrontation in Laos. In a foretaste of Vietnam, this conflict pitted the Pathet Lao communists against CIA-backed General Phoumi Nosavan. Upon entering office, Kennedy was advised by everyone from outgoing President Eisenhower to the Joint Chiefs of Staff to send troops to support Nosavan. CFR members Secretary of Defense Robert Strange McNamara and Walt Rostow, head of the State Department's Policy Planning Council vocally supported the use of troops. Kennedy declined.

The CFR had been concerned with Vietnam right from the start. In 1951 the CFR, along with the Royal Institute for International Affairs, created a study group funded by the Rockefeller Foundation to study Southeast Asia among other things. The group recommended joint British-American domination of the region in accordance with the agreements at Yalta. During the Eisenhower years, CFR founder and Secretary of State John Foster Dulles, along with his brother CFR founder and CIA Director Allen Dulles, oversaw implementation of this policy which grew to include the arrival of U.S. military advisers following the defeat of the French.

In September 1954, just four months after the fall of Dien Bien Phu, U.S. Secretary of State John Foster Dulles, a founder of the CFR, convened the Manila Conference, which resulted in the Southeast Asia Treaty Organization (SEATO). This action locked the United States, Great Britain (including Australia and New Zealand), France, the Philippines, and others into a mutual defense pact in Indochina.

C. L. Sulzberger of the *New York Times* in 1966 said, "Dulles fathered SEATO with the deliberate purpose, as he explained to me, of providing the U.S. President with legal authority to intervene in Indochina. When Congress approved SEATO, it signed the first of a series of blank checks yielding authority over Vietnam policy."

It soon became apparent that Kennedy, unlike his predecessors, was not content to be manipulated by the Eastern Establishment. "In fact the Establishment's rejection of Kennedy became increasingly intense during his time in office," wrote University of Pittsburgh Professor Donald Gibson in his well-researched 1994 book *Battling Wall Street: The Kennedy Presidency*.

Increasingly, students of the Kennedy assassination are coming to believe that his opposition to the globalists' agenda may have played a significant factor in his unsolved death.

Described by economist Seymour Harris as "by far the most knowledgeable President of all time in the general area of economics," Kennedy quickly launched a variety of sweeping initiatives to increase both the human and technological potential of the nation. "What he [tried] to do with everything from global investment patterns to tax breaks for individuals was to reshape laws and policies so that the power of property and the search for profit would not end up destroying rather than creating economic prosperity for the country," explained Gibson.

Kennedy revealed his animosity toward business titans in the spring of 1962 when he forced the major U.S. steel companies to rescind price increases. An agreement not to raise prices in exchange for labor concessions had been suddenly reversed after wage increases had been put on hold. Angered by this betrayal, Kennedy ordered his brother, Attorney General Robert Kennedy, to launch a price-fixing investigation, threatened the cancellation of steel contracts by the Defense Department and told the American public that the action by steel was unjustifiable and irresponsible. The steel companies, led by United States Steel, backed down.

Viewing the steel executives' actions as an attack on his entire proposed economic program, Kennedy told newsmen, "In my opinion, if the rise in prices had been permitted to stand, it would have been extremely difficult to secure passage of the legislation." It should be noted that board members of U.S. Steel, long controlled by Morgan interests, included many members of the CFR and other powerful institutions.

Kennedy's comptroller of the currency, James J. Saxon, grew increasingly at odds with the powerful Federal Reserve Board by encouraging broader investment and lending powers for non-Fed banks. Saxon also decided that such banks could underwrite state and local obligation bonds, further weakening the dominant Federal Reserve banks.

In June 1963 Kennedy took the ultimate step against the Fed by authorizing the issuance of more than $4 billion in "United States Notes" through the U.S. Treasury, not the Federal Reserve. "Kennedy apparently reasoned that by returning to the Constitution, which states that only Congress shall coin and regulate money, the soaring national debt could be reduced by not paying interest to the bankers of the Federal Reserve System, who print paper money then loan it to the government at interest," noted one conspiracy author.

In his attempt to level the economic playing field, Kennedy took a wide variety of actions, all of which deepened the animosity of Wall Street. As documented by author Gibson, these included:

—offering tax proposals to redirect the foreign investments of U.S. companies

—making distinctions in tax reform between productive and non-productive investment

—eliminating the tax privileges of U.S-based global investment companies

—cracking down on foreign tax havens

—supporting proposals to eliminate tax privileges for the wealthy

—proposing increased taxes for large oil and mineral companies

—revising the investment tax credit

—making a proposal to expand the powers of the president to deal with recession

Kennedy's economic policies and proposals were publicly attacked by *Fortune* magazine editor Charles J. V. Murphy, New York governor Nelson Rockefeller, David Rockefeller, and the editors of the *Wall Street Journal*. Kennedy's own Treasury Secretary, CFR member Douglas Dillon, voiced agreement with David Rockefeller in his opposition to the president's policies in 1962, and by 1965 had joined Rockefeller in creating a formal group to promote the war in Vietnam.

In foreign policy, Kennedy displayed marked antagonism toward both colonialism (open control over a country's political and economic life) and neocolonialism (covert control). "Kennedy's support for economic development and Third World nationalism and his tolerance for government economic planning, even when it involved expropriation of property owned by interests in the U.S., all led to conflicts between Kennedy and elites within both the U.S. and foreign nations," wrote Gibson.

In Vietnam, Kennedy early on assuaged his hawkish counselors by increasing the number of military advisers until by late 1963, the number had grown to about fifteen thousand. But he was having second thoughts and, following the ill-fated Bay of Pigs Invasion in 1961, he had become more and more dubious of the intelligence reports from the military and CIA. On October 11, 1963 Kennedy approved National Security Action Memorandum 263 which approved a possible disengagement in Vietnam by the end of 1965 and even ordered a quiet withdrawal of some military personnel by the end of that year.

He consistently rejected recommendations to introduce U.S. ground troops as he had earlier in Laos. "In rejecting an expanded military involvement, Kennedy went against the Joint Chiefs and a host of high-level people in his government, including (CFR members) Dean Rusk, Robert McNamara, and McGeorge and William Bundy," Gibson noted.

Another key player was Averell Harriman, a CFR man whose connections to secret society manipulation stretched back to World War I and the founding of Soviet Communism. In the fall of 1963 it was Harriman, one of JFK's inner circle, who advocated the removal of Vietnam President Diem and who sent what became known as the "green light" cable to Saigon. This cable voiced support for a movement against the corrupt Diem government. "It did not deal with the warning about a coup and therefore seemed to countenance one," noted author Michael McClear. On November 2 Diem was assassinated in a coup by his own generals, believed by many to have been inspired by the CIA, and the Vietnam War soon escalated.

"The axis of Lodge [CFR] and Harriman [CFR] was too strong for President Kennedy to thwart or overcome," observed former U.S. Ambassador to Saigon Frederick E. Nolting.

Kennedy knew he had to tread lightly in his opposition to a war supported by such powerful interests. He confided to Senator Mike Mansfield that he had decided on "a complete withdrawal from Vietnam" but said this couldn't be done until after he was given a mandate in the 1964 election. Corporate America may well have seen Kennedy as the "ambiguous leadership" that so concerned the "Iron Mountain Boys."

Although there is every indication that Kennedy planned to end U.S. military involvement in Vietnam, no one will ever know for certain. Gunfire in Dallas, Texas, on November 22, 1963, ended his presidency.

The circumstances of JFK's assassination remain controversial at best.

It might be noted that the wife of accused assassin Lee Harvey Oswald in 1994 told author A. J. Weberman, "The answer to the Kennedy assassination is with the Federal Reserve Bank. Don't underestimate that. It's wrong to blame it on [CIA official James] Angleton and the CIA per se only. This is only one finger of the same hand. The people who supply the money are above the CIA."

Two more things should be noted here. One is that Dr. Martin Luther King Jr. was assassinated in 1968 only after he turned his dynamic oratory and organizing skills to protesting the Vietnam War. Second, the overwhelming evidence of obstruction to a truthful investigation of Kennedy's death indicates the use of tremendous and lasting force wielded at the highest level of the American power structure—the level controlled by the secret societies and their Wall Street members.

ALL THE WAY WITH LBJ

Kennedy's successor, Texan Lyndon B. Johnson, the powerful Senate majority leader who had been a member of the House Armed Services Committee, was more attentive to the Joint Chiefs and the CFR crowd.

On December 2, 1963, just days after becoming president, a White House memo from Johnson to General Maxwell Taylor (CFR) only released to the public in 1998, stated, "The more I look at it, the more it is clear to me that South Vietnam is our most critical military area right now. I hope that you and your colleagues in the Joint Chiefs of Staff will see to it that the very best available officers are assigned to General [Paul] Harkins' command in all areas and for all purposes. We should put our blue ribbon men on this job at every level."

Even with this reversal of attitude toward Vietnam in Washington, the war needed a provocation to enlist public support along with congressional authority. "In hopes of provoking a North Vietnamese attack, [Johnson] authorized the resumption of destroyer patrols in the Gulf of Tonkin," wrote West Point historian Major H. R. McMaster. This tactic proved successful with the so-called Gulf of Tonkin incident.

On August 4, 1964 the U.S. destroyers *Maddox* and *Turner Joy* patrolling in the Gulf of Tonkin off Vietnam received a message that the National Security Agency had monitored preparations for an attack by North Vietnam gunboats. Defense Secretary McNamara telephoned President Johnson and confirmed an "anticipated" attack.

This came only two days after three small North Vietnamese torpedo boats had made ineffective attack runs on the *Maddox* in retaliation for raids on the North Vietnam coast by small boats operated jointly by the U.S. Navy and South Vietnamese in an action called Operation Planning (OPLAN) 34-A, a provocative scheme enthusiastically endorsed by McNamara. The destroyer's crews knew nothing of the OPLAN 34-A raids.

The crews of the destroyers went to full battle stations and for two hours Navy guns roared. When the smoke cleared, no damage or casualties were reported and no gunboats were actually seen. Naval commander Wesley McDonald, whose A-4 jet squadron was circling over the gulf, later reported, "[The destroyer crews] were calling out where they thought the torpedo boats were, but I could never find the damn torpedo boats."

Yet on the basis of this "phantom" attack, Johnson called together congressional leaders and asked for the power to respond militarily. He told them, "We want them [the North Vietnamese] to know we are not going to take it lying down" and that "some of our boys are floating around in the water."

Stampeded in those tense Cold War days, the House voted 416 to 0 to allow Johnson, as Commander in Chief, "to take all necessary steps, including the use of armed force, to assist any member or protocol state of the [CFR-inspired SEATO] Collective Defense Treaty requesting assistance in defense of its freedom."

The Joint Resolution to Promote the Maintenance of International Peace and Security in Southeast Asia, better known as the "Gulf of Tonkin Resolution," passed 88 to 2 in the Senate. One of the dissenters, Alaskan senator Ernest Gruening warned that the resolution was nothing more than "a predated declaration of war." The other, Oregon's senator Wayne Morse warned, "I believe that within the next century, future generations will look with dismay and great disappointment upon a Congress which is about to make such a historic mistake."

The resolution neatly bypassed the constitutional requirement that only Congress has the power to declare war. In late January 1965 it was McNamara and National Security Advisor McGeorge Bundy who told President Johnson it was time to end fifteen years of limited U.S. involvement in Vietnam. They said it was time for either direct military intervention or a negotiated end of the conflict. "Bob and I tend to favor the first course," Bundy later wrote. Johnson agreed and one month later a bombing campaign against North Vietnam, code named "Rolling Thunder," began. By July Johnson had ordered in 100,000 combat troops and the Vietnam War was begun in earnest.

Adding strength to this military buildup, U.S. ambassador to Saigon, CFR member Henry Cabot Lodge, was replaced by CFR member and former chairman of the Joint Chiefs, General Maxwell Taylor.

From the perspective of 1984, editors of *U.S. News & World Report* correctly saw that "the seeds were sown for today's running conflict between President Reagan and Congress over the use of U.S. military power—from Central America to Lebanon and the Persian Gulf." In 1999, with President Clinton under impeachment for dissembling about a sexual affair, no one in Congress seemed concerned that he carried on this unconstitutional heritage by attacking Iraq and Kosovo on behalf of the United Nations.

A look at members of the Council on Foreign Relations—that creation of Rockefeller-Morgan men connected back to the Rhodes-Milner secret society mentality—appears to be a who's who of the Vietnam War era: McNamara, Cyrus Vance, Walt Rostow, William and McGeorge Bundy, Dean Acheson, Dean Rusk, and Averell Harriman. U.S. ambassadors to Saigon during the war—Henry Cabot Lodge, Maxwell Taylor, and Ellsworth Bunker—all were CFR members and played prominent roles in U.S. policy. "In fact, many of the most important advocates of U.S. involvement in Vietnam, both within and outside the government, were members of the Board of Directors of the CFR," noted author Donald Gibson. This would include Allen Dulles, David Rockefeller, John J. McCloy, and Henry M. Wriston (a Morgan associate).

Noting that William "Wild Bill" Donovan, head of the Office of Strategic Services, the forerunner of the CIA, as a young man was a private agent for J. P. Morgan Jr., author Gibson observed, "By the early 1960s the Council on Foreign Relations, Morgan and Rockefeller interests, and the intelligence community were so extensively inbred as to be virtually a single entity."

According to CFR researcher James Perloff, Walt Rostow, who became President Johnson's national security adviser in 1966, not only was a CFR member but had been rejected three times for employment in the Eisenhower administration for failing security checks. In his 1960 book *The United States in the World Arena,* Rostow revealed his CFR globalist outlook by calling for an international police force. "It is a legitimate American national objective to see removed from all nations—including the United States—the right to use substantial military force to pursue their own interests. Since this residual right is the root of national sovereignty . . . it is, therefore, an American interest to see an end to nationhood as it has been historically defined," he wrote.

CFR member McNamara added to America's secret intelligence apparatus on August 1, 1961, by creating the Defense Intelligence Agency (DIA). By September he and Taylor were pushing for expanded U.S. involvement in Vietnam by recommending the addition of 16,000 troops. Opposition came from Undersecretary of State George Ball who strongly opposed this, warning that such a move would result in the deployment of at least 300,000 American troops within two years. Kennedy acceded to McNamara's advice.

Later it was McNamara, serving as Secretary of Defense until 1968, who continually cut back on U.S. military capabilities and formulated the polices forbidding strategic air strikes in North Vietnam. In 1978, after the Vietnam War ended with a communist takeover in the South, McNamara became president of the World Bank (a for-profit agency of the United Nations and CFR pet project) and coordinated a $60 million loan for the victors.

William Bundy (The Order, 1939), who joined the CIA in 1951, became a director of the CFR in 1964, the same year he was appointed Assistant Secretary of State for Far Eastern Affairs. A major planning force behind U.S. Vietnam policy, Bundy drafted the Gulf of Tonkin Resolution, according to the *Pentagon Papers*. It was Bundy who also was involved in OPLAN 34-A, the aggressive CIA-run incursions of U.S. gunboats against the North Vietnam coast (possibly in violation of international law) which provoked retaliation on the U.S. Sixth Fleet resulting in the Gulf of Tonkin incident. Bundy went on to become editor of the CFR publication *Foreign Affairs*.

Bundy's brother, CFR member McGeorge Bundy (The Order, 1940) reportedly was one of the instigators of the Report from Iron Mountain and Special Assistant for National Security Affairs to both Kennedy and Johnson, a post which could be used to screen information to his boss.

Bundy joined the U.S. Army as a private at the start of World War II and suddenly was helping to plan the invasions of Sicily and Normandy. He went on to become Assistant to the Secretary of War at age twenty-seven. He later served as president of the Ford Foundation from 1966 to 1979.

"By acting jointly, the Bundy brothers could have controlled absolutely the flow of information relating to Vietnam from Intelligence, State and D[epartment] O[f] D[efense]," postulated author Anthony C. Sutton.

Secretary of State Dean Rusk, another named as an instigator of the Report from Iron Mountain, had been deputy chief of staff with the Allied Command in Asia during World War II. A Rhodes Scholar, CFR member, and chairman of the Rockefeller Foundation, Rusk guided the policies of both Kennedy and his close friend Lyndon Johnson, who told his biographer Doris Kearns he "built his advisory system around Rusk." CFR members Dean Acheson and Robert Lovett had "enthusiastically" recommended Rusk to President Kennedy.

As documented by authors Walter Isaacson and Evan Thomas, President Lyndon Johnson met with a select group of fourteen advisers on almost a daily basis. Twelve of these advisers were CFR members, all were bankers or lawyers, and all counseled increased commitment in Vietnam. His six key advisers were Truman's Defense Secretary Robert Lovett, McCloy, Harriman, Acheson, State Department adviser Charles Bohlen, and former U.S Ambassador to Russia George Kennan—all CFR. Johnson called these close friends his "Wise Men." By 1968 these same advisers suddenly turned against the war.

Johnson was so shocked and disheartened by this betrayal by the foreign policy establishment that he went on television to announce that he would not run for reelection. When asked why Johnson's advisers had such a change of heart, General Maxwell Taylor could only respond "My Council on Foreign Relations friends were living in the cloud of *The New York Times*." In other words, these men had awakened from their self-delusions and realized that the United States was tearing itself apart over Vietnam. Even then, the war continued for another seven years.

With newly installed president Richard Nixon heading the war effort, CFR member and Trilateralist Henry Kissinger stepped in as National Security Advisor in early 1969. By the end of that year Kissinger was controlling U.S. policy in Vietnam. Some claim Kissinger was placed there for that reason. Nixon's Defense Secretary Melvin Laird admitted, "I would say that in the conceptual view of the world, President Nixon was influenced to a great degree by Kissinger, although he had not been a friend of his and did not know him before December of 1968."

In 1970 Kissinger closeted himself with staffer Winston Lord. According to Lord his boss "wanted to share and debate with his closest aides major policy decisions, so that the popular image of Kissinger as a man who doesn't like to hear dissent [was shown to be] not true." Lord and other staffers must have approved of Kissinger's plan to widen the war, since fighting soon spread into Cambodia.

Despite this expansion, the war grew static and began winding down.

Kissinger, considered America's leading diplomat even into the 1990s, prompted Eugene McCarthy to comment, "Henry Kissinger got the Nobel [Peace] Prize for watching the end of a war he's advocated—and that's pretty high diplomacy."

In 1971 Louisiana Congressman John R. Rarick was blunt in denouncing the CFR as the instigators of Vietnam. In a circular, Rarick wrote, "The My Lai massacre, the sentencing of Lt. [William] Calley to life imprisonment, 'The Selling of the Pentagon,' and the so-called *Pentagon Papers* are leading examples of attempts to shift all of the blame to the military in the eyes of the people.

"But no one identifies the Council on Foreign Relations—the CFR— a group of some 1,400 Americans which includes as members almost every top level decision and policy maker in the Vietnam War.

"CBS tells the people it wants them to know what is going on and who is to blame. Why doesn't CBS tell the American people about the CFR and let the people decide whom to blame for the Vietnam fiasco—the planners and top decision makers of a closely knit financial-industrial-intellectual aristocracy or military leaders under civilian control who have had little or no voice in the overall policies and operations and who are forbidden by law to tell the American people their side. . . . Who will tell the people the truth if those who control 'the right to know machinery' also control the government?"

Since CFR members realized the economic necessity of war but agreed that nuclear war was unthinkable, it was decided that future conflicts would have to be limited in scope. "We must be prepared to fight limited actions ourselves," wrote one contributor to the CFR's *Foreign Affairs* in 1957. "Otherwise we shall have made no advance beyond 'massive retaliation' which tied our hands in conflicts involving less than our survival. And we must be prepared to lose limited actions."

How easy it is to lose conflicts when the military is hamstrung. In 1985 the *Congressional Record* published the newly declassified "rules of engagement" by which the U.S. military fought in Vietnam. These rules filled twenty-six pages and included restrictions such as repeated refusals to allow Air Force bombing of the most strategic targets as determined by the Joint Chiefs of Staff, a general order for U.S. troops not to fire on the Viet Cong unless fired upon first, vehicles more than two hundred yards off the Ho Chi Minh Trail were not to be bombed, North Vietnamese fighter planes could not be attacked unless they were in the air and openly hostile, SAM missile sites under construction were off limits, and enemy forces could not be pursued if they crossed into Laos or Cambodia.

The United States publicly assured North Vietnam it would not bomb certain areas, which allowed their antiaircraft batteries to concentrate in areas that could be bombed, greatly increasing U.S. casualties.

In addition to such restrictions, which were totally incomprehensible to trained military officers, vital materials and supplies were allowed to move unhindered through the North Vietnamese port of Haiphong, some 80 percent coming from America's ostensible enemies—Russia and China.

TRADING WITH THE ENEMY

At the height of the war, trade with the communist nations supplying North Vietnam was actually increased—another goal of the CFR.

As far back as 1961, Trilateral Commission founder Zbigniew Brzezinski had written in *Foreign Affairs* that the United States should provide economic aid to Eastern Europe. David Rockefeller signaled his approval of such trade by making a trip to Moscow in mid-1964.

"David Rockefeller, president of Chase Manhattan Bank, briefed President Johnson today on his recent meeting with Premier Nikita S. Khrushchev of Russia. Rockefeller told Johnson that during the two-hour talk, the Red leader said the United States and the Soviet Union 'should do more trade.' Khrushchev, according to Rockefeller, said he would like to see the United States extend long-term credits [loans] to the Russians," reported the *Chicago Tribune* on September 12. The Rockefellers had a long history of trade with Russia, dating back to the 1920s when Chase Bank helped create the American-Russian Chamber of Commerce.

On October 13, 1966 the *New York Times* reported, "The United States put into effect today one of President Johnson's proposals for stimulating East-West trade by removing restrictions on the export of more than 400 commodities to the Soviet Union and Eastern Europe." On October 27, less than a month later, the *Times* reported, "The Soviet Union and its allies agreed at the conference of their leaders in Moscow last week to grant North Vietnam assistance in material and money amounting to about $1 billion."

In 1967 the Rockefellers joined with Cyrus Eaton, called "the communists' best capitalist friend" by *Parade* magazine, in financing aluminum and rubber plants in the Soviet Union. Young Eaton had been dissuaded from becoming a preacher by John D. Rockefeller and instead became the founder of Republic Steel Corporation. In the 1970s it was American technology and financing, primarily through the Rockefeller Chase Manhattan Bank, which resulted in construction of the $5 billion Kama River factory. The factory produced heavy trucks, many of which were converted to military use.

Signing the accords which authorized U.S. funding for the Kama River factory was George Pratt Shultz, who later replaced CFR member Alexander Haig as President Reagan's secretary of state. Shultz was a CFR director and a relative of Mrs. Harold Pratt, who donated the Pratt House to the council as a headquarters.

So United States troops were fighting North Vietnam while United States goods and financing went to Russia and Eastern Europe, which provided funds and materials to North Vietnam. It is now understandable why college students, many of whom were well aware of the absurdity of this situation and all of whom were susceptible to the draft, began to demonstrate against the war.

Even in the antiwar movement one can find the hand of the secret societies. In 1968 James Simon Kunen, author of an autobiography of his student activist days entitled *The Strawberry Statement: Notes of a College Revolutionary,* wrote, "Also at the [Students for a Democratic Society sponsored First International Students'] convention, men from Business International Roundtables—the meetings sponsored by *Business Interna-*

tional for their client groups and heads of government—tried to buy up a few radicals. These men are the world's leading industrialists and they convene to decide how our lives are going to go. These are the guys who wrote the Alliance for Progress [a 1961 Kennedy program designed to generate about $20 billion in loans to 22 Latin American nations for economic and social reform which passed away not long after he did]. They're the left wing of the ruling class. . . . They offered to finance our demonstrations in Chicago. We were also offered Esso—Rockefeller—money. They want us to make a lot of radical commotion so they can look more in the center as they move to the left."

Kunen caught the puzzled spirit of the youthful antiwar protesters in an opening to his book when he wrote, "Isn't it singular that no one ever goes to jail for waging wars, let alone advocating them? But the jails are filled with those who want peace. Not to kill is to be a criminal. They put you right into jail if all you do is ask them to leave you alone. It strikes me as quite singular."

For those Americans who lived through it—whether against the war or not—the costs of the Vietnam War should remain fresh in their consciences: Nearly 50,000 dead GIs, more than 300,000 physical casualties (many more with mental and emotional problems), and President Johnson's hopes for a "Great Society" dashed by a divided, hostile public saddled with a faltering economy. The cost to Vietnam was much worse—250,000 South Vietnamese dead and 600,000 wounded compared to the North Vietnamese and Viet Cong who suffered 900,000 killed and 2 million wounded. An additional hundreds of thousands of civilians in both North and South were killed, many in the U.S. bombing campaigns, and the countryside was devastated by bombs, artillery, land mines, and chemical defoliates. Total financial cost of the war has been estimated at more than $200 billion.

After all this, the United States pulled out. It is inconceivable today that anyone can view the U.S. experience in Vietnam as anything but a total defeat—a defeat incomprehensible to the brave men and women who fought there as well as most Americans.

"The Vietnam War is a mystery only if seen through the accumulated myths surrounding it—such as that it resulted from blunders, or from overconfident jingoism," explained author Perloff. "Viewed, however, as an exercise in deliberate mismanagement, it ceases to mystify, for its outcome fulfilled precisely the goals traditional to the CFR."

KOREA

Nowhere has the secret society manipulation of both sides of a conflict been more evident than in Korea in the early 1950s. As in the Persian Gulf and Vietnam, official semantics termed this conflict, which cost almost 34,000 American lives, a mere "police action," not a war.

Much documentation exists to show that the Korean conflict was the result of careful planning by men whose control extended to both the United States and the Soviet Union.

This conflict began with the founding of the United Nations at the end of World War II. The name "United Nations" had been imprinted in the mind of the American public during the war when it referred to the countries allied against Germany, Italy, and Japan.

The UN organization was merely an outgrowth of the old League of Nations, that failed attempt at fledgling world government instigated by Woodrow Wilson and members of the Milner-Rhodes secret societies. The concept was resurrected during the distraction of the world war when representatives from the United States, the Soviet Union, Great Britain, and Chiang Kai-shek's China met at the Dumbarton Oaks estate near Washington, DC, from August 21 to October 7, 1944.

A primary mover of this and subsequent actions to establish a United Nations was John Foster Dulles, who had helped found the Council on Foreign Relations. A participant in the 1917 Versailles Peace Conference, Dulles also created the Southeast Asia Treaty Organization which provided the legal rationale for the war in Vietnam.

Further details of United Nations operations were worked out during the pivotal Yalta Conference in February 1945. It was secret protocols at Yalta that agreed to partition Korea along the Thirty-eighth Parallel and allowed the Soviet Union and China control over the North.

Such action had been contemplated a year earlier. An April 1944 article in *Foreign Affairs* called for "a trusteeship for Korea . . . assumed not by a particular country, but by a group of Powers, say, the United States, Great Britain, China and Russia." The CFR leadership realized that the American public might not agree to war should such a "trusteeship" be challenged and began to develop a rationale for intervention.

An internal 1944 CFR memo stated that the "sovereignty fetish" and the "difficulty . . . arising from the Constitutional provision that only Congress may declare war" might be countered with "the contention that a treaty would override this barrier [and] . . . our participation in such police action as might be recommended by [an] international security organization need not necessarily be construed as war."

"It is not unreasonable to say that there never would have been a Communist regime in North Korea, nor would there ever have been a Korean War, had American negotiations [led by CFR members] and lend-lease shipments not brought the USSR into the Pacific theater," commented Perloff.

Formal construction of the UN began two months after Yalta at the United Nations Conference on International Organization held in San Francisco. A resulting charter was signed in June and went into effect October 24, 1945, little more than two months after World War II ended. The United Nations was created "essentially by the Council on Foreign Relations," wrote Ralph Epperson. "There were 47 members in the American delegation to the UN conference at San Francisco."

Their "senior adviser" was John Foster Dulles. "Emboldened by his formidable achievements, Dulles viewed his appointment as secretary of state by President Eisenhower, in January, 1953, as a mandate to originate foreign policy, which is normally regarded as the domain of the president," stated *The New Encyclopaedia Britannica*.

Considering Dulles and the other CFR members behind the creation of the UN, it is no surprise to find that organization today supervising the International Bank for Reconstruction and Development (commonly called the World Bank) and the International Monetary Fund (IMF). The UN also houses a number of social agencies including the International Labor Organization (ILO), Food and Agriculture Organization (FAO), World Health Organization (WHO), United Nations Educational, Scientific and Cultural Organization (UNESCO), and United Nations Children's Fund (UNICEF).

In 1947, following a breakdown in negotiations over reunification, the matter of Korea was turned over to the United Nations. By 1949 both the United States and the Soviet Union had largely withdrawn wartime occupation troops from the Korean peninsula. The U.S. withdrawal left a mere 16,000 South Koreans armed with mostly small arms to face a North Korean communist army of more than 150,000 armed with up-to-date Russian tanks, planes, and artillery. When General Albert C. Wedemeyer, sent by President Truman to evaluate the situation, reported that the communists represented a direct threat to the South, he was ignored and his report kept from the public.

In January 1950 North Korean premier Kim Il-sung proclaimed a "year of unification" and began massing troops along the Thirty-eighth Parallel. As in the future Persian Gulf war, the CFR-filled U.S. State Department did nothing. Truman's secretary of state, CFR member Dean Acheson, stated publicly that Korea was outside the defensive perimeter of the United States. "This gave a clear signal to Kim, who invaded the South that June under Soviet auspices," wrote Perloff.

American leaders professed surprise and anger over the June 25 North Korean assault and called for an emergency meeting of the UN Security Council, then composed of the U.S., Great Britain, France, the Soviet Union, and Nationalist China.

The council, with the Soviet Union absent and China represented only by anticommunist Chiang Kai-shek, voted for UN intervention in Korea. It has been noted by conspiracy authors that this vote could have been prevented by a Russian veto. But strangely, Soviet delegates had staged a walkout in protest that Communist China had not been recognized by the UN. Soon after this vote for UN-backed conflict, the Soviet delegates returned, even though the People's Republic of China still had not been recognized.

On June 27, with UN sanction, President Truman ordered American troops to assist the UN "police action" of defending South Korea. Through July and August, the outnumbered and outgunned South Korean Army, along with the four ill-equipped American divisions sent by Truman, were pushed down to the tip of the Korean peninsula. The situation looked bad until mid-September when General Douglas MacArthur launched a brilliant and daring attack on Inchon Harbor, located midway up the peninsula, that broke the North Korean battle line and cut their supply routes.

Badly shattered, the North Koreans pulled back with the UN troops— 90 percent of which were Americans—close behind. As the fight crossed the Thirty-eighth Parallel, China's Mao Tse-tung warned that any movement to the Yalu River bordering China by UN forces would be unacceptable. MacArthur warned the State Department that Chinese troops were massing north of the Yalu, but his warning was unheeded. On November 25, nearly 200,000 Chinese "volunteers" crossed the Yalu and smashed into the unprepared UN troops. Another 500,000 followed in December.

Again the Americans and their allies were pushed back but managed to regroup and later counterattacked back to the Thirty-eighth Parallel.

The war settled into a series of actions back and forth across the contested parallel.

As in Vietnam, the U.S. military was hamstrung with policy decisions which prevented them from fully prosecuting the Korean conflict. But, unlike in Vietnam, a military leader of considerable standing balked at these restrictions and appealed directly to the American public for support.

General MacArthur, the hero of World War II, ordered the Air Force to bomb the Yalu River bridges, which would have cut China's supply and communication lines. He appealed to sympathetic congressmen to support his military actions and to allow the Nationalist Chinese on Taiwan to launch a second front against China to relieve pressure on Korea.

The official response to MacArthur was swift in coming. MacArthur's bombing orders were canceled by General George Marshall (father of the Marshall Plan to rebuild Europe after World War II and a CFR member who had been called out of retirement by President Truman to serve as Secretary of Defense). This was the same Marshall who, as Army Chief of Staff, reportedly received advance word of the attack on Pearl Harbor.

MacArthur was ordered not to bomb key Chinese supply bases and to order pilots not to chase fleeing enemy aircraft. Chinese commander General Lin Piao was to say later, "I never would have made the attack and risked my men and my military reputation if I had not been assured that Washington would restrain General MacArthur from taking adequate retaliatory measures against my lines of supply and communication."

MacArthur's appeal to the public resulted in his dismissal by President Truman on April 10, 1951. He was replaced by General Matthew B. Ridgeway, who later became a CFR member.

The MacArthur plan for a diversionary attack by Taiwan was never to be. This plan had been blocked by an order from Truman only two days after the North Koreans attacked. According to government documents, Truman said, "I have ordered the Seventh Fleet to prevent any attack on Formosa [now Taiwan]. As a corollary of this action, I am calling upon the Chinese Government on Formosa to cease all air and sea operations against the mainland. The Seventh Fleet will see that this is done." General Marshall also rejected an offer by Chiang Kai-shek to send Nationalist Chinese to aid Americans in Korea.

Added to these incomprehensible orders restricting military options, was the amazing fact that Russian commanders were running the conflict on both sides. Under the agreement at Yalta and due to their supplying North Korea with military hardware and technology, Soviet military officers were largely in control of the war. Author Epperson cited a Pentagon press release which identified two Soviet officers as being in charge of movements across the Thirty-eighth Parallel. One, a General Vasilev, actually was overheard giving the order to attack on June 25, 1951.

General Vasilev's chain of command reached from Korea to Moscow to the UN Undersecretary General for Political and Security Council Affairs. At this same time, General MacArthur's chain of command went through President Truman to the UN Undersecretary General for Political and Security Council Affairs, an office held at that time by Russian Constantine Zinchenko. This meant that Soviet officers were overseeing the North Korean war strategy while reporting back to a fellow Soviet officer in the same UN office that coordinated the allied war effort.

"In effect, the Communists were directing both sides of the war," wrote author Griffin. What past conspiracy authors failed to consider was the evidence that Communist Russia was financed and controlled from the beginning by the inner circle of America's modern secret societies.

The war finally settled into a stalemate which ended with an armistice signed on July 27, 1953, six months after General Dwight Eisenhower had become president of the U.S.

MacArthur, noting that for the first time in its military history, the United States had failed to achieve victory, was later to state, "Never before has this nation been engaged in mortal combat with a hostile power without military objective, without policy other than restrictions governing operations, or indeed without even formally recognizing a state of war." This set a precedent in the United States which continues to haunt us to this day.

But was there again a hidden purpose to this seemingly pointless conflict, one that reached into the upper circles of the secret societies? A 1952 *Foreign Affairs* article explained, "The meaning of our experience in Korea as I see it, is that we have made historic progress toward the establishment of a viable system of collective security." So Korea was another step forward in realizing the CFR goals of one-world government backed by a unified military command as with the North Atlantic Treaty Organization (NATO). CFR member Dean Acheson later admitted, "The only reason I told the President to fight in Korea was to validate NATO."

Both NATO and the United Nations resulted from the most momentous event of the twentieth century—World War II—and once again the diligent researcher finds the unmistakable imprint of the secret societies

RISE OF THE NAZI CULT

As hard to believe as it may be for Americans brought up on wartime propaganda films and publications devoted merely to war technology and battles, World War II was largely the result of infighting between secret occult societies composed of wealthy businessmen that eventually led to international tensions that provoked open warfare.

As in other conflicts, the manipulation and influence of these societies is found in the origins and finances of the war, not on the battlefields. Abundant evidence now exists indicating that World War II was brought about by agents and members of secret societies connected to the Illuminati and Freemasonry in both Germany and Britain. It was in this "good war," that the older mystic societies seeking freedom from both church and state merged with the modern secret societies concerned primarily with wealth, power, and control.

"Sir Winston Churchill himself . . . was insistent that the occultism of the Nazi Party should not under any circumstances be revealed to the general public," wrote author Trevor Ravenscroft, who claimed to have worked closely with Dr. Walter Johannes Stein, a confidential adviser to Churchill. "The failure of the Nuremberg Trials to identify the nature of the evil at work behind the outer facade of National Socialism convinced him that another three decades must pass before a large enough readership would be present to comprehend the initiation rites and black magic practices of the inner core of Nazi leadership."

This remarkable statement was corroborated by Airey Neave, one of the postwar Nuremberg prosecutors, who said the occult aspect of Nazi activities was ruled inadmissible because the tribunal feared both the psychological and spiritual implications in the Western nations. They also thought that such beliefs, so contrary to public rationalism, might be used to mount an insanity defense for Nazi leaders.

History identifies Adolf Hitler as a dominant figure in the war, so to understand the involvement of the secret societies, one must first understand Hitler and the origins of his Nazi Party. Many books, articles, and even TV specials have been produced documenting the ties between Hitler's Nazis and occult societies, but few have made it plain that Hitler was their creation.

To fully understand how and why Hitler was created, a close study must be made of the secret groups operating around Hitler as well as their connections to military intelligence services.

Adolf Hitler's Nazis were far more than simply a political movement. They saw themselves leading a quasi-religious movement born out of secret organizations whose goals were the same as those found in the Illuminati and Freemasonry. "They were a cult . . . [and] as with any typical cult, its chief enemies were other cults," noted author Peter Levenda in a well-researched book dealing with Nazis and the occult.

Hitler himself acknowledged this by stating, "Anyone who interprets National Socialism merely as a political movement knows almost nothing about it. It is more than religion; it is the determination to create a new man."

This Nazi cult grew from a variety of organizations, theologies and beliefs present in Germany at the end of World War I—all stemming from the mysteries of older groups such as the Bavarian Illuminati, *Germanenorden,* Freemasonry, and the Teutonic Knights.

A prerequisite for grasping this background is understanding *The Protocols of the Learned Elders of Zion,* also known as *The Protocols of the Wise Men of Zion,* a list of procedures for world domination. This document may have wreaked more havoc than almost any other piece of literature in recent history.

A version of the *Protocols* first appeared in 1864 in France in a book entitled *Dialogue in Hell Between Machiavelli and Montesquieu or the Politics of Machiavelli in the Nineteenth Century by a Contemporary.* It was written anonymously by a French lawyer named Maurice Joly and taken as a political satire against the Machiavelli-inspired machinations of Napoléon III. Joly reportedly was a friend of Victor Hugo and both were members of the Order of the Rose-Croix or Rosicrucians, a secret society that may have influenced his writing. Joly's identity was discovered, and he received a fifteen-month prison sentence for his impertinence and his book was almost forgotten.

In the mid-1890s Joly's obscure book was rewritten and augmented with anti-Semitic material on orders of the Russian Ochrana, the czar's secret police. It was added to the work of a religious writer named Sergei Nilus and published to coincide with the founding of the first Zionist movement (seeking a return to Palestine) at the 1897 World Congress of Jewry in Basel, Switzerland. The *Protocols* were included as an appendix to Nilus's book, partially titled *The Anti-Christ is Near at Hand*.

The objective was to relieve public pressure on the czar by portraying Russian revolutionaries as pawns of an international Jewish conspiracy. The document purported that a clique of Jews and Freemasons would join forces to create a one-world government by means of liberalism and socialism, a conspiratorial theory still alive in some quarters.

The *Protocols* still chills readers with its prophetic description of the methodology for tyranny by a few. Its message fits quite well with the elitist outlooks of men like Cecil Rhodes and the Rothschilds. "We are the chosen, we are the only true men. Our minds give off the true power of the spirit; the intelligence of the rest of the world is merely instinctive and animal. They can see, but they cannot foresee; their inventions are merely corporeal. Does it not follow that nature herself has predestined us to dominate the whole world?" stated the *Protocols*. "Outwardly, however, in our 'official' utterances, we shall adopt an opposite procedure, and always do our best to appear honorable and cooperative. A statesman's words do not have to agree with his acts. If we pursue these principles, the governments and peoples which we have thus prepared will take our IOUs for cash. One day they will accept us as benefactors and saviors of the human race. If any State dared to resist us, if its neighbors make common cause with it against us, we will unleash a world war."

The *Protocols* goes on to explain that the goal of world domination will be accomplished by controlling how the public thinks by controlling what they hear, by creating new conflicts or restoring old orders, by spreading hunger, destitution and plague, by seducing and distracting the youth. "By all these methods we shall so wear down the nations that they will be forced to offer us world domination," they proclaim.

Some of the twenty-four *Protocols* bear a brief summary. If any part of them are to be believed, they provide a clear connection to Freemasonry and to the Ancient Mysteries as well as an amazing road map for world conquest. Because the *Protocols* were rewritten and attributed to Jews before World War I with the intent of inciting anti-Jewish sentiment, their use of the term *goyim,* a demeaning Jewish word for non-Jews, has been substituted with the term "masses." Pertinent points include:

—The Protocol plan "will remain invisible until the moment when it has gained such strength that no cunning can any longer undermine it." (Protocol 1)

—"Wars, so far as possible, should not result in territorial gains." (Protocol 2)

—"[The] minds [of the masses] must be diverted toward industry and trade. Thus, all the nations will be swallowed up in the pursuit of gain and . . . will not take note of their common foe." (Protocol 4)

—"We shall create an intensified centralization of government," (Protocol 5) ". . . we must develop [a] Super-Government by representing it as the Protector and Benefactor of all those who voluntarily submit. . . . We shall soon begin to establish huge monopolies. . . ." (Protocol 6)

—"The intensification of armaments, the increase of police forces . . . [so that] in all the States of the world, besides ourselves, [there will be] only the masses of the proletariat, a few millionaires devoted to our interests, police, and soldiers." (Protocol 7)

—"We shall put [government power] in the hands of persons whose past and reputations are such that between them and the people lies an abyss, persons who, in case of disobedience to our instructions, must face criminal charges. . . ." (Protocol 8)

—"We have fooled, bemused and corrupted the youth of the [masses] by rearing them in principles and theories which are known to us to be false. . . ." (Protocol 9) "We shall destroy among the [masses] the importance of the family and its educational value." (Protocol 10)

—"We have invented this whole policy and insinuated it into the minds of the [masses] . . . to obtain in a roundabout way what is . . . unattainable by the direct road. . . . It is this which has served as the basis for our organization of secret masonry which is not known to, and aims which are not even so much as suspected by, these . . . cattle, attracted by us into the 'Show' army of Masonic Lodges in order to throw dust in the eyes of their fellows." (Protocol 11)

—"What is the part played by the press today? . . . It serves selfish ends. . . . It is often vapid, unjust, mendacious and the majority of the public have not the slightest idea what ends the press really serves. We shall saddle and bridle it with a tight curb. . . . Not a single announcement will reach the public without our control. . . ." (Protocol 12)

—"The need for daily bread forces the [masses] to keep silent and be our humble servants. . . . In order that the masses themselves may not guess what they are about we further distract them with amusements, games, pastimes, passions, people's palace [no TV at that time]. Soon we shall begin through the press to propose competitions in art, in sport of all kinds. . . ." (Protocol 13)

—"It will be undesirable for us that there should exist any other religion than ours. . . . We must therefore sweep away all other forms of belief." (Protocol 14) "Freedom of conscience has been declared everywhere, so that now only years divide us from the moment of the complete wrecking of that Christian religion, as to other religions we shall have still less difficulty in dealing with them." (Protocol 17)

—"When we at last definitely come into our kingdom by the aid of *coups d'etat* prepared everywhere for one and the same day . . . we shall make it our task to see that against us such things as plots shall no longer exist. With this purpose we shall slay without mercy all who take arms in hand to oppose our coming. . . . Anything like a secret society will also be punishable with death. . . ."(Protocol 15)

—"In our program one-third of [the masses] will keep the rest under observation from a sense of duty, on the principle of volunteer service to the State. It will be no disgrace to be a spy and informer, but a merit . . . how else [are] we to . . . increase . . . disorders?" (Protocol 17) "Sedition-mongering is nothing more than the yapping of a lap-dog at an elephant. . . . In order to destroy the prestige of heroism, for political crime we shall send it for trial in the category of thieving, murder and every kind of abominable and filthy crime. Public opinion will then . . . brand it with the same contempt." (Protocol 19) "Until [dissenters] commit some overt act we shall not lay a finger on them but only introduce into their midst observation elements. . . ." (Protocol 18)

Later Protocols deal with finances. Protocol 20 called for general taxation, "the lawful confiscation of all sums of every kind for the regulation of their circulation in the State." This would be followed by "a progressive tax on property" and then finally a graduated income tax, a "tax increasing in a percentage ratio to capital" as well as taxes on sales, "receipt of money," inheritance, and property transfers. There was a discussion of "the substitution of interest-bearing paper" money since "Economic crises have been produced by us . . . by no other means than the withdrawal of money from circulation."

The *Protocols* also discuss at great length loans, which it states "hang like a sword of Damocles over the heads of rulers, who, instead of taking from their subjects by a temporary tax, come begging with outstretched palm to our bankers."

Whoever produced the *Protocols* clearly understood the secrets of banking. In a passage which could have been titled "The National Debt of the United States," Protocol 20 stated, "A loan is an issue of government bills of exchange containing a percentage obligation [interest] commensurate to the sum of the loaned capital." It proceeded to explain, "If the loan bears a charge of five percent [hefty interest in those more knowledgeable times] then in 20 years the State vainly pays away in interest a sum equal to the loan borrowed, in 40 years it is paying a double sum, in 60—treble, and all the while the debt remains an unpaid debt. . . ."

The writer also determined that no one would figure out what was happening. "We shall so hedge about our system of accounting that neither ruler nor the most insignificant public servant will be in a position to divert even the smallest sum from its destination without detection or to direct it in another direction. . . ."

The *Protocols* also demonstrate a linkage to the Ancient Mysteries, referring to bloodlines such as "the seed of David," "secret mysteries," and even the "Symbolic Snake," an icon of the earliest cults.

Nilus himself was obviously quite captivated by the *Protocols*. Sounding eerily similar to today's television evangelists, he wrote in 1905 that he hoped to "put on their guard those who still have ears to hear and eyes to see [and warned] events are precipitated in the world at a terrifying speed: quarrels, wars, rumors, famines, epidemics, earthquakes—everything which even yesterday was impossible, today is an accomplished fact. . . . Secular quarrels and schisms [must] all be forgotten in the imminent need of preparing against the coming of the Antichrist."

Despite their dubious origin, the *Protocols* were taken seriously by many powerful people, including Germany's Kaiser Wilhelm II, Russia's Czar Nicholas II, and American industrialist Henry Ford, who used them to help persuade the U.S. Senate not to join President Wilson's League of Nations.

The Ochrana's plan worked a bit too well. A counterrevolution took place and pogroms against Russian Jews were instituted by vigilantes called "The Black Guard," incensed by the Czarist propaganda. Continuing instability and violence finally resulted in the 1905 Russian Revolution, during which the *Protocols* again were trotted out by pro-czarist elements to inflame the public.

Hitler saw the *Protocols* as a real proclamation despite the evidence of fabrication. In *Mein Kampf* he wrote, "They are supposed to be a 'forgery' the *Frankfurter Zeitung* moans and cries out to the world once a week; the best proof that they are genuine after all. . . . But the best criticism applied to them is reality. He who examines the historical development of the past hundred years, from the points of view of this book [the *Protocols*], will also immediately understand the clamor of the Jewish press. For once this book has become the common property of a people, the Jewish danger is bound to be considered as broken."

Author Konrad Heiden, an anti-Nazi contemporary of Hitler, while denying the authenticity of the *Protocols,* also saw a certain reality there. "Today the forgery is incontrovertibly proved, yet something infinitely significant has remained: a textbook of world domination . . . the great principle of inequality fights to preserve its rule; the ruling class philosophy of a natural hierarchy, of innate differences between men. Once this principle is expressed in the form of historical events, it also soon assumes the aspect of conspiracy. . . . The spirit of the *Protocols,* therefore, contains historical truth, though all the facts put forward in them are forgeries."

It is the possibility of "historical truth" which has kept the *Protocols* in circulation since its inception. Today, modern conspiracy writers see it as a real program predating Nazism or Communism. Some claim the Frenchman Joly simply incorporated in his book concepts he picked up as a secret society member. Author David Icke saw a "remarkable resemblance" between the *Protocols* and confiscated secret documents of the mysterious Bavarian Illuminati of the late eighteenth century. "I call them the Illuminati Protocols," wrote Icke, with some justification considering the numerous Masonic references in them.

The authors of *Holy Blood, Holy Grail* had an even more intriguing take on the *Protocols*. They noted that the original Nilus edition contained references to a king as well as a "Masonic kingdom," concepts clearly not of Jewish origin. Furthermore, it concluded with the statement, "Signed by the representatives of Sion of the 33rd degree."

These authors argued that Nilus produced a "radically altered text" based on a legitimate original created by "some Masonic organization or Masonically oriented secret society that incorporated the word 'Sion'" and that it may indeed have been a serious blueprint for infiltrating Freemasonry and gaining global domination. They identified one secret society as a prime suspect—the mysterious Priory of Sion of which more will be said later.

The *Protocols* may indeed reflect a deeper conspiracy beyond its intended use to encourage anti-Semitism, one hidden within the secret upper ranks of the Illuminati and Freemasonry.

In the summer of 1917 a young Estonian Jew named Alfred Rosenberg was a student in Moscow where he was given a copy of the *Protocols* by a stranger. Following the Russian Revolution the following year, the anti-Bolshevik Rosenberg fled to Germany where he used the book to gain entry to a secret society in Munich, a move which was to have far-reaching effects for the world.

In late 1918 Rosenberg presented the *Protocols* to an aging Munich newspaper publisher named Dietrich Eckart. A boozing bon vivant and one of Germany's better known poets at the time, Eckart was enthralled by this plan for world domination. He introduced Rosenberg to fellow members of the *Thule Gesellschaft* or Thule Society, a "literary discussion" group founded by a Baron Rudolf Freiherr von Sebottendorff. The society proved to be merely a front for a more secret society, the *Germanenorden* or German Order. Both were anti-Semitic nationalist organizations laced with beliefs in the supernatural. Eckart claimed to be a "Christian mystic" who, according to an article written by Rosenberg after Eckart's death, was knowledgeable of the ancient Indian lore of Cosmic Consciousness (*Atman*) and the idea that reality is actually an illusion (*Maya*).

Sebottendorff, Eckart, and others within the Thule Society were greatly influenced by the beliefs of the most prominent twentieth century occult group—the Theosophical Society.

THEOSOPHISTS, THULISTS, AND OTHER CULTISTS

The term Theosophy is derived from the Greek words *theos* (god) and *sophia* (wisdom) and has been interpreted as meaning "divine wisdom."

Theosophy came into usage in 1875 when a Russian-born mystic named Helena Petrovna Blavatsky founded the Theosophical Society in New York City. Blavatsky had immigrated to America in 1873 after many years of travel and research in Europe and the Middle East.

Between 1877 and 1888 Blavatsky published occult material including her two most famous books, *Isis Unveiled* and *The Secret Doctrine*. Both were intended to present a quasi-scientific underpinning for religion, then in decline due to scientific discoveries and the theories of Charles Darwin.

In 1878 Blavatsky, along with her ardent follower U.S. Army Colonel Henry Steel Olcott, moved the society's headquarters to Madras, India, where it remains today. Theosophical societies spread throughout the East and into Europe and America, bringing significant attention to Eastern philosophies. This promotion of Buddhism and Hinduism greatly affected several religious-oriented movements including "I Am," the liberal Catholic church, Rosicrucians, the Unity church and, more recently, various "New Age" groups.

Theosophy drew its thinking from the same early philosophers venerated by the secret societies of Freemasonry, the Illuminati and the Round Tables—Plato and Pythagoras as well as the Egyptian Mystery schools. According to author Nesta Webster, it was evident that Blavatsky also drew heavily from the Hebrew Cabala and Talmud, cementing the connection with the Ancient Mysteries.

Writing in 1924, Webster warned, "The Theosophical Society is not a study group, but essentially a propagandist society which aims at substituting for the pure and simple teaching of Christianity the amazing compound of Eastern superstition, Cabalism and 18th century charlantanism. . . ."

Blavatsky's society taught the belief in one creator, that there was an underlying unity in the universe including all humans, that secret meanings are found in all religions, and, most controversial, that "Great Masters" or "Adepts," sometimes called the "Great White Brotherhood," are secretly directing the evolution of humankind.

Blavatsky, in forming the German branch of the Theosophical Society in 1884, brought her belief in channeling, reincarnation, racial superiority, and extraterrestrial visitation to people who later would form the theological basis of Nazism.

"German occultists like Lanz von Liebenfels, Guido von List and Rudolf von Sebottendorff borrowed heavily from [Blavatsky]. They sought to show that the ancient Germans had been keepers of a secret science—which had originated in Eden/Atlantis," wrote author William Henry.

"The rationale behind many later Nazi projects can be traced back . . . to ideas first popularized by Blavatsky," agreed Levenda, who detailed connections with other European secret organizations. "We have the Theosophical Society, the OTO [*Ordo Templi Orientis* or Oriental Templars], [Dr. Rudolf Steiner's] Anthroposophical Society and [the Order of] the Golden Dawn all intertwined in incestuous embrace."

Following World War I, the occult societies began to merge with political activism, particularly in southern Germany.

Munich was flooded with anticommunist Russian refugees and Dietrich Eckart was delighted to find in the *Protocols* what he saw as the final proof of the long-theorized Jewish-Masonic-Bolshevik world conspiracy. He saw to its immediate publication, and the book swiftly spread throughout Germany and Europe and even to America. "The story of the circulation of *The Protocols of the Wise Men of Zion* would seem to indicate the existence of an international network of secret connections and co-operating forces . . . described clearly enough in the *Protocols* themselves," commented author Heiden.

The *Protocols* was especially well received in Germany, where a distraught and impoverished population was asking why they had been defeated in the war. With no blacks, Hispanics, or Asians at hand, the lot of the scapegoat fell to the Eastern European Jews. The circulation of the *Protocols* ignited long-smoldering anti-Semitism into a red-hot bonfire of hatred and division.

Political factions fought throughout the nation, with the newly arrived communist philosophy gaining great inroads in a disillusioned public unaccustomed to self-rule.

To counter this communist threat and the spreading chaos, more than two dozen right-wing nationalist organizations sprang up in Munich alone. Among them was the Thule Society, named after the mythic German homeland of icebound Ultima Thule. The logo of the society was a swastika superimposed over a sword.

Thule, in the minds of German occultists, was a Teutonic Atlantis, a mystical prehistoric island in northern climes believed to be the home of a long-vanished civilization of extraterrestrials who lost awareness of their origins by interbreeding with humans. Eckart, Sebottendorff, and their followers believed that the advanced science of Thule had survived through the centuries, handed down by select initiates into this secret and esoteric wisdom. Thulists were continually seeking this wisdom through rituals designed to contact superior beings.

"The inner core within the Thule Group were all Satanists who practiced Black Magic," wrote Trevor Ravenscroft. "That is to say, they were solely concerned with raising their consciousness by means of rituals to an awareness of evil and non-human Intelligences in the Universe and with achieving a means of communication with the Intelligences. And the Master-Adept of this circle was Dietrich Eckart."

It is well known that in Munich during those turbulent postwar years, there were several hundred unsolved "political" murders and kidnappings. "And it was from among these missing persons, most of whom were either Jews or Communists, that we must look to find the 'sacrificial victims' who were murdered in the rites of 'Astrological Magic' carried out by Dietrich Eckart and the innermost circle of the *Thule Gesellschaft*," charged Ravenscroft, who claimed it was a "well-known fact" that the Thulists were a "Society of Assassins."

Assassins or not, it is true that on April 7, 1919, when communist revolutionaries held Munich for a short period proclaiming a Bavarian Soviet Republic, the only people they rounded up and executed as dangerous subversives were Thule Society members, including its young secretary and Prince von Thurn und Taxis. By May 3 army veterans comprising the *Frei Korps* (Free Corps), with their helmets festooned with the swastika of the Thule Society, rid Munich of the Bolsheviks. It was the last serious threat to Germany by Communism until after World War II.

The monarchists and industrialists of the Thule knew they had to win the support of the rank-and-file worker to defeat the socialist-laden labor unions. To this end they adopted a two-pronged strategy. While Munich's business, military, and intellectual leaders plotted at Thule Society meetings in the Four Seasons Hotel, a second, blue-collar, organization was formed—the German Workers Party run by sportswriter Karl Harrer and railroad machinist Anton Drexler. According to Time-Life editors, "The [Thule] society had contacted Drexler because it hoped to foment a workers' revolution but knew nothing about workers."

The party was created in January 1919 by merging Drexler's Committee of Independent Workmen with the Harrer-led Political Workers Circle. The Circle had been founded by the Theosophist Sebottendorff, who was also instrumental in creating the secret *Germanenorden*.

The *Germanenorden* was an order patterned after the Freemasons, but decidedly anti-Mason and anti-Jewish, with intricate initiations and ceremonies extolling the glories of German mythology and the medieval Teutonic Knights, who were formed through the Knights Templar.

Noted Hitler biographer John Toland described Sebottendorff only as a "man of mystery" and a devotee of Plato. As it turned out, Sebottendorff was actually born Rudolf Glauer, the son of a Dresden railroad engineer. The Count said he had been legally adopted by a Count Heinrich von Sebottendorff and had the right to claim the inherited title. Eckart and others declined to expose his true identity for fear of discrediting their cause.

Widely perceived as subversive, Sebottendorff's *Germanenorden* contrived the Thule Society as a cover organization. "The original conception of the modern Thulists was extremely crude and naïve," wrote Ravenscroft. "The more sophisticated versions of the legend of Thule only gradually developed in the hands of Dietrich Eckart and General Karl Haushofer, and were later refined and extended under the direction of *Reichsfuehrer SS* Heinrich Himmler, who terrorized a large section of the German academic world into lending a professional hand at perpetuating the myth of German racial superiority."

According to William Bramley, Haushofer was a member of the "Vril," another secret society based on a book by British Rosicrucian Lord Bulward Litton about the visit of an Aryan "super race" to Earth in the distant past. Haushofer was a mentor to both Hitler and his deputy Rudolf Hess. Himmler was another notable member of the Vril.

Haushofer had traveled extensively in the Far East before becoming a general in the Kaiser's army. "His early associations with influential Japanese businessmen and statesmen were crucial in forming the German-Japanese alliance of World War II," wrote Levenda. "He was also the first high-ranking Nazi to form important relationships with South American governments in anticipation of military and political action against the United States, relationships that would eventually be exploited by war criminals—and Nazi cultists—fleeing the reach of the Nuremberg prosecutors." Haushofer, as a professor at the University of Munich, worked out Hitler's policy of *Lebensraum*, "living space" for a hemmed-in Germany.

Backed by the violent thugs of Army Captain Ernst Roehm's Brownshirts and incited by anti-Jewish and anti-Bolshevik diatribes, the fledgling German Workers Party joined the growing opposition to the unstable Weimar government.

Eckart, who carried dual membership in both the fledgling party and the Thule Society, realized the German Workers Party needed a leader. "We need a fellow at the head who can stand the sound of a machine gun. The rabble need to get fear into their pants. We can't use an officer because the people don't respect them anymore. The best would be a worker who knows how to talk. . . . He doesn't need much brains. . . . He must be a bachelor, then we'll get the women," he told members during a meeting in 1919.

THE LEADER ARRIVES

Eckart found his leader in the form of an Army intelligence agent sent to infiltrate the Party—a failed Austrian-born painter named Adolf Hitler, once described as a "child of Illuminism."

It has been well documented how Hitler shared Eckart's interest in the supernatural and occult. As a child in Austria, he thrived on heroic folk tales of the Germanic Teutonic Knights.

As a destitute artist in Vienna before World War I, Hitler haunted libraries and old bookstores filling his mind with esoteric lore and anti-Jewish propaganda. An admirer of Hegel and his philosophies, he also studied ancient history, Eastern religions, Yoga, occultism, hypnotism, Theosophy, and astrology.

According to Ravenscroft, he even sought enlightenment 1960s style by ingesting hallucinogenic drugs. "It was in the small back office of the bookshop in the old quarter of the city that Ernst Pretzsche [the shop owner] unveiled for Hitler the secrets hidden behind the astrological and alchemical symbolism of the search for the Grail," he wrote. "It was here too that the sinister hunchback handed to his monstrous pupil the drug which evoked the clairvoyant vision of the Aztecs, the magic Peyotl [Peyote] venerated like a deity."

Ravenscroft, a former British commando officer, reported that while in Vienna Hitler became obsessed with the so-called "Spear of Destiny," reportedly the spear of a Roman soldier named Gaius Cassius who became known as Longinus. By legend, Longinus used the spear to pierce the side of Jesus on the cross, not as punishment, but to mercifully shorten his agony. What claims to be the same spear is still exhibited in the Hofburg Museum in Vienna.

It was here, according to Ravenscroft, that young Hitler learned of the legend that whoever possesses the *Heilige Lance*, or Holy Spear, controls the destiny of the world. In his book *The Spear of Destiny*, Ravenscroft weaves a rich tapestry of Germanic history and folklore, tying Hitler and the spear to a detailed background of magic, occultism, and secret societies.

Ravenscroft attributed his knowledge of both the spear and Hitler to his mentor, Dr. Walter Johannes Stein, a Viennese scientist and philosopher who knew Hitler but later fled to England. Stein told how Hitler entered a trance while "channeling" a nonhuman entity in proximity to the spear. "Hitler's soul life was not mature enough at that moment to maintain an awareness of himself and his surroundings when this alien entity entered him," Stein explained to Ravenscroft.

This trancelike channeling was noted by an audience member during one of Hitler's speeches: "He just spoke and spoke, like a record running in a groove, for an hour and a half until he became absolutely exhausted . . . and when he was finished and breathless, he just sat down once more a simple and nice man. . . . It was just as if he switched into another gear. And there was no in-between."

Hitler himself alluded to metaphysical control. He mentioned to several associates that an "inner voice" guided him and once remarked, "I follow my course with the precision and security of a sleepwalker."

Also during his time in Vienna, Hitler met Jorg Lanz von Liebenfels, publisher of *Ostara,* a magazine with occult and erotic themes. A Cistercian monk who founded the anti-Semitic, secret Order of the New Templars, Liebenfels and his mentor, Guido von List, sought to revive the medieval brotherhood of Teutonic Knights, which had used the swastika as an emblem.

List was a respected author on pan-German mysticism until he was chased out of Vienna following disclosures that his secret brotherhood involved sexual perversions and "medieval black magic." It was the philosophies of Liebenfels and List, extolling the glories of pagan occultism and the superiority of the Aryan race, that provided the foundation of the Thule Society. "The names List and Liebenfels soon became synonymous with the Pan-Germanic *volkisch* movement that eventually gave birth to the Nazi Party," reported author Levenda.

Whatever Hitler learned in Vienna changed him drastically. Previously a devout Catholic choirboy who had considered becoming a priest, he became openly antireligious and has even been accused of dabbling in Satanism. Author Epperson offered these connections, "So the swastika was a symbol of the Thule Society; it was a symbol of the Nazi Party; it was somehow connected to a symbol of the Sun-god; and the Sun-god was a symbol of Lucifer."

Lending support to the accusation of Satan worship, as well as reflecting Hitler's fascination with the supernatural, is a poem he wrote in 1915 while serving in the German army on the Western Front. It was reproduced in *Adolf Hitler* by John Toland:

> I often go on bitter nights
> To Wotan's oak in the quiet glade
> With dark powers to weave a union—
> The runic letter the moon makes with its magic spell
> And all who are full of impudence during the day
> Are made small by the magic formula!

Hitler's connection with the supernatural became more personal after being blinded by mustard gas during a British attack on the night of October 13–14, 1918.

Sent to a hospital in Pasewalk, Pomerania, Hitler's eyesight was improving when he learned of Germany's defeat and the signing of the armistice from a visiting pastor.

As he languished in pain and despair, Hitler experienced a supernatural vision. "Like St. Joan, he heard voices summoning him to save Germany," Toland wrote. "All at once 'a miracle came to pass'—the darkness encompassing Hitler evaporated. He could see again! He solemnly vowed, as promised, that he would 'become a politician and devote his energies to carrying out the command he had received.'"

Peter Levenda saw Hitler's experience as a "kind of mystical enlightenment, like that experienced by Guido von List many years before during his own temporary blindness—or like that of Saul, blinded on the way to Damascus—for, from that point on, Adolf Hitler was changed."

Arriving in Munich after the war, Corporal Hitler was assigned the menial job of guarding prisoners until the communist takeover in the spring of 1919. When the *Reichswehr* evacuated, Hitler remained behind to spy on the revolutionaries. Later, when the Army and the *Freikorps* retook Munich, it was Hitler who calmly walked down the ranks of communist captives singling out the ringleaders for execution.

As a reward for this undercover work, Hitler was assigned to the Press and News Bureau of the Political Department of the German army, a thinly disguised army intelligence operation. By the fall of 1919 he was assigned to spy on the various revolutionary groups springing up on the tumultuous Bavarian political scene. Hitler's commander, Captain Karl Mayr recalled that Hitler resembled "a tired stray dog looking for a master . . . ready to throw in his lot with anyone who would show him kindness" and "totally unconcerned about the German people and their destinies."

Hitler recalled, "One day I received orders from my headquarters to find out what was behind an apparently political society which, under the name of 'German Workers Party,' intended to hold a meeting. . . . I was to go there and look at the society and to report upon it." Arriving at the Sterneckerbrau beer hall, he was not overly impressed. "I met there about 20 to 25 people, chiefly from among the lower walks of life," wrote Hitler. The young military agent "astonished" the small gathering by arguing against a proposal that Bavaria break ties with Prussia.

To his surprise, a few days later a postcard arrived at his barracks informing Hitler that he had been accepted as a member of the GWP. "I did not know whether to be annoyed or to laugh at it," he wrote. "I had no intention of joining a ready-made party, but wished to found a party of my own." Nevertheless, on orders from his superiors, Hitler returned.

One of the early German Workers Party members was Eckart, often referred to as the spiritual founder of National Socialism. Eckart saw in Hitler the malleable leader he had been seeking and was soon introducing the new member to the right social circles in Munich and his intellectual friends in the Thule Society.

Although Eckart's role in metaphysical practices as well as in the foundation of the Nazi Party has been marginalized by most historians, it is significant that Hitler clearly understood Eckart's importance. He ended his infamous book *Mein Kampf* with these words, "And I want also to reckon among [Nazi heroes] that man, who, as one of the best, by words and by thoughts and finally by deeds, dedicated his life to the awakening of his, of our nation: Dietrich Eckart."

As Eckart lay dying in 1923, he said, "Follow Hitler! He will dance, but it is I who have called the tune. I have initiated him into the 'Secret Doctrine,' opened his centers in vision and given him the means to communicate with the Powers. Do not mourn for me: I shall have influenced history more than any other German."

The "Secret Doctrine" imparted to Hitler by Eckart and University of Munich Professor Haushofer was an amalgamation of concepts and philosophies largely stemming from the work of Madam Blavatsky and her Theosophical Society.

Blending Eastern mysticism, occultism, and hidden history, the doctrine concerns the effort to understand man's origins. According to Ravenscroft, "When the Third Eye [believed by many to be the pineal gland between the eyes] had been opened to a full vision of the Akashic Record [the mystical hidden record of mankind], the initiate [of the Secret Doctrine] became a living witness of the whole evolution of the world and of humanity. Traveling back through tremendous vistas of time, the very spirit origin of the earth and of man was unveiled to him, and he was able to follow the unfolding destiny of mankind through ever-changing conditions of life and cycles of development."

In this doctrine, nonhuman visitors to Earth long ago produced by genetic manipulation "divine-human hybrid beings, sort of God-men" divided into seven subraces—the Rmoahals, Tlavatli, Toltecs, Turanians, Aryans, Akkadians, and Mongols. During this process there were many mistakes, resulting in mutations such as the "giants" of biblical and Nordic mythology. These races lived through progressive life cycles during the time of fabled Atlantis.

With the destruction of Atlantis, they were scattered around the world and their mental and physical attributes began to degenerate. Their life spans decreased significantly. While their thought processes in the material world sharpened, "these faculties of thought and sense perception were gained at the price of a total loss of all magical powers over nature and over the life forces in the human organism," wrote Ravenscroft. With this loss of intuitive powers, these early humans were taught by their creators that everything on Earth was directed by invisible "gods" and that they should serve these "gods" unreservedly. "Above all, they were taught to respect and protect the purity of their blood," he added.

Hitler echoed these concepts in *Mein Kampf*, writing, "Aryan tribes . . . subjugate foreign peoples, and . . . develop the mental and organizatory [sic] abilities slumbering in them. Often, in the course of a few millenniums or even centuries, they create cultures which . . . bear the inner features of their character. . . . Finally, however, the conquerors deviate from the purity of their blood which they maintained originally, they begin to mix with the subjugated inhabitants and thus they end their own existence; for the fall of man in Paradise has always been followed by expulsion from it."

At this point, it is not necessary to decide whether or not to take any of this seriously. It is enough to understand that many educated and thoughtful people at that time did take such concepts seriously. And, as in the case of Hitler, these ideas caused serious repercussions for millions.

It is interesting to note that the term "Aryan" (a Sanskrit word meaning noble) until the time of Hitler usually referred merely to people using Indo-European languages rather than any race. However, in both scholarly and occult studies the term is also connected to an Indo-European-speaking people traceable to prehistoric times. These people were of unknown origins, but due to common language characteristics many scholars believe they came from northern Europe. One branch of these Aryans was located in present-day Iraq and is connected to ancient stories of gods who came from the sky.

A second branch entered India and intermingled with the existing population. They are mentioned in the Hindu Vedas, also in connection with gods who flew in flying machines called *vimanas*. It all begins to sound eerily similar to the Theosophist belief in extraterrestrial visitors.

Supported both by funds from Captain Mayr's army intelligence unit and the dedicated anticommunists of the Thule through Eckart, Hitler quickly gained control of the German Workers Party, which soon claimed three thousand members. Levenda reported that Mayr was reporting to wealthy industrialists and military officers operating out of the Four Seasons Hotel, indicating a connection between Army Intelligence and the Thule Society.

In April 1920 Hitler changed the party's name to the *Nationalsozialistiche Deutsche Arbeiterpartei*, the National Socialist German Workers Party, abbreviated to Nazi. Later that year, the party purchased a newspaper, the *Voelkischer Beobachter* (*Racial Observer*) with secret army funds and placed Eckart in charge. "At the beginning of 1923 the *Voelkischer Beobachter* became a daily, thus giving Hitler the prerequisite of all German political parties, a daily newspaper in which to preach the party's gospels," wrote William Shirer. From that point on, the Nazi machine rolled inexorably forward.

It is apparent that the Nazis could never have existed without the aid and support of the German *Reichswehr* and the secret Thule Society.

A study of the Twenty-five Points formulated in 1920 by Hitler, Drexler, and Eckart as the basis of the Nazi Party, reveals many which are nearly identical with the stated ideals of Marxism, indicating a common origin. Also addressed are reforms in the areas of international banking and business, particularly denouncing "interest slavery."

HITLER'S SUPPORT GROUP

Despite his clear intentions to nationalize and curtail the power of international business and finance, Hitler had little trouble getting funds from corporate sponsors who saw National Socialism as a welcome alternative to Communism.

It was, in fact, wealthy businessmen in Western industrial and banking circles who guaranteed Hitler's success. After Hitler lost a popular election to the aging war hero Field Marshal Paul von Hindenburg in 1932, thirty-nine business leaders, with familiar names like Krupp, Siemens, Thyssen, and Bosch, signed a petition to Hindenburg urging that Hitler be appointed chancellor of Germany.

This deal bringing Hitler into the government was cut at the home of banker Baron Kurt von Schroeder on January 4, 1933. According to Eustace Mullins, also attending this meeting were John Foster and Allen Dulles of the New York law firm Sullivan and Cromwell, which represented the Schroeder bank. The next year, when Rosenberg represented Hitler in England, he met with Schroeder Bank of London managing director T. C. Tiarks, who also was a director of the Bank of England. Throughout World War II, the Schroeder bank acted as financial agents for Germany in both Britain and the United States.

Schroeder, the powerful head of the J. H. Stein & Company banking house of Cologne, had long provided financial support to the Nazis in hopes they would counteract the spread of Communism. Hitler had pledged his word to von Schroeder that "National Socialism would engage in no foolish economic experiments." In other words, he would not attack banking practices except in rhetoric.

With this assurance and with Schroeder's blessing, Hitler was named chancellor of Germany by the senile President Hindenburg on January 30, 1933. A week later, the *Reichstag* (Parliament) building burned in a fire blamed on the communists. In another few days, Hitler was given dictatorial power with the passage of an emergency decree called the Enabling Act, euphemistically titled "The Law to Remove the Distress of the People and State" and began to assume control of the government.

Army and senior officials were becoming alarmed over Hitler's power, especially with some three million *Sturmabteilung* (SA) or Storm Detachment Brownshirts under the command of Hitler's SA chief Ernst Roehm. The Army proposed a deal: If the power of the SA was broken, the military would pledge loyalty to Hitler. Hitler agreed, and on June 30, 1934, trumped up charges of plotting a revolution caused Roehm and hundreds of Brownshirts to be fatally purged, and the SA quietly faded away.

With the death of the eighty-seven-year-old Hindenburg on August 2, 1934, Hitler merged the offices of president and chancellor and proclaimed himself commander-in-chief of the armed forces, the absolute leader—führer—of all Germany.

With both the government and military now firmly in hand, Hitler knew it was time to make deals with the international bankers and industrialists. This proved an easy task considering their multinational nature.

In the 1930s many people in both Britain and America viewed Nazi ideology favorably. In 1934 there was even a failed attempt by Morgan and Du Pont agents to bring about a fascist dictatorship in the United States, as detailed in my book *Alien Agenda*.

Automobile maker Henry Ford became a guiding light to Hitler, especially in the realm of anti-Semitism. In 1920 Ford had published an anti-Jewish book entitled *The International Jew*. As Hitler worked on his book *Mein Kampf* in 1924, he copied liberal portions of Ford's writing and even referred to Ford as "one great man."

Ford became an admirer of Hitler, provided funds for the Nazis, and in 1938 became the first American to receive the highest Nazi honor possible for a non-German—the Grand Cross of the Supreme Order of the German Eagle.

Like Hitler, Ford's suspicions initially were centered on international financiers. "At first he talked only about 'the big fellows' and said he had nothing against Jews in ordinary walks of life," recalled Edwin Pipp, editor of Ford's anti-Semitic newspaper, the *Dearborn Independent*. "Later he stated, 'They are all pretty much alike.'. . . He said that he believed they were in a conspiracy to bring on war for profits."

Ford said he learned this in 1915, when he chartered a ship to Europe in an unsuccessful attempt to negotiate an end to the war there. Later, he said that Jewish passengers on board had told him that it was international Jewish bankers who arranged wars for profit and that his peace effort would be in vain unless he contacted certain Jews in France and England, undoubtedly referring to the Rothschilds.

Hitler too initially kept his verbal attacks confined to international bankers, particularly the Rothschilds. In speeches during the early 1920s, Hitler praised German industrialists such as Alfred Krupp, while condemning "the rapacity of a Rothschild, who financed wars and revolutions and brought the peoples into interest-servitude through loans."

Despite these attacks, the emerging Nazi power continued to find support in Britain, even within the Rothschild-dominated Bank of England. "On New Year's Day, 1924, the financial fate of Germany was settled in London at a meeting between Hjalmar Schacht, the new Reich Commissioner for National Currency, and Montagu Norman, governor of the Bank of England," noted John Toland. "Schacht, who had already abolished emergency money, began with a frank disclosure of Germany's desperate financial situation." He then proposed to open a German credit bank second to the *Reichsbank,* but one which would issue notes in pound sterling. Schacht asked Norman to provide half the capital for this new bank and declared, "What prospects such a measure would afford for economic collaboration between Great Britain's World Empire and Germany . . .

"Within 48 hours Norman not only formally approved the loan at the exceptionally low interest of a flat five percent but convinced a group of London bankers to accept bills far exceeding the loan."

William Bramley noted these international banking connections: Max Warburg, a major German banker, and his brother Paul Warburg, who had been instrumental in establishing the Federal Reserve System in the United States, were directors of *Interssen Gemeinschaft Farben* or I.G. Farben, the giant German chemical firm that produced Zyklon B gas used in Nazi extermination camps. H. A. Metz of I.G. Farben was a director of the Warburg Bank of Manhattan, which later became part of the Rockefeller Chase Manhattan Bank. Standard Oil of New Jersey had been a cartel partner with I.G. Farben prior to the war. One American I.G. Farben director was C. E. Mitchell, who was also director of the Federal Reserve Bank of New York and of Warburg's National City Bank. The president of I.G. Farben in Germany, Hermann Schmitz, served on the boards of the Deutsche Bank and the Bank for International Settlements. In 1929 Schmitz was voted president of the board of National City Bank, now Citibank.

Paul Manning, a CBS news correspondent in Europe during World War II, wrote that Schmitz once "held as much stock in Standard Oil of New Jersey as did the Rockefellers." Schmitz also controlled eleven I.G. Farben companies in Japan. After the war, twenty-four I.G. Farben executives would stand trial at Nuremburg for crimes against humanity, including the building and maintenance of concentration camps and the use of slave labor.

I.G. Farben's American subsidiary, American I.G. Chemical Corporation, proved an ongoing source of important intelligence to the Nazis throughout the war as noted by German economic minister Dr. Max Ilgner. He wrote, "Extensive information which we receive continuously from [Chemical Corporation] is indispensable for our observations of American conditions ... [and] is, since the beginning of the war, an important source of information for governmental, economic and military offices."

Financing the rearmament of Germany in violation of the Versailles Treaty proved as profitable as it was dangerous to European peace.

Another American supporter of Hitler was Joseph P. Kennedy, father of the future president. On May 3, 1941, President Roosevelt was advised by FBI director J. Edgar Hoover that "Joseph P. Kennedy, the former ambassador to England, and Ben Smith, the Wall Street operator, some time in the past had a meeting with [Nazi Luftwaffe chief Hermann] Goering in Vichy, France, and that thereafter Kennedy and Smith had donated a considerable amount of money to the German cause. They are both described as being very anti-British and pro-German."

And support for Hitler continued to grow in Britain. According to Howard S. Katz, "In the spring of 1934, a select group of city financiers gathered around Montagu Norman . . . [head of] the Bank of England. . . . Hitler had disappointed his critics. His regime was no temporary nightmare, but a system with a good future, and Mr. Norman advised his directors to include Hitler in their plans. There was no opposition and it was decided that Hitler should get covert help from London's financial section until Mr. Norman had succeeded in putting sufficient pressure on the Government to make it abandon its pro-French policy for a more promising pro-German orientation." Considerable financial aid also came from Sir Henri Deterding, the powerful head of Royal Dutch-Shell Oil, who lived in London. His motives stemmed from his hope that Hitler, who had made it clear in *Mein Kampf* that he intended to subjugate Russia, might regain Deterding's assets in the Baku, Grozny, and Maikop oil fields.

Why would these powerful businessmen, all with financial links to the great Rothschild empire, support the overtly anti-Jewish Hitler? Part of the answer may lie in an astounding assertion that Hitler was a blood relative to the Rothschilds!

Dr. Walter C. Langer, a psychologist who produced a wartime psychoanalysis of Hitler for the American OSS, reported that a secret prewar Austrian police report proved Hitler's father was the illegitimate son of a peasant cook named Maria Anna Schicklgruber, who at the time she conceived her child was "employed as a servant in the home of Baron Rothschild" in Vienna. Upon learning of her pregnancy in 1837, she left Vienna and gave birth to Hitler's father of record, Alois. Five years later, she reportedly married an itinerant miller named Johann Georg Hiedler. Yet Alois carried his mother's name of Schicklgruber until nearly forty years of age when Heidler's brother, Johann Nepomuk Hiedler, offered him legitimacy. Due to the illegible writing of a parish priest in changing the birth register, the name Hiedler became Hitler, either by mistake or to confuse authorities.

Alois Hitler led a sad and morose life, chiefly as a government bureaucrat, and married his own second cousin, Klara Poelzl, in 1885, after obtaining special Episcopal dispensation. Adolf was born in Braunau, Austria, in 1889, when Alois was fifty-two years old.

This incredible story might be written off as fanciful wartime propaganda except for the fact that the OSS never made this story public, indicating the tale may have been considered too sensitive to publicize.

The issue came up in the late 1930s, when Hitler's English nephew, William Patrick Hitler, hinted to newsmen about the German leader's Jewish background. Hitler's personal attorney Hans Frank confirmed this scandalous information, but the name Frankenberger was substituted for Rothschild. When no record of a Frankenberger could be found in Vienna, the matter was quietly dropped by all but Hitler. Historians have long noted that the question of possible Jewish ancestry haunted Hitler throughout his life.

In case someone might question if a Rothschild would consider dallying with the servants, it is instructive that Rothschild biographer Ferguson stated that the son of one of Salomon's senior clerks "recalled that by the 1840s, [the Viennese Rothschild] had developed a somewhat reckless enthusiasm for young girls."

The late Philippe Rothschild, a descendent of Nathan, in 1984 published memoirs revealing his "scandalous love life." He wrote, "I was a tremendous success . . . leaping from bed to bed like a mountain goat. . . . I was always convinced [my father] had won his spurs riding my grandmother's chambermaids."

"It is possible that Hitler discovered his Jewish background and his relation to the Rothschilds, and aware of their enormous power to make or break European governments, reestablished contact with the family," wrote author Epperson. "This would partially explain the enormous support he received from the international banking fraternity, closely entwined with the Rothschild family, as he rose to power."

It is obvious why neither Hitler or his followers nor today's neo-Nazis nor the Rothschilds nor those who desire to profit from their international power would want the Hitler-Rothschild connection made public.

It certainly appears that with all their wealth and power, the Rothschilds suffered little during Hitler's holocaust. *The New Encyclopaedia Britannica* tactfully stated, "The Rothschilds, particularly those of

Vienna and Paris during the Nazi period, preserved the kind of family unity necessary to weather great misfortunes."

According to biographer Derek Wilson, various family members had narrow and traumatic escapes from Europe following German victories in 1940, but the fact remains that most safely gathered in New York City.

Far from being the destitute refugees as sometimes portrayed, some Rothschilds played crucial roles in the war effort. In May 1940 it was the French Maurice de Rothschild who arranged a secret meeting in Paris's Ritz Hotel between French prime minister Paul Reynaud, his minister of war Georges Mandel (whose real name was Rothschild though the claim is that there was no relation to the banking family), and Britain's Prime Minister Churchill, along with Anthony Eden, to determine the future of France. Also present was French general Charles de Gaulle, who within a month had organized the French government in exile in London.

Another family member, Lord Victor Rothschild, provided close security to Churchill during the war. He eventually was named to head Britain's powerful Central Bankers Policy Review Staff. "Lord Rothschild had access to all manner of leaders and experts," noted Wilson. "He was responsible only to the Prime Minister and answerable to neither the electorate nor the civil service chiefs."

One exception may have been a Robert Rothschild, who during World War II refused to sell his French holdings to Alfried Krupp, grandson of the great German armaments magnate Alfred Krupp. According to *The New Encyclopaedia Britannica*, the irate Krupp had Rothschild sent to the infamous death camp Auschwitz, where he was gassed. This incident, along with his exploitation of slave labor, landed grandson Krupp in front of the Nuremberg War Crimes judges.

With or without Rothschild influence, there is no question that Hitler's rise to power rested heavily on the support of the major German banks—Schroeder's Cologne banking firm, the *Deutsche Bank*, *Deutsche Kredit Gesellschaft,* and the huge insurance firm, *Allianz.*

One *Deutsche Bank* executive outlined a few of the bank's wartime loans: 150 million Reichmarks to the aircraft industry; 22 million to Bavarian Motor Works (BMW); 10 million to Daimler-Benz (Mercedes) in 1943 alone. Similar amounts were loaned again in 1944.

HITLER'S FORTUNE TURNS

At the zenith of his power, two important aspects of Hitler's position were reversed. Following the strange flight of his lieutenant Rudolf Hess to England, Hitler officially turned against occultism and the international order turned against him.

One of Hitler's early cronies was Rudolf Hess, who became deputy leader of the Nazi Party. Hess also was deeply involved in metaphysical studies, particularly astrology. He listened avidly to Professor Haushofer's explanations of the "Secret Doctrine" and was a student of Dr. Rudolf Steiner's school of anthroposophy, the use of man's higher consciousness to contact the spirit world. Hess also was an early member of the Thule Society.

On May 10, 1941, after secret but thorough preparations, Hess flew a specially prepared Messerschmitt 110 to England, where he parachuted out over the estate of the Duke of Hamilton. He apparently hoped to discuss a negotiated peace between Britain and Germany. "Twenty-five years later, in Spandau prison, Hess assured me in all seriousness that the idea had been inspired in him in a dream by supernatural forces," wrote Nazi minister of armaments and war production Albert Speer. Others thought Hess's flight was an under-the-table effort by Hitler to end fighting in the West in preparation for his coming attack on Russia.

Whatever the true purpose, nothing came of the flight. Hess was promptly imprisoned in the Tower of London and Hitler denounced him as a lone nut. According to Speer, Hitler blamed the flight on "the corrupting influence of Professor Haushofer." General Walter Schellenberg, head of the Nazi Foreign Intelligence Service who believed that British intelligence agents may have influenced Hess through Haushofer, said Hess astonished him by his belief in "old prophecies and visionary revelations. . . . He would recite whole passages out of books of prophecies, such as Nostradamus and others that I cannot remember, and also referred to old horoscopes concerning his own fate as well as that of his family and of Germany."

Fearful that Hess would reveal plans for his attack on the Soviet Union, Hitler declared him insane and vowed to put an end to "these stargazers." Hitler outlawed the public practice of astrology, palm and tea-leaf reading, and seances, as well as any "Freemasonlodge-like Organizations" to include the Theosophical Society, the Oriental Templars, the Order of the Golden Dawn, and Dr. Steiner's Anthroposophical Society. Many historians point to this crackdown as proof that Hitler disbelieved in such things.

Author Levenda argued that this was simply a case of cult infighting. "Occultists in general have no difficulty distancing themselves—with appropriate invective and astral curses—from other occultists with whom they disagree on philosophical grounds; and virtually every 'serious occultist' . . . has had nothing but disdain for tea leaf readers, palmists and cut-rate astrologers. Thus . . . [I] find no contradiction at all in Hitler's fascination with occultism on the one hand and his order to ban 'popular' occult practices on the other."

Duplicity in his approach to occultism was nothing new to Hitler. "The Fuehrer himself constantly ridiculed the *voelkisch* occult groups in his official speeches—while secretly soliciting their advice and counsel away from the prying eyes of both the press and the superstitious Christian public," noted Levenda, who also described in detail, based on captured Nazi documents, several knowledge-gathering expeditions to Tibet by the *Ahnenerbe-SS,* which in 1940 became a part of Himmler's staff.

After annexing Danzig, the Sudetenland, and Austria, Hitler had carved up Czechoslovakia by agreement with the French and British at a meeting in Munich. By mid-1939 he was ready to move into Poland, which had mutual defense pacts with the Western powers.

Again, a public pretext for war was needed. After weeks of increasing tension, dead prisoners were dressed in Polish army uniforms and left near a border radio station, which Hitler claimed had been attacked by Poland. In retaliation, on September 1, 1939, a million and a half soldiers of the German *Wehrmacht,* including fifty-five armored and motorized divisions, rolled into Poland under cover of the largest air armada every mobilized. Arrayed against this new Lightning War or blitzkrieg was a Polish army still containing cavalry units armed with lances.

Britain and France honored their collective security agreements with Poland but were helpless to stop the German onslaught due to both time and distance. Open warfare flared again on April 9, 1940, when Hitler loosed the blitzkrieg on Belgium and Holland. On June 10, with Allied forces falling back in all sectors, Italian dictator Mussolini, his courage bolstered, joined Hitler against France and Britain. France fell in a matter of weeks, leaving a desperate Britain to fight on alone. The balance of power had dangerously shifted, and the international bankers must have begun to rethink their support for Hitler.

JAPAN AGAINST THE WALL

On the other side of the world, matters were coming to a head with the Japanese Empire. Like Britain, this island nation was totally dependent on imports for survival and with the economic depression of the late 1930s, the country was in desperate straits. Fueled by its own rich history of societies involving militant knights (samurai) with a strict code of honor (Bushido), Japan sought its own *Lebensraum* by attacking Manchuria on mainland China in 1931. During the next few years, Japanese forces took ever larger portions of a China weakened by civil war between Chiang Kai-shek's nationalists and the communists.

With Britain busy fighting Hitler in 1940, it was clear that the United States was the only power capable of stopping Japanese expansion in the Pacific. Animosity between the two nations intensified when Japan was forced to seize further resources in China due to an ever-tightening American embargo which deprived the home island of vital materials.

In September 1940 Japan became partners with Germany and Italy in the Tripartite Pact, which pledged mutual assistance should the United States enter the war.

President Franklin D. Roosevelt reacted by halting Japan's importation of American petroleum, which had provided more than 90 percent of Japan's needs. On July 2, 1941, Japan entered Indochina, the nearest alternative source of fuel. President Roosevelt retaliated by freezing all Japanese assets in the United States. It was clear at the highest levels that war between Japan and the United States was inevitable.

This fact was not lost on Roosevelt, who had campaigned for a third term in office in 1940 by pledging to keep America out of the European war. However, planning for war was already underway—at least within the secretive Council on Foreign Relations.

Journalist Lucas noted, "In September, 1939, the Council offered to undertake long-range planning for the hard-pressed State Department. The Department accepted, and five study groups—on Security and Armaments, Economics and Finance, Politics, Territories and Peace Aims—were established. Over the next six years, financed by the Rockefeller Foundation, they flooded the State Department with 682 memoranda. . . . By 1942 the Council groups were virtually absorbed into the State Department."

The conclusion of this CFR undertaking—known as the War and Peace Studies Project—was made public in 1940 when a group of CFR members placed newspaper ads declaring that "the United States should immediately declare that a state of war exists between this country and Germany."

"CFR members were interested in exploiting the Second World War—as they had the first—as a justification for world government," asserted Perloff. "The globalists hoped to use the Axis threat to force the U.S. and England into a permanent Atlantic alliance—an intermediate step toward world government."

But throughout 1941, even after Hitler invaded Russia that summer, the American public stubbornly maintained a position of noninterference toward the war. A 1940 Gallup poll showed 83 percent of the public was against intervention. A good pretext was needed to gain support from an intransigent public.

Controversy has raged for years over the question of Roosevelt's foreknowledge of the December 7, 1941, attack on Pearl Harbor. While incontestable proof remains elusive, the accumulation of available information has now caused wide acceptance of the idea that the devastating attack was encouraged and tolerated in an effort to galvanize public support for America's participation in the war.

It cannot be denied that Roosevelt's Depression-era social and economic policies greatly centralized the federal government and initiated social engineering which continues to this day, and he was quite open in his allegiance to England. While proclaiming neutrality, Roosevelt sent war ships and ammunition to Britain as proposed by the Century Group composed of CFR members. He ordered the occupation of Iceland, closing it off to the Germans, and authorized attacks on U-boats. He openly approved loans to Japan's enemy, nationalist China, and quietly approved the recruitment of well-paid American "volunteers" for Chiang Kai-shek's famous "Flying Tigers." Much of this was in violation of international war rules and was guaranteed to provoke the Axis powers.

"Roosevelt was himself a prototypic Wall Streeter," wrote Perloff. "His family had been involved in New York banking since the eighteenth century. His uncle, Frederic Delano, was on the original Federal Reserve Board." Roosevelt's son-in-law, Curtis B. Dall, wrote, "Most of his [Roosevelt's] thoughts, his political 'ammunition,' as it were, were carefully manufactured for him in advance by the CFR-One World Money group."

Those who accept the idea that Roosevelt and a few other insiders knew that Pearl Harbor was to be attacked point to these suspicious facts:

—During Pacific naval exercises in 1932 and 1938, and with Japanese military attachés closely observing, U.S. Navy officers theoretically destroyed the Pacific fleet at Pearl Harbor both times.

—Roosevelt ordered the Pacific fleet moved to the exposed position at Pearl Harbor over the vigorous objections of Admiral James O. Richardson, who was replaced for refusing to issue the order.

—Roosevelt, Secretary of State Cordell Hull, and other high-level officials knew that war was inevitable and that negotiations with Japan's Kichisaburo Nomura were hopeless since the broken Japanese code revealed that Nomura was instructed not to yield to Hull's harsh demands.

—They also knew that a large Japanese task force, including six aircraft carriers, had dropped from sight after moving toward America.

—This prompted U.S. Army Chief of Staff George C. Marshall, a close associate to many CFR members, to send an oddly worded message to Pearl Harbor commanders on November 27, 1941, "Hostile action possible at any moment. If hostilities cannot, repeat CANNOT, be avoided, the United States desires that Japan commit the first overt act. This policy should not, repeat NOT, be construed as restricting you to a course of action that might jeopardize your defense." Despite this clear warning, with its accompanying suggestion not to attack any attackers, Pacific fleet ships remained at anchor and aircraft were bunched into clusters of "sitting ducks" as "security" against saboteurs.

—During the first week of December, Americans intercepted the Japanese diplomatic "Purple" code ordering their embassy in Washington to destroy all secret papers and prepare to evacuate.

—On December 4 Australian intelligence reported sighting the missing Japanese task force moving toward Pearl Harbor but Roosevelt dismissed it as a rumor begun by pro-war Republicans.

—A British agent named Dusko Popov learned of Japan's plans from German sources but his warnings to Washington were ignored.

—According to author John Toland, separate warnings regarding a pending attack on Pearl Harbor, though varying as to a specific time, came from U.S. ambassador to Japan Joseph Grew; FBI Director J. Edgar Hoover, Senator Guy Gillette, Congressman Martin Dies, Brigadier General Elliot Thorpe in Java, and Colonel F. G. L. Weijerman, the Dutch military attaché in Washington. Later, Dutch naval officer, Captain Johan Ranneft, said sources in U.S. Intelligence told him on December 6 that the Japanese carriers were only four hundred miles northwest of Hawaii.

—During investigations after the attack, Marshall and Navy Secretary Frank Knox both testified they could not recall their whereabouts the night of December 6. It was later revealed that they were both in the White House with Roosevelt.

Then there is the issue of the aircraft carriers. In 1941 the American public, as well as a few hidebound military officers, still believed that the battleship was the ultimate weapon. But anyone who had been paying attention knew that General Billy Mitchell had proven in the mid-1920s that a single bomb-loaded airplane could destroy a battleship. Battleships were obsolete. Victory in any Pacific war would go to the side with the strongest air power and that meant aircraft carriers.

Not one aircraft carrier was present when Pearl Harbor was attacked.

On November 25, 1941, Secretary of War Henry Stimson had a conversation with Roosevelt, after which he wrote in his diary, "The question was how we should maneuver them into the position of firing the first shot without too much danger to ourselves. . . . It was desirable to make sure the Japanese be the ones to do this so that there should remain no doubt in anyone's mind as to who were the aggressors."

The answer to this dilemma came within twenty-four hours. The most damning evidence yet of Roosevelt's foreknowledge of an attack came from the 1948 interrogation of Germany's Gestapo chief Heinrich Mueller. In a 1995 book by Gregory Douglas based on previously secret files, Mueller stated that on November 26, 1941, the Germans in Holland had intercepted a private trans-Atlantic telephone conversation between Roosevelt and British Prime Minister Churchill.

Churchill informed Roosevelt of the movements of the missing Japanese fleet and stated, "I can assure you that their goal is the (conversation broken) fleet in Hawaii, at Pearl Harbor."

"This is monstrous," exclaimed Roosevelt. "Can you tell me . . . indicate . . . the nature of your intelligence?" "Reliable," answered Churchill, who mentioned agents within the Japanese military and foreign service as well as their broken code.

"The obvious implication is that the Japs are going to do a Port Arthur on us at Pearl Harbor. Do you concur?" asked Roosevelt. Churchill replied, "I do indeed unless they add an attack on the Panama Canal to this vile business." Port Arthur, today called Pinyun Lu-shun, was a strategic Russian port on China's Liaodong Peninsula. The Japanese launched a surprise torpedo attack against the port, which began the 1904–05 Russo-Japanese War.

Roosevelt then said, "I will have to consider the entire problem. . . . A Japanese attack on us, which would result in war between—and certainly you as well—would certainly fulfill two of the most important requirements of our policy." Roosevelt speaks about absenting himself from the White House on some pretext, adding, "What I don't know, can't hurt me and I cannot understand messages at a distance."

Addressing the unlikely proposition that U.S. military officers would have knowingly allowed American units to be attacked, author Douglas explained, "The warning did not come to Roosevelt from below but on a parallel level and from a foreign intelligence source which was far better equipped to decode and translate the Japanese transmissions."

WORLD WAR II

Foreknowledge of the December 7 attack gives new meaning to Roosevelt's words concerning, "a date that will live on in infamy." On that day, the American public was shocked to learn that its forces in Hawaii had suffered 2,400 dead, 1,200 wounded, four battleships sunk with another three badly damaged, and many other smaller vessels and hundreds of aircraft destroyed.

The next day, Roosevelt addressed Congress, asking for a declaration of war. It was quickly granted with only one dissenting vote—Representative Jeannette Rankin of Montana, the first woman to hold a seat in either house of Congress. Rankin had also been among the forty-nine Congress members who voted against Wilson's declaration of war in 1917, and in 1968, at age eighty-seven, she led five thousand women of the "Jeannette Rankin Brigade" in a march on Capitol Hill to protest the Vietnam War. Widely despised as a "pacifist," perhaps Rankin understood the hidden machinations behind these wars better than her fellow citizens.

A special commission was appointed by Roosevelt to determine responsibility for the Pearl Harbor attack. It was headed by his friend Supreme Court Justice Owen Roberts along with two CFR members on the five-person panel. The Roberts Commission blamed dereliction of duty by Pearl Harbor commanders, Admiral Husband Kimmel and General Walter C. Short, for the tragedy and disbanded.

Incensed, the two officers sought a court martial to clear their names, which was finally mandated by Congress in 1944. During these proceedings, internal investigations by both the army and navy were shown to have fixed blame for the surprise attack on Marshall and other Washington chiefs. Kimmel was exonerated and Short was given a light reprimand. Like the future Warren Commission, the Roberts Commission had operated on a presumption of guilt and had selectively chosen evidence to fit this bias. Furthermore, investigators concluded that if decoded messages had been forwarded to Kimmel in Hawaii, they may have provided "the probable exact hour and date of the attack."

"The court-martial findings were buried in a 40-volume government report on Pearl Harbor and few Americans ever learned the truth," noted Perloff.

With the entire world now ablaze in war and nearly all of Europe under Hitler's control, the international war financiers finally realized they had produced a Frankenstein monster, a creation out of control. Their loathing of Communism as well as an offensive against the Japanese Empire were placed on a back burner while they mobilized to stop the man who had vowed to eliminate war profiteers, Freemasons, Jews, and international bankers.

BUSINESS AS USUAL

Even after more than two dozen nations formed an alliance to combat Hitler and the Japanese militarists, there were some businessmen—most connected with secret societies—who could not resist the temptation to profit from the world's misery.

A good example was Walter C. Teagle, chairman of Standard Oil of New Jersey, owned by Rockefeller's Chase Bank. Teagle also was a director of American I.G. Chemical Corp., a subsidiary of the giant I.G. Farben conglomerate.

Author Charles Higham described how Teagle, through Rockefeller banking and oil interests, made his employers a handsome profit just prior to the war. "[Teagle] remained in partnership with Farben in the matter of tetraethyl lead, an additive used in aviation gasoline," Higham wrote in his book *Trading with the Enemy: An Expose of the Nazi-American Money Plot 1933–1949*.

"[German Luftwaffe chief Hermann] Goering's air force couldn't fly without it. Only Standard, Du Pont, and General Motors had the rights to it. Teagle helped organize a sale of the precious substance to [Farben chairman] Schmitz, who in 1938 traveled to London and 'borrowed' 500 tons from Ethyl, the British Standard subsidiary. Next year, Schmitz and his partners returned to London and obtained $15 million worth. The result was that Hitler's air force was rendered capable of bombing London, the city that had provided the supplies. Also, by supplying Japan with tetraethyl, Teagle helped make it possible for the Japanese to wage World War II."

Curiously, it was this same Walter Teagle who helped created the National Recovery Administration, one of President Roosevelt's New Deal agencies designed to regulate American business. This was an odd choice if the captains of industry were as opposed to Roosevelt's social policies as they claimed. Some researchers see such activity as evidence that secret agendas were taking place behind seemingly innocuous scenes.

As war approached, the business and banking connections tightened. In 1936 the Schroeder and Rockefeller families formed Schroeder, Rockefeller and Company which *Time* magazine described as "the economic booster of the Rome-Berlin Axis." Partners in this company were John D. Rockefeller's nephew, Avery, Baron Bruno von Schroeder in London and Kurt von Schroeder in Cologne. Their lawyers were John Foster and Allen

Dulles's law firm. The younger Dulles along with Edsel Ford served on the firm's board of directors.

I.G. Farben and Rockefeller's Standard Oil had become so intertwined that in 1942 Thurman Arnold, head of the U.S. Justice Department's Anti-Trust Division, produced documents for Senator Harry S. Truman's defense committee showing that "Standard and Farben in Germany had literally carved up the world markets, with oil and chemical monopolies established all over the map."

Even after the United States entered the war, this cozy relationship continued. Through complicated business transactions, the Rockefellers continued selling petroleum products to Germany through third-party nations. "While American civilians and the armed services suffered alike from restrictions, more gasoline went to Spain [then transferred to Germany] than it did to domestic customers," wrote author Higham.

Higham called the international cabal of interconnected businessmen and bankers "The Fraternity," linked by "the ideology of Business as Usual. . . . Bound by identical reactionary ideas, the members sought a common future in fascist domination, regardless of which world leader might further that ambition," he explained. "Thus, the bosses of the multinationals as we know them today had a six-spot on every side of the dice cube. Whichever side won the war, the powers that really ran nations would not be adversely affected.

"When it was clear that Germany was losing the war the businessmen became notably more 'loyal.' Then, when war was over, the survivors pushed into Germany, protected their assets, restored Nazi friends to high office, helped provoke the Cold War, and insured the permanent future of The Fraternity."

It has been carefully documented how Standard Oil of New Jersey shipped fuel to Germany through Switzerland in 1942; how Chase Bank in occupied Paris conducted business with the full knowledge of its New York headquarters; how Ford trucks were produced for the German army with home office approval; how Colonel Sosthenes Behn, the head of International Telephone and Telegraph Corp. and a director of National City Bank, worked to improve Nazi telephone communications and produce fighter planes along with the V-1 buzz bomb.

All this was done legally thanks to President Roosevelt. Only six days after Pearl Harbor, on December 13, 1941, Roosevelt ordered, "A general license is hereby granted, licensing any transaction or act proscribed by section 3(a) of the Trading with the Enemy Act, as amended, provided . . . that such transaction or act is authorized by the Secretary of the Treasury . . . pursuant to the Executive Order No. 8389, as amended."

This meant any kind of business transaction could be made legal with the approval of Roosevelt's Secretary of the Treasury, Henry Morgenthau, whose father helped found the Council on Foreign Relations.

A considerable amount of the funds used to perpetuate the war came through the Bank for International Settlements (BIS), owned by the Morgan-affiliated First National Bank of New York, the Bank of England, Germany's *Reichsbank*, the Bank of Italy, the Bank of France, and other major central banks. Created in 1930 in Basel, Switzerland, ostensibly to handle German war reparations, the BIS was actually a creature of secret society manipulators. According to historian Quigley, it was part of a plan "to create a world system of financial control in private hands able to dominate the political system of each country and the economy of the world as a whole . . . to be controlled in a feudalist fashion by the central banks of the world acting in concert by secret agreements arrived at in frequent meetings and conferences."

The BIS soon fell under the control of Hitler associates Kurt von Schroeder, *Reichsbank* president Hjalmar Horace Greeley Schacht, and vice president Emil Puhl. According to author Higham, the bank became "a money funnel for American and British funds to flow into Hitler's coffers and to help Hitler build up his war machine." The first president of the BIS was Rockefeller banker Gates W. McGarrah, a former officer with Chase National Bank and the Federal Reserve Bank as well as grandfather to future CIA director Richard Helms. According to several conspiracy writers, the BIS continues to be a hub of drug money laundering and interconnected banking control.

Many of the complex and intertwined financial dealings during the war took place in neutral Switzerland, which by 1939 had 2,278 registered international corporations, 2,026 holding companies whose owners were not Swiss, and was the home of 214 international banks.

The connections between the German and American steel industries were outlined in 1944 by an *SS Obergruppenfuehrer* who explained to German industrialists and government officials that "patents for stainless steel belonged to the Chemical Foundation, Inc., New York, and the Krupp Company of Germany, jointly, and that of the United States Steel Company, Carnegie, Illinois, American Steel & Wire, National

Tube, etc. were thereby under obligation to work with the Krupp concern." It had been German steel magnate Fritz Thyssen, an early Nazi, who had funded Hitler and introduced him into important business circles.

In a 1942 deal involving Karl Lindemann, Standard Oil's Berlin representative; SS counterintelligence chief Schellenberg; banker Kurt von Schroeder; and ITT head Behn, Hitler's government entered into partnership with ITT. Thanks to these interconnected business ties, "After Pearl Harbor, the German army, navy and air force contracted with ITT for the manufacture of switchboards, telephones, alarm gongs, buoys, air raid warning devices, radar equipment and 30 thousand fuses per month for artillery shells used to kill British and American troops," reported Higham. "This was increased to 50 thousand per month by 1944. In addition, ITT supplied ingredients for the rocket bombs that fell on London, selenium cells for dry rectifiers, high-frequency radio equipment and fortification and field communication sets."

General Motors prior to 1939 invested more than $30 million in German I.G. Farben plants although executives were well aware that one-half percent of the total wage and salary payroll was being donated to the Nazis. Furthermore, Germany's biggest manufacturers of armored fighting vehicles were Opel, a wholly owned General Motors subsidiary controlled by Morgan interests, and the Germany subsidiary of Ford Motor Company. Reuters News Service reported that Nazi armaments chief Albert Speer said that Hitler would never have considered invading Poland without the synthetic fuel technology provided Germany by General Motors.

Thanks to the political and social clout of secret society members on both sides of the Atlantic, Higham said, "The Nuremberg Trials successfully buried the truth of the Fraternity connections."

This "Fraternity" of men tied together by clandestine individual and business intrigues continued after the gunfire ceased. A U.S. Justice Department attorney named James Steward Martin arrived with an investigative team in Germany after the war and tried to sort out the tangled web of business dealings. He was blocked continually and finally resigned in frustration.

In his 1950 book entitled *All Honorable Men,* Martin wrote, "We had not been stopped in Germany by German business. We had been stopped in Germany by American business. The forces that stopped us had operated from the United States but had not operated in the open. We were not stopped by a law of Congress, by an Executive Order of the President, or even by a change of policy approved by the President . . . in short, whatever it was that stopped us was not 'the government.' But it clearly had command of channels through which the government normally operates. The relative powerlessness of governments . . . is of course not new . . . national governments [have] stood on the sidelines while bigger operators arranged the world's affairs."

None of the information presented here should be construed to mean that it was unnecessary to fight the Nazis and Japanese militarists. Obviously, however the world situation is viewed today, it must be better than a string of intercontinental concentration camps filled with non-Aryans lorded over by jackbooted SS troopers and Japanese guards.

But it is important to understand the manipulation of the public by secret societies in order to prevent future recurrences. And it must be pointed out that the secret society men who propagated and financed the war continued to profit throughout the hostilities. Exhibiting no allegiance to the countries in which they prospered, these men and their companies continued to provide support to the deadliest of enemies during the most perilous of times for the United States and Great Britain.

Lest anyone think that this is all dry ancient history with no connection to today's world, consider that in late 1998 there were a multiplicity of lawsuits still pending against Ford Motor Co., Chase Manhattan Bank, J. P. Morgan & Co., several Swiss banks, and other firms in connection with their wartime dealings with Nazi Germany.

The German insurance giant *Allianz AG,* which in 1990 purchased America's Fireman's Fund Insurance Co. in a $3.3 billion deal, was sued for failing to pay off life insurance policies of Jewish customers. The firm also was found to have insured buildings and civilian employees of the infamous death camp Auschwitz against "careless or malicious actions on the part of prisoners."

In early 1999 Germany's *Deutsche Bank* officials were concerned that their admission that the bank loaned the money to build Auschwitz might jeopardize the bank's $9.8 billion buyout of New York's Bankers Trust Corp. Why the late admission? Dr. Hermann Josef Abs, the central bank's founder and a leading banker for Hitler and the Nazis, had remained as the bank's honorary chairman until his death in 1994.

WORLD WAR I

The hand of the secret societies with its attendant banking and business manipulation of war can be seen even more clearly in the "wars to end all wars," commonly known as World War I.

Contrary to the high school textbook explanation that the war was caused by the assassination of Archduke Francis Ferdinand of Austria-Hungary by a Serb in 1914, researchers have found that planning for this conflagration began many years before and, once again, involved members of secret societies.

"Since the latter part of the 18th century, the Rothschild Formula [pitting nation against nation while making loans to both] had controlled the political climate of Europe," wrote author Griffin. "An arms race had been in progress for many years. . . . The assassination of Ferdinand was not the cause but the trigger."

Just as today, the Balkan states were locked in a cycle of war, revolution, and ethnic conflict. Following wars during 1912–13, Colonel Dragutin Dimitrijevic, chief of Serbian military intelligence, conspired to assassinate Ferdinand as part of a plan to liberate Serbs in South Austria-Hungary. He operated under the name "Apis" in a secret society known as "The Black Hand."

According to a 1952 Masonic publication, Ferdinand's assassin, the Bosnian Serb Gavrilo Princep, and others were Freemasons, encouraged by Apis and incensed by disclosure of a secret treaty between the Vatican and Serbia. The death of Ferdinand caused a chain reaction of ultimatums and mobilizations which ultimately spread war from the Balkans to the whole of Europe.

Prior to this, trustees of the Andrew Carnegie Foundation's Endowment for International Peace met in 1909 to discuss changing life in America. Bonesman Daniel Coit Gilman was a former president of the Carnegie Institution, and fellow members of The Order sat as trustees of this study. According to one congressional researcher, the trustees came to the same conclusion as the Report from Iron Mountain, "There are no known means more efficient than war, assuming the objective is altering the life of an entire people. . . . How do we involve the United States in a war?"

It was a very good question, since the American people were overwhelmingly isolationist, adhering to the advice of President George

Washington "to steer clear of permanent alliance with any portion of the foreign world."

Author Gary Allen in his 1971 underground classic *None Dare Call It Conspiracy* also saw an evil design in this war. He wrote, "Woodrow Wilson was re-elected by a hair. He had based his campaign on the slogan: 'He Kept Us Out of War!'. . . Just five months later we were in it. The same crowd which manipulated the passage of the income tax and the Federal Reserve System wanted America in the war. J. P. Morgan, John D. Rockefeller, 'Colonel' House, Jacob Schiff, Paul Warburg and the rest of the Jeykll Island conspirators were all deeply involved."

"Even before the actual clash of arms, the French firm of Rothschild Freres cabled to Morgan and Company in New York suggesting the floatation of a loan of $100 million, a substantial part of which was to be left in the United States to pay for French purchases of American goods," wrote author Charles Callan Tansill in *America Goes to War.*

This loan involved banker J. P. Morgan Jr., who had taken control of the Morgan financial empire after the death of his famed father in 1913. Morgan as the Rothschild's American representative—some say partner—was a pivotal character in the coming bloodbath.

President Woodrow Wilson, who was put in office by the largess of bankers Morgan, Bernard Baruch, Jacob Schiff, and Cleveland Dodge, chose the younger Morgan as chief purchasing agent for the United States even as he was acting as the sole purchasing agent for Britain, France, Russian, Italy, and Canada. In this capacity, Morgan oversaw the transfer of tremendous amounts of money as the war continued. He bought more than $3 billion in American military and other materials on behalf of the Allied powers while organizing more than two thousand U.S. banks to underwrite more than $1.5 billion in Allied bonds. After the war, Morgan's firm arranged loans totaling more than $10 billion to reconstruct the European nations.

Banker Bernard Baruch, who later helped fund the Council on Foreign Relations, was named by President Wilson to head the War Industries Board where he controlled all domestic war material contracts. "It was widely rumored in Wall Street that out of the war to make the world safe for international bankers he netted $200 million for himself," wrote Allen.

Morgan and Baruch were not the sole beneficiaries of war profits. According to published statistics, yearly profits to the Du Ponts, manufacturers of gunpowder, rose from $6 million in 1914 to $58 million by 1918, a 950 percent increase. In the five years proceeding the war, U.S. Steel's yearly earnings averaged $105 million. This jumped to $240 million during the war years of 1914–18. Profits for the International Nickel Company went from $4 million a year to $73.5 million by 1918, an increase of more than 1,700 percent.

Was this massive amount of money well spent? Not according to Marine Major General Smedley D. Butler. In his 1935 book *War is a Racket*, Butler commented, "Take the shoe people. . . . For instance, they sold Uncle Sam 35,000,000 pairs of hobnailed service shoes. There were 4,000,000 [U.S.] soldiers. Eight pairs, and more, to the soldier. My regiment during the war had only a pair to a soldier. Some of the shoes probably are still in existence. . . . There was still lots of leather left. So the leather people sold your Uncle Sam hundreds of thousands of McClellan saddles for the cavalry. But there wasn't any American cavalry overseas! . . . They sold your Uncle Sam 20,000,000 mosquito nets for the use of the soldiers overseas. . . . Well, not one of these mosquito nets ever got to France! . . . Some 6,000 buckboards [horse-drawn wagons] were sold to Uncle Sam for the use of colonels! Not one of them was used. But the buckboard manufacturer got his war profit."

But trouble soon developed for these gigantic money transactions—Germany appeared to be winning the war and the treasuries of both England and France were empty. British and French bankers, faced with total loss if Germany ended the balance of power by victory, looked to the United States for rescue. U.S. ambassador Walter Hines Page, who also was a trustee of Rockefeller's General Education Board and was being paid a $25,000-a-year allowance by Rockefeller's National City Bank, outlined the problem to the State Department in a March 15, 1917, telegram, "I think that the pressure of this approaching crisis has gone beyond the ability of the Morgan Financial Agency for the British and French Governments. . . . Unless we go to war with Germany, our Government, of course, cannot make . . . a direct grant of credit."

The leaders wanted America in the war but President Wilson had pledged not to get involved. But quietly he made other arrangements. On March 9, 1916, eight months before the presidential election, Wilson authorized a secret agreement arranged by his right-hand man, Colonel House, to enter the war on the Allied side. "After the war, the text of the agreement leaked out," wrote German sympathizer George Viereck.

"[Britain's Sir Edward] Gray was the first to tattle. Page discussed it at length. Colonel House tells its history. . . . But for some incomprehensible reason the enormous significance of the revelation never penetrated the consciousness of the American people."

Yet the American public still resisted going to war. Clearly, the public's attitudes had to be changed.

Attitudes are shaped by the media, and even in World War I much of the major media was under the control of Rockefeller-Morgan interests. As recorded in the Congressional Record of 1917, "In March, 1915, the J. P. Morgan interests . . . got together 12 men high up in the newspaper world and employed them to select the most influential newspapers in the United States and [the] sufficient number of them to control generally the policy of the daily press. . . . They found it was only necessary to purchase the control of 25 of the greatest papers.

"An agreement was reached; the policy of the papers was bought, to be paid for by the month; an editor was furnished for each paper to properly supervise and edit information regarding the questions of preparedness, militarism, financial policies, and other things of national and international nature considered vital to the interests of the purchasers."

Any publication which was not controlled outright was intimidated by the strength of Rockefeller-Morgan advertising dollars. Griffin noted, "After the J. P. Morgan bloc, the Rockefellers have the most advertising of any group to dispose of. And when advertising alone is not sufficient to insure the fealty of a newspaper, the Rockefeller companies have been known to make direct payments in return for a friendly editorial attitude."

But even this money-backed media blitz, coupled with anti-German rhetoric from the Rockefeller-Morgan foundations and universities, failed to convince the American public to enter the war. Public polls showed opposition to entering the European war at nearly ten-to-one.

A STIMULUS FOR WAR

As throughout history, a provocation was needed to push a recalcitrant public into war. This provocation was the sinking of the ocean liner *Lusitania*. How this cruel act played out is an intriguing study in behind-the-scenes manipulation.

Britain's Winston Churchill, who was appointed first lord of the admiralty in 1911, was desperate for America to join England as an ally. In a later book, *The World Crisis,* Churchill wrote, "The maneuver which brings an ally into the field is as serviceable as that which wins a great battle."

Under existing rules of war, both British and German warships were to give the crew of enemy vessels a chance to escape before sinking them. For submarines this meant surfacing and challenging the enemy. In 1914 Churchill ordered British merchant ships to disregard any challenge, even counterattack if they were armed. This order forced German U-boat commanders to launch torpedoes while submerged for protection. Churchill also ordered British ships to remove their hull names and to fly the flags of neutral nations when in port.

Churchill freely admitted his orders were a ploy to involve other nations in the war. "The submerged U-boat had to rely increasingly on underwater attack and thus ran the greater risk of mistaking neutral for British ships and of drowning neutral crews and thus embroiling Germany with other Great Powers."

Just such a "mistake" occurred on May 7, 1915, when a German U-boat commander torpedoed the British liner *Lusitania* en route from New York to Liverpool.

Nearly 2,000 persons went down with the ship, including 128 Americans. This act set off a firestorm of anti-German feeling throughout the United States, fanned by the Rockefeller-Morgan dominated press.

Only in later years did the facts of the *Lusitania*'s demise become public. Contrary to United States claims of neutrality, the ship carried 600 tons of gun cotton explosive, 6 million rounds of ammunition, 1,248 cases of shrapnel shells, plus other war materials. "When the *Lusitania* left New York harbor on her final voyage, she was virtually a floating ammunition dump," commented Griffin. According to author Colin Simpson, the ship's original manifest listing these armaments was ordered hidden away in Treasury archives by Wilson.

Griffin also pointed out that the *Lusitania* was registered as an armed auxiliary cruiser by the British Admiralty and owned by the Cunard Company, the closest competitor to J. P. Morgan's international shipping trust, which included Germany's two largest lines along with Britain's White Star line. "Morgan had attempted in 1902 to take over the . . . Cunard Company, but was blocked by the British Admiralty, which wanted to keep Cunard out of foreign control so her ships could be pressed into military service, if necessary, in time of war," noted Griffin.

The imperial German embassy in Washington, fully aware that tons of war materials were being carried into the war zone around England, aside from vainly protesting to the U.S. government, made an effort to prevent tragedy. Embassy officials attempted to place ads in fifty East Coast newspapers.

The ad read: "NOTICE! TRAVELERS intending to embark on the Atlantic voyage are reminded that a state of war exists between Germany and her allies and Great Britain and her allies; that the zone of war includes the waters adjacent to the British Isles; that, in accordance with formal notice given by the Imperial German Government, vessels flying the flag of Great Britain, or of any of her allies, are liable to destruction in those waters and that travelers sailing in the war zone on ships of Great Britain or her allies do so at their own risk."

Of the fifty newspapers slated to carry this notice, only the *Des Moines Register* ran it on the date requested. The other papers pulled the ad because of intervention by the U.S. State Department. Government officials cowed editors by claiming that, due to the possibility of libel suits, they should first obtain approval by State Department lawyers.

President Wilson was alerted to the situation. Years later, author Simpson wrote, "There can be no doubt that President Wilson was told of the character of the cargo destined for the *Lusitania*. He did nothing, but was to concede on the day he was told of her sinking that his foreknowledge had given him many sleepless hours."

Adding support to those who believed the *Lusitania* was consciously sent to her fate, British commander Joseph Kenworthy, on duty when the ship was sunk, later revealed that her military escort was withdrawn at the last minute and her captain ordered to enter at reduced speed an area where a German U-boat was known to be operating. It is clear why Germany attacked this ship, and Britain would have done the same if U.S. munitions were being shipped to Germany. "The Germans, whose torpedo struck the liner, were the unwitting accomplices or victims of a plot probably concocted by Winston Churchill," concluded author Simpson.

Survivors and later investigations revealed that the German torpedo did not sink the *Lusitania*. Its destruction was caused instead by a secondary internal explosion, most probably the tons of stored explosives and ammunition.

Whether the sinking of the *Lusitania* was contrived or not, the incident still was not enough to propel the American people into war. "Torpedoings of merchant ships and loss of noncombatant lives, including American, convinced Americans of German frightfulness but not of German hostility to themselves," wrote author Barbara W. Tuchman.

The German high command, in a studious effort to avoid antagonizing the United States following the sinking of several merchant ships including the *Lusitania,* in September 1915 suspended unrestricted submarine warfare.

Despite all the maneuvering on the part of Wilson and Churchill, it was the Germans themselves that finally pushed America into the war. This event involved Mexico and, more specifically, the one man who more than any other launched World War I. This was Arthur Zimmermann, who as acting German foreign secretary in 1914 helped start the war in the first place by drafting the telegram that announced Germany's decision to support Austria-Hungary against Serbia following the assassination of Archduke Ferdinand. This action angered Russia and precipitated war.

By January 1917 Zimmermann had been appointed foreign secretary and was a strong supporter of unrestricted U-boat warfare. On January 16 he sent a coded telegram to the German minister in Mexico by way of the German ambassador in Washington authorizing the proposal of an alliance with Mexico and Japan. Both of these nations had strained relations with the United States. Brigadier General John "Blackjack" Pershing, who would become the commander of the American Expeditionary Force in France, was chasing Mexican revolutionary Pancho Villa at the time; meanwhile, the Japanese cruiser *Asama* was causing concern in California by maneuvering off the west coast of Mexico.

Zimmermann advised Mexican president Venustiano Carranza that Germany was about to resume unrestricted submarine warfare. In the event that war with the United States ensued, Germany promised to assist Mexico "to regain by conquest her lost territory in Texas, Arizona, and New Mexico."

While this promise in all likelihood was merely the usual wartime diplomatic maneuvering, it was just the catalyst needed to put America into the war. The sensational telegram was intercepted by British cryptographers, who spent days deciphering the document before it was given to the American ambassador on February 25. It was made public on March 1 and initially was greeted with great skepticism.

Former senator Elihu Root—who later became honorary president of the CFR—and other New York elitists meeting at the Round Table Dining Club, forerunner of the Council on Foreign Relations, couldn't believe their good fortune. Former U.S. ambassador to England Joseph H. Choate, "as warm an Anglophile as any in America . . . openly said that the Zimmermann note was a forgery and was practically unanimously supported by the whole bunch," reported author Tuchman.

But questions regarding the authenticity of the telegram were laid to rest on March 3 at a Berlin news conference. Here a Hearst news correspondent, who later turned out to be a German agent, gave Zimmermann every chance to deny the telegram. "Of course Your Excellency will deny this story," urged the correspondent. Zimmermann then inexplicably announced "I cannot deny it. It is true."

This simple confession produced the desired effect in America. Newspaper editorials railed against the "Hun," and public pressure for war against the German Kaiser grew irresistible. Wilson, who had fought so long and hard for a negotiated peace with himself as leader of a "league" of nations, was forced to declare war on April 6, 1917. Eight days later, money began to flow when passage of the War Loan Act authorized $1 billion in credit to the empty banks of the Allies.

While the Zimmermann telegram apparently was authentic, no one will ever know why something so audacious was produced or why it was acknowledged once discovered.

World War I cost 323,000 American casualties, a pittance compared to 9 million Russians, 6 million Frenchmen, and 3 million British. The war also effectively ended any meaningful gold standard for money, although several nations tried to return to it in the 1920s.

Not only did the total expenditure of the United States for the war years rise to an unprecedented $35 trillion, but the fiat money supply—paper backed only by government edict—nearly doubled from $20.6 to $39.8 billion, which caused the purchasing power of the dollar to drop by almost 50 percent. Tremendous amounts of debt were created, while only those who collected the interest benefited. As always, it was the American public that suffered the real losses in dead relatives, devalued money, and enduring foreign commitments.

The entry of America and the withdrawal of Russia following revolution guaranteed victory for the Allies in World War I. Hostilities were ended by the Treaty of Versailles, signed by the belligerent nations on June 28, 1919. Attending was Paul Warburg, who as chairman of the Federal Reserve System represented American banking interests, and his brother Max Warburg, who represented the German central bank, his own M. M. Warburg and Company, and who reportedly was involved with German Intelligence during the war.

President Wilson, who grew up in the South under the harsh Reconstruction policies of the Republicans, knew firsthand the long-term misery and devastation caused by war. It seems clear that his attempt to keep America out of the European war was based on a sincere personal conviction. It is equally clear that this noble impulse was subverted at every turn by schemers in England and by his own advisers.

Perhaps the most tragic aspect of the "war to end all wars" was that it didn't settle much of anything. The harsh terms of Versailles only prompted resentment in Germany and paved the way for Hitler. All sides soon began to rebuild and rearm, enriching lenders by ever greater spending and borrowing.

British foreign secretary Lord George Nathaniel Curzon, another delegate, said he felt the treaty only set the stage for more war and even predicted the date. "This is no peace; this is only a truce for twenty years," he stated at the 1919 Versailles conference. His comment—or was it informed prophecy?—generated much comment among conspiracy researchers since World War II indeed began in 1939, exactly twenty years later.

Curzon may have known precisely what he was talking about, as he had attended both Oxford and All Souls College, the home ground of Cecil Rhodes and John Ruskin. Following his marriage to the daughter of a Chicago millionaire, he became leader of the House of Lords in 1915 and was a member of the inner cabinet that dictated the policies of World War I.

Marriage, it seems, played an important role in connecting these early secret society members together. "Money Barons such as the Rockefellers of National City Bank and Chase Bank, J. P. Morgan of Morgan and Company, Jacob Schiff of Kuhn, Loeb Company and, most important, the brothers Warburg . . . tied the plot into a neat knot with Paul marrying

Schiff's daughter, Felix [Warburg] marrying Loeb's daughter, and Max staying home in Germany where he could influence the Kaiser and help finance the Russian Revolution," noted Neal Wilgus in his nonfiction book *The Illuminoids*.

THE RUSSIAN REVOLUTION

There indeed exists a wealth of documentation indicating that the Russian Revolution—indeed the very creation of Communism—sprang from Western conspiracies beginning even before World War I.

"One of the greatest myths of contemporary history is that the Bolshevik Revolution in Russia was a popular uprising of the downtrodden masses against the hated ruling class of the Czars," wrote author Griffin, who claimed that both planning and funding for the revolution came from financiers in Germany, Britain, and the United States.

In January 1917 Leon Trotsky was living in New York City working as a reporter for *The New World*, a communist newspaper. Trotsky had escaped an earlier failed attempt at revolution in Russia and fled to France, where he was expelled for his revolutionary behavior. "He soon discovered that there were wealthy Wall Street bankers who were willing to finance a revolution in Russia," wrote journalist Still.

One of these bankers was Jacob Schiff, whose family had lived with the Rothschilds in Frankfurt. Another was Elihu Root, attorney for Paul Warburg's Kuhn, Loeb & Company. According to the *New York Journal-American*, "It is estimated by Jacob's grandson, John Schiff, that the old man sank about $20 million for the final triumph of Bolshevism in Russia." Root, a CFR member, contributed yet another $20 million, according to the Congressional Record of September 2, 1919.

Schiff and Root were not alone. Arsene de Goulevitch, who was present during the early days of the Bolsheviks, later wrote, "In private interviews, I have been told that over 21 million roubles were spent by Lord Milner in financing the Russian Revolution." Recall that it was Alfred Milner who was the primary force behind Rhodes's Round Tables, that grand ancestor of the modern secret societies.

"In 1915, the American International Corporation was formed to fund the Russian Revolution," wrote Icke. "Its directors represented the interests of the Rockefeller, Rothschilds, Du Pont, Kuhn, Loeb, Harriman, and the Federal Reserve. They included Frank Vanderlip (one of the Jekyll Island group which created the Federal Reserve) and George Herbert Walker, the grandfather of President George Bush."

Gary Allen noted, "In the Bolshevik Revolution we have some of the world's richest and most powerful men financing a movement which claims its very existence is based on the concept of stripping of their wealth men like the Rothschilds, Rockefellers, Schiffs, Warburgs, Morgans, Harrimans and Milners. But obviously these men have no fear of international communism. It is only logical to assume that if they financed it and do not fear it, it must be because they control it. Can there be any other explanation that makes sense?"

This conspiratorial view was echoed by none other than Winston Churchill, who in 1920 wrote, "From the days of Spartacus-Weishaupt [head of the mysterious Illuminati] to those of Karl Marx, to those of [socialists Leon] Trotsky, Béla Kun, Rosa Luxemburg, and Emma Goldman, this worldwide conspiracy for the overthrow of civilization . . . has been steadily growing.

"It played a definitely recognizable role in the tragedy of the French Revolution. It has been the mainspring of every subversive movement during the nineteenth century, and now at last this band of extraordinary personalities from the underworld of the great cities of Europe and America have gripped the Russian people by the hair of their heads, and have become practically the undisputed masters of that enormous empire."

If there can be identified one single motivating factor behind the horror and tragedy experienced in the twentieth century, it is surely anti-Communism. The animosity between the so-called democracies of the West and the Communism of the East produced continuous turmoil from 1918 through the end of the century.

The flight of the privileged elite from Russia in 1918 and from China in 1949 sent shock waves through the capitals of Europe and America and prompted a backlash that lasted for decades. The cry of "Workers of the world unite!" struck fear in the capitalists of Western industry, banking, and commerce who were not in the know. This fear trickled through their political representatives, employees, and on into virtually every home.

Mystified conspiracy researchers for years were puzzled how such high-level capitalists as the Morgans, Warburgs, Schiffs, and Rockefellers could condone, much less support, an ideology which overtly threatened their position and wealth.

To understand this seeming dichotomy, indeed to understand how the secret society members operate, one must study the philosopher who influenced these men through Rhodes and Ruskin, Georg Wilhelm Friedrich Hegel.

Coming on the heels of the Age of Reason—the intellectual revolt against the authority of the church—German philosophers Hegel, Johann Gottlieb Fichte, and Immanuel Kant inspired future generations with the idea that modern man need not be chained by religious dogma and tradition. These iconoclasts differed only in that Kant believed that things which cannot be experienced in the material world cannot be known to man, while the metaphysical Fichte and Hegel believed that man's reason is "the candle of the Lord," that intuition and love create a unity of man with the Divine which brings understanding and equality.

Hegel's claim to the rational interpretation of the human essence, termed the Hegelian System, was an attempt to reconcile opposites, to comprehend the entire universe as a systematic whole. It was a mind-boggling effort and has not yet been fully completed. Adherents and opponents of Hegel will continue to philosophize well into the coming millennium. It is easy to understand why such abstract thinking has been interpreted in so many ways by Hegel's followers, including Karl Marx and Hitler.

Hegel's fellow idealist and the man who most influenced his work, Fichte, was a member of secret societies. "It is interesting that Fichte, who developed these ideas before Hegel, was a Freemason, almost certainly Illuminati, and certainly was promoted by the Illuminati," wrote author Sutton. It has even been suggested that Hegel himself may have been a member of the revolutionary German Illuminati lodge outlawed by the government in 1784, though no conclusive documentation has been found. He certainly espoused the Freemason theology of rationalism.

Marx turned Hegel's theoretical philosophy to the material world and developed an exceptional tool for manipulating people and events. This has become known as the Hegelian dialectic, the process in which opposites—thesis and antithesis—are reconciled in compromise or synthesis.

The application relevant here is the idea that Western capitalists created Communism on one side (thesis) as a perceived enemy to the democratic nations (antithesis) on the other side. The ensuing conflict produced huge markets for finance and armaments and eventually a leveling of both sides (synthesis). Often during the past fifty years it was said, the U.S. is getting more like Russia, and they are getting more like the U.S.

The members of secret societies traceable to Rhodes's Round Tables understood the Hegelian dialectic well. Their predecessors had successfully used it for centuries without the name of Hegel. These early-day Machiavellis had found it was but a small step to the realization that one needn't wait for crisis and turmoil. Social upheaval could be created and controlled to their own benefit. Hence came the cycles of financial booms and busts, crises and revolutions, wars and threats of war, all of which maintained a balance of power.

Social activists and bureaucrats alike have learned this both-ends-against-the-middle stratagem well, whether by experience, intuition, or study. Demand more than you really need (thesis) from your opposition (antithesis) and, after compromises, you'll usually end up with what you wanted in the first place (synthesis).

"This revolutionary method—the systematic working of thesis vs. antithesis = synthesis—is the key to understanding world history," declared conspiracy author Texe Marrs.

Returning to Trotsky, we find he left the United States by ship on March 27, 1917—just days before America entered the war—along with nearly three hundred revolutionaries and funds provided by Wall Street. Trotsky, whose real name was Lev Davidovich Bronstein, was being trailed by British agents who suspected him of working with German Intelligence since his stay in prewar Vienna. In a speech before leaving New York, Trotsky stated, "I am going back to Russia to overthrow the provisional government and stop the war with Germany."

When the ship carrying Trotsky and his entourage stopped in Halifax, Nova Scotia, they and their funds were impounded by Canadian authorities, who rightly feared that a revolution in Russia might free German troops to fight Allied soldiers on the Western Front.

But this well-grounded concern was overcome by President Wilson's alter ego, Colonel House, who told the chief of the British Secret Service, Sir William Wiseman, that Wilson wanted Trotsky released. On April 21, 1917, less than a month after the United States entered the war, the British Admiralty ordered the release of Trotsky, who, armed with an American passport authorized by Wilson, continued on his journey to Russia and history.

After an abortive revolution in 1905, thousands of Russian activists had been exiled, including Trotsky and Vladimir Ilyich Lenin, a revolutionary intellectual who adapted the theories of Hegel, Fichte, Ruskin, and Marx to Russia's political and economic predicament. After years of attempts at reform, the czar was forced to abdicate on March 15, 1917, following riots in Saint Petersburg (then Petrograd) believed by many to have been instigated by British agents.

As Trotsky traveled to Russia with an American passport and Wall Street funding, Lenin also left exile. Aided by the Germans and accompanied by about 150 trained revolutionaries, "[He] was put on the infamous 'sealed train' in Switzerland along with at least $5 million," wrote Still. The train passed through Germany unhindered, as arranged by Max Warburg and the German High Command. Lenin, like Trotsky, was labeled a German agent by the government of Aleksandr Kerensky, the second of provisional governments created following the czar's abdication. By November 1917 Lenin and Trotsky, backed by Western funds, had instigated a successful revolt and seized the Russian government for the Bolsheviks.

But the communist grip on Russia was not secure. Internal strife between the "Reds" and the "Whites" lasted until 1922 and cost some twenty-eight million Russian lives, many times the war loss. Lenin died in 1924 from a series of strokes after helping form the Third International or Comintern, an organization to export Communism worldwide. Trotsky fled Russia when Stalin took dictatorial control and in 1940 was murdered in Mexico by a Stalinist agent.

Author Icke saw a "multidimensional" aspect to the funding of the Bolsheviks. "The Russian 'revolutionaries' such as Lenin and Trotsky were being used to get Russia out of the war, to the benefit of Germany. But at the Elite level, the bogeyman called Communism was being created to stimulate the division of fear and mistrust presented as communism vs. capitalism vs. fascism."

Even Lenin apparently came to understand that he was being manipulated by more powerful forces. "The state does not function as we desired," he wrote. "A man is at the wheel and seems to lead it, but the car does not drive in the desired direction. It moves as another force wishes."

This other "force" were the members of the secret societies that were behind the birth of Communism itself, "monopoly finance capitalists" as Lenin described them.

THE RISE OF COMMUNISM

Many varied secret societies were involved in the movement which eventually led to Communism. One of the earliest may have been the *Carbonari*, or charcoal burners, of Italy of the Middle Ages. According to author Arkon Daraul, the *Carbonari* claimed to have begun in Scotland where they lived a free and communal life in the wild forests burning wood to make charcoal. They created a government consisting of three *vendite*, or lodges, for administration, legislation, and judicial matters. The lodges were ruled by a High Lodge led by a Grand Master, who headed a form of primitive Masonry.

"Under the pretense of carrying their charcoal for sale, they introduced themselves into the villages, and bearing the name of real *Carbonari* they easily met their supporters and communicated their mutual plans," wrote Daraul. "They made themselves known to each other by signs, touches and words." The anticleric doctrine of the *Carbonari,* which became known as "forest Masonry," spread widely after initiating the French king, Francis I. At one point members so filled Italy, they nearly dominated the country.

"In the early 1820s, they were more than just a power in the land," wrote Daraul. "[They] boasted branches and sub-societies as far afield as Poland, France and Germany."

He added, "The Bolsheviks and their theoreticians of the Communist persuasion are traced by many as offspring of the Charcoal-burners. . . ."

The antiauthoritarian socialism of the *Carbonari,* Illuminated Freemasonry, and other rationalist and humanist groups that grew during the Age of Enlightenment coalesced during the early nineteenth century, greatly aggravating the Roman Catholic church.

"In our day, if Masonry does not found Jacobite or other clubs, it originates and cherishes movements fully as satanic and as dangerous. Communism, just like Carbonism, is but a form of the illuminated Masonry of [Illuminati founder] Weishaupt," warned Monsignor George Dillon in 1885.

One such movement was the International Working Men's Association—better known as the First International—the direct forerunner to Communism, convened in London in 1864 and soon under the leadership of Karl Marx.

Marx was born in 1818 in Trier, Germany, to Heinrich and Henrietta Marx, both descended from a long line of Jewish rabbis and hence undoubtedly familiar with the mystical traditions of the Torah and Cabala. To deter anti-Semitism, both Karl and his father were baptized in the Evangelical Established church. And both were greatly influenced by the humanism of the Age of Enlightenment.

Following his graduation from the University of Bonn, Marx enrolled in the University of Berlin in 1836 where he joined a secret society called the Doctor Club filled with devotees of Hegel and his philosophy. Although he had earlier expressed devout Christian ideals, Marx joined these Hegelians in moving from a belief that the Christian Gospels were "human fantasies arising from emotional needs" to outright atheism.

Some modern conspiracy writers even claim that Marx eventually became a Satanist. They point to his eventual criticism of Hegel as not material enough in his thinking, the antisocial societies in which he moved, and a work written by Marx as a student which stated, "If there is a Something which devours, I'll leap within it, though I bring the world to ruins . . . that would be really living." Again the metaphysical views of both Marx and his detractors cannot be ignored.

In 1843 Marx married and moved to Paris, a hotbed of socialism and extremist groups known as communists. It was in Paris that Marx befriended Friedrich Engels, scion of a well-to-do English textile mill owner. Marx and Engels both became confirmed communists and collaborated in writing a number of revolutionary pamphlets and books, the most famous being three volumes discussing capital, *Das Kapital*. Ironically, it was Engels—the capitalist's son—who would financially subsidize Marx—the champion of the working class—most of his life.

Engels, also a devoted Hegelian, had been converted to socialist humanism by Moses Hess, called the "communist rabbi," and by Robert Owen, a utopian socialist and spiritualist openly hostile to traditional religion.

Marx and Engels eventually moved to Brussels and then on to London, where in 1847 they joined another secret society called the League of the Just, composed primarily of German emigrants, many of whom were thought to be escaped members of the outlawed Illuminati.

The group soon changed its name to the Communist League and Marx along with Engels produced its famous proclamation, *The Communist Manifesto*.

Marx's manifesto set forth the ten immediate steps to create an ideal communist state. They bear a striking resemblance to the *Protocols of the Learned Elders of Zion*, suggesting some common origin. These steps include:

—abolition of private property
—a progressive or graduated income tax
—abolition of all inheritance
—confiscation of all property of dissidents and emigrants
—creation of a monopolistic central bank with state capital to control credit
—centralization of all communication and transport
—state control over factories and farm production
—state ownership of all capital and the creation of a deployable labor force
—combining agriculture with manufacturing industries and the gradual distribution of the population to blur the distinction between towns and rural country
—free public education to all children

This list was also remarkably similar to the steps for creating the ideal society proposed by the Bavarian Illuminati, strongly indicating a close connection between the two. "In fact, the Internationale can hardly be viewed as anything but Illuminated Masonry in a new disguise," commented author Still.

In 1848 Marx failed to incite a socialist revolution in Prussia and, after evading prison, returned to London. Personality clashes, petty bickering, and fractious fights over ideology prevented the Communist League from becoming an effective force. Militant factions chided Marx for being more concerned with speeches than revolutions, and he gradually withdrew into isolation which only ended with his attendance at the 1864 First International.

Marx's life of struggle and poverty made a tremendous impact on world history by providing a philosophical platform for the modern secret societies based on the tenets of the older ones. He died of apparent lung abscesses on March 14, 1883, depressed over the suicides of his two daughters and just two months after the death of his wife.

It is clear that Communism did not spring spontaneously from poor, downtrodden masses of workers, but was the result of long-range schemes and intrigues by secret societies. "There is no proletarian, not even Communist, movement that has not operated in the interests of money . . . and without the idealists among its leaders having the slightest suspicion of the fact," wrote German philosopher Oswald Spengler, author of *The Decline of the West*.

COMMENTARY

The imprint of the secret societies can be found in every war and conflict of the twentieth century.

The historic record is unmistakable. The same society members turn up in every instance—passing from father to son, business partner to close associate, fraternity brother to brother. It would seem, based on the public's demonstrated antipathy toward war, that occasionally there would be governmental house cleaning, a complete changeover of leadership and officials. Yet the same old secret society faces keep returning to power, as noted by President Kennedy. The mass media appears unconcerned and the public is asked to believe that this is all sheer coincidence—simply a case of the most competent man for the job.

The Report from Iron Mountain, whether provable as historic fact or not, accurately reflects the thinking of secret society members. For example, in a 1981 interview concerning overpopulation, CFR member Maxwell Taylor blithely stated, "I have already written off more than a billion people. These people are in places in Africa, Asia, Latin America. We can't save them. The population crisis and the food-supply question dictate that we should not even try. It's a waste of time."

While some conflicts arguably were necessary—such as World War II—others like Vietnam and the Gulf War appear less so. Yet all were immensely profitable to secret society members and all advanced their goal of one-world government.

The Royal Institute of International Affairs and the CFR made plans for a conflict in Southeast Asia as far back as 1951. The creation of the Southeast Asia Treaty Organization in 1954 was a calculated scheme to provide U.S. officials a legal basis for intervention in Vietnam. President Kennedy, who was assassinated before he could withdraw troops, had been at increasing odds with secret society members on Wall Street, several of whom passed judgment on his death as members of the Warren Commission.

President Johnson and his CFR advisers were deceitful in their maneuvering to obtain unconstitutional war powers from Congress following the phony "Gulf of Tonkin" incident in 1964. These same advisers continued to support that war until it became apparent that the costs—both in lives, money, and national unity—were becoming greater than the profits, at which time they turned against Johnson.

Korea was a prototype conflict to judge how the American public would react to a winless United Nations "police action." It set the precedent of American GIs fighting outside the United States under foreign commanders, an activity which continues today. Ironically, ranking Russian officials commanded the North Koreans on one side and the United Nations troops on the other.

World War II was fought to stop fascists in Germany, Italy, and Japan, who had been created and financed by secret society members in the West. Despite the deadly nature of this war, American and British society members continued to do business with the enemy and then arranged their reconstruction afterward. Nowhere was this duplicity more evident than in President Roosevelt's failure to alert American troops at Pearl Harbor of the impending Japanese attack brought on by his own containment policies.

Hitler, that great scourge of the twentieth century, was clearly a creation of both secret societies and their Western financiers. Explanations for this extraordinary circumstance range from the desire to create a balance of power with Communism to the extraordinary possibility that Hitler was directly related to the Viennese Rothschilds. His Nazis were more a cult than a political party and reflected both the esoteric knowledge and obsessions of elder European secret societies which can be traced back to the Ancient Mysteries.

These societies had been active during World War I and the Russian Revolution, which was directly encouraged and financed by American and British secret society members. The goals of the Russian communists and Karl Marx were largely the same goals of the Illuminati and continental Freemasonry. It was all a real-world model of the theory of Hegel, who saw one side of a conflict (thesis) pitted against the other (antithesis) created a compromise (synthesis). This formula—with the added element of actually creating the conflict—has been used success-fully by the students of Hegel, which include the Illuminati, Cecil Rhodes, Hitler, and members of the modern secret societies.

It is evident that, to whatever degree, individuals connected by blood, titles, marriage, or membership in secret societies have manipu-lated and controlled the destinies of entire nations through the fomen-tation and funding of war. These people consider themselves above the morality and ethics of the average man. They obviously look to some higher purpose—whether that be sheer wealth and power or perhaps some hidden agenda concerning mankind's origin, destiny, and spiritu-ality.

Even as Marx, Engels, and their followers were creating Commu-nism in London during the mid-nineteenth century, the long-standing plans of the Illuminati and its descendent societies to foment internal strife within the United States were being brought to fruition in a great rebellion.

PART III

REBELLION AND REVOLUTION

It was not my intention to doubt that the doctrines of the Illuminati, and the principles of Jacobinism, had not spread in the United States. On the contrary, no one is more fully satisfied of this fact than I am.

—PRESIDENT GEORGE WASHINGTON IN AN 1782 LETTER

The stability of both America's finances and her people in the early nineteenth century must have been a source of great irritation to the wealthy schemers of Europe's secret societies, even then in the process of changing their focus from ecclesiastical control to debt manipulation.

Russia was under the tyranny of the czar, who had steadfastly refused to create a central bank. Western Europe was financially drained following the French Revolution and the Napoleonic Wars. And since no loans meant no profits, European bankers looked to the Americas for new revenue.

Following the War of 1812, also called the Second War for American Independence, the United States was in extremely enviable circumstances: It had defeated the British empire, and its borders with the less-populated countries of Mexico and Canada were secure.

As previously noted, President Andrew Jackson had put an end to repeated attempts at creating a central bank, and by 1835 he had even paid off the national debt. The next year, he halted inflation caused by land speculation by ordering that public lands be sold only for gold or silver.

The lure of America must have been irresistible. However, President James Madison in 1823 had warned off all European intervention and exploitation in the Americas by issuing the Monroe Doctrine. To thwart this policy, a slow and stealthy infiltration process by foreigners was needed, and it may have begun as far back as 1837, the year of Jackson's retirement. In that year a German-born representative of the Rothschild banking empire arrived in the United States and changed his name from August Schoenberg to August Belmont. According to a sympathetic Rothschild biography, Belmont was actually dispatched to Cuba by Amshel Rothschild and his son but took it upon himself to go to New York instead. He was even rumored to be an illegitimate Rothschild himself. Whatever the truth, Belmont was in daily correspondence with the Rothschilds and became their acknowledged representative in the U.S.

With no apparent capital of his own, Belmont soon was buying up government bonds, and within a few short years had created one of the largest banking firms in the nation, August Belmont & Company. Because of his known ties to the family, the firm has always been considered by conspiracy researchers as a Rothschild enterprise.

At the outbreak of the Mexican War in 1846, it was Belmont who bought the greater portion of U.S. government bonds. Thanks to his aggressive business tactics, the Rothschilds soon had investments in American industry, banks, railroads, federal and state bonds, tobacco, cotton, and, of course, gold. Belmont was instrumental in later financing both North and South during the Rebellion which began in 1861.

From 1853 to 1857, due in part to substantial donations to the Democratic Party, Belmont represented the United States at the Hague, the seat of government for the Netherlands. He also insinuated himself into American society by marrying the daughter of the famous U.S. Naval Commodore Matthew Perry, hero of the Mexican War and Tokyo Bay. An avid equestrian, Belmont introduced Thoroughbred horse racing to the United States and served as president of the American Jockey Club.

In 1849 Alphonse Rothschild traveled to New York to determine if the family should replace their agent Belmont with a permanent banking firm. Rothschild was impressed with the obvious opportunities in America and wrote to his brothers that a bank should be established, adding, "Without the slightest doubt, this is the cradle of a new civilization."

Yet, despite the obvious opportunity, the Rothschilds apparently made the mistake of not making a major investment in the United States—at least not openly.

"Had they established a bank in New York at this early stage in the nation's growth, there can be little doubt that the wealth derived from that one source would have dwarfed, within a generation, all that they had amassed so far in Europe," wrote Rothschild biographer Derek Wilson. "It is difficult to understand why James and Lionel [Rothschild] ignored Alphonse's powerful advocacy."

It was indeed difficult to understand from a straightforward business viewpoint, but this decision might make eminently good sense when seen from the conspiratorial view of history.

First there is the long-standing allegation that the Rothschilds, due to both anti-Semitism and suspicion of Europeans by Americans, decided to exercise their power through intermediaries such as Belmont, the Rocke-fellers, Morgans, and others. And there is now abundant evidence that the bankers of Europe were already conspiring to destroy the economically strong, but politically fragile, American union.

WAR BETWEEN THE STATES

Author Epperson reported that an authorized biography of the Roth-schilds mentioned a London meeting where the "International Banking Syndicate" decided to pit the American North against the South in a "divide and conquer" strategy. Such a plan would provide the solvent U.S. federal government with an enemy that would require massive war expenditures and subsequent debt.

And in the event of Southern independence, "each state could with-draw from the confederation, re-establish its sovereign nature and set up its own central bank. The Southern states could then have a series of European-controlled banks, the Bank of Georgia, the Bank of South Car-olina, etc., and then any two could have a series of wars, such as in Europe for centuries, in the perpetual game of Balance of Power politics. It would be a successful method of insuring that large profits could be made on the loaning of money to the states involved," Epperson explained.

Griffin quoted German chancellor Otto von Bismarck as stating, "The division of the United States into federations of equal force was decided long before the Civil War by the high financial powers of Europe. These bankers were afraid that the United States, if they remained in one block and as one nation, would attain economic and financial independence, which would upset their financial domination over the world. The voice of the Rothschilds prevailed. . . . Therefore they sent their emissaries into the field to exploit the question of slavery and to open an abyss between the two sections of the Union."

It is historical fact that for some years the Rothschilds had financed major projects in the United States on both sides of the Mason-Dixon Line. Nathan Rothschild, who owned a large Manchester textile plant, bought his cotton from Southern interests and financed the importation of Southern cotton prior to the war. At the same time, wrote Rothschild biographer Wilson, "He had made loans to various states of the Union, had been, for a time, the official European banker for the U.S. government and was a pledged supporter of the Bank of the United States."

"Europe's aristocracies had never been happy about the prodigious success of the Yankee democracy. If the nation now broke into halves, proving that democracy did not contain the stuff of survival, the rulers of Europe would be well pleased," noted historian Bruce Catton. Lending support to the idea of European manipulation of the American situation, another Rothschild biographer, Niall Ferguson, noted there is a "substantial and unexplained gap" in private Rothschild correspondence between 1854 and 1860 and that nearly all copies of outgoing letters from the London Rothschilds "were destroyed at the orders of successive senior partners."

If this indeed was the gambit, presidential aspirant Abraham Lincoln saw it clearly. He often tried to explain that his goal was to save the American union, not emancipate the slaves. During his famous debates with Stephen Douglas in 1858, Lincoln made his personal position on race quite clear: "I will say, then, that I am not, nor ever have been, in favor of bringing about in any way, the social and political equality of the white and black races. . . . I, as much as any other man, am in favor of having the superior position assigned to the white race."

But equally clear was Lincoln's determination to preserve the federal union. In late 1862 he proclaimed, "My paramount object in this struggle is to save the union. . . . If I could save the union without freeing any slaves, I would do it; if I could save it by freeing some and leaving others alone, I would also do that."

Lincoln understood that the true reason for sectional friction in the United States was not slavery, but economics. The South desired to buy cheaper imported European products, but the powerful Northern manufacturers imposed stiff import tariffs. These tariffs were quickly increased after Southern congressmen left Washington in 1861. The industrial North, filling rapidly with immigrants willing to work for a pittance, had no need for slaves, while the major planters of the agrarian South were totally dependent on human labor. Although Southern leaders had continually demonstrated a willingness to compromise on the slavery issue, they felt they could not suddenly abandon their "peculiar institution."

Antislavery advocates in both North and South realized that technological advances meant the demise of slavery was only a matter of time.

But extremists on both sides, encouraged by agents of the European financiers, continually fanned the fires of discontent.

The spearhead of this agitation came in the form of yet another secret society: the Knights of the Golden Circle (KGC).

SECRET SOCIETY AGITATION

The secretive Knights organization was the creation of surgeon and author Dr. George W. L. Bickley, who in 1854 founded his first knightly "castle" in Cincinnati, Ohio, drawing heavily from local Freemasons. This society "had close ties with a secret society in France called The Seasons, which itself was a branch of the Illuminati," charged G. Edward Griffin.

Patterned after Masonic lodges, the Knights had similar passwords, handshakes, "temples," and grand, lesser, and supreme councils. Initiates were sworn to secrecy with a live snake held over their head accompanied by this bloodcurdling oath:

> Whoever dares our cause reveal,
> Shall test the strength of Knightly steel;
> And when the torture proves too dull,
> We'll scrape the brains from out his skull
> And place a lamp within the shell
> To light his soul from here to hell.

The name Knights of the Golden Circle was derived from Bickley's grandiose plan to create a huge slaveholding circular empire 2,400 miles in circumference with Cuba as the center point. This new nation was to include the southern United States, Mexico, part of Central America, and the West Indies in order to gain a dominance over the world's supply of tobacco, sugar, rice, and coffee.

While modern historians either ignore or downplay the significance of the KGC, it is evident from contemporary writings and newspaper coverage that the organization was considered an extremely credible threat at the time. Bickley was certainly a mysterious individual, always claiming to be in need of money, yet constantly traveling and entertaining dignitaries.

The "financial nucleus" of his order was the American Colonization and Steamship Company, organized in Veracruz, Mexico, and capitalized for $5 million. Somebody other than Bickley was paying the bills.

He also had demonstrable ties to Great Britain, claiming to have been an 1842 graduate of the University of London. Early in the war Bickley was in the Confederate capital of Montgomery, Alabama, identifying himself as a correspondent for the London *Times,* and after the war he lectured extensively in England.

Bickley appeared to have shifting allegiances and philosophies. Previously, he had founded a society called the Wayne Circle of the Brotherhood of the Union, which purported to seek constitutional unity. Just before the war started, Bickley wrote an article for his Cincinnati paper *Scientific Artisan* in which he predicted the end of slavery, stating "this institution is one altogether unenviable, [as] every reasonable man in America will at once admit."

Despite the ideas put forth in his article, the first step in Bickley's plans for the Knights of the Golden Circle was to create a separate slaveholding Southern nation, then move southward to Mexico. Like the Nazis much later, the KGC were concerned with purity of blood, as demonstrated by his call for "Anglo-Saxon blood" for the "Texasizing" of the Mexican population.

By 1860 there were more than fifty thousand Knights, mostly in Texas, awaiting orders to march on Mexico. Headquartered in San Antonio, Bickley gained popularity by pledging to "kill Wall Street" bankers, who he said were scheming against the South. He also said that if Lincoln was elected president, "Washington, not Mexico, would become the target" of the Knights.

In fact there were two tentative invasions of Mexico in the spring of 1860, but both were repulsed after Bickley failed to provide his men with promised reinforcements and supplies.

Texas hero and governor Sam Houston reportedly was a member of the Knights at the time but resigned when the Knights turned their attention from the invasion of Mexico to the secessionist movement.

It was in the cause of Southern secession that Bickley proved more successful, as the KGC came to form the nucleus of the Southern military. According to writer Ollinger Crenshaw, "The Southern press received the plans of the order with enthusiasm and many newspapers became its exponents. . . . The Vicksburg *Sun* said the Knights of the Golden Circle gave the South a military organization capable of defending her rights at home and abroad."

The KGC was divided into three sections or "degrees"—the "Foreign and Home Guard Militia," the "Foreign and Home Guard Corps" of civilian support, and the "American Legion" which was the political and governing arm. Reportedly, by 1860 membership in the KGC was more than sixty-five thousand and constituted the "brains" of the South. Bickley made their objective clear when he declared, "The fact is, we want a fight, but how to get it is the question."

Through constant agitation, the Knights stirred up hatreds and fears throughout the North and South. "After Abraham Lincoln was elected in 1860, this minority of the Southern minority conspired to bring off a last gamble. In 1861, to the extremists' amazement, disunion triumphed," wrote historian William W. Freehling.

KGC activity in Northern states involved a plan to create a "Northwest Confederacy" composed of pro-Southerners in several states, including Ohio, Indiana, Minnesota, and Michigan. Illinois alone was reported to have a KGC membership of some twenty thousand. The plan was to seize federal arsenals, then take control of the states and release all Confederate prisoners. One state official, Edmund Wright, tried to opposed the Knights, only to have his wife poisoned and his home burned. In August 1862 sixty KGC members—out of a reported fifteen thousand members in Indiana—were indicted for conspiracy and treason but later released. Federal prosecutors were fearful of creating martyrs and the conspiracy cases were weak.

The Knights' actions created havoc with the national government, prompting President Lincoln to lament, "The enemy behind us is more dangerous to the country than the enemy before us."

The Lincoln administration was compelled to imprison more than thirteen thousand people on charges of "disloyalty," which meant anything from speaking against the government to discouraging military enlistment. "Those who before the war had been called 'the loyal opposition' found themselves after 1861 commonly referred to as traitors," wrote author Larry Starkey.

Such repression incensed Democrats and anti-Republicans, who charged federal officials with exaggerating the KGC threat in order to suppress criticism of the administration. Membership in the Knights' organization and its spin-offs, the Order of American Knights and the

Sons of Liberty, grew to number in the hundreds of thousands. According to Griffin, the Knights went underground after the war, eventually emerging as the Ku Klux Klan.

In 1863 Bickley was arrested as a spy in Indiana and held without trial until his release in 1865. A broken man, Bickley died in Baltimore on August 10, 1867.

With national attention focused on the Southern Rebellion and disunity in the North, far-reaching financial measures were being taken in Washington.

In mid-1861, with the war just beginning, U.S. Treasury secretary Salmon Chase (the namesake of Chase Manhattan Bank) asked for and received from Congress the first income tax instituted in America. It began as a meager three percent federal tax on all income, but only a year later the tax was raised to five percent on all income over $10,000. "It was a graduated income tax, just as proposed by Karl Marx just 13 years before," noted Epperson, intimating that hidden agendas were being pressed behind the contingencies of war.

As the war progressed, Lincoln desperately needed more money. Instead of borrowing from the European banks as expected, in 1862 he issued about $450 million in currency printed with green ink called "greenbacks." This paper money was legalized by an act of Congress with nothing to secure it. Endorsing this debt-free, fiat money, Lincoln proclaimed, "Government, possessing power to create and issue currency . . . need not and should not borrow capital at interest. . . . The privilege of creating and issuing money is not only the supreme prerogative of the government but it is the government's greatest creative opportunity."

It is fascinating to note that the two U.S. presidents who have issued debt-free currency—Lincoln in 1862 and John F. Kennedy in 1963—were assassinated. Lincoln's assassin, Southern sympathizer John Wilkes Booth, has been established as a member of the Knights of the Golden Circle (along with the famous outlaw Jesse James). Various conspiracy researchers have connected Booth to the previously mentioned Illuminati, the Italian *Carbonari,* and through Southern secretary of state Judah Benjamin to the House of Rothschild. After the war, Benjamin, often called the "sinister power behind the throne" of Southern president Jefferson Davis, fled to England where he became a successful attorney.

As in the Kennedy assassination, Lincoln's death sparked cries of conspiracy which still echo today. The Lincoln assassination conspiracy involved several persons, four of whom were hanged, including Mary Surratt, the first woman executed in this country for a capital offense. It is historic fact that the Lincoln assassination case was a complex plot including smuggling and kidnapping plans that involved Knights of the Golden Circle agents. "The fact remains that the story of why Abraham Lincoln was murdered can only be completed within the confines of the Confederate cabal in Canada [which included KGC members as well as British agents] . . . " noted author Starkey. The plot also involved some of the highest offices in Washington, including Lincoln's secretary of war Edwin Stanton. The full story of this plot has yet to reach a wide audience.

Despite pervasive use of the term, the conflict between 1861 and 1865 was never truly a civil war, which is defined as a conflict between factions or sections within a nation. The majority of citizens in each Southern state freely elected to leave the Union. Confederate President Davis, a former United States senator and secretary of war, in his inaugural address on February 18, 1861, cited "the American idea that governments rest on the consent of the governed, and that it is the right of the people to alter or abolish them at will whenever they become destructive of the ends for which they were established. . . . Thus the sovereign states here represented have proceeded to form this Confederacy; and it is by abuse of language that their act has been denominated a revolution."

"Secession—or rebellion, as the Jacobins preferred to call it—might be treason, but no court had ever said so—or ever would say so—no matter what the opinion the radicals had on the matter," observed historian Shelby Foote.

But Lincoln and the radical Republicans did proclaim that secession was treason and prepared huge armies and a naval blockade to force the Southern states back into the Union. And while twenty-two million Northerners were locked in strife with nine million Southerners, France and Britain made moves to encircle the conflicted nation.

With regimental bands playing "Dixie," Britain sent eleven thousand additional troops to Canada, which had become a haven for Confederate agents. France's Napoléon III installed Austrian Archduke Maximilian as emperor of Mexico, which promptly opened negotiations with the Confederacy and allowed the transportation of supplies into Texas, bypassing the Union blockade. French troops were poised on the Texas border. Both France and England were ready to step in just as soon as the North and South had bled each other dry.

Two eventualities forestalled the complete breakup of the United States: Lincoln's proclamation freeing slaves in Confederate states and the quiet intervention of Russia.

PREEMPTIVE STRIKES

On September 22, 1862, just days after the federal army stopped a Confederate advance at the battle of Antietam, Lincoln announced his plans to order the freeing of Southern slaves unless the Southern states returned to the Union. This decree had been held in abeyance for nine months awaiting a Union battlefield victory.

With no response from the South, Lincoln issued his Emancipation Proclamation on January 1, 1863. He proclaimed freedom for all slaves in Rebel-held territory. It was a purely political act, since obviously he had no authority in those areas. But it brought the issue of slavery to the forefront of the conflict. Lincoln later explained this pragmatic gesture by saying, "Things had gone from bad to worse until I felt that we had reached the end of our rope on the plan of operations we had been pursuing; that we had about played our last card, and must change our tactics or lose the game. I now determined upon the adoption of the emancipation policy." In other words, it was halfway through this fratricidal war that slavery became a central issue.

The proclamation was a brilliant strategic maneuver as the citizens of neither Britain nor France would have accepted their nation's support of slavery—and it strengthened Lincoln's hand at home.

When Lincoln instituted the first military draft in 1863, there were riots in several major cities including New York. Between July 13 and 16 more than one thousand people were killed or wounded as army troops restored peace at gunpoint. "After the passage of many years, it is easy to forget that Lincoln had an insurrection on his hands in the North as well as in the South," commented Griffin dryly. "To control [this Northern] insurrection, Lincoln ignored the Constitution once again by suspending the right of habeas corpus, which made it possible for the government to imprison its critics without formal charges and without trial. Thus, under the banner of opposing slavery, American citizens in the North, not only were killed on the streets of their own cities, they were put into military combat against their will and thrown into prison without due process of law. In other words, free men were enslaved so that slaves could be made free. Even if the pretended crusade had been genuine, it was a bad exchange."

By the fall of 1863 Lincoln was becoming increasingly concerned with the foreign military presence in Canada and Mexico. His concern over the French in Mexico led to a hasty attack at Sabine Pass at the mouth of the Sabine River separating Texas from Louisiana. On September 8, 1863, a mere forty-seven Texas militiamen with six cannons chased off a flotilla of Union ships composed of twenty-two transports carrying five thousand Yankee troops escorted by four gunboats.

With France and Britain coming dangerously close to both recognizing and aiding the South, it was Russia's pro-North Czar Alexander II who tipped the balance the other way. After receiving information that England and France were plotting war to divide up the Russian Empire, Alexander ordered two Russian fleets to the United States in the fall of 1863. One anchored off the coast of Virginia while the other rested at San Francisco. Both were in perfect position to attack British and French commerce shipping lines. No threats or ultimatums were made public, but it was clear that should war come, the Russian Navy was in a position to wreak havoc. "Without the inhibiting effect of the presence of the Russian fleets, the course of the war could have been significantly different," commented Griffin.

Due chiefly to the presence of these fleets, coupled with the effect of the Emancipation Proclamation on their constituents, Britain and France declined to intervene for the South as planned.

By early 1865 the South had been bled dry, both in men and materials. The Mississippi River was in federal hands and Union general William T. Sherman had cut the Confederacy in two with his infamous "march to the sea" through Georgia. "The [Confederate] nation was able to keep an army in the field at all only because of the matchless endurance and determination of its surviving soldiers," wrote Catton. "Opposing it was a nation which the war had strengthened instead of weakened—a nation which had had the greater strength to begin with and which had now become one of the strongest powers on the globe. The war could end only as it did. The Confederacy died because the war had finally worn it out."

The blood cost of the war was horrendous—the 365,000 Yankee deaths combined with 258,000 Confederates totaled more dead than all other U.S. wars combined.

And the financial cost was staggering. At the end of 1861 government spending was $67 million. By 1865 this number had grown to more than $1 billion. The national debt, which was a mere $2.80 per capita for a population of 33 million in 1861, rose to $75 per person by 1865. It was estimated in 1910 that the total cost of the war, including pensions and the burial of veterans, totaled almost $12 billion, a preposterous sum at that time.

In the middle of this immense flow of money was Rothschild agent Belmont, financing both sides. He strongly influenced bankers in both England and France to support the Union war effort by the purchase of government bonds. At the same time, he quietly bought up the increasingly worthless bank bonds of the South at great discounts, with the idea that the South would be forced to honor them in full after the war. In 1863 the *Chicago Tribune* assailed "Belmont, the Rothschilds, and the whole tribe of Jews, who have been buying up Confederate bonds." Much later, this charge was styled a "libel" by those who could not understand the duplicity of Belmont and his employers with their public pro-North sentiments.

One of the younger Rothschilds visited America at the onset of the war and was as openly pro-Confederate as their agent Belmont was pro-Union. Concerning Lincoln, Salomon Rothschild wrote, "He rejects all forms of compromise and thinks only of repression by force of arms. He has the appearance of a peasant and can only tell barroom stories."

The Rothschilds played both sides and apparently felt little compassion for the American tragedy. Baron Jacob Rothschild rationalized the carnage by telling U.S. minister to Brussels Henry Sanford, "When your patient is desperately sick, you try desperate measures, even to bloodletting."

"The boot print of the Rothschild formula is unmistakable across the graves of American soldiers on both sides," concluded Griffin.

If indeed the War Between the States was a plot by the secret societies to split the United States—as claimed by a Knights of the Golden Circle tract published in 1861—backed by the European Rothschilds, it very nearly succeeded. The harsh Reconstruction policies of the Republican government, which caused the South to suffer under punitive economic policies well into the 1960s, generated enduring hatred and bitterness into the twentieth century as well as the growth of other secret societies in the South, such as the Ku Klux Klan.

Historian Foote used the term "Jacobins" to describe the secessionists of the era—disrupters of the established social, religious, and political order—who had been operating in America since the late eighteenth century. The Jacobins, a form of "Illuminized" Freemasonry, were the connective tissue that tied the secret societies of the Old World to hidden manipulation in the New World.

They had crossed the Atlantic after successfully destroying the "Old World Order" in France and were looking for new worlds to conquer. These fugitives were former members and the offspring of members of elder secret societies such as the Bavarian Illuminati, which traced its origins back to the dawn of humankind.

The men who created societies such as the Knights of the Golden Circle, the *Thule Gesellschaft,* and Cecil Rhodes's Round Table Groups drew from a long history of these clandestine European organizations.

However, by the time of the War Between the States, much of the secret society machinations had been forgotten by the American public thanks to the Anti-Masonic Movement of the early nineteenth century.

THE ANTI-MASONIC MOVEMENT

Freemasonry, the oldest and most powerful secret society in the history of the world, had planted firm roots in early-day America and even played a significant role in the American Revolution. It played an even greater role in the subsequent French Revolution, which initially was greeted with great joy and approval in the United States. The number of Masonic lodges grew and membership increased. By 1826 it was estimated that Masons in the United States numbered nearly fifty thousand, mostly educated and professional men.

But in that year, one Mason broke ranks. It became known that a Captain William Morgan of Batavia, New York, was planning to publish a book revealing the secret symbols, handshakes, oaths, and purposes of the Freemasons. Morgan, a thirty-year member of the order, wrote, "The bane of our civil institutions is to be found in Masonry, already powerful and daily becoming more so. I owe my country an exposure of its dangers."

Before the book could be printed, Morgan and his publisher were kidnapped in Batavia. Irate friends and neighbors pursued the kidnappers and managed to rescue the publisher, but Morgan was not so fortunate. He was never seen again.

Years later, a Mason named Henry L. Valance confided to his doctor as he lay dying that he and two other Masons had dropped Morgan into the Niagara River. Valance said since that night he had suffered from a guilty conscience—"the mark of Cain"—and sought absolution for his sin.

Yet at the time of the kidnapping, no one could seem to get a straight answer regarding Morgan's fate. According to the Reverend Charles G. Finney, writing in 1869, the wheels of justice were slowed by brother Masons in the courts and law enforcement, and among witnesses and jurors. Rumors that Morgan had been abducted and murdered by the Masons spread through New York and on into the New England and mid-Atlantic states and a major scandal erupted.

Due to the public backlash against the secrecy and exclusiveness of Masonry, Finney claimed that about forty-five thousand members left the order and more than two thousand lodges closed. "Thousands of Masons burned their aprons. In a few years' time, membership in the New York lodges dropped from 30,000 to 300 as a direct result of the Morgan incident," wrote author William J. Whaley.

In 1827 Morgan's book, *Illustrations of Masonry by one of the Fraternity Who Has Devoted Thirty Years to the Subject,* was published posthumously. For the first time, non-Masons were able to learn of the order's inner workings.

The chilling "blood oaths" of punishments for revealing Masonic secrets renewed the widespread belief that Morgan had been murdered by his fellows members. Morgan disclosed that the initiate into the order's beginning or First Degree of the Blue Lodge pledged to "binding myself under no less penalty than to have my throat cut across, my tongue torn out by the roots, and my body buried in the rough sands of the sea at low-water mark, where the tide ebbs and flows twice in 24 hours. . . ." The penalties in higher degrees grew progressively more gruesome.

In 1829, under public pressure, the New York State Senate investigated Freemasonry and reported that wealthy and powerful Masons were found at every level of government. The Senate also criticized the "silent as the grave" news media, reporting, "This self-proclaimed sentinel of freedom, has felt the force of Masonic influence. . . ."

Opponents of President Andrew Jackson—himself a Freemason—took advantage of the scandal to form the Anti-Masonic Party, the first time a third party was created in the United States. Anti-Masonic candidates were successful in state and local elections but failed to unseat Jackson in 1832. By the late-1830s the Anti-Masonic Party had turned to agitation against slavery and the strictly anti-Jackson members had joined the newly formed Whig Party. Nevertheless, a serious blow had been delivered from which Masonry was not to recover for decades.

Suspicions and sentiment against Masonry had been growing in the years prior to the abduction of Morgan as many Americans understood how the organization had played a role in the nation's two earliest, but long forgotten, insurrections.

Early in 1787 about one thousand Massachusetts farmers, led by Revolutionary War veteran Daniel Shays, attacked the Springfield arsenal to seize arms. Their uprising resulted from anger over increased taxes, the banning of paper money, and laws that only the wealthy could hold state office.

Irate and overburdened farmers demonstrated in several towns. Samuel Adams, who claimed European "emissaries" were secretly stirring up the people, helped draw up a Massachusetts resolution suspending habeas corpus as well as the famous Riot Act which was read without much effect to the unruly farmers.

Men who less than ten years earlier had been rebels against English rule were now calling for the death penalty for Shays's rebels. Only Thomas Jefferson, far from the scene as U.S. ambassador to France, offered sympathy. "I hold it that a little rebellion now and then is a good thing," he wrote to a friend. "God forbid that we should ever be twenty years without such a rebellion. . . . The tree of liberty must be refreshed from time to time with the blood of patriots and tyrants." Shays's small army finally marched on Boston but was turned back, more by a winter storm than by the hastily assembled militia funded by Boston merchants.

The American union was far from stable, especially in the western areas. In 1791 Secretary of the Treasury Alexander Hamilton—a Mason—had pressed through Congress a series of tax laws intended to support the newly created Bank of the United States and force full repayment of the government bonds held by his friends. It was also an exercise to assert the power of the fledgling federal government. His actions resulted in the Whiskey Rebellion of 1794.

One group hardest hit by Hamilton's taxes was the Scotch-Irish farmers of western Pennsylvania, who were particularly incensed at a tax on whiskey. Aside from their imbibing, most farmers converted their grain to whiskey for easy transport to Eastern markets. They saw the whiskey tax as a direct attack on their livelihood and tax collectors were met with weapons. A few were tarred and feathered.

According to some researchers of this period, the involvement of secret societies influenced by foreigners was demonstrable. For example, the natural disobedience of the angry farmers was heightened by agitation from French ambassador to the U.S. Edmond Genet.

Expelled from Russia for inciting revolution, Genet had arrived in America in the spring of 1793 and began organizing secret societies called "Democratic Clubs." They were direct replicas of the Illuminati-inspired clubs then advocating revolution in France. John Quincy Adams noted that the Democratic Clubs "are so perfectly affiliated with the Parisian Jacobins that their origin from a common parent cannot possibly be mistaken."

President George Washington also voiced concern, stating, "I gave it as my opinion . . . that if these societies were not counteracted . . . they would shake the government to its foundations."

In July 1794 Washington donned his old military uniform and reviewed an army of thirteen thousand men led by Robert E. Lee's father, General Henry "Light-Horse Harry" Lee. The militia army, gathered from neighboring states, moved into Pennsylvania and the few hundred farmers opposing it quickly scattered. Two farmers were convicted of treason but later pardoned by Washington after Jefferson's Republicans expressed dismay over what they saw as overreaction by the government. The Federalists saw the incident as a victory since it was their first opportunity to establish federal authority by military means within state boundaries.

But critics saw it as further imposition of elitist authority under a different name. "Why did Messrs. Hamilton and Washington bother participating in the American Revolution?" wondered author Bramley. "They simply used their influence to create the very same institutions in America that the colonists found so odious under British rule."

With a full-blown revolution underway in France, under criticism by

Jeffersonian Republicans and fearful of Illuminati influence in the nation's Masonic lodges and Democratic Clubs, Federalists in Congress in 1798 passed the four Alien and Sedition Acts. These unpopular laws, "designed to protect the United States from the extensive French Jacobin conspiracy, paid agents of which were even in high places in the government," empowered the president to expel or imprison foreigners, curtailed immigration, and provided punishment for anyone writing or speaking "with intent to defame" the government.

Many thought these laws were a thinly disguised attempt to consolidate unwarranted federal power, and resolutions were passed in the Kentucky and Virginia legislatures essentially negating the acts. These states declared that since the federal government was the result of a compact between the states, if the federal government assumed powers not specifically granted by the Constitution, the states had the right to declare such powers unconstitutional. This was the beginning of the constitutional argument that supported secession in the mid-nineteenth century.

The religious nature of early Northeastern America, founded in great part by the Pilgrims and Puritans, proved resistant to the anarchistic ideas imported by Illuminized Freemasonry—but such was not the case in France.

THE FRENCH REVOLUTION

If one desires to point to a major world event proven to have been inspired by secret society machinations, one need look no further than the French Revolution, which devastated that nation between 1787 and 1799. Revolutionary leaders, in seeking to overthrow the decadent monarchy of King Louis XVI, launched the first national revolution of modern times.

Although popularly believed to have begun due to a public uprising over lack of food and government representation, the record is quite clear that the revolution was instigated by cells of French Masonry and the German Illuminati.

The New Encyclopaedia Britannica tells us that in France "there arose a political system and a philosophical outlook that no longer took Christianity for granted, that in fact explicitly opposed it. . . . The brotherhood taught by such groups as the Freemasons, members of secret fraternal societies, and the Illuminati, a rationalist secret society, provided a rival to the Catholic sense of community."

Secret society researcher and author Nesta H. Webster was even more pointed, writing in 1924, "[The Masonic book *A Ritual and Illustrations of Freemasonry*] contains the following passage, 'The Masons . . . originated the Revolution with the infamous Duke of Orleans at their head.'"

Author Bramley wrote, "During the first French Revolution, a key rebel leader was the Duke of Orleans, who was grand master of French Masonry before his resignation at the height of the Revolution. Marquis de Lafayette, the man who had been initiated into the Masonic fraternity by George Washington, also played an important role in the French revolutionary cause. The Jacobin Club, which was the radical nucleus of the French revolutionary movement, was founded by prominent Freemasons."

It was the Duke of Orleans, grand master of the Grand Orient Lodge of Freemasons, who reportedly bought all the grain in 1789 and either sold it abroad or hid it away, thus creating near starvation among the commoners. Galart de Montjoie, a contemporary, blamed the Revolution almost solely on the Duke of Orleans, adding that he "was moved by that invisible hand which seems to have created all the events of our revolution in order to lead us towards a goal that we do not see at present. . . ."

Drawing on an impressive number of contemporary writings, Webster added, "If, then, it is said that the [French] Revolution was prepared in the lodges of Freemasons—and many French Masons have boasted of the fact—let it always be added that it was *Illuminized Freemasonry* that made the Revolution, and that the Masons who acclaim it are Illuminized Masons, inheritors of the same tradition introduced into the lodges of France in 1787 by the disciples of Weishaupt, 'patriarch of the Jacobins.'" (emphasis in the original)

Giuseppe Balsamo, a student of the Jewish Cabala, a Freemason, and a Rosicrucian, became known as Louis XIV's court magician Cagliostro. He wrote how the German Illuminati had infiltrated the French Freemason lodges for years and added, "By March 1789, the 266 lodges controlled by the Grand Orient were all 'illuminized' without knowing it, for the Freemasons in general, were not told the name of the sect that brought them these mysteries, and only a very small number were really initiated into the secret."

JACOBINS AND JACOBITES

Pro-revolutionary members of France's National Constituent Assembly had formed a group which became known as Society of the Friends of the Constitution. After the assembly moved to Paris, this group met there in a hall leased from the Jacobins' convent of Catholic Dominican friars. These revolutionaries, sworn to protect the revolution from the aristocrats, soon were known as the Jacobin Club. Since that time, all revolutionaries have been called Jacobins.

At least that is the official story of the Jacobins. As usual, the Jacobins are tied to earlier secret societies, in this case a movement to restore a kingship in Britain.

In 1688 England's unpopular and pro-Catholic Stuart king, James II, was deposed by his Dutch son-in-law, the Protestant William of Orange. James—whose name in Latin was Jacobus, hence the name Jacobites— fled to France. There he continued to be supported by Freemasons in Scotland and Wales who sought to restore him to the English throne. They were accused by French Freemasons of converting Masonic rituals and titles into political support for this restoration.

According to some versions of Masonic history, James was ensconced in the Chateau of Saint-Germain by his friend, French king Louis XIV, where, with the help of Catholic Jesuits, he established a system of Masonry that became the basis of Masonic traditions such as the "Scottish Rite."

"The theory that connects the royal house of the Stuarts with Freemasonry . . . as a political engine to be wielded for the restoration of an exiled family to a throne . . . is so repugnant to all . . . that one would hardly believe that such a theory was ever seriously entertained, were it not for many too conclusive proofs of the fact," was the convoluted admission of this political involvement by Masonic author Albert Mackey writing in the nineteenth century.

After a series of failed rebellions, the Jacobites in Scotland were finally crushed at the battle of Culloden Moor near Inverness in 1746. Their leader, Charles Edward Stuart, "Bonnie Prince Charlie, the young pretender," escaped to France, taking with him Jacobites imbued with Freemasonic ideals. A year later in Arras, France, Charles chartered a Masonic Sovereign Primordial Chapter of Rose Croix known as "Scottish Jacobite."

"The organization of this chapter was intended only as the beginning of a plan to enlist other Masons . . . to create a chapter in whatever town they might think proper, which they actually did . . . among them one at Paris in 1780, which in 1801 was united to the Grand Orient [Lodge] of France," explained Mackey.

"The Jacobite character of the Paris lodge is not a matter of dispute," wrote Webster. But she argued that "the founders of the Grand Lodge in Paris did not derive from the Grand Lodge in London, from which they held no warrant, but . . . took their Freemasonry with them to France before the Grand Lodge of London was instituted; they were therefore in no way bound by its regulations." This may be where English and Continental Freemasonry began to diverge.

According to Mackey, the attempt to connect Masonic traditions with the Stuart claims to the English throne was the first time politics had been introduced into the "speculative philosophy" of freemasonry. It certainly was not the last.

French Masons too were heavily involved in the political events of that day. Webster noted, "All the revolutionaries of the Constituent Assembly were initiated into the third degree" of Illuminized Masonry, including revolutionary leaders such as the Duke of Orleans, Valance, Lafayette, Mirabeau, Garat, Rabaud, Marat, Robespierre, Danton, and Desmoulins.

Honore-Gabriel Riquetti, Comte de Mirabeau, a leading revolutionary, indeed espoused ideals which were identical to those of Adam Weishaupt, founder of Bavarian Illuminized Masonry. In personal papers, Mirabeau called for the overthrow of all order, all laws, and all power to "leave the people in anarchy." He said the public must be promised "power to the people" and lower taxes but never given real power "for the people as legislators are very dangerous [as] they only establish laws which coincide with their passions." He said the clergy should be destroyed by "ridiculing religion."

Mirabeau ended his tirade by proclaiming, "What matter the means as long as one arrives at the end?"—the same end-justifies-the-means philosophy preached from Weishaupt to Lenin to Hitler.

As is common in world events, the issues that sparked revolution originally centered on finances. France had spent a considerable amount of money supporting the American Revolution. In February 1787 French noblemen were summoned to an assembly by the controller general of finances, who proposed increasing taxes on the wealthy to reduce the national debt. Needless to say, the wealthy noblemen rejected this idea and instead called for a meeting of Estates-General, France's parliament composed of the three Estates of the nobles, the clergy, and the commoners. It had not met in nearly two hundred years.

Agitation for the Estates-General to consider political reforms continued through 1788, with disturbances in major French cities, including Paris. During this period, representatives of the three Estates were elected.

The three Estates met at Versailles on May 5, 1789, and were immediately divided over how voting should be tabulated. Popular votes would favor the majority, primarily the commoners, while a vote by the Estates would favor the nobles and clergy.

Third Estate commoners, gaining support from some of the priests, won out, and King Louis XVI grudgingly called for a National Constituent Assembly to devise a new French constitution while secretly gathering troops to suppress the gathering.

Word of these troop movements spread, and in the ensuing Great Fear of July 1789, a crowd in Paris stormed the king's chief prison, the Bastille, where they released only seven prisoners—most were mentally ill—but acquired much-needed guns and powder.

Contrary to popular history, this attack was not the spontaneous action of a downtrodden mob. "That brigands from the South were deliberately enticed to Paris in 1789, employed and paid by the revolutionary leaders, is a fact confirmed by authorities too numerous to quote at length. . . . In other words, the importation of the contingent of hired brigands conclusively refutes the theory that the Revolution was an irrepressible rising of the people," wrote Webster.

Meanwhile mounted couriers dispatched by the secret societies rode from town to town warning the fearful peasants that conspirators against the nation were hiding in the aristocrats' castles and manors. They were told the king had ordered them attacked. Chaos and violence were soon widespread and hailed as a revolution.

"We see in the French Revolution the first time where grievances were systematically created in order to exploit them," wrote author Still.

Such exploitation began with the Freemasons as early as 1772 when the Grand Orient Lodge was firmly established in France, counting 104 lodges. This number grew to 2,000 lodges by the time of the Revolution, with 447 lodge members participating in the 605-member Estates-General. According to several researchers, the Grand Orient Lodges were the core of the Illuminati penetration of Freemasonry.

This penetration began in the early years of the eighteenth century when the Jacobites and Templar remnants fought for control of the French lodges of Freemasonry. Author Webster believed that "Scots Masonry" was merely a veil for Templarism and that the Grand Lodge of France was "invaded by intriguers" (meaning the Jacobites).

French Masonry soon split into two factions—the Grand Lodge of France with its Templar tradition infused with Illuminism, and the expelled Grand Lodge Lacorne, which in 1772 became the Grand Orient Lodge with the future Duke of Orleans at its head.

"The Grand Orient then invited the [Grand Lodge of France] to revoke the decree of expulsion and unite with it, and this offer being accepted, the revolutionary party inevitably carried all before it, and the Duc de Chartes [soon to be Duke of Orleans] was declared Grand Master of all the councils, chapters and Scotch lodges of France. In 1782 the 'Council of Emperors' and the 'Knights of the East' combined to form the 'Grand Chapitre General de France,' which in 1786 joined up with the Grand Orient. The victory of the revolutionary party was then complete," explained Webster.

Alarmed over the spreading havoc, the national assembly in 1789 hastily introduced a Declaration of the Rights of Man and of the Citizen, proclaiming liberty, equality, the inviolability of property, and the right to resist oppression—all basic longtime tenants of Masonry.

When the king refused to approve the declaration, a Parisian mob marched to Versailles and took him to Paris, where the assembly continued to hammer out new laws and policies. One was to nationalize property of the Roman Catholic church to pay off the national debt. This action drove a wedge between the commoners and their supporters within the clergy, increasing hostility on both sides. The assembly then attempted to create a constitutional monarchy similar to England's, but the weak and fearful Louis tried to flee the country in June 1791. He was captured at Varennes and returned to Paris under guard.

Meanwhile, buoyed by the situation in France, Masonic-based revolutionary clubs sprang up in other countries, including England, Ireland, the German states, Austria, Belgium, Italy, and Switzerland. Tensions between outside nations and France rose until 1792 when France declared war on Austria and Prussia.

Confronted with both a war and a revolution, France degenerated into the Reign of Terror, during which time King Louis XVI, Marie Antoinette, and many thousands, chiefly aristocrats, were executed.

In a move similar to Hitler's action 150 years later, the Jacobins closed down all Masonic lodges in 1791, ironically fearful that Freemasonry's organizing power might be turned against them.

"Behind the Convention, behind the clubs, behind the Revolutionary Tribunal, there existed . . . that most secret convention which directed everything . . . an occult and terrible power of which the other Convention became the slave and which was composed of the prime initiates of Illumanism," noted Webster.

Author Epperson, after an exhaustive study of the subject, agreed. He wrote, "The invisible hand that guided the entire French Revolution was the Illuminati, only 13 years in existence, yet powerful enough to cause a revolution in one of the major countries of the world."

Wars, riots, and coups continued in France until a young General Napoléon Bonaparte finally seized complete control in 1799. Although he carried on his own brand of terror in Europe for years, Napoléon proclaimed an end to the revolution. France was in a shambles. Hundreds of thousands had died of starvation, war, violence, and the guillotine. The power of both the monarchy and the monolithic church had been largely destroyed.

"So in the 'great shipwreck of civilization,' as a contemporary has described it, the projects of the Cabalists, the Gnostics, and the secret societies which for nearly eighteen centuries had sapped the foundations of Christianity found their fulfillment," commented Webster.

The confidence to initiate a major revolt such as the French Revolution may have been gained in the new lands of America. While the American Revolution was not the sole creation of secret societies as in France, there was nevertheless a definite undercurrent of secret society connections based on both religious and philosophical differences.

SIR FRANCIS BACON AND THE NEW ATLANTIS

In the early seventeenth century, two distinct groups of Englishmen made their way to the new land of America: "Illuminized" Freemasons who founded the ill-fated Jamestown colony, and the religious Pilgrims who fared better at Plymouth. It is instructive to briefly consider both.

Jamestown was named after England's King James I, who commissioned the first "authorized" version of the Bible. It became the first permanent English settlement in America after its founding by Captain John Smith in 1607. The colony was strictly a business venture of the Virginia Company of London, a firm formed in 1606 by secret society members including Sir Francis Bacon, who might rightfully be viewed as the founder of modern America.

The well-educated son of the lord keeper of Britain's Great Seal, Bacon became a lawyer and member of Parliament. Despite a quarrel with Queen Elizabeth, he was knighted in 1603.

Sir Francis Bacon served as England's grand chancellor under King James I and was described by author Marie Bauer Hall as "the founder of [English] Freemasonry . . . the guiding light of the Rosicrucian Order, the members of which kept the torch of true universal knowledge, the Secret Doctrine of the ages, alive during the dark night of the Middle Ages." British author Icke said Bacon was "a Grand Commander of the Brotherhood Order called the Rosecrusians, and very much involved in the underground operations of the Knights Templar traditions."

Bacon indeed was a fascinating figure, largely ignored in history except for his scientific work.

Despite his attacks on scholastic orthodoxy, Bacon gained renown as a scientist and philosopher. Twenty years after Bacon's death in 1626, his "Invisible College" of followers formed a society of learned men, which in 1660 became the Royal Society of London for the Promotion of Natural Knowledge. According to Masonic historian Albert Mackey, many members of the original society were also members of the Company of Masons.

"This was the reason of their holding their [Society] meetings at Mason's Hall, in Masons' Alley, Basinghall Street," wrote Mackey. "They all entered the Company and assumed the name of Free and Accepted Masons . . . [which] gave birth to that denomination of Freemasons which afterward became so famous."

"In Stuart England, the early Freemasons of Charles I and Charles II were men of philosophy, astronomy, physics, architecture, chemistry and generally advanced learning. Many were members of the country's most important scientific academy, the Royal Society, which had been styled the *Invisible College* after it was forced underground during the Cromwellian

Protectorate. . . . Early members included Robert Boyle, Isaac Newton, Robert Hooke, Christopher Wren and Samuel Pepys," wrote author Laurence Gardner. He noted of the men of the Royal Society that "like the early Templars, they were endowed with very special knowledge."

For nearly three decades, according to authors Michael Baigent and Richard Prince, "'Rosicrucianism,' Freemasonry and the Royal Society were not just to overlap, but virtually to be indistinguishable from one another." According to some Masonic writers, the only meaningful difference between the Freemasons and the Royal Society was that the latter conducted open meetings.

England's first recorded Masonic initiation was for Sir Robert Moray in 1641. Moray also was one of the founders of the Royal Society and said to be its "soul" and "guiding spirit." He also was said to be a chemist and a patron of the Rosicrucians, yet another example of that sect's penetration of Freemasonry.

Bacon for many years has even been identified by some as the true author of the writings of William Shakespeare, an allegation not as ludicrous as it sounds. There is ample evidence to support it, and believers included Mark Twain, Walt Whitman, Henry James, Sigmund Freud, and Ralph Waldo Emerson.

It was alleged that William Shakespeare was merely an illiterate stable hand and actor whose name was used to mask the radical political writings of a secret Elizabethan society which included Bacon, Sir Walter Raleigh, and Edmund Spenser. It was even rumored that Bacon was actually the illegitimate child of Queen Elizabeth.

Adding to the suspicions concerning Shakespeare's true identity was the fact that no biography of the Bard was written for more than one hundred years after his death in 1616. In addition, not one remnant of an original Shakespeare script has ever been found—not even correspondence with producers, patrons, or fellow actors—and there is really no proof of his official biography as an actor and playwright other than that a certain Shakespeare did exist. In his last will, this Shakespeare made no mention of his literary works, left his wife merely his "2nd-best bed and furniture," and signed the document "William Shackspeare."

Another valid argument against Shakespeare's authorship was that the dramas and comedies evinced a knowledge of history, politics, geography, and court etiquette unlikely in a commoner. In Love's Labour's Lost there supposedly was found an anagram in Latin which translated, "These plays, the offspring of F. Bacon, are preserved for the world." Acknowledged as a "master of English prose," the courtly Bacon would certainly seem the prime candidate as author of the Shakespeare material.

Bacon's Masonic beliefs were advanced in two books—*De Sapientia Veterum* (The Wisdom of the Ancients) and *New Atlantis*. In the latter, according to occult researcher Andre Nataf, "Bacon is here describing a utopia which underlies many secret societies, including modern Freemasonry."

Masonic writer Manly P. Hall said the reason *New Atlantis* was not published until after Bacon's death was that "it told too much . . . [revealing] the entire pattern of the secret societies which had been working for thousands of years to achieve the ideal commonwealth in the political world."

This "ideal commonwealth" proved to be America, hailed as a land of boundless opportunity and the site of the Masonic "Great Plan" to build a "New Atlantis."

"Time will reveal that the continent now known as America was actually discovered, and, to a considerable degree, explored more than a thousand years before the beginning of the Christian era," wrote Hall. "The true story was in the keeping of the Mystery Schools, and passed from them to the Secret Societies of the medieval world. The Esoteric orders of Europe, Asia, and the Near East were in at least irregular communication with the priesthoods of the more advanced Amerindian nations.

"Plans for the development of the Western Hemisphere were formulated in Alexandria, Mecca, Delhi, and Lhasa [Tibet] long before most European statesmen were aware of the great Utopian program."

Following this ancient secret society plan, Sir Walter Raleigh and other members of the "Baconian Circle" made an ill-fated expedition to America, landing on Roanoke Island, North Carolina, in 1584. Raleigh, who was executed by King James I in 1618 for treason, was accused by the Catholic Jesuits of operating a "School of Atheism" because of his Freemason connections and philosophy.

With the failure of Raleigh's colony, interest about America waned in England until the posthumous publication of Bacon's *New Atlantis*.

Many of the subsequent Jamestown colonists led by Captain John Smith were Rosicrucian Freemasons and, some have said, relatives of Bacon. They certainly were for the most part aristocratic Englishmen who relied on their utopian ideals rather than hard work for success. The colony suffered severe hardships and would have disappeared but for the aid of friendly Indians and the arrival in 1610 of Thomas West, Lord De La Warr, and reinforcements.

Meanwhile two groups of religious dissenters were colonizing America further north.

In 1534 King Henry VIII broke with Catholicism and formed the Church of England. Those who sought to purify the new church of any taint of Catholicism were called Puritans and a splinter group who wanted nothing whatsoever to do with the church were known as Separatists. Collectively these dissenters became known as Pilgrims when they journeyed to America.

The Pilgrims set up colonies in Plymouth, Massachusetts, and elsewhere in New England. Plymouth leader William Bradford quickly decided that the communal style of living advocated by the London merchants who financed the colony was not working well.

"Everyone was fed from common stores," wrote Still. "The lack of incentive was threatening to turn Plymouth into a another Jamestown. . . . So Bradford instituted an incentive system. He assigned a plot of land to be worked by each family. From then on, the little community was never again in need of food. . . .

"The first two colonies in America were excellent examples of two rival systems," Still continued, "one based on the concept of individually-held property driven by incentive, the other based on the communal theories of Plato and Francis Bacon."

As America grew, so did English Freemasonry. A Freemason center was founded in London on June 24, 1717, when four lodges united to form the Grand Lodge of England, also called the Mother Grand Lodge of the World. "Encouraged by the Mother Grand Lodge in London, the Freemasonic lodges in the colonies of America began to plot and agitate against British rule," wrote author Icke.

One of the earliest revolts was led by Nathaniel Bacon, a descendant of Sir Francis, according to journalist Still. Bacon in 1676 organized a militia supposedly to fight Indians, but instead he took control of Jamestown, thus starting the first revolution in America. His rebellion disintegrated with his sudden death at age twenty-nine.

According to several sources, American Masons included George Washington, Thomas Jefferson, Alexander Hamilton, James Madison, Ethan Allen, Henry Knox, Patrick Henry, John Hancock, Paul Revere, and John Marshall. Benjamin Franklin became grand master of the Philadelphia Lodge in 1734.

Colonel LaVon P. Linn, a Masonic chronicler, wrote that of the estimated 14,000 officers in the Continental Army, 2,018 of them were Freemasons representing 218 Lodges, many of them "field lodges" that moved with the army from camp to camp. British Freemasons recruited members from among the American troops they trained prior to the revolution, thus "most of the military personnel involved, commanders and men on both sides, were either practicing Freemasons themselves or were steeped in the values and attitudes of Freemasonry," noted authors Baigent and Leigh.

According to one theory, it was Washington, who became a Mason at age twenty, who helped initiate revolution in the British colonies. In 1754 Washington led a military foray into the Ohio Valley, where his troops fired upon French soldiers. These Frenchmen later said they were ambassadors under diplomatic immunity, a claim dismissed by Washington. French retaliatory action forced Washington's force to surrender at Fort Necessity, Pennsylvania. The incident turned long-standing frontier tensions into the French and Indian War, which spread to Europe as the Seven Years War. This war drained Britain's finances, forcing Parliament to saddle the American colonies with higher taxes, a key issue of the revolution.

THE AMERICAN REVOLUTION

According to *A New Encyclopedia of Freemasonry,* "In the tense times before the American Revolution the secrecy of the Masonic Lodges offered the colonial patriots the opportunity to meet and plan their strategy. The Boston Tea Party was entirely Masonic, carried out by members of St. John's Lodge during an adjourned meeting." Others have identified the lodge as Saint Andrew's, but the point is made.

Of the fifty-six signers of the Declaration of Independence, only one was known not to be a Freemason, asserted Masonic writer Manly P. Hall, who in *The Secret Teachings of All Ages* also told of a most mysterious incident at the time of the signing of this historic document. As the debate over their future reached a crescendo and many hesitated to sign the declaration realizing they would be putting their life on the line, suddenly a tall stranger with a pale face spoke out. No one knew who he was or where he came from, but the force of his oration was transfixing. His stirring words ended with the cry, "God has given America to be free!" Amid cheers filled with emotion, every man rushed forward to sign the declaration except the stranger. "He had disappeared," wrote Hall, "nor was he ever seen again or his identity established." Hall said this episode paralleled similar incidents in world history, when strange unknown men suddenly appeared just in time for the creation of some new nation. "Are they coincidences," he asked, "or do they demonstrate that the divine wisdom of the Ancient Mysteries is still present in the world, serving mankind as it did of old?"

Recall that England in 1764 had outlawed the creation of colonial scrip. This forced the colonists to sell bonds of indebtedness to the Bank of England and use its banknotes. "The colonies would gladly have borne the little tax on tea and other matters had not it been that England took away from the colonies their money, which created unemployment and dissatisfaction," wrote Benjamin Franklin.

Author Epperson commented, "Franklin acknowledged that the cause of the Revolution was the resistance of the colonies to the idea of borrowed money, resulting in debt and inflation as well as interest payments, and not 'taxation without representation' as is commonly believed." Again, this is an issue that we of modern-day America are not supposed to consider, much less understand.

"When speaking of deficit spending," explained author Griffin, ". . . the colonists discovered, every government building, public work, and cannon of war is paid out of current labor and current wealth. These things must be built *today* with *today's* labor, and the man who performs that labor must also be paid *today*. It is true that *interest* payments fall partly to future generations, but the *initial cost* is paid by those in the present. It is paid by loss of value in the monetary unit and loss of purchasing power for one's wages." (emphasis in original)

Faced with the staggering costs of the American Revolution, the colonists found that the unrestricted printing of money offered no lasting solution. In an attempt to avoid interest on borrowed money, the new states began printing their own paper fiat money eventually called "Continentals." The total money supply grew from $12 million in 1775 to $425 million by the end of 1779. By that year the one-dollar Continental note was worth less than a penny, hence the old slogan "not worth a Continental."

Working to agitate these financial problems into open revolution were the secret societies. Freemasons were drawn to Samuel Adams's Committees of Correspondence and the Sons of Liberty, which organized boycotts of British goods. Purposeful violent acts, such as the Boston Tea Party, were instigated by the inner-core members of the Freemason lodges, although sometimes even peaceful demonstrations got out of hand.

In the summer of 1765, wealthy Boston merchants, including many Masons, formed a group opposed to England's Stamp Act called the Loyal Nine. This group organized a procession of more than two thousand demonstrators who marched on the home of the local stampmaster and burned his effigy. After the initial instigators left, the aroused crowd began destroying property. Armed citizen patrols were organized and the very merchants who formed the Loyal Nine denounced the violence of the crowd.

Thomas Paine clearly advocated Masonic ideals, as when he attacked the divine right of kings in his book *Common Sense*. Referring to the Norman invasion of England by William the Conqueror in 1066, Paine wrote, "A French bastard landing with an armed Banditti and establishing himself king of England against the consent of the natives, is in plain terms a very paltry rascally original. It certainly hath no divinity in it."

Author A. Ralph Epperson concluded that Masons controlled the American Revolution, while William Bramley noted, "There was clearly something deeper driving the revolutionary cause: the rebels were out to establish a whole new social order . . . A 'Who's Who' of the American Revolution is almost a 'Who's Who' of American colonial Freemasonry."

Most of the patriots never realized this hidden manipulation. "Few of these men, if any, knew of the 'plan' of which only the leaders of Masonry were aware," noted Still. "Most believed they were simply involved in the cause of gaining independence from a tyrant. Masonry was to most of them, as it is to most of the membership today, merely a fraternal organization promoting social skills and providing fellowship to its members."

Further proof of Freemasonic influence in the American Revolution can be found in an examination of the U.S. dollar bill—with Mason George Washington on the front and Masonic symbols on the reverse. One finds a pyramid with a missing capstone but topped by an "All-Seeing Eye," both significant and long-standing Masonic symbols. There are also the Latin phrases *Annuit Coeptis* (He hath prospered our beginning) and *Novus Ordo Seclorum (*New Worldly Order).

Charles Thompson, designer of the Great Seal of the United States, was a Freemason and a member of Benjamin Franklin's American Philosophical Society, an American counterpart to Britain's "Invisible College." According to author Laurence Gardner, "The imagery of the *Seal* is directly related to alchemical tradition, inherited from the allegory of the ancient Egyptian Therapeutate [medicine]. The eagle, the olive branch, the arrows and the pentagrams are all occult symbols of opposites: good and evil, male and female, war and peace, darkness and light. On the reverse—as repeated on the dollar bill—is the truncated pyramid, indicating the loss of the Old Wisdom, severed and forced underground by the Church establishment. But above this are the rays of ever-hopeful light, incorporating the 'all-seeing eye,' used as a symbol during the French Revolution."

Author Bramly noted that the official seal of the United States bears the words *E Pluribus Unum* (One out of many) originally depicted a Phoenix bird rising from ashes, a Masonic symbol traced to ancient Egypt. But so many people mistook the long-necked Phoenix for a turkey that the Bald Eagle was substituted in 1841.

With these undeniably Masonic symbols prominently displayed on money and considering the wealth of information available to the scholar, Washington was clearly correct in his 1782 quote acknowledging the role of Illuminized Freemason doctrine in the early United States.

Many conspiracy writers view one particular secret society—the Illuminati—as an early stage manager of world affairs from behind the scenes, a group powerful and dedicated enough to infiltrate and control even the Freemasons. To understand the mysterious and elusive Illuminati or Illuminated (enlightened) Ones, one must first turn to Germany in the eighteenth century.

THE ILLUMINATI

Although Illumimati concepts can be traced back through history to the earliest sects claiming esoteric knowledge, the order was first publicly identified in 1776. On May 1 of that year—a day long honored by communists who some believe formed their philosophy based on the

Illuminati doctrine—the Bavarian Illuminati was formed by Adam Weishaupt, a professor of Canon Law at Ingolstadt University of Bavaria, Germany.

One of his cofounders reportedly was William of Hesse, the employer of Mayer Rothschild. It is certainly true that the Rothschilds and German royalty were connected through Freemasonry: Rothschild biographer Niall Ferguson wrote that Mayer's son Salomon was a member of the same Masonic lodge as Mayer's bookkeeper Seligmann Geisenheimer.

Studying to be a Jesuit priest, Weishaupt was undoubtedly angered over the 1773 banning of the order by Pope Clement XIV. While this act eventually led Weishaupt to break with the church, he remained fascinated with Jesuit theology. He also was greatly influenced by a merchant known only as Kolmer, termed by author Webster "the most mysterious of all the mystery men."

Kolmer, suspected by some researchers to be the same man called Altotas who was admired and mentioned by the French court magician and revolutionary Cagliostro, learned the esoteric knowledge of Egypt and Persia while living in the Near East for many years. Kolmer preached a secret doctrine based on an ancient form of Gnosticism called Manichaeanism or Mandaeanism that had used the word "Illuminated" prior to the third century.

Kolmer reportedly met Cagliostro on the Island of Malta, the old Knights Templar stronghold, while on his way to France and Germany in the early 1770s. Cagliostro, the future French revolutionary, then became involved in Masonic activities with the famed Venician lover Giovanni Giacomo Casanova, as well as the mysterious Count of Saint-Germain.

In Germany, Kolmer passed his secrets along to Weishaupt, who then spent several years determining how to consolidate all occult systems into his new "Illuminated" order. Weishaupt's devotion to the ancient mysteries of Mesopotamia is shown by the fact that he had the Illuminati adopt the Persian calendar.

Considering his deep knowledge of the Jesuits, Weishaupt may have taken the name "Illuminati" from a secret splinter group called the "Alumbrados" (enlightened or illuminated) of Spain, which was created by Jesuit founder, the Spaniard Ignatius Loyola. The Alumbrados taught a form of Gnosticism, believing that the human spirit could attain direct knowledge of God and that the trappings of formal religion were unnecessary for those who found the "light." It is no wonder that the Spanish Inquisition issued edicts against this group in 1568, 1574, and 1623. Weishaupt wrote that with his formation of the Illuminati, he, too, incurred "the implacable enmity of the Jesuits, to whose intrigues he was incessantly exposed."

Despite this enmity, Weishaupt created a pyramid structure of degrees for his initiates based on the Jesuit and Freemason structure, with key personnel located within only the top nine degrees. To his fellow Illuminati, Weishaupt was known by his code name "Spartacus" in honor of the slave who led a bloody revolt against the Romans in 73 B.C.

According to a 1969 magazine article, the Illuminati originated within the Muslim Ismaili sect, a group closely connected to the venerated Knights Templar who may have brought Illuminati ideals to Europe centuries before Weishaupt. This article stated that Weishaupt studied the teachings of the leader of the infamous Muslim Assassins, named for their consumption of hashish, and himself achieved "illumination" by ingesting homegrown marijuana. A harbinger of the psychedelic 1960s, the Illuminati slogan *Ewige Blumenkraft* meant "Eternal Flower Power."

The Illuminati were indoctrinated with ancient esoteric knowledge and were opposed to what they saw as the tyranny of the Catholic church and the national governments it supported. "Man is not bad," Weishaupt wrote, "except as he is made so by arbitrary morality. He is bad because religion, the state, and bad examples pervert him. When at last reason becomes the religion of men, then will the problem be solved."

Weishaupt also evoked a philosophy which has been used with terrible results down through the years by Hitler and many other tyrants. "Behold our secret. Remember that the end justifies the means," he wrote, "and that the wise ought to take all the means to do good which the wicked take to do evil." So, for the enlightened or illuminated, any means to gain their ends is acceptable—whether this means lies, deceit, theft, murder, or war.

The key to Illuminati control was secrecy. Edinburgh University professor John Robison was a Mason invited to join the Illuminati in the late eighteenth century. After investigating the order, Robison published a book which offered his conclusions in its title, *Proofs of a Conspiracy Against All the Religions and Governments of Europe Carried on in the Secret Meetings of the Free Masons, Illuminati, and Reading Societies.*

He quoted from Weishaupt's letters to fellow Illuminati. One 1794 work, *Die neuesten Arbeiten des Spartacus und Philo in dem Illuminaten-Orden,* stated:

"The great strength of our Order lies in its concealment. Let it never appear in any place in its own name, but always covered by another name, and another occupation. None is fitter than the three lower degrees of Freemasonry; the public is accustomed to it, expect little from it, and therefore takes little notice of it. Next to this, the form of a learned or literary society [the Thule Society] is best suited to our purpose. . . . By establishing reading societies and subscription libraries . . . we may turn the public mind which way we will. In like manner we must try to obtain an influence in . . . all offices which have any effect, either in forming, or in managing, or even in directing the mind of man."

Weishaupt not only set out to deceive the public, but he reminded his top leaders they should hide their true intentions from their own initiates by "speaking sometimes in one way, sometimes in another, so that one's real purpose should remain impenetrable to one's inferiors."

"Weishaupt's followers were enlisted by the most subtle methods of deception and led on towards a goal entirely unknown to them," noted Webster. "It is this that . . . constitutes the whole difference between honest and dishonest secret societies."

Unlike anarchists that seek an end to all government, Weishaupt and his Illuminati sought a world government based on their philosophy of human-centered rationalism. This world government, of course, would be administered by themselves. "The pupils [of the Illuminati] are convinced that the order will rule the world. Every member therefore becomes a ruler," he proclaimed.

In 1777 Weishaupt blended his brand of Illuminism with Freemasonry after joining the Masonic Order's Lodge Theodore of Good Counsel in Munich. The French Revolutionary leader and Illuminati member Mirabeau noted in his memoirs, "The *Lodge Theodore de Bon Conseil* at Munich, where there were a few men with brains and hearts . . . resolved to graft on to their branch another secret association to which they gave the name of the Order of the *Illumines.* They modeled it on the Society of Jesus [Jesuits], while proposing to themselves views diametrically opposed." It was here that the anticlerical message of Freemasonry combined with one against established government. In this Freemason lodge Mirabeau and the Illuminati formulated the very political agenda proposed at France's Constituent Assembly twelve years later.

The Illuminati philosophy was further spread—although unwittingly—by the Bavarian government which cracked down on the order in 1783. Authorities saw the Illuminati as a direct threat to the established order and outlawed the organization. This action prompted many members to flee Germany, which only spread their philosophies farther. Secret Illuminati orders sprang up in France, Italy, England, and even the new lands of America.

Mason, Founding Father, and former president Thomas Jefferson wrote with admiration, "Weishaupt seems to be an enthusiastic philanthropist. Weishaupt believes that to promote the perfection of the human character was the object of Jesus Christ. [Weishaupt's] precepts are the love of God and love of our neighbor." Either Jefferson lacked knowledge of the inner Illuminati teachings or, as was charged in his time, he himself was a secret member.

Warnings against the Illuminati came from many quarters. Professor Robison, utilizing the order's own internal papers, made it perfectly clear that the organization was created for the ". . . express purpose of rooting out all the religious establishments and overturning all the existing governments of Europe."

But Weishaupt presented yet another dimension to this goal of political and religious upheaval, one which may provide the basic motivation for all secret societies right up to today: the desire for power. He wrote, "Do you realize sufficiently what it means to rule—to rule in a secret society? Not only over the lesser or more important of the populace, but over the best men, over men of all ranks, nations, and religions, to rule without external force, to unite them indissoluby, to breathe one spirit and soul into them, men distributed over all parts of the world?"

Weishaupt achieved such power himself by creating a pyramid chain of command so secure that no one knew he was the head of the Illuminati until Bavarian authorities seized the group's internal papers. In these documents, Weishaupt described his organization, "I have two immediately below me into whom I breathe my whole spirit, and each of these two has again two others, and so on. In this way I can set a thousand men in motion and on fire in the simplest manner, and in this way one must impart orders and operate on politics."

By 1790 the Illuminati appeared to have disbanded, but many members had simply fled to other countries while retaining their loyalty to the group's ideals. The Bavarian government tried to alert the leaders of other nations to what they saw as the danger of the Illuminati. Officials collected Illuminati documents into a publication entitled *Original Writings of the Order of the Illuminati* and distributed it to other European governments. But their warning fell on deaf ears.

Webster wrote, "The extravagance of the [Illuminati] scheme . . . rendered it unbelievable, and the rulers of Europe, refusing to take Illuminism seriously, put it aside. . . ." Many researchers claim this same incredulous attitude has helped protect the descendants of the Illuminati even today.

It was easy enough for the Illuminati to elude Bavarian authorities in the late 1780s. They simply went further underground, having successfully merged with Continental Freemasonry earlier in that decade.

Masonic historian Waite tried to distance Freemasonry from the Illuminati by writing, "The connection of the Illuminati with the older Institution is simply that they adopted some of its Degrees and pressed them into their own service."

Despite Waite's attempt to make this distinction, it was recorded that Weishaupt's group had formed an earlier alliance with the "Order of Strict Observance" of Freemasons in Frankfurt, Germany. This order was based on an earlier Rosicrucian group called the Order of the Gold and Rosy Cross.

One prestigious member of the Order of Strict Observance was the Hanoverian Baron Adolph Franz Friedrich Ludwig von Knigge. Though himself long proposing reforms in Masonry, once Knigge discovered the strength of Weishaupt's Illuminati, he joined and took up their cause.

Although Weishaupt was absent, Knigge represented the Illuminati at the Masonic Convention of Wilhelmsbad in Hesse, convened on July 16, 1782, under the chairmanship of the Duke of Brunswick and attended by Masonic representatives from all over Europe. Leading the Illuminati contingent under his Illuminati name "Philo," Knigge "effected a kind of marriage between Masonic advanced Degrees and those of Illuminism," wrote Waite. Although Knigge and Weishaupt later quarreled and parted ways, the baron proved instrumental in merging the Illuminati with the higher degrees of Freemasonry.

According to Webster, Knigge, "who had been traveling about Germany proclaiming himself the reformer of Freemasonry, presented himself at Wilhelmsbad, armed with full authority from Weishaupt, and succeeded in enrolling a number of magistrates, savants, ecclesiastics and ministers of state as Illuminati. . . . Illuminism was left in possession of the field."

The same year of the Wilhelmsbad congress, according to author Still, "the headquarters of Illuminized Freemasonry was moved to Frankfurt, the stronghold of German finance, and controlled by the Rothschilds." He added, "For the first time, Jews were admitted into the Order. Previously, Jews had only been admitted to a division of the Order called 'the small and constant Sanhedrin of Europe.'"

Jacob Katz, in his *Jews and Freemasonry in Europe*, wrote that founders of the Frankfurt Lodge of Freemasonry included Frankfurt rabbi Zvi Hirsch, Rothschild chief clerk Sigismund Geisenheimer, and all of Frankfurt's leading bankers, including the Rothschilds, who would later fund Cecil Rhodes and his societies.

Although the Order of Strict Observance officially disappeared after the Wilhelmsbad convention, authors Lynn Picknett and Clive Prince argued that the Rectified Scottish Rite accepted there was merely the Strict Observance under a different name. The idea that the Strict Observance, which claimed lineage through the Knights Templar to the Ancient Mysteries, simply changed names to camouflage itself is well supported by the fact that the Wilhelmsbad chairman, the Duke of Brunswick, "one of the most active and influential Freemasons of the age," was himself a member of the Strict Observance. Additionally, according to Masonic author Waite, "It would seem that we can trace [to the Order of Strict Observance]—practically without exception—every important personality in connection with French Freemasonry, not to speak of Germany itself." Waite admitted that, following the Wilhelmsbad convention, Strict Observance was "transformed" into other rites and "Hidden Grades."

With divisive issues settled and the Illuminati safely hidden away within the Freemasons, the Convent of Wilhelmsbad proved a turning point for the order. Although attendees were sworn to secrecy, the Count de Virieu later wrote in a biography, "The conspiracy which is being woven is so well thought out that it will be . . . impossible for the Monarchy and the Church to escape it."

"From the Frankfurt Lodge, the gigantic plan of world revolution was carried forward," Still wrote. "The facts show that the Illuminati, and its lower house, Masonry, was a secret society within a secret society."

Weishaupt's Illuminism was the public manifestation of a centuries-old struggle between organized religious dogma and a humanism based on ancient esoteric knowledge both theological and secular. Such knowledge required great secrecy because of the unrelenting attacks by both the church and the monarchies. But where many of the older Gnostic sects, including the *Carbonari,* advanced honest beliefs and values, Weishaupt had a more cynical and disruptive agenda of his own.

"Weishaupt . . . knew how to take from every association, past and present, the portions he required and to wield them all into a working system of terrible efficiency," wrote critic Webster, " . . . the disintegrating doctrines of the Gnostics and Manicheans, of the modern philosophers and Encyclopaedists, the methods of the Ismailis and the Assassins, the discipline of the Jesuits and Templars, the organization and secrecy of the Freemasons, the philosophy of Machiavelli, the mystery of the Rosecrusians—he knew moreover, how to enlist the right elements in all existing associations as well as isolated individuals and turn them to his purpose."

Considering what this one German professor achieved in the eighteenth century, it is clear why recent conspiracy writers have expressed a concern over what a modern Illuminati, armed with technology and influence over the mass media, might accomplish.

Many researchers today believe the Illuminati still exist and that the order's goals are nothing less than the abolition of all government, private property, inheritance, nationalism, the family unit, and organized religion. This belief partially comes from the intriguing notion that the much-denounced *Protocols of the Elders of Zion*—used widely since its publication in 1864 to justify anti-Semitism—was actually an Illuminati document with Jewish elements added for disinformation purposes.

"Even though the Illuminati faded from public view, the monolithic apparatus set in motion by Weishaupt may still exist today," Still commented. "Certainly, the goals and methods of operation still exist. Whether the name Illuminati still exists is really irrelevant."

FREEMASONRY

The ongoing connective tissue between the modern and ancient secret societies has been Freemasonry, which existed as a formidable force long before certain lodges became "Illuminized."

During the late Middle Ages when any opposition to the Holy Roman Universal (Catholic) church was forced deep underground, among the only organized groups able to move freely throughout Europe were the guilds of stone masons, who maintained meeting halls or "lodges" in every major city.

The masons, who traced their own secret knowledge of architecture and building back to Egypt and beyond, were essential in the construction of Europe's churches and cathedrals. They were the direct descendants of early guilds of masons which existed both in Egypt and Greece and utilized esoteric construction techniques in their craft. These techniques had been passed down through the sects and mystery schools and some continue to confound modern builders.

According to *The New Encyclopaedia Britannica*, Freemasonry is the largest worldwide secret society and was spread largely by the advance of the British empire in the nineteenth century. There were even Masonic lodges established in China under the auspices of the Grand Lodge of England beginning in 1788. The infamous Chinese Triad Society began as a Masonic order, along with one called the Order of the Swastika, according to the author of *A New Encyclopedia of Freemasonry*. These Chinese Masons conducted identical rites, wore similar jeweled symbols and leather aprons. They referred to the deity as the "First Builder."

There are several organizations that, while not officially Masonic, draw from the Masons. These include such social or "fun" organizations as Ancient Arabic Order of the Nobles of the Mystic Shrine (Shriners) and the Orders of the Eastern Star, DeMolay, Builders, and Rainbow. These groups are predominately American as British Masons are expressly forbidden to join such affiliates.

According to journalist George Johnson, "Early on, Masonry developed an aura of mystique. Its members possessed a power based not on royal or ecclesiastical authority but on knowledge, not only of stone cutting and mortaring but of the mysteries of ancient Greek geometers [experts in geometry]." Already possessing certain esoteric or secret knowledge, the Masons were an ideal vehicle for the covert distribution of anticlerical teachings.

The most famous of the Masonic symbols—the letter *G* inside a square and compass—in fact stands for geometry, according to Masonic historian Albert Mackey, who added that Masons have been taught that "Masonry and Geometry are synonymous terms" and "the geometrical symbols found in the ritual of modern Freemasonry may be considered as the debris of the geometrical secrets of the Medieval Mason, which are now admitted to be lost." Occult geometry, sometimes called "sacred geometry," long has utilized geometrical symbols such as the circle, the triangle, the pentagram, etc., as symbols for metaphysical and philosophical concepts.

Authors Christopher Knight and Robert Lomas had an interesting take on the well-known Masonic symbol of the square and compass. They claimed it originated as a stylized form of the ancient symbol for a king's power—a pyramid with its base at the bottom representing earthly power—superimposed with a reversed pyramid representing the heavenly power of the priest. Together, these pyramids of power create the symbol which has come to be known as the Star of David. "It first came into popular use on a large number of Christian churches in the Middle Ages," they wrote, "and the earliest examples were, we were amazed to find, on buildings erected by the Knights Templar. Its use in synagogues came very much later."

One Masonic tradition claimed that Abraham, the patriarch of the Hebrews, taught the Egyptians special knowledge predating the Great Flood. Later, this knowledge—reported as the work of the legendary Hermes Trismegistus—was collected by the Greek philosopher Euclid, who studied the work under the name geometry. The Greeks and later Romans called this discipline architecture.

Critics of Freemasonry have claimed the prominent G stands for Gnosticism, a philosophy of Gnostic sects such as the Alumbrados, which was outlawed by the early church.

Authorities disagree as to the actual origin of Freemasonry but all acknowledge that it predates ancient Egypt. Masonic lore traces its origins back to the construction of the biblical Tower of Babel and King Solomon's Temple of Jerusalem.

Writing in the nineteenth century, Mackey stated that the Masons of the Middle Ages derived their knowledge of building as well as organization from the "Architects of Lombardy." This guild in northern Italy was the first to assume the name "Freemasons," which has become the shortened name for the fraternal Order of Free and Accepted Masons. The term "Accepted" applied to later members who were not connected to the original stone masons. One paper on alchemy specifically mentioning "Freemason" can be dated to the 1450s.

Other Masonic scholars claim to historically date the order to Rome's

Collegium Fabrorum or College of Workmen, a group of builders and architects that became a prototype of the later guilds. Most writers trace Masonic secrets through those warrior-priests of the Crusades, the Knights Templar. One eighteenth century writer claimed modern Freemasonry was founded by Godfrey de Bouillon, leader of the First Crusade, which captured Jerusalem, and reportedly also the founder of the mysterious Priory of Sion.

The secrets of the origins of Freemasonry have been tightly held despite the publication of numerous books and literature on the subject. Walter Leslie Wilmshurst, a ranking Mason and author of *The Meaning of Masonry*, wrote, "The true, inner history of Masonry has never yet been given forth even to the Craft itself." Many researchers believe that even most Masons themselves have lost sight of the organization's true origin and purpose. "The overall picture is one of an organization that has forgotten its original meaning," wrote the authors of *The Templar Revelation*.

This allegation was echoed by the Masonic authors of *The Hiram Key*, Knight and Lomas, who wrote, "Not only are the origins of Freemasonry no longer known, but the 'true secrets' of the Order are admitted to have been lost, with 'substituted secrets' being used in their place in Masonic ceremony. . . ."

Yet, following an exhaustive study of the Knights Templar, they concluded, "We now could be certain, without any shadow of a doubt, that the starting place for Freemasonry was the construction of Rosslyn Chapel in the mid-fifteenth century." Rosslyn, near Edinburgh, Scotland, was built by the Saint-Clair family. The Saint-Clairs were close to the original Knights Templar and William Saint-Clair of Rosslyn became the first grand master of Scottish Freemasonry. Catherine de Saint-Clair was married to the first grand master of the Knights Templar.

Much of the confusion over Freemasonry's origins and growth dates from the rift between the Roman Catholic church and the Protestant Church of England when many Masonic records were lost. Wars and revolutions took their toll on Masonic libraries in all nations.

King Henry VIII, in breaking with Rome, not only discontinued the church's building programs in England, causing widespread unemployment, but looted the assets of the Masons under the guise of taxes and tribute. To survive, the lodges began opening their memberships to non-Masons. These outsider merchants, landowners, and others—many with Templar backgrounds—became known as "Speculative" Masons. They embraced a mystical and esoteric doctrine based on traditions predating Freemasonry and brought to the order by Knights Templar members fleeing persecution by the church.

By the time four London lodges formed a United Grand Lodge in 1717, Speculative Freemasonry completely dominated the original guild stonemasons or "Operative" Masons. It is primarily from Speculative Masonry that the order derived its esoteric knowledge.

Author Webster stated that the origins of Freemasonry cannot be traced to any one source, but that the order resulted from a combination of traditions that evolved and merged over a period of time. "Thus Operative Masonry may have descended from the Roman Collegia and through the operative masons of the Middle Ages, whilst Speculative Masonry may have derived from the [Hebrew] patriarchs and the mysteries of the pagans. But the source of inspiration which admits of no denial is the Jewish Cabala. . . . The fact remains that when the ritual and constitutions of Masonry were drawn up in 1717, although certain fragments of the ancient Egyptian and Pythagorean doctrines were retained, the Judaic version of the secret tradition was the one selected by the founders of the Grand Lodge on which to build up their system."

Freemasonry continued to broaden its appeal. In 1720 Masonic lodges were established in France under the auspices of England's United Grand Lodge. They formed a Grand Lodge in Paris in 1735. These were distinct from the Scottish lodges which had been formed after Charles Stuart I fled England. Tensions between the two branches of French Masonry were heightened in 1746 with the exile of Charles Edward "Bonnie Prince Charlie" Stuart, the "Young Pretender" and his followers, who encouraged political use of the order.

It was during this time that the true lineage of Freemasonry became publicly known. In 1737 the tutor of Prince Charles Edward's sons and Royal Society member Andrew Michael Ramsey delivered a speech to the Freemasons of Paris. In what became known as "Ramsey's Oration," he clearly stated that "our Order formed an intimate union with the Knights of St. John of Jerusalem," an order closely associated with the Knights Templar. Ramsey also said that Freemasonry was connected to the ancient mystery schools of the Greek goddess Diana and the Egyptian goddess Isis.

German Mason Baron Karl Gottlieb von Hund had joined the Frankfurt lodge and in 1751 he formed an extension of the Scottish Rite called the Order of the Strict Observance after its oath of unquestioning obedience to mysterious and unseen "superiors." As previously described, this order ended with the fusion of the Illuminati and German Freemasonry during the Wilhelmsbad Convention.

Von Hund admitted carrying on the traditions of Knights Templar forced into exile in Scotland in the early 1300s. Order members proclaimed themselves "Knights of the Temple." He claimed to be carrying out the orders of "unknown superiors" who were never identified or located. While some claimed these "superiors" were not human, most researchers believe they probably were Jacobite supporters of the Stuarts who died or lost faith following the defeat of the "Young Pretender."

These superiors did provide von Hund with a list of names reported to have been ongoing grand masters of the Knights Templar, thought to have become extinct in the mid-1300s. A nearly identical list discovered recently was connected to the mysterious Priory of Sion headquartered in Rennes-le-Château in southern France, through an Austrian historian named Leo Schidlof, reportedly the author of genealogical lists entitled *Dossiers secrets* or secret files. "Save for the spelling of a single surname, the list Hund produced agreed precisely with the one in the *Dossiers secrets*. In short, Hund had somehow obtained a list of Templar grand masters more accurate than any other known at the time," wrote the authors of *Holy Blood, Holy Grail*. They felt this provided strong support for the belief that both the Priory and Freemason Hund were directly tied to the Knights Templar.

After years of clashes with the Roman Catholic church, Freemasons in England—now under the Church of England—announced in 1723 that the organization would accept persons from all religions. Today there are an estimated six million Freemasons active in the world in nearly one hundred thousand lodges.

Freemasonry is formed into three basic lodges: the Blue Lodge, the beginning step which is divided into three stages or degrees; the York Rite, composed of ten more degrees; and the Scottish Rite with its total of thirty-two degrees of initiation. The invitation-only thirty-third degree represents the human head atop the thirty-three vertebrae of the back. This is the highest publicly known degree.

The vast majority of members look upon their affiliation with Freemasonry as little different from joining the Lion's Club, the Optimists, or the chamber of commerce. And from their standpoint, this is true. Even Masonic literature makes clear that only those initiates who progress beyond thirty-third–degree status are educated in the group's true goals and secrets.

This hierarchy is readily admitted by Masonic authors. "There has always existed an external, elementary, popular doctrine which has served for the instruction of the masses who are insufficiently prepared for deeper teaching," wrote Mason Wilmshurst. "There has been an interior, advanced doctrine, a more secret knowledge, which has been reserved for riper minds and into which only proficient and properly prepared candidates, who voluntarily sought to participate in it, were initiated."

The thirty-third–degree Mason Manly P. Hall wrote, "Freemasonry is a fraternity within a fraternity—an outer organization concealing an inner brotherhood of the elect . . . the one visible and the other invisible. The visible society is a splendid camaraderie of 'free and accepted' men enjoined to devote themselves to ethical, educational, fraternal, patriotic and humanitarian concerns. The invisible society is a secret and most august fraternity whose members are dedicated to the service of an . . . *arcanum arcandrum* [a sacred secret]."

Prominent nineteenth-century Mason Albert Pike admitted that Freemasonry has "two doctrines, one concealed and reserved for the Masters, . . . the other public. . . ." Past Provincial Grand Registrar Wilmshurst confirmed that the "first stage" or initial degrees of Masonry are "concerned merely with the surface-value of the doctrine" and that "beyond this stage the vast majority of Masons, it is to be feared, never passes."

Even many high-ranking Masons are never brought into the inner circle of knowledge. In his memoirs, the famous Freemason Casanova wrote, "That those even who have occupied the Chair of the Master [Mason] for 50 years may yet be unacquainted with its Mysteries."

Author Epperson made the interesting observation that every Mason will deny that there exists an inner and outer circle to the order because the "average Mason" is truly unaware of this system while the "Illuminated Mason" is pledged not to reveal it. "This second layer is protected by an oath of secrecy, which means that if you knew about its existence, you would be obligated by an oath not to tell anyone," he explained.

The power structure of the order also caused concern among many researchers. "World Freemasonry is a massive pyramid of manipulation," wrote conspiracy author Icke. "The pyramid structure allows the Elite, the few at the top of Freemasonry, to control the majority by misleading them and keeping them in the dark."

This deception has been accomplished by providing both initiate Masons and the inquiring public alike with such a mass of contradictory and confusing information, traditions, and history that even Masonic scholars cannot agree on many issues. Author Mackey acknowledges that Masonic records are "replete with historical inaccuracies, with anachronisms, and even with absurdities."

There was a reason for this obfuscation. "The growth [of Freemasonry] synchronizes with a corresponding defection of interest in orthodox religion and public worship," noted Wilmshurst. "The simple principles of faith and the humanitarian ideals of Masonry are with some men taking the place of the theology offered in the various Churches."

Though its leaders deny it to be a religion, Freemasonry nevertheless offered a substitute for religion. No wonder it had to be circumspect in its teachings. Up to within living memory, anyone speaking concepts popularly believed to be sacrilegious or blasphemous risked serious community censure, bodily injury, or even death.

Wilmshurst explained that one seeking enlightenment "in the form of new enhanced consciousness and enlarged perceptive faculty . . . must be prepared to divest himself of all past preconceptions and thought-habits and, with childlike meekness and docility, surrender his mind to the reception of some perhaps novel and unexpected truths. . . ."

Referring to the teachings of Masonry as "veiled" and "cryptic," he wrote, "The meaning of Masonry . . . is a subject usually left entirely unexpounded and that accordingly remains largely unrealized by its members save such few as make it their private study. . . ."

However, Wilmshurst gave some clues to the hidden history of Freemasonry when he wrote of a "Golden Age" when "men were once in conscious conversation with the unseen world and were shepherded, taught and guided by the 'gods.'. . . " He noted that humankind lost its way after a "fall" due to its attempt to gain the same knowledge as its creators, a concept comparable with the biblical "fall from grace."

This "fall" of mankind, according to Wilmshurt writing in 1927, was not due to any individual transgression but to "some weakness or defect in the collective or group-soul of the Adamic race" so that "within the Divine counsels" it was decided that "humanity should be redeemed and restored to its pristine state," a process which required "vast time-cycles for its achievement." He added that this restoration also required "skilled scientific assistance" from "those 'gods' and angelic guardians of the erring race of whom all the ancient traditions and sacred writings tell."

Masonic author Manly P. Hall demonstrated that Wilmshurst was not merely speaking allegorically, explaining, "In the remote past the gods walked with men and . . . they chose from among the sons of men the wisest and the truest.

"With these specially ordained and illumined sons they left the keys of their great wisdom. . . . They ordained these anointed and appointed ones to be priests or mediators between themselves—the gods—and that humanity which had not yet developed the eyes which permitted them to gaze into the face of Truth and live. . . . These illumined ones founded what we know as the Ancient Mysteries."

So one inner Masonic secret has to do with their awareness of prehistoric "gods" who left their knowledge to certain individuals, thus illuminizing them. This knowledge was passed down through ancient Mystery Schools to the founders of both the Jewish and Christian religions, whose traditions were learned by the Knights Templar and brought to the inner core of modern Freemasonry.

The transition from ancient secret societies to more modern secret organizations was invigorated by the introduction of this "Illuminized" Freemasonry in the late eighteenth century, itself a blending of elder esoteric lore with Cabalistic traditions. These secrets continue to lurk at the inner core of Freemasonry even as its unknowing millions of members enjoy its outward philanthropy and fellowship.

The diligent researcher can begin to understand these ancient secrets only after the most laborious and serious study—much is still not being told in a direct manner, as admitted by Masonic authors.

Another of the ancient secrets concerned the concept of reincarnation, which, apologized Wilmshurst, "will be novel and probably unacceptable to some readers." He added, "We are merely recording what the Secret Doctrine teaches."

It was this hidden and esoteric side of Freemasonry that prompted critics to charge the order as antireligious. "Accusations that the Freemasons have cultivated the occult sciences—particularly alchemy, astrology and ceremonial magic—have pursued the order throughout its history," acknowledged the modern editors of Mackey's book.

Within early Freemasonry were men called magicians—not the stage illusionists of today but men who took the name from the term *Magi*, or wise men. Until the Enlightenment of the eighteenth century, magic was merely another name for science. These magicians seriously claimed to have the ancient knowledge of metal transmutation, matter manipulation, and eternal youth.

One of the most magical of these Masons was a person known as a "Wonderman," who was thought to have lived for hundreds of years.

COUNT SAINT-GERMAIN AND OTHER MAGICIANS

People who knew the Count of Saint-Germain either characterized him as a charlatan or an immortal magician. The truth probably lay somewhere between, although there was a definite strangeness about the man.

No one ever learned his true origins, but rumors were thick. Some claimed this brilliant man who spoke all European languages and evinced a deep knowledge in many fields was actually the third son of Leopold-George, third son of Francis II of Transylvania and Charlotte Amalie of Hesse-Reinfels. Occult author Hall reported that Saint-Germain once told William of Hesse that he was actually Prince Ragoczy of Transylvania and had been educated by the last Duke of Medici. As Saint-Germain claimed to have discovered the secret of immortality, perhaps memory of the count provided some of the modern Count Dracula legend.

Others said this noted violinist was the son of the king of Portugal while others said he was merely the offspring of a wandering Portuguese Jew or, according to some reports, a Strasburg doctor's son named Daniel Wolf. One account even claimed he was the result of a liaison between an Arabian princess and a reptile.

Whoever he was, the Count of Saint-Germain, called a "Wonderman" due to his vast knowledge and social skills, proved to be one of the most successful agents of the secret societies in his time. He first appeared in London about 1743 where, two years later, he was arrested as a Jacobite spy but later released.

Leaving London, the count traveled through Germany and Austria. He met Marshal de Belle-Isle, France's minister of war, who introduced Saint-Germain to the French court. He was immediately popular, claiming to have lived for centuries after discovering the "Elixir of Life," a formula for physical immortality. As recounted by author Richard Cavendish, the count told courtiers he had been among the guests at Cana when Jesus turned water into wine and had known Egyptian Queen Cleopatra. His knowledge of history was extraordinary, as he described details of events that astounded the most scholarly historians. Considered one of the world's greatest minds, French literary giant François-Marie Arouet, better known as Voltaire, once stated that Saint-Germain "is a man who knows everything."

He obviously was quite a showman. Once he spoke of being friends with the legendary King Richard the Lion Heart ". . . turning to his manservant for confirmation. 'You forget, sir,' the valet said solemnly, 'I have been only 500 years in your service.'"

Saint-Germain also claimed to possess the secrets of removing flaws from diamonds and transmuting various metals. He was given a laboratory for his alchemical experiments by King Louis XV, who also employed the count on secret diplomatic and spying missions. Saint-Germain made it clear where he had received his extraordinary knowledge. "One needs to have studied in the pyramids as I have studied," he once said.

In 1762 the count traveled to Saint Petersburg, where he assisted in placing the daughter of a friend, the Princess of Anhalt-Zerbst, on the Russian throne following the death of Peter III. His friend's daughter became known as "Catherine the Great." "St. Germain's involvement in the overthrow of Peter of Russia was not a petty scam," noted author Bramley, "it was a major coup which altered the political landscape of Europe."

The significance of Saint-Germain lies in his close associations. After leaving Russia, the count made connections with important Freemasons such as Casanova and the future French revolutionary Cagliostro. It was in Germany, according to Cagliostro, that Saint-Germain helped establish Freemasonry and initiated him into the Order of the Strict Observance in an underground chamber near Frankfurt. Sharing leadership in this order were the Duke of Brunswick and Prince Karl of Hesse, "head of all German Freemasons" and brother of William IX, the patron of Mayer Rothschild. "One of Saint-Germain's best friends and pupils was Prince Karl von Hesse-Kassel," noted Tomas, "who wrote *Memories de Mon Temps* [Memories of My Time], in which he calls the count 'one of the greatest philosophers who ever lived.'"

"Saint-Germain was the 'Grand Master of Freemasonry' and it was he who initiated Cagliostro into the mysteries of Egyptian masonry," confirmed author Webster, who added that Cagliostro soon "far eclipsed his master." Cagliostro founded his own Egyptian branch of Freemasonry drawn from the teachings of Saint-Germain and his knowledge of the Jewish Cabala. All of this laid the foundation for the Illuminati takeover of German Freemasonry.

While in Germany in 1774, Saint-Germain stayed for a time with William IX of Hesse. Perhaps during his stay, Saint-Germain exchanged secrets with William and his financial adviser Mayer Rothschild. Considering Rothschild's interest in antiquities as well as the Cabala, one can imagine his fascination with Saint-Germain's knowledge of the Egyptian Mysteries.

"St. Germain's activities are important because his movements provide a fascinating link between the wars going on in Europe, the deeper levels of the Brotherhood, and the clique of German princes—particularly the House of Hesse," wrote author Bramley.

Another connection between Rothschild's royal mentor and occult Freemasonry was Jean-Baptiste Willermoz, who, as a Mason since 1753 and a wealthy silk manufacturer from Lyons, undoubtedly moved in the same circles as Mayer Rothschild. Willermoz, who also claimed to receive instruction from "unknown superiors," stayed for a time with the Prince of Hesse-Kassal. A member of the Masonic "Rite of Elect Cohen," Willermoz was a moving force during the 1782 Wilhelmsbad Conference and is considered by many to be a founder of modern spiritualism.

Willermoz may have had contact with Saint-Germain, as an old work entitled *Freimaurer Bruderschaft in Frankreich* [The Freemason Brotherhood in France], Vol. II, stated: "Amongst the Freemasons invited to the great conference at Wilhelmsbad . . . we find St. Germain included with St. Martin and many others."

Saint-Germain and Cagliostro may not have been the only connections between the Hebrew Cabala and Freemasonry. Another contender was a mysterious and little-known person named Hayyim Samuel Jacob Falk. "Whilst St. Germain and Cagliostro figure in every account of 18th century magicians, it is only in exclusively Judaic or Masonic works, not intended for the general public, that we shall find any reference to Falk," noted author Webster.

The German poet Gotthold Ephraim Lessing, a close friend of Cabalist philosopher Moses Mendelssohn and librarian for the Duke of Brunswick, a ranking Masonic official, wrote several important Masonic tracts entitled *Ernst und Falk: Gesprache für Freimaurer (Ernst and Falk: Speak for Freemasonry)*. Although not documented, Lessing's title would indicate a connection between Falk and German Freemasons, which included the Rothschilds.

Falk fled Germany to avoid being burned at the stake as a sorcerer and arrived in London in 1742, apparently with only the shirt on his back. Yet, soon Falk had purchased a comfortable home containing much silver and gold as well as his own private synagogue.

Webster connects Falk not only with the Cabala but with the French Revolution. "The Duke [of Orleans] was in touch with Falk when in London and Falk supported his scheme of ursurpation," wrote Webster, wondering if "in Falk's 'chests of gold' that we might find the source of some of those loans raised in London by the Duc d'Orleans to finance the riots of the Revolution. . . ."

Webster saw in Falk the most likely person in the historic record—next to the Rothschild connection—who might have introduced Cabalist teachings into the higher degrees of Freemasonry. "Falk indeed was far more than a Mason," she wrote, "he was a high initiate—the supreme oracle to which the secret societies applied for guidance." Webster added that the "inaccessible" Falk may well have been one of the "real initiates whose identity has been so carefully kept dark . . . whilst St. Germain and Cagliostro . . . emerge into the limelight. . . ."

Whether Falk or Rothschild or both provided the connection, it is plain that both Freemasonry and the Knights Templar drew heavily from the Cabala for both concepts and rituals.

MASONIC PLOTS

Over the years there has been much concern—even outright paranoia as in the anti-Masonic movement—regarding the role of the Masonic orders in world affairs beginning with the American and French Revolutions and continuing up to today.

This mindset can be better understood by a listing of a mere handful of significant Masons, beginning with the American Presidents Washington, Monroe, Jackson, Polk, Buchanan, Andrew Johnson, Garfield, Taft, Harding, Truman, Ford, and both Teddy and Franklin Roosevelt. Other famous American Masons include John Hancock, Benjamin Franklin, Paul Revere, Sam Houston, Davy Crockett, Jim Bowie, Douglas MacArthur, J. Edgar Hoover, and Hubert Humphrey. Historical foreign Masons include Winston Churchill, Cecil Rhodes, Horatio Nelson, Duke Arthur Wellington, Sir John Moore, Simón Bolívar, Giuseppe Garibaldi, Franz Joseph Haydn (who provided the melody to *Deutschland über Alles*), Wolfgang Amadeus Mozart, Johann Wolfgang von Goethe, Voltaire (François-Marie Arouet), Giuseppe Mazzini, Mikhail Bakunin, Aleksandr Kerensky, Aleksandr Pushkin, Benito Juárez, and José de San Martín.

Such a wide divergence of personalities prompted authors Baigent and Leigh to argue "the impossibility of ascribing any political orientation, or even political consistency, to Freemasonry." However, in their detailed study of early Masonry and the Knights Templar, Beigent and Leigh took no notice of the infusion of Illuminati into Freemasonry in late eighteenth century. This infusion brought the philosophies of Hegel and Weishaupt which included "the end justifies the means" and "to achieve synthesis requires two opposing forces." Conspiracy researchers make it clear that Illuminized Freemasons have used any and every opportunity to advance their cause regardless of which side they may support at the moment.

The Masonic slogan *Ordo ab Chao*, or Order out of Chaos, generally is regarded as referring to the order's attempt to bring an order of knowledge to the chaos of the various human beliefs and philosophies in the world—a New World Order.

Conspiracy author Epperson explained that the slogan actually means the "'order' of Lucifer will replace the 'chaos' of God." Author Texe Marrs places his interpretation on a more mundane level, writing that *Ordo ab Chao* is a "Secret Doctrine of the Illuminati" based on the Hegelian concept that "crisis leads to opportunity." Marrs stated, "They work to invent chaos, to generate anger and frustration on the part of humans and thus, take advantage of peoples' desperate need for order."

Author Bramley saw this very mechanism in operation early on in England following the overthrow of Catholic King James II in 1688. Noting that the Mother Grand Lodge had conferred Masonic degrees on his Hanoverian successor, Bramley said, "The English Grand Lodge was decidedly pro-Hanoverian and its proscription against political controversy really amounted to a support of the Hanoverian status quo. In light of the Machiavellian nature of Brotherhood activity, if we were to view the Mother Grand Lodge as a Brotherhood faction designed to keep alive a controversial political cause, i.e. Hanoverian rule in Britain, we would expect the Brotherhood network to be the source of a faction supporting the opposition. That is precisely what happened. Shortly after the founding of the Mother Grand Lodge, another system of Freemasonry was launched [Freemason Jacobites] that directly opposed the Hanoverians!"

Allegations of Masonic plots—hard to find in mainstream publications and even harder to prove—are not restricted to dimly recalled history. One largely unreported story during the Ronald Reagan presidency clearly indicated that at least one Freemason lodge was conspiring to overthrow the government of Italy.

This scandal also involved a little-known group connected to the Freemasons called the Knights of Malta, which inherited the military orders of the old Knights Templar.

John J. Raskob, one of the thirteen founders of the American Order of the Knights of Malta, was involved in the abortive coup against President Roosevelt in the early 1930s, foiled only after Marine major general Smedley Butler blew the whistle on the scheme.

Modern American Knights included CIA directors John McCone and William Casey. Casey, along with Reagan's first secretary of state, Alexander Haig, have been connected to a fellow Knight named Licio Gelli, who during the 1980s turned a little-used Italian Masonic lodge into what was termed a "worldwide fascist conspiracy" with the help of the Mafia, the Vatican Bank, and the CIA.

Propaganda Masonica Due (2), better known as the P2 Lodge, was founded in Italy in 1877 to serve Italian Freemasons visiting Rome. Gelli, who became a Mason in 1963, had gained control over P2 by 1966 and increased the membership from fourteen to nearly one thousand. Obviously, Gelli had help. Italian journalist Mino Pecorelli, a P2 member himself, claimed the CIA was funding P2, a charge echoed by CIA contract agent Richard Brenneke in 1990. Pecorelli later was found fatally shot in the mouth in a classic gangland slaying. According to Icke, the P2 Lodge was connected not only to the CIA but to "the *Carbonari,* an amalgamation of Freemasons, the Mafia and the [Italian] military. . . ."

Gelli—a "business partner of [Nazi war criminal] Klaus Barbie, a financial backer of [fascist South American dictator] Juan Perón, a paid

CIA contact and an honored guest at Ronald Reagan's 1980 inauguration"—created what an Italian court indictment called a "secret structure [that] had the incredible capacity to control a state's institutions to the point of virtually becoming a state-within-a-state." Gelli also claimed to be on friendly terms with former CIA director and president George Bush, who some claimed was an "honorary" P2 Lodge member.

By 1981 Italian authorities had discovered the P2 plot. In searching Gelli's home, they found a list of the Masonic conspirators' names, which included three cabinet ministers, forty members of Parliament, forty-three military generals, eight admirals, security service chiefs, the police chiefs of four major cities, industrialists, financiers, entertainment celebrities, twenty-four journalists, and hundreds of diplomats and civil servants.

They also found a document entitled "The Strategy of Tension," a carefully designed plan to fabricate so much leftist terrorism that the Italians would demand an authoritarian or even fascist government. This plan evolved from an operation named "Gladio" created just after World War II by CIA official James Jesus Angleton in an effort to prevent a communist takeover in Italy. Gladio tactics involved creating alliances between the Mafia and Vatican officials as well as the CIA and the Knights of Malta.

Several investigators have claimed that a major force behind the P2 Lodge was the highly secret Freemason Grand Alpine Lodge of Switzerland, whose membership includes almost everyone of any importance in that nation of banks. Former British prime minister and Bilderberger Harold Wilson called Alpine Lodge members "the Gnomes of Zurich," claiming they had more power than any government.

P2 was implicated in several acts of terrorism beginning with the 1980 bombing of the Bologna train station which killed eighty-five persons and possibly even the December 1988 bombing of Pan Am Flight 103 over Lockerbie, Scotland. According to a little-publicized report by investigators for the airline's insurance company, the Pan Am flight's victims included a CIA team which was on its way to Washington to report its discovery of CIA drug smuggling and gun running activities in the Middle East with financing through P2 members. These extralegal activities were being run from Washington in the same manner as the Iran-Contra activities and reportedly involved high-ranking officials. Other CIA agents quickly arrived at the crash site and reportedly made off with vital evidence.

Conspiracy author Jonathan Vankin reported Italian media allegations that the P2 Lodge was funded through the Panamanian company Amitalia and that President Bush's invasion of Panama in 1989 was partially a cover for the destruction of records linking him, the P2 Lodge, and the CIA to the Pan Am 103 bombing. Vankin disparaged this allegation as "another demon raised from conspiratoriological hell," yet provided many intriguing bits of evidence in support of this thesis.

During subsequent trials in Italy involving P2 members, one prominent American name kept cropping up—a name with close connections to secret societies in the United States. Italian prime minister Giulio Andreotti, a close friend of Gelli who was tried for Mafia involvement, named Henry Kissinger as a character witness. In addition, both a close associate and the widow of former Italian prime minister Aldo Moro— kidnapped and murdered reportedly by the leftist Red Brigade in 1978—testified that Moro had been told by Kissinger to halt his stabilizing policies or "you will pay dearly for it."

A London *Independent* article stated that Moro's murder may have been contrived by the CIA through P2 members in the Italian government. Others even claimed the entire P2 scandal may have been orchestrated by the mysterious and most secret Priory of Sion.

The P2 story caused a major scandal in Europe but received scant attention in the American media, even when it grew to implicate top Vatican officials, American bishop Paul Marcinkus, and Kissinger.

Michele Sindona and Roberto Calvi, two prominent members of the seditious P2 Lodge, were involved in numerous questionable business deals with Marcinkus, the American Catholic bishop in charge of the Vatican Bank at the time. Sindona later was accused of laundering money for both the Sicilian and American Mafia and Calvi used Vatican money for investments in banks and enterprises all over the world, including Washington's infamous Watergate complex.

Markcinkus and the Vatican Bank became major shareholders in *Banco Ambrosiano,* owned by Sindona's partner, Calvi (called "God's banker" due to his Vatican connections). In mid-1982, as this Mafia-Freemason-fascist-Vatican scheme began to further unravel, the convicted Calvi fled to London, where he was found hanging from scaffolding underneath Blackfriars Bridge under conditions with Masonic connotations. Only a few hours earlier, Calvi's secretary, Graziella Corrocher—who also happened to be the P2 Lodge bookkeeper—fell or was pushed through a fourth floor window of the *Ambrosiano* bank building.

In 1986 Sindona and an accomplice were convicted of ordering the death of Giorgio Ambrosoli. An estate liquidator, Ambrosoli was fatally shot in 1979 after he found evidence of criminal activity in Sindona's papers while working in Sindona's home. Just two days after being sentenced to life in prison, Sindona was found dead of cyanide poisoning in his cell. While it is still debated whether Sindona's death was suicide or homicide, just before he died, he said, "They are afraid I could reveal some very delicate information that they don't want divulged."

Markcinkus, after assurances he would not be prosecuted by the Italian authorities, left the Vatican in disgrace and returned to the United States to settle into semiretirement. Ironically enough, it was *Banco Ambrosiano*'s namesake—Saint Ambrose of Milan—who in the fourth century denounced any interest on loans as "against nature."

"New York DA Frank Hogan, who prosecuted several local Mafiosi for [the P2] caper, attempted to extradite and prosecute Marcinkus also, but was blocked by White House intervention," noted author Wilson. Gelli, under several indictments in Italy, apparently remains free and in hiding.

These Masons "engineered frauds that led to the largest bank failures in American and Italian history," reported Vankin and Whalen, yet coverage of this billion-dollar disaster was almost nonexistent in the American media.

British conspiracy author Icke echoed the fears of many conspiracy writers when he wrote, "I believe strongly that something similar is happening in the United Kingdom and many other countries [the United States?], which mirrors the methods and aims of P2."

FREEMASONRY VS. CHRISTIANITY

Any attempt at an in-depth discussion of the inner workings and philosophies of Freemasonry would bog down in endless details and unresolved controversies. They are, after all, a secret fraternity and require some secrets.

Suffice it to say that Freemasonry has provided an overt bridge to the modern era for the covert teachings of the Ancient Mysteries, incurring the wrath of both church and state along the way.

This was stated clearly by Masonic author Hall, who wrote, "Freemasonry is therefore more than a mere social organization a few centuries old, and can be regarded as a perpetuation of the philosophical mysteries and initiations of the ancients."

Wilmshurst was even more to the point. He wrote, "When Christianity became a state religion and the church a world power, the materialization of its doctrine proceeded apace and has only increased with the centuries. Instead of becoming the unifying force its leaders meant it to be, its association with 'worldly possessions' has resulted in making it a disintegrative one. Abuses led to schisms and sectarianism . . . whilst the Protestant communities and so-called 'free' churches have unhappily become self-severed altogether from the original tradition and their imagined liberty and independence are in fact but a captivity to ideas of their own, having no relation to the primitive gnosis and no understanding of those Mysteries which must always lie deeper than the exoteric popular religion of a given period. . . . Since the suppression of the Mysteries in the sixth century, their tradition and teaching have been continued in secret and under various concealments and to that continuation our present Masonic system is due."

So another secret is out. Freemasonry and its progenitors have passed along knowledge inimical and dangerous to organized religion.

While espousing the Christian ideals of brotherly love, charity, and truth, even Masonic authors make it clear that Freemasonry is not an adjunct to the Christian religion. The innermost secrets of the order, some of which appear to be the antithesis of Christianity, have raised considerable suspicion and concern over the years, including an early church prohibition.

On April 28, 1738, just one year after the Mason Ramsey publicly connected Freemasonry to the outlawed Knights Templar, Pope Clement XII issued his famous bull, *In Eminenti*. He condemned Freemasonry as pagan and unlawful and threatened any Catholic who joined with excommunication.

Modern Christian authors have continued this condemnation of the order. "The Masons have but one purpose": concluded author Epperson, "They exist to utterly destroy Christianity. . . ."

Others see in Freemasonry an ambivalent public view on religion at best. Journalist Still, who conducted a lengthy study of the group, wrote in 1990, "Every aspect of Masonry seems to have both a good and a bad side to it—an evil interpretation and a benign interpretation. Those who wish to find a Christian interpretation in its symbols can find ample published Masonic justifications. Those who wish to show that Masonry is really a form of Deism—built for all religions and faiths—can easily do so."

Webster, that earlier Freemason researcher and author, concurred, writing in 1924, "The truth is that Freemasonry in a generic sense is simply a system of binding men together for any given purpose, since it is obvious that allegories and symbols, like the x and y of Algebra, can be interpreted in a hundred different manners."

Yet Masonic authors themselves reveal that the order is not without metaphysical thought, rather it is very much devoted to divine under-standing. "Freed of limitations of creed and sect, [the Mason] stands master of all faiths," wrote Manly P. Hall. "Freemasonry . . . is not a creed or doctrine but a universal expression of Divine Wisdom . . . revealing itself through a secret hierarchy of illumined minds."

Hall saw Freemasonry as a "world-wide university, teaching the lib-eral arts and sciences of the soul to all who will hearken to its words." He said the traditions of hundreds of religions and the knowledge of a thousand ages spawned Masonic philosophy.

Wilmshurst stated clearly that Masonry "is a system of religious phi-losophy in that it provides us with a doctrine of the universe and of our place in it."

Though writing in the 1920s, Wilmshurst sounded like a consummate New Ager. He wrote of "positive energy," reincarnation or regeneration of the spirit, as well as a person's "aura," by which he explained the bib-lical Joseph's coat of many colors. He even went so far as to state that "Just as our Craft organization has its higher assemblies and councils . . . so in the mighty system of the universal structure there are grades of higher life, hierarchies of celestial beings working and ministering . . . beyond our ken."

Having addressed all this, Wilmshurst stated that the "secrets" of Freemasonry deal with introspection of the human soul but that "beyond this brief reference to the subject it is inexpedient here to say more." Obviously, all Masonic secrets are not publicly available despite a wealth of published material.

One can readily see why authors Still, Epperson, Webster, and others saw in Freemasonry an insidious attempt to subvert Christianity. Still claimed Masonic initiation rites "provide a system to gradually and gently realign a man's religious beliefs. Thus, a Christian is slowly encouraged to become a Deist [one who believes in no supernatural intervention by God in human affairs]; a Deist becomes an Atheist; an Atheist to a Satanist."

At another point, journalist Still backed away from the claim that Masons are Satanists. He stated the god of Masonry is actually Lucifer and explained that the difference is that "Luciferians think they are doing good [while] Satanists know they are evil."

Epperson concurred with this Luciferian interpretation, writing, "So the secret inside the Masonic Order is that Lucifer is their secret god." He quotes Master Mason Pike as writing, "You may repeat it to the 32nd, 31st and 30th degrees—The Masonic religion should be, by all of us initiates of the high degrees, maintained in the purity of the Luciferian doctrine."

Wilmshurst explained with typical Masonic obscurity, "To clear vision, Christian and Masonic doctrine are identical in intention though different in method. The one says '*Via Crucis*' [through the Cross]; the other '*Via Lucis*' [through Lucifer]; yet the two ways are but one way."

This belief in two separate but equal gods provides significant support to those connecting Freemasonry directly to the Cathars of France and the earlier Gnostics, both of which were mercilessly exterminated by the Catholic church. Both of these sects were known dualists, those that believe in the equal power of good and evil, light and dark.

It is illustrative to note that in the 1980s fundamentalist Christians were upset to learn that the Lucis Trust, a New York tax-exempt, non-profit "New Age" organization concerned with topics dear to the secret societies such as economics and environmentalism, originally had incorporated as a publishing house under the name the Lucifer Publishing Company. The firm published the works of Alice Bailey and Madame Blavatsky, both advocates of Theosophy. Trust officials explained "Lucifer as here used means 'bringer of light or the morning star' and has no connection whatsoever with Satan as conventional wisdom would have it."

Contrary to the idea that Pike and his fellow Masons were simply secret Satan worshipers, several Masonic writers demonstrate that less simplistic issues are involved. Even anti-Mason author Epperson demonstrates that Pike made a deeper examination of his subject by quoting

Pike's book *Magnum Opus* as stating, "All have admitted two gods with different occupations, one making the good and the other the evil found in nature. The former has been styled 'God,' and the latter 'Demon.' The Persians or Zoroaster named the former Ormuzd and the latter Ahriman; of whom they said one was of the nature of Light, and the other that of Darkness. The Egyptians called the former Osiris, and the latter Typhon, his eternal enemy."

Author Still explained that to Luciferians, God has a dual nature—the loving side, Lucifer, and the bad side, Adonai, both equal in power but opposite in intent. "This idea is symbolized by the circular yin-yang symbol of the Buddhists or the black-and-white checkerboard pattern seen on the floor of Masonic lodges or buildings," he wrote.

Mason Pike wrote that Adonai, one of the biblical names for God, was the rival of Osiris, the Egyptian sun god, a prominent figure in Masonic traditions.

Some anti-Masonic writers saw in the Masonic symbols of ancient Egypt a return to the worship of the pagan sun god. However, Pike, in his book *Morals and Dogma* intended only for the inner core of Masonry, made it clear that worship of the sun was an adulteration of an earlier belief. "Thousands of years ago, men worshipped the sun. . . . Originally they looked beyond the orb [our solar system's sun] to the invisible God. . . . The worship of the Sun [the invisible God] became the basis of all of the religions of antiquity," he wrote.

This secret becomes clearer when closer study reveals that this Great Architect of the Universe is a supreme creative being, while, according to Pike, "[Osiris] the Sun God . . . created nothing."

Masonic authors draw a distinction between the celestial "sun" and the "Sun" god which, they say, is the bringer of light. The gift of light—light usually being interpreted as knowledge—is greatly venerated in Masonic rituals. Interestingly enough, the appellation "Morning Star" and "Bringer of Light" were at times applied to Jesus.

So one inner Masonic secret echoes the belief of the ancient Gnostics and Cathars, namely that there is only one great creative cosmic God, referred to in Masonic literature as the Great Architect of the Universe, but that there may be two opposing aspects to this deity. A hidden aspect of this belief is the idea that in the distant past on Earth there walked "gods," or powerful nonhuman beings of the Hebrew Bible and the even earlier Babylonian and Sumerian legends. According to various traditions, it was these "gods" who brought humans civilization and science.

That inner-core Freemasons understood scientific principles as well as metaphysical ones is exemplified by their veneration of the collection of Greek writings that Plato's disciples called Hermes Trismegistus after the Greek god Hermes, who established alchemy and geometry. Freemasons also trace their philosophies to the Greek philosopher Pythagoras, who greatly influenced Plato, the idol of Cecil Rhodes and John Ruskin.

Both Pythagoras, who stated the Earth moved around the sun, and the Hermetic writings were said to have utilized secret "science" that survived Noah's Flood. Hermes, deified as Thoth by the Egyptians and thought to have intimate knowledge of the gods and the stars, voiced the principle "As above, so below." This indicated a knowledge of universal unity, comparing favorably with Albert Einstein's unified field theory. "From the smallest cell to the widest expanse of the galaxies, a repetitive geometric law prevails and this was understood from the very earliest of times," explained author Laurence Gardner.

Wilmshurst said the person who reaches "the summit of the Mason's profession" will become "conscious of being the measure of the universe; he realizes that the earth, the heavens, and all their contents, are externalizations, projected images, of corresponding realities present within himself."

Alchemy became known as the "Hermetic science" and Freemasonry contains both Hermetic branches and Hermetic rites. The mythical and magical practice of alchemy was passed down from the Egyptians. "It was more than science," explained authors Picknett and Prince. "The practice embraced a fine web of interlinking activities and modes of thinking, from magic to chemistry, from philosophy and hermeticism to sacred geometry and cosmology. It also concerned itself with what people today call genetic engineering and methods of delaying the aging process, and of trying to attain physical immortality."

"There can be no doubt that in some of what are called the [Masonic] High Degrees there is a very palpable infusion of a Hermetic element. This cannot be denied," wrote Masonic historian Mackey. This Hermetic tradition was focused in a companion secret society to Freemasonry—the Rosicrucians.

ROSICRUCIANS

Some researchers believe that Freemasonry grew out of the earlier mystical traditions of the Rosicrucians, a secret brotherhood with knowledge said to reach back into antiquity.

Documents available in France today contend that an Order of the Rosy Cross was founded in 1188 by a pre-Masonic Templar named Jean de Gisors, vassal of English King Henry II and the first independent grand master of the Order of Sion.

Some recent writers, however, believed that Rosicrucianism and Freemasonry were separate philosophies which only merged in the late eighteenth century as with the Illuminati influence.

Whatever the truth, the fact remained, as acknowledged by Mackey, that "a Rosicrucian element was very largely diffused in the *Hautes Grades* or High Degrees [of Freemasonry coming from] the continent of Europe about the middle of the 18th century."

Although the Rosicrucians claim to trace a lineage back to ancient Egypt and beyond, the name only came to the fore between 1614 and 1615 with the publication of two tracts. One, entitled *Fama Fraternitatis Rosae Crusis* or *Report of the Rosicrucian Brotherhood,* was supposed to have been written by a Christian Rosencreutz (translated literally as Rosy Cross) and detailed his journeys through the Holy Land and the Mediterranean area gaining esoteric Eastern knowledge. After studying with the illuminated Alumbrados of Spain, Rosencreutz returned to Germany, where he formed the Order of the Rosy Cross.

The name has variously been interpreted as a play on the name Rosencreutz; derived from the Latin *ros* or dew and *crux* or cross; a chemical symbol for "light"—hence knowledge; or a reference to the blood-covered cross of Jesus or the red cross on the shields of the Knights Templar. Count Mirabeau, the Freemason French Revolution leader, claimed the Rosicrucians were, in fact, nothing more than the outlawed Knights Templar continued under another name.

The fictional tracts, known as the "Rosicrucian Manifestos," disclosed the existence of this secret brotherhood and promised a coming age of enlightenment along with the revelation of ancient secrets. They most probably were written by Johann Valentin Andrea, a German Lutheran cleric who traveled extensively through Europe before becoming spiritual counselor to the Duke of Brunswick, chairman of the Freemason Convention of Wilhelmsbad, and the Freemason leader connected to William of Hesse and the Rothschilds.

According to Mackey, Andrea concocted the tracts in an effort to jump-start a society by which "the condition of his fellow-men might be ameliorated and the dry, effete theology of the church be converted into some more living, active, humanizing system."

A third Rosicrucian publication, the fantasy *Chemische Hochzeit* or *The Chemical Wedding* by Christian Rosencreutz, was so filled with symbolic references to the outlawed Knights Templar that the Catholic church condemned it along with the Rosicrucian Manifestos. One early German Rosicrucian society called the Order of the Gold and Rosy Cross became the basis of the Freemason Strict Observance Lodge which many years later hid the Illuminati.

Rosicrucians were seen by the church as Satanists and accused of making compacts with the devil and sacrificing children. Others saw them as the progenitors of today's scientific inquiry as well as the protectors of ancient secrets.

Prominent Rosicrucians included Dante Alighieri (author of *The Divine Comedy*), Dr. John Dee (scientist and "007" spy for Queen Elizabeth I), Robert Fludd (who participated in translating the Bible into English for King James I), and Sir Francis Bacon, whose writings inspired the colonization of America. Although he predated the order, authors Picknett and Prince found Rosicrucian ideals in Leonardo de Vinci, who they claimed created the famous Shroud of Turin through an early photographic technique, using his own features as a model.

Most researchers saw the Rosicrucian movement as a major force in the ongoing struggle between scientific rationalism and church dogma that resulted in the breakup of the Holy Roman Empire, the creation of Protestantism and the resulting Church of England, as well as the Renaissance. According to Picknett and Prince, "It is scarcely an exaggeration to say that Rosicrucianism *was* the Renaissance." (emphasis in the original)

Gardner added, "Following the [Protestant] Reformation, the Rosicrucian Order was largely responsible for the establishment of a new spiritually aware environment. People discovered that the Apostolic history of the Roman bishops was an outright fraud, and that the Church had deliberately sabotaged the story of Jesus. It also became apparent that the Rosicrucians—like the Cathars and Templars before them—had access to an ancient knowledge which held more substance than anything promulgated by Rome."

But the rise of the Protestant orders did little to decrease the violence aimed at anyone diverting from the public mindset of the day. Gardner reported that, ironically, "the Rosecrusian scientists, astronomers, mathematicians, navigators and architects became victims of the pernicious Protestant establishment. The Anglican clerics called them pagans, occultists and heretics, just as the Roman Church had done before."

So the rational humanist Rosicrucians were forced underground by the church. By the time of the formation of the Grand Mother Lodge of Freemasonry in 1717, Rosicrucian leaders Christopher Wren and Elias Ashmole had firmly established Rosicrucian-based Speculative Masonry deep within the order. It was the avowed Rosicrucian Ashmole, according to Webster, who drew up the three existent basic Masonic degrees adopted by the Grand Lodge. Nineteenth-century Masonic author J. M. Ragon asserted that the Rosicrucians and Freemasons merged during this time, even meeting in the same room at Masons' Hall in London.

"After 1750 . . . where once there were clear distinctions between Masons, Rosicrucians and organizations that claimed Templar origins, suddenly all such groups became so intimately entwined as to seem virtually one and the same," reported Picknett and Prince.

Two competing orders of Rosicrucians are still active in the United States today. Both claim to hold secrets handed down from ancient Egypt and both are the object of scorn and derision by religious fundamentalists.

Rosicrucian publications have indeed evinced knowledge from far beyond its founders' times. Author Gardner flatly stated that Rosicrucian philosophy could be traced through Plato and Pythagoras to the Egyptian Mystery School of Pharaoh Tuthmosis III, some 1,500 years before Christ. This linkage agreed with Webster's findings. She wrote, "Rosicrucianism was a combination of the ancient secret tradition handed down from the patriarchs through the philosophers of Greece and of the first Cabala of the Jews."

COMMENTARY

As with the wars and conflicts of the twentieth century, the traces of secret society agitation and manipulation are found in earlier rebellions and revolutions, including the War Between the States and the French and American Revolutions.

In the case of America's sectional conflict, it becomes clear that European agents incited violence in both the North and the South. This agitation found fertile ground in homegrown fanatics such as John Wilkes Booth, a member of the secret Knights of the Golden Circle.

The bankers and lenders of Europe, led by the ubiquitous Rothschilds, financed both sides. Essentially, the War Between the States was a struggle for control between the European bankers and Abraham Lincoln—the one man in the United States who appeared to comprehend the forces at play.

Once open warfare broke out, Britain and France concentrated troops in Canada and Mexico awaiting the right opportunity to exploit the situation. Only President Lincoln's Emancipation Proclamation elevating slavery as the cause célèbre of the conflict and the quiet intervention of the Russian navy prevented this plan to break up the United States from succeeding.

It was a setback for the European secret societies, who had been so successful in destroying both the church and the monarchy in France between 1789 and 1799. First with agitation by the Jacobin societies and later using paid agents who led the mobs against the Bastille and aristocrats' homes, society members instigated the Revolution and subsequent Reign of Terror.

The role of the Freemasons, and particularly the newly "Illuminized" Lodges, was blatant in this French tragedy. Some Masonic publications proudly admit Freemason involvement. Many Masons, including President Thomas Jefferson, were supportive of the French Revolution as well as early rebellions in the young United States.

There was even documented involvement of Freemasons in the American Revolution, with many colonists recruited into the British "field lodges" prior to the break with Britain. It may well have been the brother-against-brother nature of the revolt that prevented the vastly superior English military from vigorously prosecuting the war against the ragtag colonial rebels, thus securing them success in their rebellion.

Freemasonry, which grew to a prominent and powerful force following the Revolution, suffered a severe setback beginning with the kidnapping of Captain William Morgan in 1826. The suspicious members of the Anti-Masonic Movement caused a loss of membership and prestige in the order for many years.

This may have been just as well, since the documented history of the German Illuminati clearly indicated the existence of a secret society bent on subverting any and all government and religion. Despite laws against this order, Illuminati members merely hid themselves away within the ranks of Freemasons. Their ideals were advanced right on through the secret Round Tables of Cecil Rhodes, backed by the might of the Frankfurt Lodge, which was under the control of Hessian royalty, the Rothschilds, and their associates.

The Count of Saint-Germain and other "magicians" brought ancient knowledge from the Middle East to the inner core of Freemasonry. This knowledge involved secret traditions concerning the biblical account of Jesus' life as well as the origins and purposes of mankind, much of which was at variance with church dogma of the time. In fact, many critics of Freemasonry, then and now, accuse the order of being anti-Christian if not outright Satanists. Such accusations have necessitated extreme secrecy as dissidents from the church have long been subjected to community censure, and even physical violence.

Secrecy remained commonplace within the societies right up to the late twentieth century, when members of Italy's *Propaganda Due* lodge were found to be fomenting a fascist plot involving the Vatican, certain large banks, the Mafia, and the CIA.

The secrets of Freemasonry must be most profound and compelling to have caused members over the centuries to persevere in their effort to protect and propagate their knowledge against official and clerical censure and oppression. It is abundantly clear that this knowledge, passed down largely through ritual allegory and symbols, predates the ancient Egyptians.

It is highly significant that so many esoteric beliefs are traced back to Egypt and, more specifically, the ancient cultures of Persia.

But any discussion concerning philosophies, magic, and religion is quickly enmeshed in a quagmire of definitions, interpretations, and personal beliefs. The uncontestable fact here is that there are significant prehistorical overtones to the doctrines of both Freemasonry and Rosicrucianism. These shall be inspected more closely in connection with the Ancient Mysteries.

However, consideration first must be given as to how the several threads of such ancient knowledge were brought into Freemasonry. A major source of those ancient secrets seems to have been through the discoveries of a group of Medieval knights: the legendary Knights Templar.

PART IV

ELDER SECRET SOCIETIES

The knowledge of the Templars concerning the early history of Christianity was undoubtedly one of the main reasons for their persecution and final annihilation.

—Masonic philosopher Manly P. Hall

In the Dark Ages following the collapse of the Roman Empire, one religion gained absolute supremacy in the Western world: Christianity. While ostensibly based on the teachings of Jesus Christ, scholars today can trace Christianity's evolution back through the ideologies of ancient Greece, Egypt, and Babylon to the much older culture of Sumer.

The discovery in recent years of lost writings dating from before the time of Jesus has provided much-needed information to fill in the gaps of knowledge about both the man and his times.

Due to a lack of first-hand accounts of Jesus, acrimonious debates over Christian beliefs and theology continued for centuries from the time the secular power of the Holy Roman Catholic "Universal" church emerged during medieval times.

Until the fall of Constantinople in 1453, the Roman church stood as the ultimate authority in the Western world. Through the lending of both its money and blessings, the Vatican dominated kings and queens and controlled the lives of ordinary citizens through fear of excommunication and its infamous Inquisition.

Europe's best and brightest men were exhorted by the clergy to battle for God and country, and Christian Europe launched Crusade after Crusade against the Muslims holding the Holy Land of the Middle East. The power of the church became further centralized and all powerful.

Some of these men, particularly in southern France with its association to certain legends concerning Mary Magdalene and her descendants, had knowledge of secret traditions which ran counter to the teachings of the church. The Crusades presented a convenient excuse to take the Holy Land and search for verification of these traditions.

Some researchers even suggest that the Crusades may have been inspired by this search for hidden knowledge. According to French author Gerard de Sede, Peter the Hermit—generally considered to be instrumental in promoting the First Crusade along with Saint Bernard—was a personal tutor to the Crusade's leader, Godfrey de Bouillon, a man later associated with the Knights Templar.

Once in the Holy Land, the Crusaders apparently found some verification of heretical ideas which supported elder traditions, principally those circulating in southern France, and differed from the teachings of the church. It was this conflict that led to the creation of societies which used secrecy as protection from the Roman church, which, in turn, began to guard its established theology with increasingly violent means.

By many recent accounts, at least one group of Crusaders brought back more than just heretical hearsay—they reportedly returned to Europe with hard evidence of error and duplicity in church dogma. These Crusaders over time became known as heretics and blasphemers and an attempt was made by the church to exterminate them. They were the Knights Templar, whose traditions live on today within Freemasonry.

KNIGHTS TEMPLAR

A religious-military knighthood called the Order of the Poor Knights of Christ and of the Temple of Solomon was formed in 1118 when nine French Crusaders appeared before King Baldwin of Jerusalem and asked to be allowed to protect pilgrims traveling to the Holy Land. They also asked permission to stay in the ruins of Solomon's Temple.

Their requests were granted and the order became known as the Knights of the Temple, soon shortened to Knights Templar.

Scant attention has been paid to the Knights in traditional history books and their role in shaping future events has been mostly relegated to footnotes. It is known that the order flourished, becoming extraordinarily wealthy and powerful, until in the year 1307 they were crushed by an envious French king and a pope fearful of their secrets.

As with much of history, there was more to this story than has been told to a general audience. With the destruction of the Templars, the church attempted to wipe out all evidence of the order and their secrets, which involved the innermost mysteries of Christianity—issues so volatile that the Templars had to be destroyed by the very church that ordained them.

Until recently, most of what was known about the origins of the Templars came from the Frankish historian Guillaume de Tyre, writing more than fifty years after the events. His account is sketchy, incomplete, and perhaps even wrong in some instances. Today, thanks to the effort of a number of scholars, the record is more complete and Templar contributions are being reappraised.

The Middle East at the time was in turmoil. In 1099 the knights of the First Crusade, under Godfrey de Bouillon, had captured the Holy City of Jerusalem from the Muslims and created a Christian kingdom under that name. But the countryside was far from pacified and the journey from the eastern Mediterranean ports to the Holy City was perilous.

So nine knights petitioned Jerusalem's King Baldwin II of Le Bourg to be allowed to form a military order and to be quartered in the east wing of his palace which was adjacent to the recently captured Al-Aqsa Mosque, former site of King Solomon's Temple. Baldwin agreed and even paid the knights a small stipend. This act was thought by some researchers to indicate that Baldwin may have had ulterior knowledge of their activities.

These knights were led by Hugh de Payens—a nobleman in the service of his cousin, Hughes, Count of Champagne—and Andre de Montbard, the uncle of Bernard of Clairvaux, later known as the Cistercian Saint Bernard. Montbard also was a vassal of the Count of Champagne. At least two of the original knights, Rosal and Gondemare, were Cistercian monks prior to their departure for Jerusalem. In fact, the entire group was closely related both by family ties and by connections to the Cistercian monks and Flemish royalty.

"Payens and his nine companions all came from either Champagne or the Languedoc, and included the Count of Provence, and it is quite apparent that they went to the Holy Land with a specific mission in mind," wrote Picknett and Prince. Provence lies adjacent to the Languedoc and includes Marseilles, where Mary Magdalene reportedly arrived in Europe after the crucifixion of Jesus Christ.

A letter to Champagne from the Bishop of Chartres dated 1114 congratulated the count on his intention to join *la Milice du Christ* (Soldiers of Christ), a prototype for the Knights Templar. Furthermore, author Graham Hancock wrote that he had established that both Payens and Champagne had journeyed together to the Holy Land in 1104 and were together back in France in 1113, indicating that plans for such an order had been underway for several years prior to the audience with King Baldwin.

One irony was that sometime later Champagne himself joined the Templars, in effect becoming a vassal to his own vassal. One explanation for this strange occurrence—and a significant point concerning the order itself—was that their oath of allegiance was to neither king nor to their grand master but to their religious benefactor, Bernard, Abbot of Clairvaux, who continued to support the group as he rose to prominence. He was canonized in 1174.

During the first nine years of their existence, this unofficial order recruited no new members, an odd circumstance for a small group claiming to protect Jerusalem's roadways. Furthermore, the protection of pilgrims had already been undertaken by another order, the Knights of the Hospital of Saint John of Jerusalem known as the Hospitallers.

The idea that a mere nine knights could effectively patrol the roads leading to Jerusalem is preposterous. It is obvious that the Templars had another reason altogether for journeying to the Holy Land. They made little effort to guard the roads, leaving such protection to the Hospitallers. Instead, the Templars kept close to their quarters and excavated for treasure deep under the ruins of the first permanent Hebrew Temple.

Solomon's Temple, first constructed some three thousand years ago, was actually planned by his father, the biblical King David. King Solomon constructed the temple on Mount Moriah in Jerusalem.

Prior to the temple's construction in Jerusalem, the Hebrew temple said to house Yahweh since the exodus from Egypt was a simple tent. Traditionally, this portable temple housed the Ark of the Covenant, said to be the means of communication with God. One Hebrew name for their temple was *hekal,* a Sumerian term meaning "Great House." In fact, some experts have claimed that Solomon's Temple was "almost a carbon copy of a Sumerian temple erected for the god Ninurta a thousand years earlier."

Solomon's Temple was destroyed during the Babylonian conquest about 586 B.C., then rebuilt by King Zerubbabel after the Jews returned from captivity. Much of the new design was based on a vision by the prophet Ezekiel, who in the Old Testament described his experiences with flying devices. In the time of Jesus, Zerubbabel's temple was greatly reworked to become the temple of Herod the Great. It was destroyed only four years after its completion in A.D. 70 during the Jewish revolt against the Romans. Today, remnants of the Jewish temples are enclosed within the Dome of the Rock mosque, an Islamic holy shrine second only to Mecca and Medina.

There is no question that Templar excavations were extensive. In 1894 a group of British Royal Engineers led by a Lieutenant Charles Wilson discovered evidence of the Templars while mapping vaults under Mount Moriah. They found vaulted passageways with keystone arches, typical of Templar handiwork. They also found artifacts consisting of a spur, parts of a sword and lance, and a small Templar cross, which are still on display in Scotland.

It was during their excavations, according to several accounts, that the Templars acquired scrolls of hidden knowledge, again most probably dealing with the life of Jesus and his associations with the Essenes and Gnostics. They also reportedly acquired the legendary Tables of Testimony given to Moses as well as other holy relics—perhaps even the legendary Ark of the Covenant and the Spear of Longinus—which could have been used to validate their claims as an alternative religious authority to the Roman church.

Such reports were well supported by the discovery of a document etched on copper among the Dead Sea Scrolls found at Qumran on the northwest shore of the Dead Sea in 1947. This "Copper Scroll," translated in the mid-1950s at Manchester University, not only mentioned a vast treasure of both gold and literature but actually described their hiding place—the site of the Templar excavations beneath Solomon's Temple. It apparently was one of several copies, another of which may have come into the hands of the Templars. With its detailed directions to hidden Hebrew valuables, the "Copper Scroll" was literally a treasure map.

Author Hancock thought the Templars' search was only partially successful. "If the Templars had found the Ark, they would certainly have brought it back to Europe in triumph. Since that had not happened it seemed to me quite safe to conclude that they had not found it," he wrote. Hancock theorized that the Ark had long since been transported to Ethiopia, where it remains hidden.

According to author Laurence Gardner, in addition to gold, the Templar excavators also recovered "a wealth of ancient manuscript books in Hebrew and Syriac . . . many of these predated the Gospels, providing first-hand accounts that had not been edited by any ecclesiastical authority.

"It was widely accepted that the Knights possessed an insight which eclipsed orthodox Christianity, an insight that permitted them the certainty that the Church had misinterpreted both the Virgin Birth and the Resurrection."

Their newfound wealth as well as their possession of lost documents also could explain the rapid acceptance of the Templars by awestruck church leaders. According to Knight and Lomas, "The Templars clearly had possession of the purest 'Christian' documents possible—far more important than the Synoptic Gospels!" With this knowledge the Templar leaders, either directly or by implication, must have greatly intimidated church officials, leading to great growth and power.

Having accepted no new members for almost a decade and claiming to be poor even though most of them were members of or connected to royal families—their original seal depicted two knights sharing one horse—the order's fortunes suddenly soared.

Their leaders began traveling, recruiting members and gaining acceptance from both the church and European royalty.

On January 31, 1128, Templar grand master Payens and Montbard traveled to Troyes about seventy-five miles southeast of Paris to plead the case for official recognition by the church before a specially convened council. This Council of Troyes was made up of Catholic archbishops, bishops, and abbots, including Montbard's nephew, Saint Bernard, by then head of the powerful Cistercian order. With the added endorsement of King Baldwin, the council approved the Templars as an official military and religious order. This resulted in Pope Honarius II approving a "Rule" or constitution for the Knights Templar which sanctioned contributions to the order.

This Rule was prepared by Saint Bernard and copied the structure of his Cistercian order. To support the religious side of the order, the Rule, among other things, ordered all new Templars to make a vow of chastity and of poverty, which included turning over all their property to the order. On the military side, Templars were forbidden to retreat in combat unless their opponents outnumbered them more than three to one and their commander approved a withdrawal.

The structure of the order was a forerunner of Freemasonry. Each local branch was called a "Temple" and its ruling commander reported to and pledged obedience to the grand master.

Within the ranks there were four classifications—knights, sergeants, chaplains, and servants. As in later Freemasonry, there was great emphasis on keeping secrets from both the public and their fellow Templars. Picknett and Prince wrote that with the order's rigid pyramid command structure, "It is likely that the majority of the Knights Templar were no more than the simple Christian soldiers they appeared to be, but the inner circle was different."

The power and prestige of the order increased rapidly, and at the zenith of its popularity counted a membership of about twenty thousand knights. The distinctive white surcoat emblazoned with a red cross worn only by the Knights Templar was always seen in the thick of battle. Quickly their reputation rivaled that of modern fighting elites such as the U.S. Marines, Britain's Special Air Service, or the earlier German *Waffen SS*."

"They [Payens and Montbard] had gone west with nothing and came back with a Papal Rule, money, precious objects, landed wealth and no less than 300 recruited noblemen to follow Hugh de Payens' lead as Grand Master of a major order," noted Knight and Lomas.

"Within a year [of the Council of Troyes], they owned lands in France, England, Scotland, Spain and Portugal," reported Baigent and Leigh. "Within a decade, their possessions would extend to Italy, Austria, Germany, Hungary and Constantinople. In 1131 the king of Aragon bequeathed to them a third of his domains. By the mid-twelfth century, the Temple had already begun to establish itself as the single most wealthy and powerful institution in Christendom, with the sole exception of the Papacy."

Contributions from royalty and the nobles were not just in coin or land. Members received lordships, baronies, landlord status, and castles. Grand Master Payens had many high-level connections. He was married to Catherine de Saint-Clair, daughter of a prominent Scottish family that donated land south of Edinburgh where the first Templar study center or preceptory outside the Holy Land was built.

Saint Bernard—who had supported the Templars so well at Troyes—and his Cistercian order also prospered. According to Baigent, Leigh, and Lincoln, the Cistercians were practically insolvent prior to the formation of the Templars, but then showed sudden and rapid growth. "Within the next few years a half dozen abbeys were established," they wrote. "By 1153 there were more than 300, of which Saint Bernard himself personally founded 69. This extraordinary growth directly parallels that of the Order of the Temple."

In 1139 Pope Innocent II—a protégé of Saint Bernard—proclaimed that the Templars would henceforth answer to no other authority but the papacy. This license to operate outside any local control meant an exemption from taxes, which considerably increased the wealth of the order. The pope also granted the Templars the most unusual right to build their own churches. According to Baigent and Leigh, within Templar enclaves "the knights were a law unto themselves. They offered right of sanctuary, like any church. They convened their own courts to try cases of local crime. They ran their own markets and fairs. They were exempt from tolls on roads, bridges and rivers."

Obviously, whatever the Templars had unearthed beneath Solomon's Temple brought them power and recognition from church and political leaders alike.

This power only increased after 1129 when King Baldwin II asked Payens and his Templars to aid in an ill-fated attack on the Muslim city of Damascus. This somewhat hasty and ill-conceived operation may have been instigated by Count Fulk V of Anjou. Fulk had rushed to Jerusalem near the end of the Templar excavations. Pledging allegiance to the fledgling order, Fulk had contributed an annuity to continue their operations. His reward for such generosity may have come in 1128 when French king Louis VI selected Fulk to marry Baldwin's daughter Melisende. Following Baldwin's death in the aftermath of the failure to take Damascus, son-in-law Fulk, the Templar, became king of Jerusalem.

On his return to the Holy Land following a visit in Europe, Payens, along with three hundred knights, shepherded a large throng of pilgrims. The Templars then joined with the Christian forces in the attack on Damascus.

It was here that the Knights Templar had yet another opportunity to learn Holy Land secrets. During this action the Christians became allied with an Islamic secret society that also claimed to be privy to ancient knowledge: the notorious Assassins.

ASSASSINS

The Assassins, a fanatical Islamic sect that developed a dictatorial pyramid command structure copied by all subsequent secret societies, were so infamous that even today their very name is synonymous with terror and sudden death.

The name reportedly was derived from the cannabis drug hashish, which members smoked in preparation for killing. Sect killers, who were taught that murder was a religious duty, became known as "hashshasin," Arabic for hashish smoker, which over time became simply "assassin." This is the popular origin of the name. However, author Daraul and others have suggested that it may well have stemmed from the Arabic word "Assasseen" denoting "guardians of the secrets."

Assassin founder, Hasan bin Sabah, was a schoolmate of the Persian poet laureate Omar Khayyám and Nizam ul Mulk, who later became the grand vizier to the Turkish sultan of Persia. He had his own secrets to guard. He had gained esoteric knowledge from the former and royal privileges from the latter. After being caught in a money pilfering scandal, Hasan was forced to flee Persia for Egypt, where he was further indoctrinated in ancient secrets, to include an intimate knowledge of the Hebrew Cabala.

While in Egypt Hasan may have laid his plans for the formation of his Assassin sect while studying the organization and practices of the *Dar ul Hikmat* (House of Knowledge) or Grand Lodge of Cairo. This lodge was a repository for ancient knowledge and wisdom brought forward from the days of Adam, Noah, Abraham, and Moses. According to author Webster, lodge members perfected the techniques used centuries later by Weishaupt to organize the Illuminati. Also stemming from this lodge was the cult of Roshaniya or the Illuminated Ones, which became such a terror to authorities in Afghanistan under the leadership of Bayezid Ansari in the sixteenth century.

Tracing their ties to the prophet Mohammed, the Assassins were an outgrowth of the Islamic sects of Hakim, Fatima, the Batinis, and Shiahs. It was about A.D. 872 that one Abdullah ibn Maymun created the Batinis sect, which set the tone for the development of the Assassins. A dedicated materialist, Abdullah was schooled in Gnosticism and became determined to abolish all structured religion, including the Ismailis to which he belonged. To achieve this end, Abdullah was forced to pose as a pious member of the Ismailis. The Ismailis believed they were descended from Ishmael, the son of the Hebrew patriarch Abraham and his surrogate wife, Hagar, demonstrating again the intertwined histories of the Israelites and their Mideast neighbors.

Webster quoted an earlier researcher, Reinhart Dozy, who described

Abdullah's program as one dedicated to forming a vast secret society filled with both freethinkers and bigots for the purpose of discrediting and destroying religion. After elaborate initiations, he would "unfold the final mystery, and reveal that Imams [spiritual leaders], religions and morality were nothing but an imposture and an absurdity." He also sought to overthrow the reigning regimes and take power for himself, first by subterfuge and then by force. Exhibiting disdain for the public, he won over the credulous with magic tricks passed off as miracles, the religious leaders by displays of piety, and the mystics by lengthy dissertations on the ancient mysteries. Through such duplicity, "a multitude of men of diverse beliefs were all working together for an object known only to a few of them."

After years of schisms within the Ismailis, the followers of Abdullah and others joined in "societies of wisdom," which in 1004 became the Grand Lodge of Cairo, where members were turned into fanatics. It was here that the later Druses sect held sway.

The Druses apparently continued Abdullah's duplicitous methods as they claimed to be both Muslims and Christians at the same time. They also used recognition signs which can still be found in Grand Orient Freemasonry. As in all secret societies, while most members were simply fervent worshippers, the top leadership had other agendas. It was through the Druse-led Grand Lodge of Cairo that Hasan learned well the techniques he employed within his own society.

Hasan's killer cult came into existence about 1094 when he and some Persian allies took the mountain fortress of Alamut on the Caspian Sea in Iran. He created his own Shiah Ismaili sect which came to be known as the Assassins. While proclaiming himself as a great spiritual leader, Hasan forged a personality cult centered on himself backed by lethal violence. According to Webster, "The final object was domination by a few men consumed with the lust of power under the cloak of religion and piety, and the method by which this was to be established was the wholesale assassination of those who opposed them."

The higher initiates were taught the Assassin secret doctrines, one of which was that "Nothing is true and all is allowed." Another secret was that there is only one God and everything in creation, including humankind, is part of a universal whole, a concept along the lines of Einstein's unified field theory, which continues to be seriously studied by modern scientists. Finally, the Assassin dogma that the end justifies the means may well have been a precursor of that same philosophy which passed into "Illuminized" Freemasonry.

Hasan's method of recruitment was so extraordinary as to be thought a myth. According to several sources, including the writings of Marco Polo, who passed his way, Hasan found and developed a secret valley that he filled with gracious palaces and landscaped gardens well stocked with exotic animals and beautiful women. Local youths would find themselves befriended by strangers in drinking places. They would awake from a drug-induced stupor to find themselves surrounded by such beauty and luxury that it could only have been the promised paradise. After a few days of living beyond all expectation, the recruits were again drugged and woke up back in their dull reality.

After a few such experiences, Hasan had no trouble in enlisting their allegiance by promising to return them to "paradise" permanently in exchange for their deadly work. Entranced by the promise of eternal heaven, these brainwashed goatherders proved eager soldiers, even to the point of sacrificing themselves when required.

Calling himself the Grand Master or Shaikh-al-Jabal, Hasan operated this early-day Murder, Incorporated, from his highland fortress, gaining the title of "Old Man of the Mountain," a name that struck terror in the hearts of his neighbors.

The power of the Assassins increased until by the mid-twelfth century the cult boasted a string of strongholds stretching throughout Persia and Iraq. Their influence may have even reached to the secret society of Thugs in India, who were known to use recognition signs similar to the Assassins.

As Grand Master, Hasan created a system of apprentices, fellows of the craft, and masters, which has been compared with the later Masonic degrees. Masonic historian Mackey admitted the Assassins "whose connection with the Templars, as historically proved, may have had some influence over that Order in molding, or at least in suggesting, some of its esoteric dogmas and ceremonies."

Author Daraul quoted an Orientalist named Syed Ameer Ali as stating, "From the Ismailis the Crusaders borrowed the conception which led to the formation of all secret societies, religious and secular, of Europe. . . . The Knights Templar especially, with their system of grand masters, grand priors and religious devotees, and their degrees of initiation, bear the strongest analogy to the Eastern Ismailis."

Several accounts have connected the Templars with the Assassins in joint operations during the Crusades, including the attack on Damascus in 1129 led by King Baldwin of Jerusalem. One eighteenth century author lamented the fact that the Templars would "ally themselves with that horrible and sanguinary prince named the Old Man of the Mountain, Prince of the Assassins."

"Those who think that the Assassins were fanatical Muslims, and therefore would not form any alliance with those who to them were infidels, should be reminded that to the followers of the Old Man of the Mountain only he was right, and the Saracens who were fighting the Holy War for Allah against the Crusaders were as bad as anyone else who did not accept the Assassin doctrine," commented Daraul.

Sometime prior to his attack on Damascus, Baldwin had entered into an agreement with the Assassins, who counted many members within the walls of the city. With the aid of this Fifth Column, the city would be taken. The Assassins had been promised the city of Tyre for their assistance. The plot, however, was discovered and all Assassins in Damascus were rounded up and lynched by the inhabitants.

Buoyed by the return from Europe of Grand Master Payens and his Templars, Baldwin decided to make an outright attack on the city but was repulsed with heavy losses.

This battle along with other later combined operations could have provided the opportunity for the Templars and Assassins to share esoteric ancient knowledge as well as important military intelligence, since it is recorded that the Assassins had deeply penetrated the Muslim hierarchy.

"The Templars entered at various times into amicable arrangements and treaty stipulations with the Assassins," confirmed Mackey, ". . . we may therefore readily believe that at those periods, when war was not raging, there might have been a mutual interchange of courtesies, of visits and of conferences."

The murderous nature of the Assassins proved their downfall. Hasan, the Old Man of the Mountain, was assassinated by his son, Mohammed, who in turn was poisoned by his son, who had learned of Mohammed's plan to kill him. By 1250 invading Mongol hordes had captured the last Assassin stronghold, effectively eliminating the order. Although, according to some researchers, pockets of Assassins still exist in the Middle East today.

It must be noted that there were only slight differences between the average fighting man of both the Templars and the Assassins. Both groups were filled with brutish, ignorant, and bloodthirsty men who merely did what they were told. Only their leaders knew the underlying truths of their order.

Brutish as the rank-and-file knights may have been, the Templar leadership was brilliant and rapidly built up one of the most powerful nongovernment organizations ever seen. Payens died in 1136 and was succeeded as Templar grand master by a Lord Robert, son-in-law of the Archbishop of Canterbury, another indication of the aristocratic nature of the Templar hierarchy.

By the thirteenth century, the Templars owned about nine thousand castles and manors throughout Europe, yet as a religious order paid no taxes. Their investments included basic industries, particularly in the building trades. They owned more than five thousand properties in England and Wales alone. Their empire stretched from Denmark to Palestine. "If their eventual aim was world hegemony, they could not have organized themselves better, or planned their aristocratic hierarchy more thoroughly," commented Daraul.

They used the revenue from these holdings to build a huge fleet of ships and underwrite a vast banking system. The concept of using money to produce more money was coming into focus.

TEMPLAR BANKERS AND BUILDERS

Although conventional history traces the development of modern banking to early Jewish and Italian lending institutions, it was the Knights Templar who predated the Rothschilds and the Medicis.

"They pioneered the concept of credit facilities, as well as the allocation of credit for commercial development and expansion. They performed, in fact, virtually all the functions of a 20th century merchant bank," wrote Baigent and Leigh, noting, "At the peak of their power, the Templars handled much, if not most, of the available capital in Western Europe."

Christians were prohibited from the practice of usury, which then meant charging any interest on loans, but the Templars managed to avoid this restriction, probably by emphasizing the military rather than the religious aspects of their order. In one case, old documents revealed that the Templars charged as much as 60 percent interest per year, a much higher rate than the moneylenders of the time.

In a practice which continues today in Swiss banks, the Templars held long-term private trust funds, accessible only by the originators of the account.

It can also be argued that the Templars first introduced the credit card and packaged tours as they developed fund transfers by note, a Muslim technique most probably obtained from the Assassins and other contacts in the Middle East.

Pilgrims, merchants, officials, and the clergy faced many hazards and obstacles traveling in Europe and the Holy Land. They were prey for ferrymen, toll collectors, innkeepers, and even church authorities demanding alms, not to mention highway robbers and thieves.

To protect against such misfortunes, the Templars developed a system whereby the traveler could deposit funds to cover travel expenses with the commander of the local Temple and receive a specially coded receipt. This receipt or chit was issued in the form of a letter of credit, redeemable from any Temple. At the end of his journey, the traveler would receive either a cash refund of his account balance or a bill to cover any overdraft. It was a system which closely resembled both a bank check and the modern credit card.

"In England, the Templars also acted as tax collectors," Baigent and Leigh noted. "Not only did they collect papal taxes, tithes and donations, they collected taxes and revenues for the crown as well—and seemed to have been even more fearsome in that capacity than [Britain's] Inland Revenue [or the U.S. Internal Revenue Service]. In 1294, they organized the conversion of old to new money. They frequently acted as trustees of funds or property placed in their custody, as brokers and as debt collectors. They mediated in disputes involving ransom payments, dowries, pensions and a multitude of other transactions."

Along with banking practices, the Templars brought to Europe their acquired knowledge of architecture, astronomy, mathematics, medicine, and medical techniques. In less than one hundred years after formation of the order, the Knights Templar had evolved into the medieval equivalent of today's multinational corporation.

The Templars were not content to simply acquire existing castles and other structures. They were avid builders, constructing immense fortified estates, particularly in southern France and the Holy Land. Many were built on peninsulas or mountaintops, making them practically impregnable. Granted the privilege to build their own churches, the Templars became the prime movers behind the construction of the great medieval cathedrals of Europe.

One of the best-known Templar works is the famous Chartres Cathedral located southwest of Paris on the Eure River. Chartres was built on the site of an ancient Druid center and, in fact, is named after one of the Celtic tribes, the Carnutes. "It was a pagan site," wrote author Laurence Gardner, "dedicated to the traditional Mother Goddess—a site to which pilgrims traveled long before the time of Jesus."

Completed in 1134, a remarkably short thirty years after it was begun, the cathedral at Chartres is said to be the first of the Gothic style of architecture. Many believe such innovation was brought from the Middle East to Europe by the Templars, especially since Chartres was greatly inspired by the Templar-connected Saint Bernard, who held almost daily conferences with the builders. Considering the history of the Templars, author Hancock said he was "satisfied that they could indeed have unearthed on the Temple Mount some repository of ancient knowledge concerning the science of building and that they could have passed on what they had learned to Saint Bernard in return for his support."

The name Gothic is believed to have been derived from the Germanic tribes of Goths that overran the Roman Empire. However, Gardner and others argue that, at least when pertaining to architecture, the name may have come from the Greek *goetik,* meaning something magical. And the Goths certainly had nothing to do with the magical architecture of an amazing number of cathedrals constructed during the twelfth century— just after the Templars brought their secrets back to Europe.

Prior to this time European buildings had been squat, thick block structures built for expediency and defense. Suddenly, people were astounded by the impossibly high vaulted ceilings and flying buttresses of the new cathedrals. Pointed arches and vaulting coupled with magnificent stained glass windows reflected new techniques inspired by Templar knowledge of sacred geometry and metallurgy techniques.

It was the Templars who instigated the first stonemason guilds. According to Picknett and Prince, the Templars "were behind the formation of builders' guilds, including that of the stonemasons—who became lay members of the Templar Order and who had all their advantages, such as exemption from paying tax."

The stained glass in Chartres has evoked much comment. "Nothing like it had ever been seen before, and nothing like it has been seen since," commented Gardner. "Even in twilight, this glass retains its brilliance way beyond that of any other. Gothic stained glass also has the unique power to transform harmful ultra-violet rays into beneficial light, but the secret of its manufacture was never revealed. . . . No modern scientific process or chemical analysis has yet managed to penetrate its mystery." Gardner also noted that among those perfecting this Gothic stained glass was Omar Khayyám, which again tied the Templar builders to the Eastern knowledge of the Assassins.

Author Hancock noted that the power and grandeur of Egypt's Karnak Temple, the Zoser "step" pyramid and the Great Pyramid were unmatched until the time of the Templar cathedrals. He added that he became even more convinced of some connection between the Ancient Mysteries and the cathedrals when he recalled that Saint Bernard once defined God as "length, width, height and depth," a clear evocation of the knowledge of Pythagoras, Plato, and the ancient Egyptians.

There is also physical evidence within Chartres Cathedral that lends strong support to the idea that the Templars had acquired hidden knowledge regarding the story of Jesus. At the north door of Chartres above a small column is a carving of the Ark of the Covenant being carried in a wheeled wagon. Since the Ark had been missing since the destruction of the Jewish temple in A.D. 70 and since prior to that time all accounts depicted the Ark being carried by hand, many researchers believe this engraving offers proof that the Templars found the ark and transported it to Europe. This carving is tied conclusively to the Ark as a Latin inscription just below it reads, "In this place, the Ark is loved and obeyed," although it also could mean "In this place, the Ark is hidden." In another part of Chartres Cathedral is a stone carving believed to represent the Virgin Mary connected to an inscription reading *arcis foederis,* or Ark of the Covenant.

While it is true that various Christian traditions depicted the Virgin Mary as a "living" Ark of the Covenant for bearing Jesus, the carving of the Ark on a wheeled wagon clearly indicates that this carving may well refer to the tangible Old Testament Ark.

All this concern with a Mary and the Ark greatly supports the idea that many learned men in the Middle Ages knew of a tradition which claimed that both at one time may have resided in Europe.

The true fate of the legendary Ark remains a great mystery. Some researchers believe it was destroyed, while others believe it still exists in some secret society hiding place or perhaps stored away in the catacombs beneath the Vatican for safekeeping. Author Graham Hancock, former East Africa correspondent for *The Economist*, made an in-depth study of the Ark and concluded that it was secreted away to Ethiopia where it remains today. At least one modern researcher believes this sacred object may still be hidden beneath Mount Moriah in Jerusalem.

Another clear connection between the Templars and their work within Solomon's Temple can be found in Rosslyn Chapel, a miniature cathedral in the small Scottish town of Roslin south of Edinburgh. William Sinclair, a descendant of the prominent Saint-Clair family connected by marriage to Grand Master Payens, founded the chapel in 1446, but it was finished in 1486 by his son, Oliver. It was intended to be the first part of a larger church which was never completed.

Ostensibly a Christian place of worship, questions have arisen regarding Rosslyn. "It is actually a strange combination of Nordic, Celtic and Gothic styles," noted Gardner. "Upon checking with the official history we found that Rosslyn had to be reconsecrated in 1862," wrote authors Knight and Lomas. "Prior to that date there is uncertainty about its consecrated status. . . . [Rosslyn's] symbolism is Egyptian, Celtic, Jewish, Templar and Masonic in profusion; a star-studded ceiling, vegetative growths coming from the mouths of the Celtic Green Men, entangled pyramids, images of Moses, towers of the Heavenly Jerusalem, engrailed crosses as well as squares and compasses. The only certain Christian imagery was in later Victorian alterations. . . ."

Knight and Lomas discovered that the floor plan of the Rosslyn Chapel was an exact match for that of Solomon's Temple in Jerusalem, even including two important columns at the entrance. These columns are called Jachin and Boaz, names tied to the Ancient Mysteries, and which still carry mythical and mystical significance for both Jews and Freemasons.

"Rosslyn was not a simple chapel," Knight and Lomas concluded, "it was a post-Templar shrine built to house the scrolls found by Hugh de Payens and his team under the Holy of Holies of the last temple at

Jerusalem! . . . Rosslyn Chapel was a deliberate replication of the burial place of the secret scrolls!" These authors wrote that the scrolls hidden beneath the Jerusalem temple were the most highly prized writings of the Jews, particularly of the more devout sects, and represented the "most priceless treasure in Christendom" perhaps to include the long lost "Q" document said to be the basis for the books of Matthew, Mark, Luke, and John. "More mundane material, such as the Community Rule, was deposited around Judea in places as humble as the caves at Qumran," they added.

It should also be noted that at the time the Templars built their Gothic cathedrals, not one carried a depiction of the Crucifixion, a most strange anomaly for a Christian order but strong evidence that the Templars indeed denied the orthodox view of this event.

Yet another factor connecting the Templars to heresies of the day was the romanticized writings of Wolfram von Eschenbach, whose hero Parsival became the Parsifal of Wagner's famous opera. *Parsifal,* said to be one of Wagner's most visionary and esoteric works, connects Wagner's outlook to Templar traditions. A poor Bavarian knight, Wolfram was believed by many to have been a Templar himself, as he certainly demonstrated a very personal knowledge of the Templars as well as their equipment and fighting techniques. He described a brotherhood of knights dressed in white mantles decorated with red crosses guarding some great sacred secret and even called them *Templeis,* which could be translated as Templars.

It was Wolfram who was among the first to popularize the legend of the Holy Grail, that elusive goal of many medieval quests. Grail mythology—King Arthur, Merlin, the Round Table—actually began with a poem by Chrétien de Troyes written in the late twelfth century. It was Chrétien who first named Arthur's residence as Camelot. Since Chrétien lived in Troyes, site of the official sanctioning of the order, and was employed by the Count of Champagne, Templar grand master Payens's liege lord, he may have had access to the Templar knowledge brought from the Holy Land which he incorporated into his writing.

In Wolfram's *Parsival,* the Grail is a magical stone which bestows youth on those who possess it. This stone was guarded by Knights of the Temple at a great temple on *Munsalvaesche,* or Mountain of Salvation, believed to be connected to the mountain fortress of Montsegur in southern France, the last bastion of the Cathars.

Wolfram tied himself even closer to the Templars when he related that his source for *Parsival* came from an old Arabic manuscript which had been kept by the House of Anjou. Recall that it was Count Fulk of Anjou, later king of Jerusalem, who had worked closely with and funded the original Knights Templar. Interestingly enough, Wolfram began writing *Parsival* about the time work on the Chartres Cathedral was completed.

Beginning with the Templars, then working its way through the Cistercians of Saint Bernard on into the symbolic architecture of the Gothic cathedrals, the seeds of their heresy spread far and wide.

The Templars thrived, thanks to the technologies and philosophies discovered in Jerusalem, while the church became more and more antagonistic, gradually realizing the threat posed by their knowledge. The Templars, in their turn, grew antagonistic toward the church. Researcher and author David Hatcher Childress observed, "To the Templars, the true church, one that taught mysticism, reincarnation and good works, was being suppressed by a dark power that called itself the one true faith."

Through the centuries of its power, the church—then an irresistible attraction to corrupt officials, scalawags, and conmen as well as the pious—often instigated bloody massacres against its enemies, which eventually came to mean anyone who failed to acquiesce to its authority. For example, between the years 1208 and 1244 tens of thousands of people were killed by a papal army sent by the Vatican to the province of Languedoc in southwestern France, the long-standing home of the Knights Templar—as well as home to some very unorthodox ideas.

CATHARS

The object of this papal attack was a people known as the Cathars, forefathers of the Italian and Scottish *Carbonari*, who so influenced the Illuminati. They were followers of the earlier Gnostics, who were more committed to matters of the spirit than material wealth.

The Cathars, whose name meant Pure Ones as they believed their religious views were more "pure" than those of the Catholic church, were ideally situated for acquiring unorthodox beliefs. The Languedoc, formerly known as Occitania, encompassed the Mediterranean coast west of Marseilles, the Black and Corbieres Mountains and the Pyrenees, which separated the area from Spain. An independent state, the region was more closely tied to the Spanish frontier and the vestiges of the old Septimanian kingdom than to the newly forming French nation. Languedoc was a crossroads where travelers passed to and from the Middle East via Muslim Iberia and the sea.

With the breakup of the Carolingian empire created by Charlemagne following his hard-won conquest of the area in A.D. 801, this corner of the old Roman Empire fell under the control of various kings of the *Francia* or Franks, the name of which soon would be applied to the entire nation—France.

Languedoc was home to a number of ancient towns, many of which traced their origin to the Greeks and early Romans. It had its own traditions, culture, and its own language. The language of Occitania or *Langue d'Oc* gave the area both its identification and its name.

Perhaps due to this convergence of ideas and traditions, the Languedoc was more cultured and prosperous than its neighbors. "Prejudice against Jews was common, but . . . persecution was not," noted Michael Costen, Senior Lecturer in Adult Education at the University of Bristol and author. "Organized and official persecution of the Jews became a normal feature of life in the south only after the Crusade because it was only then that the Church became powerful enough to insist on . . . discrimination." The Cathars also got along reasonably well with the Cistercian monks, the predominant church representatives in the region.

After a visit to Rennes-le-Chateau in the Languedoc, authors Picknett and Prince said they "found evidence for a complex series of connections that led back to a Gnostic tradition in the area, a place that has been notorious for its 'heretics,' be they Cathars, Templars or so-called 'witches.'"

According to Costen, Catharism was "the most serious and widespread of all the heretical movements which challenged the Catholic Church in the 12th century." Until very recently, little was known of the Cathars other than that they were considered heretics. This was because the only available information on them came from their implacable enemy, the Roman church, which saw that any material supporting the Cathars was destroyed.

The Cathars were known widely as *bons hommes* or good men who led simple, religion-centered lives. They preferred to meet in nature rather than in elaborate churches. Cathar priests, known as *perfecti* or the perfect ones, dressed in long dark robes and were very ascetic, having pledged to forgo worldly possessions. "There is a very considerable similarity between Catharism and Buddhism," wrote Dr. Arthur Guirdham, a psychiatrist who made a close study of that group. "Both believe in reincarnation, in abstention from flesh foods—though fish was allowed in Catharism—in non-resistance, that it was sinful to take the life of any living creature, even an animal."

"Their way of life was an attempt to obey the teachings of Jesus," explained Picknett and Prince. "All baptized members were spiritually equal and regarded as priests. Perhaps more surprising for those days was their emphasis on equality of the sexes. . . . They were also itinerant preachers, traveling in pairs, living in the utmost poverty and simplicity, stopping to help and to heal wherever they could. In many ways the Good Men would have appeared to pose no threat to anyone—except the Church."

Costen said it would be wrong to simply accept the official view that the Cathars were dangerous heretics. "Rather it should be seen as a positive choice made by people who were given a very unusual opportunity to hear a new theology [the accounts of Jesus and Mary Magdalene circulating in southern France at the time] and to choose for themselves as a result of the uncoupling of the powers of Church and secular authority," said Costen, adding, "It was impossible for the Medieval church . . . to ignore the challenge presented to it within its own territories."

Dr. Guirdham explained that Catharism was a form of dualism, a belief which "has existed from time immemorial" and connected to the ancient sects of Mithras and the Manichaeans. The Cathars also viewed Jesus as the spiritual Son of God. "To them Christ did not exist in a human but in a spirit body. The Inquisition wrongly translated this as meaning that to the Cathars, Christ was a kind of phantom. The Cathar view was in accordance with that expressed by modern spiritualists and by the adherents of [Rudolf] Steiner [who was to influence the Nazi cult]," said Dr. Guirdham.

In their dualist theology, the Cathars believed that good and evil are opposites of the same cosmic energy force and that a good god created and rules the heavens while an evil god created man and the material world. "Because of this belief, it was obvious that the God of the Old Testament was Satan," stated Costen, who said the Cathars thought that when people died, ". . . they could either leave for their true home [in

Heaven] or stay where they were . . . where they were . . . where they would have to suffer . . . seven reincarnations . . . other writers quoted nine. Thereafter the soul was irretrievably lost."

"I saw how there had been a thread throughout all time," commented Dr. Guirdham, "the Manicheans, the cult of Mithras, the [Cathars], all completely massacred, very, very completely, and among other things because of this reincarnation business."

Other researchers thought the Cathars' only problem was a lack of proper obedience to the church. Picknett and Prince wrote, "The overriding reason why the Cathars fell afoul of the Church was that they refused to acknowledge the Pope's authority."

Author Gardner agreed, writing, "The Cathars were not heretics; they were simply non-conformists, preaching without license, and having no requirement for appointed priests, nor the richly adorned churches of their Catholic neighbors." However, Gardner also saw a connection between the Cathars and the Knights Templar potentially dangerous to the church. "The Cathars were known also to be adepts of the occult symbolism of the Cabala, an expertise that would have been of significant use to the Knights Templar who were thought to have transported the Ark and their Jerusalem hoard to the region."

Something about the peaceful, if unorthodox, Cathars was certainly upsetting to the Vatican. Interestingly enough, in 1145, Pope Eugenius III sent none other than that Templar patron Saint Bernard to preach against Catharism in Languedoc. According to Gardner, Bernard instead reported, "No sermons are more Christian than theirs, and their morals are pure." Did this mean Saint Bernard was oblivious to their theology? Or did his defensive words add substance to the allegation that he and the Templars secretly held Cathar beliefs?

The answer is immaterial since, justified or not, the Vatican began laying plans to eradicate the Cathars. And it is quite clear that some of the Cathar beliefs were directly opposite those of the church.

The beginning of the Cathar heresy is hard to pin down. Some of the Languedoc clergy traced their predecessors back to the earliest days of Christianity, which may have resulted in their belief of a more pure interpretation of church origins. Others believed the Knights Templar had passed along knowledge they gained while excavating in Jerusalem. Then there is the fact that even today in that area of France one may still find traces of a remarkable belief—that Mary Magdalene, viewed as either the wife or consort of Jesus, migrated to the area following the crucifixion. It was said that the Cathars had knowledge of a tradition that spoke of Jesus as both a husband and father.

The concept of Mary Magdalene and Jesus as a couple is one supported by the Gnostic writings discovered at Nag Hammadi, Egypt, in 1945. In the Gospel of Philip, named for the apostle Philip and believed written in the second half of the third century, it is written, "And the companion of the Savior is Mary Magdalene. But Christ loved her more than all the disciples and used to kiss her often on her mouth. The rest of the disciples were offended by it and expressed disapproval. They said to him, 'Why do you love her more than all of us?'" Jesus answered them with a lengthy discourse on how "Great is the mystery of marriage!" and how it was "a great power" necessary to the existence of the world.

There is an important connection between the gospels only discovered in 1945 and a tract published in the 1330s reportedly by the German mystic Meister Eckehart under the name *Schwester Katrei* or Sister Catherine. According to authors Picknett and Prince, "This unusual and outspoken tract . . . contains ideas regarding Mary Magdalene that are *only otherwise found in the Nag Hammadi Gospels.*. . . She is portrayed as being superior to Peter because of her greater understanding of Jesus, and there is the same tension between Mary and Peter [found in the *Nag Hammadi Gospels*]. Moreover, actual incidents that are described in the Nag Hammadi texts are mentioned in Sister Catherine's tract." (emphasis in the original)

Picknett and Prince see this tract as evidence that documents identical to the recently discovered texts were known to the Cathars, most probably through the discoveries of the Knights Templar.

Another real possibility is that the Cathars already had an oral tradition of an intimate relationship between Jesus and Mary but lacked any substantiation of their theology until the Templars returned to Languedoc from Jerusalem with their newly found scrolls. The Templar discoveries may have only reinforced and intensified an existing belief.

Another factor may be a connection made by authors Baigent, Leigh, and Lincoln in *Holy Blood, Holy Grail*, between the Jesus bloodline and the Merovingian kings of southern France.

"If our hypothesis is correct," they wrote, "Jesus' wife and offspring—and he could have fathered a number of children between the ages of 16 or 17 and his supposed death—after fleeing the Holy Land, found refuge in the south of France, and in a Jewish community there preserved their lineage. During the 5th century this lineage appears to have intermarried with the royal line of the Franks, thus engendering the Merovingian dynasty. In 496 A.D. the church made a pact with this dynasty, pledging itself in perpetuity of the Merovingian bloodline— presumably in the full knowledge of that bloodline's true identity. . . . When the Church colluded in . . . the subsequent betrayal of the Merovingian bloodline, it rendered itself guilty of a crime that could neither be rationalized nor expunged, it could only be suppressed. . . ."

Author Laurence Gardner, as an internationally recognized expert on sovereign and chivalric genealogy, was permitted to study the private records of thirty-three European royal families. He confirmed that the Merovingians were related to Jesus, but through his brother James, who Gardner claimed was the same person as Joseph of Arimathea.

Gardner also made a persuasive argument for Mary Magdalene as the spouse of Jesus in his 1996 book *Bloodline of the Holy Grail*.

"It was never any secret . . . for the majority of these people [European royalty], that Jesus was married and that Jesus had heirs, because it is written as such in very many family archives. . . . The published papers of Mary, Queen of Scots talk about it at length. The papers of James II of England, who wasn't deposed until 1688, talk of it at length. . . . I was actually in a position where I was presented with . . . some very, very old documentation, not only last opened in seventeen-whatever, but actually documented and written down hundreds of years before that," he explained, adding, "I also had access to Templar documents, to the very documents that the Knights Templar brought out in Europe in 1128 and confronted the Church establishment with, and frightened the life out of them with, because these were documents that talked about bloodline and genealogy. . . . The early Christian Church leaders adopted scriptures and teachings that would obscure the truth about the royal bloodline of Jesus."

The early church was fearful not only of Jesus' descendants but of women in general. Women were prohibited from teaching or becoming priests—a prohibition only now being relaxed. Clergymen were required to be celibate and never marry, despite the clear admonition by Paul in I Timothy 3:2 that a bishop or church leader should have a wife.

According to Gardner and other recent authors, women were denigrated by the early church in order to preserve the power and authority of its insider "old boy" network of cardinals and bishops. Today many diverse Bible scholars are taking a second look at the role of women as defined by the early church. "Most Christian movements we know to have been characterized by the prominence of women were ultimately judged heretical," observed University of Pennsylvania scholar Ross S. Kraemer.

To discourage any attention toward Mary Magdalene, Gardner said church fathers made much of New Testament scriptures which described Mary as a "sinner," the original word being a mistranslation of the word *almah,* actually meaning a virgin undergoing a ritual prior to marriage. "The duplicitous bishops decided, however, that a sinful woman must be a whore," commented Gardner, "and Mary was thereafter branded as a harlot!" Other scholars, such as Jane Schaberg of the University of Detroit-Mercy, concluded that the persona of Mary Magdalene may even be a composite of other biblical women and that such conflation was deliberate.

According to the traditions of southern France as well as William Caxton's 1483 work *Legenda Aurea* or *Golden Legend,* one of the first publications of England's Westminster, Mary Magdalene, her brother Lazarus and sister Martha, with her maid Marcella and the children of Jesus, journeyed by ship to Marseilles, France, after the crucifixion. The party then moved farther westward where "they converted the inhabitants to the faith."

Gardner wrote that Mary was "nine years younger than Jesus . . . Mary was aged 30 at her [symbolic] Second Marriage, during which year—33 A.D.—she bore her daughter Tamar. Four years later she gave birth to Jesus the younger, and in 44 A.D., when she was 41 years old, her second son, Joseph, was born. By that time Mary was in Marseilles—Massilia—where the official language was Greek until the 5th century." By these same reports, Mary died at what is now Saint Baume in southern France in A.D. 63 at age sixty.

Returning from the Seventh Crusade with King Louis IX, one Jean de Joinville in 1254 wrote they "came to the city of Aix in Provence to honor the Blessed Magdalene. . . . We went to the place called Baume, on a very steep and craggy rock, in which it was said that the Holy Magdalene long resided at a hermitage."

"For centuries after her death, Mary's legacy remained the greatest of all threats to a fearful church that had bypassed Messianic descent in favor of Apostolic succession," wrote Gardner, noting, "The most active Magdalene cult was eventually based at Rennes le Chateau in the Langue-doc region."

There is a tantalizing hint that perhaps in that same region was evidence more tangible than stories about the Magdalene. According to Baigent, Leigh, and Lincoln, the very same Joinville wrote that his friend Louis IX once told him of a time when Cathar leaders had approached the commander of the papal army and cryptically asked if he would "come and look at the body of Our Lord, which had become flesh and blood in the hands of their priests."

In addition to the traditions regarding Mary and reincarnation, the Cathars also were greatly persuaded by the beliefs of an itinerant preacher named Peter Valdes of Lyon. His followers, or Waldensians as they were known, read from scriptures translated into their own vernacular Occitan and believed that a personal calling to preach was more important than church training. They also disdained bloodshed, even that instigated by the church or state. When the Waldensians refused to stop preaching openly, they were excommunicated and expelled from Lyon by local church officials.

Many people believed the Cathars originated with a Bulgarian priest named Bogomil, whose Bogomilism sect was widely spread through the Byzantine Empire. Bogomils rejected many aspects of the orthodox church, such as mass, the Eucharist, Old Testament miracles and prophesy, baptism, marriage, and the priesthood. "They believed that the physical world was the work of the Devil and intrinsically evil," wrote Costen. "They developed for themselves a rich mythology of the Creation and Fall which acted as a substitute for much of the Bible which they rejected. These dualists accepted that matter was the creation of the Good God, but believed that Satan had fashioned the world and the material bodies of men from it, either trapping the spirit of an angel within the material body to form Adam or having the clay animated by the Good God."

However, authors Picknett and Prince argued that all of the Cathar beliefs could not have come from the Bogomils. They quoted the research of Yuri Stoyanov, who wrote, "The teaching of Mary Magdalene as the 'wife' or 'concubine' of Christ appears, moreover, an original Cathar tradition which does not have any counterpart in the Bogomil doctrines."

Whatever the truth of their origins, these Cathar beliefs had evolved over a long period of time, as did the decision to move against them. Despite whatever agreements might have been made, papal authorities must have finally decided that something had to be done about whatever relics, treasure, or writings might be concealed in the Languedoc.

THE ALBIGENSIAN CRUSADE

Proclaimed heretics by King Philip II of France at the insistence of Pope Innocent III, beginning in 1209, the Cathars were hunted down and exterminated during what became known as the Albigensian Crusade. The Cathars were sometimes called Albigenses for their large presence in the central Languedoc city of Albi. This was an operation in which the much vaunted Knights Templar were conspicuously absent.

It was a long, bitter, and bloody affair, which ended in 1229 but was not fully concluded until after the fall of the fortress of Monsegur in 1244. Even then, the church did not entirely extinguish the Cathar heresy. In Languedoc today there remains some instinctive wariness and distrust of both church and state, according to several authors.

For some time after becoming pope, Innocent III had tried to bring ecclesiastical pressure to bear on the Cathars with notable lack of success. A man whose fondest dream was spearheading a great Crusade to capture the Holy Land, this pope had to settle for a Crusade in Languedoc, where the nobles as well as the general population saw little to be concerned about in the simple and gentle Cathars.

In an effort to subdue the power of the Crusader knights, the church had long instituted a policy known as the "Peace of God." Based on an alliance between the church and the military powers, this "Peace" was intended to place church authorities in firm control of any military activities.

"The agency which was supposed to oversee the enforcement of the Peace in the Languedoc was the Order of the Temple and to that end they were able to collect a small tax on each ox used by the peasantry," wrote Costen. "There is little evidence that the Templars ever did anything effective to enforce the Peace."

Proving unsuccessful in the use of anti-Cathar preaching and Templar suppression, Pope Innocent III by 1204 decided it was time to act. He began writing to King Philippe-Auguste of France urging a move against the southern heretics. He also reinstated Raymond VI, Count of Toulouse, who had been excommunicated by a predecessor, after Raymond rather reluctantly agreed to support his Crusade. Despite Raymond's agreement, little action was taken.

Raymond was again excommunicated for failing to act against the Cathars, and when a representative of the pope met with him over Christmas 1207 in an attempt to revive the issue, he was murdered by one of Raymond's men. Thoroughly fed up with the situation, Pope Innocent III set his Crusade into motion.

Although seen today as a war by Christians against Christians, at the time, many people, particularly outside the Languedoc, supported the war as one against a deadly enemy in their own midst. To Pope Innocent, the Crusade was necessary not only to subdue heresy but to demonstrate the power of the church over recalcitrant secular leaders like Raymond.

Innocent promised the status of a Crusade to anyone joining his army. This meant both absolution of any sins committed in the process as well as a share in any loot. "Many saw an opportunity for plunder and profit and were not to be entirely disappointed," said Costen. "On the whole, though, the Crusaders were primarily motivated by religious zeal."

Soon the pope's army, "the biggest ever to assemble in the Christian world," gathered at Lyon under the leadership of Arnald-Amalric along with a number of noblemen and bishops.

As this massive force—about thirty thousand strong—moved down the Rhone valley, Raymond had second thoughts and decided to join. After pledging to join the Crusade, Raymond was reconciled with the church and promised immunity from attack.

The first major attack came at the city of Béziers. Here, despite their bishop's call to surrender, the townspeople decided to resist. According to Costen, the army's loot-hungry camp followers stormed the city's gates and were soon joined by the soldiers acting without orders. "Both church and town were looted and the inhabitants massacred, with clerics, women and children being killed inside the churches," he wrote. "When the leaders of the army confiscated booty from the camp followers the town was fired and burnt down." According to the official report, twenty thousand inhabitants were slain.

It was at Béziers that Arnald-Amalric, when asked how his troops should distinguish between Catholic and heretic, replied, "Kill them all, God will know his own."

In view of the massacre at Béziers, town after town throughout the Languedoc fell to the papal army without a fight. Internal strife was rampant as inhabitants outdid each other in handing over known and suspected heretics. At the town of Castres, Cathars handed over to the army were burnt at the stake, a practice which was to continue throughout the Crusade.

By 1229 the campaign was effectively ended by a Treaty of Paris. Though the treaty ended the independence of southern French royalty, it did not stop the heresy. Cathar *perfecti* retreated to the mountainous redoubt at Montsegur, in the foothills of the Pyrenees. Beginning in the spring of 1243, the papal army besieged the fortress for more than ten months. According to Picknett and Prince, here "a curious phenomenon took place. Several of the besieging soldiers *defected to the Cathars* despite the certain knowledge of how it would end for them." (emphasis in the original) The Cathars certainly must have possessed something to commend their beliefs to these veteran soldiers.

Finally, in March 1244, the siege of Montsegur was ended by the Cathars' surrender. Picknett and Prince noted several "mysteries" connected with the fall of Montsegur. One was "for reasons that have never been explained [the Cathars] were given permission to remain in the citadel for another 15 days—after which time they gave themselves up to be burned. Some accounts go further and describe them as having actually run down the mountainside and jumped into the waiting bonfires in the field below." Costen supported this story somewhat, noting, "There is no suggestion that the Cathars of Montsegur resisted the massacre."

"The most persistent mystery of all concerns the so-called Treasure of the Cathars," commented Picknett and Prince, "which four of them managed to carry off in the night before the rest were massacred. These intrepid heretics somehow managed to get away by being lowered down on ropes over the particularly precipitous side of the mountain in the middle of the night."

The Cathars, many of whom were wealthy, did indeed have a considerable cache of gold and silver. But, according to Baigent, Leigh, and Lincoln, this pecuniary treasure was smuggled out of Montsegur and lost to history three months before the massacre of the fortress's Cathars.

No one knows for certain what secret knowledge or "treasure" the Cathars might have felt needed to be sent from Montsegur at the last minute, but it is generally believed that it was writings concerning the perpetuation of the Jesus bloodline after Mary's arrival in southern France, a subject closely connected with the Knights Templar.

"The Templars were hungry for knowledge, and their search for it was their main driving force," wrote Picknett and Prince. "They seized knowledge wherever they found it: from the Arabs they took the principles of sacred geometry, and their apparent close contacts with the Cathars added an extra Gnostic gloss to their already heterodox religious ideas."

"From its earliest years the [Templars] had maintained a certain warm rapport with the Cathars, especially in the Languedoc," noted Baigent, Leigh, and Lincoln. "Many wealthy landowners—Cathars themselves or sympathetic to the Cathars—had donated vast tracts of land to the Order. . . . It is beyond dispute that Bertrand de Blanchefort, fourth Grand Master of the Order, came from a Cathar family. . . . In the Languedoc, Temple officials were more frequently Cathar than Catholic."

Blanchefort, who headed the Templars from 1153 to 1170, was "the most significant of all Templar grand masters," according to these three authors. "It was Bertrand who transformed the Knights Templar into the superbly efficient, well-organized, and magnificently disciplined hierarchical institution they then became."

There is evidence that many other Templars were themselves Cathars, and it has been established that the Templars hid many Cathars within their order and buried them in sacred ground. Along with their failure to participate in the Albigensian Crusade, Picknett and Prince found the fact that the close connections between the Templars and the Cathars were not brought up in subsequent charges against the order, evidence that such connections were an embarrassment to a church hierarchy wanting nothing more than to forget both the Cathars and their beliefs.

Following the Albigensian Crusade, those Cathars that survived either fled to neighboring countries—Italy was a favorite for ironically this home nation of the pope was not strenuous in hunting the heretics—or went into hiding with the aid of sympathetic neighbors. "By the early 14th century the Cathars of the Languedoc were becoming isolated and poor," Costen stated. "Their destruction was caused by the methodical pursuit of the Church with its new weapon, the Inquisition. . . ."

"The Languedoc saw the first act of European genocide, when over

100,000 members of the Cathar heresy were massacred on the orders of the Pope during the Albigensian Crusade . . . ," noted Picknett and Prince. "It was specifically for the interrogation and extermination of the Cathars that the Inquisition was first created."

As the result of the Crusade, "The Church retained its monopoly of religious activity, its control of belief and strengthened its control over the private lives of individuals. The new French State gained the Church as an ally in strengthening control over towns and nobility," wrote Costen, noting that as recently as the 1920s, much like suppression of Native American languages during the past century, children in the region were punished for speaking the old Occitan language on public school playgrounds.

The extermination of the peaceful Cathars was also a foretaste of what church leaders had in mind for their rivals in power, the Knights Templar.

THE TEMPLARS' DEMISE

For sixty-two years after the fall of the Cathar stronghold at Montsegur, the Knights Templar empire stood against the growing power of the Vatican and the nation states.

Their control over industry and finance was tremendous, and they had grown into a fearful military power, complete with their own naval fleet based in the French Atlantic port of La Rochelle. It was the Languedoc that connected La Rochelle to Mediterranean ports, allowing commerce with Portugal and the British Isles without passing through the Muslim-held Strait of Gibraltar. Templar vessels, among the first to use magnetic compasses, carried weapons and supplies to the Holy Land as well as an estimated six thousand pilgrims a year.

But as their power and wealth grew, so did their pride and arrogance, as evidenced in 1252, when a Templar master threatened England's King Henry III with these words, "So long as thou dost exercise justice, thou wilt reign. But if thou infringe it, thou wilt cease to be king."

That the Templar order was closely connected to the royalty of England is clearly demonstrated by the fact that King John was residing part-time in the London Temple in 1215 when an alliance of noble-men—many of them Templars—forced him to sign the Magna Carta or Great Charter creating a constitutional monarchy in that nation.

But while the Templar order flourished in Europe, things went badly in the Holy Land. Less than a century after its capture, Jerusalem again fell into the hands of the Muslims. Soon only the city of Acre remained under Christian control. In 1291 this fortress port fell and the order, along with the Hospitallers, was forced to relocate to the island of Cyprus, which the Templars had purchased from Richard the Lion Heart during an earlier Crusade. With the loss of the Holy Land, so too was lost the principal justification for the existence of the Templars.

Near the end of the twelfth century, the Templars had aided in the creation of another military order—the formidable Teutonic Knights, those childhood heroes of Adolf Hitler. The Teutonic Knights had created a gigantic principality of their own—called the *Ordenstaat*—which extended from Prussia through the Baltic to the Gulf of Finland. This Teutonic independent state may have inspired dreams within the Templar leadership of a similar autonomous empire in the Languedoc.

But this was not to be. Beginning in the early fourteenth century, the Templars were doomed to the same fate as that of the Cathars.

A key instigator of the Templars' demise was France's King Philip IV, a ruler envious of the Templars' wealth and fearful of their military strength. At one time, Philip sought refuge in the Paris Temple to escape a rebellious mob. He knew from personal experience the wealth of the Templars and was heavily in debt to them. Adding to his rage against the Templars was the fact that he had been turned down as a member of the order.

In 1305 Philip journeyed to Rome and convinced Pope Clement V that the Templars were actually plotting the destruction of the Roman church. The pope accepted Philip's word, as the French king has been the power behind his own ascension to the papacy. "Between 1303 and 1305 the French king and his ministers engineered the kidnapping and death of one Pope—Boniface VIII—and quite possibly the murder by poison of another—Benedict XI. Then, in 1305, Philip managed to secure the election of his own candidate, the archbishop of Bordeaux, to the vacant papal throne. The new Pontiff took the name Clement V," explained Baigent, Leigh, and Lincoln.

According to Masonic author Albert Mackey, Philip had agreed to support Clement's bid for the papacy in return for a secret commitment to crush the Knights Templar.

Furthermore, since it was widely whispered that the Templars were attempting to restore the ancient Merovingian kings both in France and other states, Philip's charges fell on receptive ears. The Merovingians were said to trace their bloodline back to Jesus, which presented a grave challenge to Rome's authority and supported the idea that the Templars had gained secret knowledge of the true life of Christ.

With the blessing of Pope Clement V, King Philip returned to France and began to move against the Templars. Drawing up a list of charges that ranged from subversion to heresy, Philip issued secret orders to officers throughout the country that were not to be opened until a predetermined time.

This was dawn of Friday, October 13, 1307, a date which from that time onward brought a sinister connotation to any Friday the thirteenth. Authorities spread out over France and quickly rounded up all the Templars at hand.

"Captured knights were imprisoned, interrogated, tortured and burned," said Gardner. "Paid witnesses were called to give evidence against the Order and some truly bizarre statements were obtained. The Templars were accused of a number of assorted practices deemed unsavory, including necromancy, homosexuality, abortion, blasphemy and [use of] the black arts. Once they had given their evidence, under whatever circumstances of bribery or duress, the witnesses disappeared without trace."

It is still a matter of controversy as to whether the Templars were truly guilty of such accusations. It is apparent that many of the charges against this erstwhile Christian order were spurious and contrived. But there is also evidence that the inner circles of the Templars were sympathetic to, if not adherents of, the heresies dealing with Mary Magdalene, John the Baptist, and the crucifixion and resurrection of Jesus. Some researchers have even speculated that the Templar skull and crossbones flag may have pertained to the remains of Mary, the Baptist, or both. Vestigial memory of this Templar symbol may have inspired the pirate flags of later centuries as well as the Skull and Bones order.

"We strongly feel that while the highest-ranking knights may have had radically atypical views on the divinity of Jesus Christ, the Templars were, throughout their entire existence, a faithful Catholic Order. . . . The

Knights Templar were betrayed by a Church and a Pope that they had served well," commented the Masonic authors Knight and Lomas in defense of the order.

It was apparent that, despite the suddenness of the arrests and the secrecy of the orders, many Templars were forewarned. "Shortly before the arrests, for example, the Grand Master, Jacques de Molay, called in many of the Order's books and extant rules and had them burned," noted Baigent, Leigh, and Lincoln.

Many French Templars were arrested without a fight apparently hoping the situation would turn around, but many others fled the country. The biggest mystery was the disappearance of both the Templar fleet and the accumulated treasure in the Paris Temple. Most researchers have connected the disappearance of the Templar fleet with the missing treasure.

Author Gardner claimed the Templar treasure remained in France at the time of the arrests. "[Philip's] minions had scoured the length and breadth of Champagne and Languedoc—but all the while the hoard was hidden away in the Treasury vaults of Paris," he wrote.

Later, according to Gardner, Grand Master Molay had the treasure transferred to La Rochelle, where a fleet of eighteen galleys transported the hoard to safety in Scotland.

Authors Baigent and Leigh generally agreed with this, pointing out that there were "five years of legal wrangling, negotiation, intrigue, horse-trading and general dithering before the Order was officially dissolved," plenty enough time to disperse the treasure.

Knight and Lomas added a fascinating addition to the story of the Templar escape—that a segment of the Templar fleet may have made its way to America 185 years before Christopher Columbus set sail.

This claim begins with the Mandaean sect, those who believed that John the Baptist was the true messiah and that Jesus perverted his teachings. The Mandaeans have been connected to Nazoreans thought to be part of the Qumran community whose scrolls were found in 1945. Muslims forced the Mandaeans from the banks of the Jordan River into Persia where remnants of the sect still exist.

The Mandaeans, like the Essenes, believed that the souls of good people would go to a wonderful and peaceful land across the sea when they died, a land they believed was marked by a star called "Merica." Since it is likely the documents discovered by the Templars in Jerusalem were duplicates of those found at the Qumran community, the Templars may have found a reference to the new lands as well as the name "Merica."

Knight and Lomas conjectured that at least one part of the Templar fleet provisioned in Portugal then sailed west for "la Merica." They said these intrepid sailors, flying their well-known skull and crossbones battle flag, arrived in New England in the year 1308.

Compelling evidence of such a landing can be found in Westford, Massachusetts, where today a punched-holes engraving of a knight can be found on a rock. This figure, dressed in the style of a fourteenth-century knight, carries a shield containing a picture of a sailing ship following a single star. In Newport, Rhode Island, a landmark tower matches the rounded architecture of the Templars and is dated back to the fourteenth century. "There is no doubt that the building is extremely old," noted Knight and Lomas, "because on a map of 1524 recording the European discovery of this coastline, Italian navigator Giovanni da Verrazano marked the location of the Newport Tower as an existing 'Norman Villa.'"

Recently discovered ruins in Patagonia, thought to be the lost *La ciudad de los Cesares* (the City of the Caesars), revealed an ancient pier and docks along with a slab of dressed stone marked with a Templar cross, which prompted investigator Flugberto Ramos to speculate that Templars may have journeyed there in pre-Columbian times.

More persuasive evidence of previously unknown Templar exploration can be found in Scotland's Rosslyn Chapel, where clear depictions of ears of corn and aloe cactus are found on archways and ceiling. "According to official history, seed grains on Indian maize were first brought to Europe and Africa by 16th century explorers . . . ," noted Knight and Lomas. Since Rosslyn Chapel was completed in 1486, six years before Columbus ventured out over the Atlantic, and the carvings are an integral part of construction, "we have certain evidence that the men that instructed the masons of Rosslyn Chapel must have visited America at least a quarter of a century before Columbus," commented Knight and Lomas.

While these authors admit that indications of a Templar presence in the pre-Columbian New World are not conclusive, they do add to the suspicion that the later Templar-inspired Freemasons Bacon and Raleigh knew more about the "New Atlantis" than previously imagined.

They also explained that a sixteenth-century German monk named Waldseemueller, who first wrote that America was named for explorer

Amerigo Vespucci, knew nothing about the Templar-Mandaean legend of "Merica." The monk had heard about the new land of "America" and also of the explorer Vespucci and simply put the two together. "Wald-seemueller got the name right but the explanation wrong," said Knight and Lomas. "Very shortly after he had written these words, he realized his mistake and publicly retracted his assertion that Amerigo Vespucci was the discoverer of the New World—but by then it was too late. . . ."

"The standard historical line that is routinely trotted out for the origin of the name of the New World, comes entirely from a silly misunder-standing by an obscure clergyman who never ventured more than a few miles from [his] monastery . . . on the French/German border," they com-mented.

Whether or not there was a Templar landing in "la Merica" in the early fourteenth century, there could well have been a Templar connection to its discovery. According to Baigent and Leigh, Templars in sympathetic Por-tugal were cleared by an inquiry and then changed their name to Knights of Christ, devoting themselves chiefly to sea exploration. "Vasco da Gama was a Knight of Christ and Prince Henry the Navigator was a grand mas-ter of the Order," they noted. "Ships of the Knights of Christ sailed under the familiar red pattee cross. And it was under the same cross that Christopher Columbus's three caravels crossed the Atlantic to the New World. Columbus himself was married to the daughter of a former Knight of Christ and had access to his father-in-law's charts and diaries."

While Templar connections to America will be debated for some time, there seems little doubt that many members of the order—as well as their treasure of both gold and documents—made their way to Scot-land by way of their fleet.

Scotland, then being fought over by England and Robert the Bruce, was the perfect refuge from the persecution of the order, which soon spread outside France. At the urging of Pope Clement V, other nations began rounding up Templars and attaching their property. England's King Edward II was initially slow to move against the Templars, but, as King Philip's son-in-law, he was finally spurred to halfhearted action. A few Templars were arrested but generally given light sentences such as penance in a monastery or abbey. Templar property was handed over to the Hospitallers order.

It was two years after the attack against the order began that Edward finally ordered the arrest of all Templars remaining under his control in

English-occupied Scotland. His men managed to secure exactly two men, one of them Walter de Clifton, the Templar master. Under interrogation, Clifton revealed that his fellow Templars had fled "across the sea," more evidence that Templars may have set out for America.

Robert the Bruce's Scotland was a different story, with its long history of involvement with the Templars. According to Gardner, Grand Master Payens had met with the Scottish king just after the Council of Troyes, and Saint Bernard had merged the Celtic church with his own Cistercian order. The Knights Templar had been encouraged and supported by a succession of Scottish kings beginning with King David and had gained a considerable amount of property there.

During the time of the Templar persecution, King Robert had every reason not to prosecute the Templars—he was one by birth based on the support of his ancestors, he was at war with Edward II, and he had been excommunicated by the Roman church for warring with Edward, Philip's son-in-law. Cut off from both the church and his neighbors, Robert welcomed any help he could get.

English blockades closed off most of the normal routes from the continent to Scotland. "But one important route was open," stated Baigent and Leigh, "from the north coast of Ireland, including the mouth of the Foyle at Londonderry, to Bruce's domains in Argyll, Kintyre and the Sound of Jura. . . . Thus Templar ships, Templar arms and material, Templar fighting men and, just possibly, the Templar treasure would have found their way to Scotland, providing vital reinforcements and resources for Bruce's cause."

While official history does not credit the Templars with Bruce's victory against the English, researchers have found considerable reason to believe that was the case. Several Masonic authors flatly state that Templars were among Bruce's army.

The Battle of Bannockburn, which secured Scottish independence, was fought on June 24, 1314. Intriguingly enough, this was Saint John's Day, one of the most significant days of the year for Templars, who venerated the saint.

Ostensibly to relieve a besieged garrison at Stirling Castle, gateway to the Highlands, King Edward mobilized an army of well more than twenty thousand in addition to the nearly ten thousand in the Stirling garrison. It was plain that he sought to destroy Bruce rather than simply reinforce Stirling. King Robert could only muster a force of less than ten thousand, so outnumbered nearly three to one, his chances for victory appeared dim.

The two forces clashed in the vicinity of Stirling Castle and fought viciously all day. Although specifics of the battle are vague, it appeared that a "fresh force" arrived just as the battle hung in the balance.

This new force was enough to cause King Edward and five hundred of his best knights to leave the field, which caused a panic among the remaining English forces. "The withdrawal deteriorated quickly into a full-scale rout, the entire English army abandoning their supplies, their baggage, their money, their gold and silver plate, their arms, armor and equipment," reported Baigent and Leigh.

These authors believed that a contingent of Templars, with their distinctive flowing beards and red-cross banners, was the "fresh force" that struck fear in the hearts of Edward and his men. Other authors confirm this. Gardner wrote that a member of the Saint-Clair family commanded Knights Templar at the Battle of Bannockburn. Mackey wrote that Masonic historians mentioned orders "first conferred on the field of Bannockburn, as a reward for the valor that had been displayed by a body of Templars who aided Bruce in that memorable victory."

By the date of this battle, the Templars supposedly no longer existed. In 1312 the order had been officially dissolved by the pope at the insistence of King Philip, and in 1314, the order's last official grand master, Jacques Molay, was burned at the stake in Paris.

Molay, according to nineteenth century author Eliphas Levi, had organized "Occult Masonry," namely adding the Johannite heresy to the Templars' secret knowledge concerning Mary Magdalene's journey to Europe with the children of Jesus.

Johannites were named for John the Baptist, who they considered the true biblical messiah with Jesus merely a secondary figure during the time prior to the Jewish revolt in Palestine. The Johannites, who claimed to have inherited their secret knowledge, believed that Jesus or "Yeshu the Anointed" was actually a mortal man who was initiated into the cult of Osiris. They believed that the story of the Virgin Mary was a fabrication by later writers to explain away his illegitimate birth.

"The Johannite sect recognized that the title 'Christ' was not unique to Jesus": explained Picknett and Prince, "the original Greek *Christos* merely meant 'Anointed'—a term that could have been applied to many, including kings and Roman officials. Consequently, the Johannite leaders always took the title of 'Christ' themselves—Significantly, the Nag Hammadi *Gospel of Philip* applies the term 'Christ' to all Gnostic initiates."

Levi even claimed that Grand Master Payens had been initiated into the ideas of the Johannite sect prior to heading the Knights Templar. This idea was supported by the claim of the Masonic leader Baron von Hund, who claimed he had been presented the "true history" of Freemasonry. Recall that von Hund created the "Strict Observance" lodge in Germany. It was initially known as the Brethren of John the Baptist. It has also been suggested that the Masonic ritual involving the death of a Hiram Abif actually symbolizes the martyrdom of Templar master Molay.

If indeed the Templar elite were infused with the teachings of the Johannites passed through Grand Master Molay, it is clear why church authorities persisted in his death sentence. Another reason may have been that Molay recanted an earlier confession that some of the charges against the Knights Templar were true.

Molay, who entered the Templar order in 1265, had fought in Syria and later was stationed at the Templar base on Cyprus. He was elected grand master about 1298. In late 1306 or early 1307 Molay was summoned to appear before Pope Clement V, supposedly to discuss regaining the Holy Land. Instead he was questioned about the charges against the order being leveled by King Philip. On that fateful Friday thirteenth, Molay was arrested and made his initial confession, most probably under torture.

Molay also was coerced into writing to his brother Templars and urging them to turn themselves in and confess. Appeals from Molay for a personal judgment by the pope proved fruitless. And in March 1314, after three cardinals condemned him to life imprisonment, Molay retracted his confession. As a relapsed heretic, he was handed over to Philip's officers, who burned him at the stake near the Templar-inspired Notre-Dame cathedral.

Legend has it that, as the flames licked around him, Molay called out for both Pope Clement and King Philip to join him before God within a year. Both men were indeed dead before a year had lapsed. Some believed that secret Templars poisoned them while others believed their deaths resulted from Molay's curse.

Authors Knight and Lomas claimed to have connected Molay's death to a modern controversy. "The Qumranian/Masonic style shroud that was taken from the Paris temple of the Knights Templar and used to wrap the damaged figure of the Grand Master traveled with de Molay to the home of Geoffrey de Charney, where it was washed, folded up and placed in a drawer. Exactly 50 years later, in 1357, this 14-foot-long piece of linen was taken out of store and put on public display at Livey . . . that length of cloth is today called the Shroud of Turin," they wrote.

In other parts of Europe, most Templars shaved their conspicuous beards and blended into the general population. A few were tried, found not guilty, and released. In Germany, intimidated judges released Templars, who promptly joined other orders such as the Knights of Christ, the Teutonic Knights, or the Hospitallers.

The Hospitallers began about 1070—before the First Crusade—when a group of Italian merchants established a hospital dedicated to Saint John in Jerusalem. After Crusaders took the city in 1099, the Hospitallers organized as an order and a grand master was selected. While not initially a military order, the Knights of Saint John, known simply as Hospitallers, became more militant as the Templars rose to prominence.

With the loss of the Holy Land, the Hospitallers fell back to Cyprus along with the Templars. After the destruction of the Templars, the Hospitallers gained much of their property, which only increased their already prosperous and powerful order. Later they were forced to retreat to Rhodes. When a third siege by the Turks finally took the island in 1522, the order relocated to the island of Malta, where they would become the Sovereign and Military Order of Malta or simply the Knights of Malta.

Today, the Knights of Malta are headquartered in Rome under the direct supervision of the pope and are recognized by more than forty countries as a sovereign nation. A British offshoot, known as the Knights of Saint John of Jerusalem, is a Protestant order headquartered in London and headed by the king or queen. According to author David Icke, "The Catholic and the Protestant wings are in fact the same organization at the highest level. . . . Both were the same force, as were, and are, the Teutonic Knights. All were involved in the same things, including banking, and used the same vicious, unscrupulous methods to get their way."

Modern Americans connected to the Knights of Malta include the late CIA directors William Casey and John McCone, Chrysler chairman Lee Iacocca, columnist William F. Buckley, Joseph P. Kennedy, U.S. ambassador to the Vatican William Wilson, Clare Boothe Luce, and former U.S. secretary of state Alexander Haig. Dr. Luigi Gedda, the head of Catholic

Action, was decorated by the Knights of Malta for his liaison work between the Vatican, the CIA, and the European Movement of Joseph Retinger, the "Father of the Bilderbergers." "Today, the Order of Malta is believed to be one of the primary channels of communication between the Vatican and the CIA," wrote Baigent, Leigh, and Lincoln.

"Today, there are no fewer than five organizations in existence alleging one or another species of direct descent from the [Templars]," noted Baigent and Leigh. The Hospitallers, Knights of Malta, Knights of Saint John, Freemasonry, and the Rosicrucians, and perhaps others, all trace their lineage to the Knights Templar with their esoteric knowledge recovered from under Solomon's Temple.

As these groups became more and more intertwined, the lines of membership blurred. Baigent and Leigh noted that the disposition of Templar property in Scotland involved "something quite extraordinary—something which has been almost entirely neglected by historians. . . . For more than two centuries in Scotland—from the beginning of the 14th to the middle of the 16th—the Templars, it appears, were actually *merged* with the Hospitallers. Thus, during the period in question, there are frequent references to a *single joint order*—the 'Order of the Knights of St. John *and* the Temple.'" (emphasis in the original)

The Knights of Malta survived the Medieval persecution by allying themselves with the Vatican and even participating in the persecution of its enemies. Likewise, many of Europe's royal families, themselves usurpers of the thrones of the Merovingians and others, worked in partnership with the Vatican to maintain the status quo. These royals are sometimes referred to as the "Black Nobility."

Yet another order which was created specifically to combat the Vatican's enemies and to protect the secrets of the church was the Jesuits. This order, officially known as the Society of Jesus, was formed in 1540 by Ignatius of Loyola, a soldier turned priest, who swiftly turned the organization into an aggressive militant force against both heretics and Protestants alike. It was the structure of the Jesuits that Adam Weishaupt used as a template for his Illuminati.

But even the militant Jesuits were susceptible to the lure of the secret knowledge of the Templars. Over time, many Jesuits may have gotten too close to the heresies of the period. They began to resist the authority of the Roman church and its power over governments, resulting in a ban against the order by Pope Clement XIV in 1773. But the imperative of protecting the church forced a reinstatement of the Jesuits, including all former rights and privileges, by Pope Pius VII in 1814.

Since King Philip's move against the Templars had failed to entirely exterminate adherents of the order, and even the militant Jesuits were not entirely reliable, the effort to remove all enemies of the church was taken up by the infamous Inquisition, which came close to completing this task over the next few centuries.

Operating on behalf of a succession of popes, the Franciscan Gray Friars and the Dominican Black Friars conducted unspeakable tortures during the Catholic Inquisition. In 1480 the Inquisition recovered lost momentum when the grand Inquisitor, the Dominican Tomás de Torquemada, initiated the Spanish Inquisition, aimed primarily at Muslims and Jews. By 1486 the list of ecclesiastical crimes had grown to include Satan worshippers, herbalists, midwives, and just about anyone who disagreed with church dogma or local social values.

The dreaded Inquisition, first initiated to control the Cathars during the Albigensian Crusade, was not entirely dissolved until 1820. "Meanwhile, those of the privileged class who possessed true esoteric skills and Hermetic knowledge were obliged to conduct their business in the secrecy of their lodges and underground clubs," noted Gardner.

"The once revered knowledge of the Templars caused their persecution by the savage Dominicans of the 14th century Inquisition. It was at that point in the history of Christianity that the last vestige of free thinking disappeared," he added.

While Molay's death ended the overt power of the Knights Templar, there seems to be no question that the order survived and was fused into other secret societies. "These days, history books and encyclopedias are almost unanimous in declaring that the Knights Templar became extinct in the 1300s. They are quite wrong," declared Gardner. "The Chivalric Military Order of the Temple of Jerusalem [an updated title for the Knights Templar]—as distinct from the later contrived Masonic Templars—is still flourishing in continental Europe and Scotland."

"After the sinister events surrounding the official suppression of the Templars, the Order went underground and continued to exert its influence on many other organizations," agreed Picknett and Prince. "Gradually it has emerged that the Templars have continued to exist as Rosecrucianism and Freemasonry, and the knowledge they had acquired passed into these societies."

Behind the Knights Templar lurked one of the most mysterious secret societies of all: the little-known Priory of Sion, another group obsessed not only with politics but with unorthodox religious views.

THE PRIORY OF SION

If the claims of several recent authors are correct, the *Prieure de Sion* or Priory of Sion, may be one of the oldest and most powerful secret societies in history.

It reportedly was the moving force behind the creation of the mighty Knights Templar and records show that past Priory leadership involved such names as Leonardo da Vinci, Robert Fludd, Sir Isaac Newton, Victor Hugo and artist Jean Cocteau. It lists twenty-six past grand masters going back through seven hundred years of history. Yet the public had no knowledge of this group until mid-twentieth century, which has fueled charges that the whole issue is a hoax.

It was in the mid-1950s that the public—mostly in France—first learned of the Priory, which means a religious house, something like an abbey.

Scattered newspaper and magazine articles beginning in 1956 spoke of a "mystery" surrounding the small Languedoc town of Rennes-le-Chateau. At first this story appeared little different from other stories of local hidden treasure found almost anywhere. But, as the years passed and more information came to light, the story of the Priory took on much greater significance.

The "mystery" of Rennes-le-Chateau involved a Catholic priest named Francois Berenger Sauniere, who was assigned to the town's parish in 1885. Young and well-educated, Sauniere was given this backwater assignment after apparently evoking the ire of some superior. Yet, the thirty-three-year-old priest decided to make the best of it.

Sauniere, working closely with an eighteen-year-old housekeeper named Marie Denarnaud, cared for his parish and still found time to hunt and fish. "He read voraciously, perfected his Latin, learned Greek [and] embarked on the study of Hebrew," noted authors Baigent, Leigh, and Lincoln. He also decided to restore the town church, which had been consecrated to Mary Magdalene in 1059 and stood on Visigoth ruins dating to the sixth century.

In 1891, while working in the church, Sauniere removed the alter stone and discovered that one of its supports was hollow and contained four parchment documents—two genealogies dating from 1244 and 1644 along with two missives written in the 1780s by a former parish priest, Abbot Antoine Bigou.

The Bigou texts were unusual and appeared to be written in different codes. "Some of them are fantastically complex, defying even a computer, and insoluble without the requisite key," stated Baigent, Leigh, and Lincoln.

Sauniere took his discovery to his superior, the bishop of nearby Carcassonne, who sent him on to Paris to meet with the director general of the Saint Sulpice Seminary. Later it was found that in earlier years, this seminary had been the center for an unorthodox society called the *Compagnie du Saint-Sacrement,* thought to be a front for the Priory of Sion. If this was the case, it would explain how Priory members learned of Sauniere's discovery.

Whatever was in the documents, it set Sauniere's life on an entirely new course. "For during his short stay in Paris, Sauniere began to mix with the city's cultural elite, many of whom had dabbled in the occult arts," noted authors Vankin and Whalen. "Contemporary gossip had it that the country priest had an affair with Emma Calve, the famous opera diva who was also the high priestess of the Parisian esoteric underground. She would later visit him frequently in Rennes-le-Chateau."

Not only did Sauniere's reported Paris visit gain him new friends in high places, he also came into great wealth. Before his sudden death in 1917, researchers estimated he had spent several million dollars on construction and renovations in the town. During his work upon returning from Paris, Sauniere made yet another discovery—a small crypt beneath the church reportedly containing skeletons.

His behavior became quite odd. Sauniere scraped off a Latin inscription on the headstone of a member of the prominent local Blanchefort family, not realizing that copies had already been made. Translated, the inscription read, "To Dagobert II King and to Sion belongs this treasure and he is there dead." He began collecting worthless postage stamps and valueless rocks along with costly rare china and fabrics.

But he also had the town's road and water supply upgraded, assembled a massive library, and built a zoological garden, a lavish country house named Villa Bethania and a round tower named *Tour Magdala* or Tower of Magdalene, all of which indicated sudden wealth.

Within the renovated church, Sauniere erected a strange statue of the demon Asmodeas—"custodian of secrets, guardian of hidden treasures, and, according to ancient Judaic legend, builder of Solomon's temple." He filled the renovated church with unusual painted panels, one depicting Jesus' body being carried to his tomb. But a full moon in this panel caused authors Baigent, Leigh, and Lincoln to suspect it might mean that the body was slipped out of the tomb in the dead of night. Over the church entrance, he had inscribed the Latin words *Terribilis Est Locus Iste,* meaning "This place is terrible." Perhaps Sauniere was echoing the words of Jacob in Genesis 28:17, who said "This is a terrible place!" upon realizing he had found the "Gate of Heaven."

Unusual visitors came to the town, including Archduke Johann von Habsburg, cousin to the Austrian emperor Franz Joseph. "Bank statements subsequently revealed that Sauniere and the archduke had opened consecutive accounts on the same day," noted the author trio, "and that the latter had [transferred a] substantial sum over to the former."

Sauniere began to exhibit a defiant independence toward his church superiors, refusing to disclose the source of his new-found wealth or accept a transfer from Rennes-le-Chateau, where he and his housekeeper were seen digging incessantly in the graveyard around the church. When push came to shove, the Vatican supported Sauniere, a good indication of the significance of his discoveries.

On January 17, 1917—the official Feast Day of the Saint Sulpice Seminary where he first consulted experts on his discovered documents as well as the day that was on the Blanchefort tombstone he obliterated and just five days after his housekeeper had inexplicably ordered a coffin—Sauniere suffered a sudden stroke. A nearby priest was called to administer Last Rites but, "visibly shaken" refused to do so after hearing Sauniere's confession, which has never been made public.

Marie Denarnaud kept her silence about Sauniere's activities, living quietly in the Villa Bethania. Toward the end of her life she sold the villa to a man whom she promised she would tell a secret which would make him both wealthy and powerful. Unfortunately, she too died of a stroke before passing along this secret.

Thus began the mystery of Rennes-le-Chateau. "Speculation has varied over the years as to the true nature of Sauniere's discovery": wrote Picknett and Prince, "most prosaically it has been suggested that he found a hoard of treasure, while others believe it was something considerably more stupendous, such as the Ark of the Covenant, the treasure of the Jerusalem Temple, the Holy Grail—or even the tomb of Christ. . . . The Priory claim that what Sauniere had discovered were parchments containing genealogical information that prove the survival of the Merovingian dynasty."

Two things seem certain about this story—that Sauniere obviously found something for which some person or group of people were willing to pay him large sums of money and that he continued looking for something else his entire life. It seems equally clear that his superiors in the church acquiesced in whatever Sauniere was up to. One Priory official even suggested that Sauniere was being well paid by ranking church officials for both his efforts and his silence.

According to one account, another clergyman named Antoine Gelis was close to Sauniere and also came into a considerable amount of money. Whatever Gelis knew about the situation died with him in November 1897, when the elderly priest was found beaten to death in his home. Details of his murder disappeared from church records and had to be reconstructed from police and court reports.

In 1969 British BBC television documentary producer Henry Lincoln read of the mystery while vacationing in France. He soon joined forces with novelist Richard Leigh and photojournalist Michael Baigent to research the story that ultimately provided them several TV programs as well as the best-selling 1982 book, *Holy Blood, Holy Grail*. This book brought the story of the Priory to an international audience.

Their research led them from Rennes-le-Chateau and the Blanchefort family to the Knights Templar and the Cathars to the order called Priory of Sion. A Bertrand de Blanchefort was the fourth grand master of the Knights Templar and operated from a preceptory in the vicinity of Rennes-le-Chateau. It has been established that the Blancheforts fought on the side of the Cathars and that Bertrand was a protégé of Templar founder Andre de Montbard.

Baigent, Leigh, and Lincoln discovered that during the time Blanchefort guided the order, Templars were dispatched to the vicinity of Rennes-le-Chateau, where they engaged in extensive excavations. They theorized this may have been a mission to bury and safeguard the treasure recovered from under their Jerusalem quarters. Their suspicion was heightened when they learned that as King Philip launched his nationwide arrests of the order in 1307, only those Templars near Rennes-le-Chateau remained unmolested. It should be noted that during World War II, German troops also reportedly excavated extensively around Rennes-le-Chateau, apparently hunting Holy relics as dramatized in two Indiana Jones films by director Steven Spielberg.

The three British researchers gathered an assortment of material on the Priory, including a number of books by French author Gerard de Sede, who was found to be connected to one Pierre Plantard de Saint-Clair, an official of the modern Priory of Sion. Researching in the National Library of France, they studied microfilm of documents called *Dossiers secrets* or Secret Files that purported to trace the Priory of Sion back to the time of the Crusades and closely tied the society to the Knights Templar. These files named past grand masters of the Priory, presented detailed history, and even stated that Sauniere was working for the order while in Rennes-le-Chateau. Since these papers were dated to the 1950s, yet not placed in the archives until the mid-1960s, controversy over the legitimacy of these documents has raged with no final proof forthcoming on either side, much like the MJ–12 documents in the United States.

"One curious feature of the dossiers is the constant and underlying implication that the authors had access to official government and police files," noted authors Picknett and Prince, who were generally more cynical of Priory information than other writers. They reported that critics of the Priory story claimed the group was nonexistent until the name first appeared publicly in the 1950s and that the whole idea is a scheme of "royalists with unlimited delusions of grandeur."

Baigent, Leigh, and Lincoln countered this by stating that at least one charter for the *Ordre de Sion* at Orleans from King Louis VII along with a papal bull confirming the order's possessions and dated 1178 still exist. They explained that many documents pertaining to the order were destroyed when Orleans was bombed by the Germans in 1940.

Names connected to the Templars and Freemasonry cropped up in their investigation: Marie de Saint-Clair, a descendent of Henry Saint Clair of the Rosslyn Chapel connection, reportedly was married to Jean de Gisors, reportedly the first independent grand master of the Priory of Sion; Rene d'Anjou, who, among others, carried the title "King of Jerusalem" which indicated a descendency from the Templar Count of Anjou, was listed as Grand Master of Sion from 1418 to 1480; the great Leonardo da Vinci was listed as Priory grand master from 1510 to 1519; Robert Fludd, that friend of Sir Francis Bacon and English kings, was listed as Priory grand master from 1595 to 1637; Johann Valentin Andrea, the cleric connected to Hessian Freemasonry and considered the author of the Rosicrucian Manifestos, was listed as Sion grand master from 1637 to 1654; Robert Boyle, member of Bacon's "Invisible College" who reportedly taught alchemy to Sir Isaac Newton, served between 1654 and 1691; while the famous Freemason Newton reportedly replaced Boyle as Grand Master of Sion from 1691 to 1727.

Other grand masters of Sion listed in the *Dossiers secrets* give good indication of the depth and reach of the Priory. They include Charles Radclyffe, a cousin to Bonnie Prince Charlie; Charles de Lorraine, who also served as grand master of the Templar-inspired Teutonic order; Maximillian de Lorraine, nephew to Charles and mentor to musicians Franz Joseph Haydn, Wolfgang Amadeus Mozart, and Ludwig von Beethoven; Victor Hugo, a Lorraine aristocrat and author of *The Hunchback of Notre Dame* and *Les Miserables;* the composer Claude Debussy, whose associates included writer Oscar Wilde, poet W. B. Yeats, novelist Marcel Proust; opera diva Emma Calve; and the young priest from Rennes-le-Chateau, Berenger Sauniere.

Based on their research, Baigent, Leigh, and Lincoln came to accept as "indisputable historical fact" that the Priory of Sion, under different names at different times, was the secret society behind the Knights Templar and survived the destruction of the Templars in the fourteenth century. At the very least, the *Dossiers secret* state that members of the Priory—members of the Gisors, Anjou, and Saint-Clair families to include Hugh de Payens and Godfrey de Bouillon—were among the founders of the Templars.

They also believed that the Priory exists today and "acting in the shadows, behind the scenes, it has orchestrated certain of the critical events in Western history." Unstated was the implication that Priory members were involved within the nucleus of Freemasonry, the Illuminati, and the Round Tables.

"The avowed and declared objective of the *Prieure de Sion,*" according to the trio, "is the restoration of the Merovingian dynasty and bloodline—not only to the throne of France, but to the thrones of other European nations as well."

They said Priory members worked through Freemasonry in the nineteenth century to revive the Holy Roman Empire, to be ruled jointly by the Habsburg family and a reformed Roman church. This scheme apparently was only thwarted by World War I and the fall of Europe's royal dynasties.

Throughout the years, the Priory—which apparently inherited, if not initiated, the Templar discoveries in Jerusalem—had been preoccupied not only with royal bloodlines but with the heretical knowledge of the Cathars and earlier sects.

"Suddenly, the meandering history of Europe develops a dramatic, cohesive plot line," noted Vankin and Whalen. "The persecution of the Cathars by the church, the collusion of Rome in the assassination of [Merovingian] King Dagobert, the successful conspiracy of the Pope Clement V and Philip IV of France to suppress the powerful Templars— all were efforts to eradicate . . . Jesus' bloodline. . . . For [it] constituted nothing less than a rival church with a more direct link to J.C.'s legacy than the Vatican could ever claim."

In an earlier work, Vankin argued the case for his belief that the church suppressed documents pertaining to Jesus, as implied by the accounts of the Templars and the Priory. "There are two possible explanations for the absence of a Holy Paper Trail," he wrote. "First, Jesus never existed—he is a purely fictional character. Second, and more likely in my view, is that historical writings about Jesus have been censored to insure that no extant information could contradict the 'official' biography of Jesus that gave the Church a rationale for power. Under either scenario, the story of Jesus holds many dangerous secrets."

As previously mentioned, Baigent, Leigh, and Lincoln came to believe that the notorious *Protocols of the Elders of Zion* actually pertained to the Priory. After much research, the trio concluded that the protocols were based on a real document which had nothing to do with an international Jewish conspiracy but instead was issued through "some Masonic organization or Masonically oriented secret society that incorporated the word 'Sion' . . . [and] may very well have included a program for gaining power, for infiltrating Freemasonry, for controlling social, political and economic institutions."

Whatever the Priory is today, according to the *Dossiers secrets* it was founded in 1090 by Godfrey de Bouillon, Duke of Lower Lorraine and the handsome descendent of Charlemagne, who led the First Crusade to capture Jerusalem. However, other Priory documents state the order was not founded until 1099, the year Jerusalem was taken and its inhabitants massacred. This text also said that Bouillon's youngest brother owed his throne to the Priory and, indeed, his brother Baldwin I of Le Bourg became king of Jerusalem. Baldwin II, who authorized the Knights Templar order, followed.

Whatever year the Priory was founded, once Jerusalem was taken, some knights were housed in an abbey built by Bouillon over the ruins of a Byzantine church on Mount Sion just south of the city. This became the Abbey of Notre Dame du Mont Sion, from which the order took the name Knights of the Order of Notre Dame de Sion. The word Sion was believed to be a transliteration of Zion, itself a transliteration of the ancient Hebrew name for Jerusalem.

Baigent, Leigh, and Lincoln claimed to have found an original charter for the Priory, dated 1125, with Templar grand master Hugh de Payens's name on it which would definitely tie the two orders together.

Picknett and Prince said the Priory and the Templars were "virtually the same organization, presided over by the same Grand Master, until they suffered a schism and went their separate ways in 1188."

Gardner generally concurred, but wrote that the Order of Sion had been founded by the Knights Templar to serve Jews and Muslims within their Christian order and that both shared the same grand master. "Although the early Templars had a Christian affiliation, they were noted exponents of religious toleration, which enabled them to be influential diplomats in both Jewish and Islamic communities. However, their liberal association with Jews and Muslims was denounced as 'heresy' by the Catholic bishops and was instrumental in the Knights' excommunication by the Church of Rome in 1306," he added.

Apparently, the Order of Sion was restructured in 1188, a year after Jerusalem was retaken by the Muslims and all involved had returned to France. Here there was some sort of rupture between the order and the Templars at a town called Gisors. Afterward, the order became more concerned with the French Merovingian bloodline, while the Templars, as previously noted, fell back to Cyprus and Rhodes and became more associated with England and Scotland and their royal bloodlines.

Jean de Gisors, according to the Priory documents, was the first grand master of the order after its separation from the Templars, which they called the "Cutting of the Elm." The order was already connected to the Rosicrucians through Johann Andrea. According to a priest writing in 1629, Gisors in fact founded the Rose-Croix order in 1188. This same contention is found in the *Dossiers secret*, according to Baigent, Leigh, and Lincoln. The idea that both Gisors and Andrea were officials of Sion, added much credence to the claim that they were involved in the creation of Rosicrucianism.

It is clear that shortly after the First Crusade, there was a blending of ideas, theology, and ancient secrets from which came the Rosicrucians, the Knights Templar, and the Priory of Sion.

Following the break with the Templars, a large priory of the *Ordre de Sion* was established in the mid–twelfth century at Orleans by a charter from King Louis VII, the original of which is still in municipal archives.

The history of the Priory from that time until the present is veiled in mystery. The first definite public notice of the Priory's existence came in July 1956 when a *Prieure de Sion,* with the professed goal of "studies and mutual aid to members," was registered with French authorities. Even then the address listed was untraceable and little could be learned about the group. About that time, the Priory claimed a membership of almost ten thousand divided into "grades" starting with a grand master, although this information is considered highly questionable. It also claimed not to be a secret society, yet efforts to gain solid information on the order are still met with denials, circumvention, and dissembling.

One of the Priory officers was listed as Pierre Plantard, the same man connected to de Sede, the French journalist who wrote about the order in later years. Plantard was said to be secretary-general of the Department of Documentation, implying there were other departments within the order.

Meanwhile, more Priory documents were made public, but only in small private editions and quantities. "Whatever the motivation behind [them], it was clearly not financial gain," noted Baigent, Leigh, and Lincoln, who came to believe that the paced and deliberate release of Priory information was "calculated to 'pave the way' for some astonishing disclosure."

The three authors claimed that a 1981 notice in the French press reported that none other than Pierre Plantard had been elected grand master of the Priory of Sion, his election being "a decisive step in the evolution of the order's conception and spirit in relation to the world; for the 121 dignitaries of the *Prieure de Sion* are all *eminences grises* [gray eminences or elder statesmen] of high finance and of international political or philosophical societies; and Pierre Plantard is the direct descendant, through Dagobert II, of the Merovingian kings."

The late Plantard was indeed connected with the Priory throughout his life. Not only was he the apparent source of Priory information to selected researchers, but he owned property in the vicinity of Rennes-le-Chateau, and his father reportedly knew the priest Sauniere. He reportedly worked with the French Resistance during World War II and was held by the German Gestapo for more than a year toward the end of the war. Interestingly enough, the code name for one of the plotters against Hitler toward the end of the war was "Gray Eminence." In 1958, along with French minister André Malraux, he helped organize the movement that returned Charles de Gaulle to power in France. Clearly Plantard was not just some nobody off the street.

After much arduous work, authors Baigent, Leigh, and Lincoln managed a series of interviews with Plantard beginning in 1979. They found him aristocratic and courtly, eloquent with a dry sense of humor. Although for the most part vague and evasive about the order, Plantard did claim that the Priory does in fact have the lost "treasure" of Solomon's Temple and plans to return it to Israel "when the time is right." He also indicated that in the near future, a monarchy would be reestablished in France and perhaps other nations.

"Again, we considered dismissing the *Prieure de Sion* as a minor 'lunatic fringe' sect, if not an outright hoax," stated the authors. "And yet all our own research had indicated that the Order, in the past, had had real power and been involved in matters of high-level international import."

Other authors also questioned the statements of Plantard as well as the *Dossiers secret*. "On the evidence given in the secret dossiers, the case for the survival of the [Merovingian] dynasty beyond King Dagobert II, not to mention the continuation of a clear line of descent right through to the late 20th century, is at best fragile and at worst demonstrably fictitious," commented Picknett and Prince.

Robert Richardson, writing in the Spring 1999 issue of *Gnosis Magazine,* was more to the point when he stated unequivocally that the whole Priory story was a "fraud." He loosely connected Plantard to prewar esoteric organizations and concluded, "The fraudulent history of the 'Priory of Sion' and its false bloodline was created by utilizing the vast amount of esoteric documents publicly available in French libraries and by depositing its own documents among them."

While confirming that a real Catholic monastic order named Priory of Sion existed at Crusades-era Jerusalem, Richardson said it was absorbed into the Jesuits and disappeared in 1617. He claimed Plantard and other right-wing members of a group called Alpha Galates concocted the Priory story "by placing fabricated histories in libraries, by falsely associating itself with ancient esoteric groups, and by usurping the heritage of prewar esoteric groups."

"The group the 'Priory' has plagiarized most from is the Order of the Rose-Croix of the Temple and the Grail, founded by Josephin Peladan in 1891," wrote Richardson. "This group is intimately connected with the real affair of Rennes-le-Chateau." He said Peladan's secretary, the Scottish Rite Mason Georges "Count Israel" Monti, was denounced by the French Masonic Grand Lodge as a false claimant to nobility. He tars Plantard with the same charge by stating, "It is highly likely that Alpha Galates [and hence Plantard] was a front for Monti's group and that Monti's group continued on, subsequently implementing a plan which would be carried out under the guise of the 'Priory of Sion.'"

Richardson, while certainly entitled to his opinions, also made questionable statements. For example, he disputed a description by authors Baigent, Leigh, and Lincoln regarding Bertrand de Blanchefort. "Blanchefort was the home of a Cathar noble by that name," he noted, "not a Templar Grand Master. Few researchers have bothered to investigate this or innumerable other outright fictions."

Yet Masonic author Charles G. Addison, writing in 1842, a century before the time of Plantard and Alpha Galates and citing even older sources, wrote at length on Bertrand de Blanchefort and listed him as Templar grand master between the years of 1156 and 1169. There is obviously more to this story than a simple hoax, although truth appears to be elusive.

While also disbelieving the story of trying to preserve the Merovingian bloodline, Picknett and Prince concluded that behind this "smokescreen of full-scale nonsense, prevarication and obfuscation, there lies a very serious, very single-minded intent."

An attempt to discern this intent requires a study of the Merovingian royalty.

MEROVINGIANS

The Merovingian dynasty of Franks has been traditionally considered the first race of kings in what is now France. France was named for the Franks and their first ruler, Francio, was said to be a descendant of Noah.

Francio's race migrated from the legendary city of Troy in northwest Turkey, bringing their royal bloodline to Gaul. They named their settlement Troyes after their hometown. Paris was named for the Greek hero Paris whose elopement with Helen to Troy precipitated the Trojan War.

The name Merovingian refers to Meroveus, the father of Childeric I, ruler of the Salian Franks. According to genealogist Gardner, Meroveus traced his lineage through his father, Clodion, back through Joseph of Arimathea to Jesus. "Despite the carefully listed genealogies of his time, the heritage of Meroveus was strangely obscured in the monastic annals," noted Gardner. "Although the rightful son of Clodion, he was nevertheless said by the historian Priscus to have been sired by an arcane sea creature, the *Bistea Neptunis* [sea beast]. . . . There was evidently something very special about King Meroveus and his priestly successors, for they were accorded special veneration and were widely known for their esoteric knowledge and occult skills."

Authors Baigent, Leigh, and Lincoln saw the legend of the sea creature fathering Meroveus as alluding to, or concealing, the idea of some sort of dynastic alliance or intermarriage. Some authors have suggested that the "sea beast" story was a misinterpretation of the idea that Meroveus was half-fish, the fish being a long-standing symbol of Christ.

French author Gerard de Sede raised eyebrows by declaring that the Merovingians were, in fact, descended from extraterrestrials who interbred with selected ancient Israelites. This allegation was echoed by author David Wood, who wrote that this royal line, as well as all humans, were descendants of an extraterrestrial "super-race."

Meroveus's grandson, Clovis I, took control in about A.D. 482 (about ten years after the fall of the Roman Empire) and eventually extended his rule to include most of Gaul. Paris was his capital, a status which the city retained when Hugh Capet became king of France in 987.

According to the Priory of Sion's *Dossiers secret,* the Merovingians were of Jewish origin. "They were the lost tribe of Benjamin, who migrated to Greece and then on to Germany, where they became the

Sicambrians [Franks]," reported Picknett and Prince. Others pointed out there was so much intermarriage in the region that the terms "Goth" and "Jew" became interchangeable.

The *Dossiers secret* declared that the descendants of Jesus and Mary Magdalene, living in southern France, intermarried with the Sicambrian Franks and founded the Merovingian royal lineage. Priory members claimed that the parchments discovered by the priest Sauniere at Rennes-le-Chateau were genealogical lists tracing the Merovingian lineage right up to descendants living in Europe today—to include the evasive Pierre Plantard.

Some support for this idea can be found in the Jewish principality of Septimania, created in the mid-eighth century after the Jewish inhabitants of Narbonne aided King Pépin in taking the city from the Muslims. The first king of Septimania was a Frankish noble named Theodoric (the Grail romances refer to him as Aymery), a Jew "recognized by both Pepin and the caliph of Baghdad as 'the seed of the royal house of David.'" Theodoric is thought by many to have also been a Merovingian. His son, Guillem de Gellone, also rose to prominence as both a Merovingian and Jew of royal blood.

"Jesus was of the Tribe of Judah and the royal house of David. The Magdalene is said to have carried the Grail—the *Sangraal* or 'royal blood'—into France," noted Baigent, Leigh, and Lincoln. "And in the 8th century there was, in the south of France, a potentate [Guillem] of the Tribe of Judah and the royal house of David, who was acknowledged as king of the Jews. He was not only a practicing Jew, however; he was also a Merovingian."

Clovis converted to Christianity after evoking the name of Jesus, at the urging of his Catholic wife, Clotilde, during a crucial and ultimately successful battle in 496. This came at a time of decline for the Roman church, then locked in a continuous battle against Arianism.

Arianism, named after the Alexandrian priest Arius, taught that God created everything including Jesus and therefore, Jesus was not himself God, but rather a heavenly teacher, a messiah. This concept, perhaps strengthened by the Magdalene tradition in southern France, gained considerable popularity at the time.

To counter Arianism, Roman emperor Constantine had convened the Council of Nicaea in A.D. 325. When Arius rose to argue his views, he was punched in the face. The council, under firm control of the Roman church, declared that God was a Trinity—Father, son, and spirit. Arius and his followers were banished. "There were now only two official objects of worship": commented Gardner. "The Holy Trinity of God and the Emperor himself—the newly designated Savior of the World. Anyone who disputed this in any way was at once declared a heretic. Christians who attempted to retain loyalty to Jesus as the Messianic Christ were discounted by the Imperial Church as heathens."

Despite edicts from Rome, Arianism remained strong in western Europe. "If the early Merovingians, prior to Clovis, were at all receptive to Christianity, it would have been the Arian Christianity of their immediate neighbors, the Visigoths and Burgundians," commented Baigent, Leigh, and Lincoln.

When Clovis was baptized into Catholicism, nearly half of his troops followed his example. "A great wave of conversions followed, and the Roman church was effectively saved from almost inevitable collapse," noted Gardner. "In fact, were it not for the baptism of King Clovis, the ultimate Christian religion of Western Europe might well now be Arian rather than Catholic." The Roman authorities, in turn, proclaimed Clovis the "new Constantine" and pledged allegiance to both him and his descendants, a pledge they soon repudiated.

Upon the death of Clovis in 511, his realm was shared by his four sons—Theuderic, Chodomir, Childebert, and Lothar. The emblems of the Merovingian kings were the fish (still a symbol of Jesus), the Lion of Judah (further indication of their Hebraic heritage), and the fleur-de-lis (which became the symbol of French royalty). Despite strife between the brothers, Merovingian rule grew to include Septimania along the Mediterranean coast between Provence and Spain to Saxony in the north and eastward to Bavaria.

By 561 the realm had been divided between Clovis's grandsons, Charibert I, Guntram, Sigebert, and Chilperic I. These brothers also intrigued against each other, causing weakness within the kingdom, which was quickly exploited by their neighbors. By 613 Chlotar II—son of Chilperic I—had regained some unity within the kingdom.

His son, Dagobert, was abducted at the age of five and taken to a monastery near Dublin, Ireland, where he was educated and later married the Celtic princess Matilda. After his surprise return to France, Dagobert proved even more effective in consolidating the Merovingian sovereignty, but in 679, while hunting, he was murdered by a retainer of Pépin the Fat, one of his own officials with close ties to the Roman church.

According to Gardner, papal authorities deliberately obscured the history of the Merovingians to secure their own power and prominence. "The inevitable result was that accounts of Dagobert's life were suppressed to the point of his non-existence in the chronicles," he wrote. "Not for another thousand years were the true facts of his existence to be made public once more. And only then did it become apparent that Dagobert had a son called Sigebert, who was rescued from the mayoral clutches in 679. Following his father's murder he was removed to his mother's home at Rennes-le-Chateau in Languedoc. . . . In time, the deposed Merovingian line from Sigebert included the famous crusader, Godfrey de Bouillon, Defender of the Holy Sepulchre."

Here again can be found the connections between the Priory of Sion, the Knights Templar, and elder traditions involving Jesus' bloodline. Although, as pointed out by Baigent, Leigh, and Lincoln, "while the Merovingian royal blood was credited with a sacred, miraculous, and divine nature, it was not explicitly stated anywhere that this blood was in fact Jesus."

Yet the connection was there as evidenced by the linkage of the Jewish Franks to the Merovingians Dagobert and Guillem de Gellone through a Hugh de Plantard to Eustache, first count of Boulogne and the grandfather of the Crusade leader Godfrey de Bouillon. "And from Godfrey there issued a dynasty and a 'royal tradition' that, by virtue of being founded on the 'rock of Sion,' was equal to those presiding over France, England and Germany," they added.

"By dint of dynastic alliances and intermarriages, this line came to include Godfrey de Bouillon . . . and various other noble and royal families, past and present—Blanchefort, Gisors, Saint-Clair—Sinclair in England . . . Plantard, and Habsburg-Lorraine."

Following the death of Dagobert there was again division in the land. The surviving Merovingians were forced to yield power to court officials known as "Mayors of the Palace," known to be under the control of the Catholic church.

In 750 the last Merovingian king, Childeric III, was deposed by one of these mayors—Pépin III the Short—who established the Carolingian dynasty so named for his father, Carolus or Charles Martel. "The

Merovingian monarchy had been strictly dynastic," explained Gardner, "but that tradition was destined to be overturned when Rome grasped the opportunity to *create* kings by papal authority. . . . The Church's long-awaited ideal had come to fruition—and from that time onwards kings were endorsed and crowned only by self-styled Roman prerogative." (emphasis in the original)

"The Merovingian kings did not rule the land nor were they politically active," wrote Gardner. "They were avid students of proper kingly practice in the ancient tradition and their model was King Solomon, the son of David. Their disciplines were largely based on Old Testament scripture—but the Roman Church nevertheless proclaimed them irreligious."

Heresies aside, it is clear why the early church was fearful of the Merovingians. If indeed their heritage connected to the "royal house of David" and specifically to Jesus, they represented a distinct threat to the theology being formulated by the church at the time and later by European dynasties.

"The Thule Society's early mission was to put a member of Jesus' family—a Merovingian—on the throne of Europe," wrote author Henry. "When Hitler came along he dismantled this operation."

According to several modern writers, the picture that is becoming clear in light of recent research and literature is this: Mary Magdalene, as the wife of Jesus, arrived in the south of France following the crucifixion, along with Jesus' children. They preserved their bloodline while living in the large Jewish community of the region and, in the fifth century, intermarried with Frankish royalty to create the Merovingian dynasty. The Roman church pledged allegiance to this dynasty, in full knowledge of its messianic lineage.

But church authorities, fearful and jealous of this dynasty born of both priestly and political bloodlines, fomented the assassination of Dagobert and the usurpation of Childeric III to gain complete control over what was to become the nation of France. And throughout this intrigue wound the threads of the Plantards, the Bouillons, the Knights Templar, and the Priory of Sion.

By the twelfth century, these families, knowing full well their heritage, mounted the expedition to Jerusalem—if not the entire First Crusade—to recover family genealogies from beneath Solomon's Temple. They also created the secret Priory of Sion, and the Knights Templar as a front organization, to achieve this purpose. At this point restoration of the Merovingian monarchy may indeed have been a primary goal.

As discussed, the Templars apparently were successful in their attempt to gain the Temple treasure, whether it was merely historical records or something more substantive, such as the Ark of the Covenant or even the mummified body of Jesus. Whatever it may have been was transported back to the area of Rennes-le-Chateau and so strengthened the beliefs of the Cathars that they were quite willing to die for them. The Templars, being less willing to sacrifice themselves, simply melded their beliefs into other secret societies.

Over the years there were repeated attempts to take the throne of France for royalty of Merovingian lineage, but only one in the eighteenth century came close to success. According to Baigent, Leigh, and Lincoln, "By virtue of its intermarriage with the Habsburgs, the house of Lorraine [a family descended from the Merovingians] had actually acquired the throne of Austria, the Holy Roman Empire [which finally ceased to exist in 1806]. When Marie Antoinette, daughter of Francois de Lorraine, became Queen of France, the throne of France, too, was only a generation or so away. Had not the French Revolution intervened, the house of Habsburg-Lorraine might well, by the early 1800s, have been on its way to establishing dominion over all Europe."

The Habsburg dynasty was believed to be an integral part of the Priory of Sion and even related to the Rothschilds through Holy Roman Emperor Frederick Barbarossa's second son Albrecht, or Archibald, II. The family origins go back to a Swiss estate named *Habichtburg* (Hawk Castle), or Habsburg, built in 1020 by the Bishop of Strasbourg. Through strategic marriages, the Habsburgs grew to be the most powerful of the European royal houses. Emperor Maximilian, whose French troops were poised in Mexico during the War Between the States, was a Habsburg, as was Holy Roman Emperor Charles V.

There may have been another attempt to recreate the Holy Roman Empire in the late nineteenth century. According to French author Jean-Luc Chaumeil, several of the characters involved in the Rennes-le-Chateau mystery—including the priest Sauniere—were members of an ultra-secret group of Scottish Rite Freemasons who, just as the Illuminati before them, sought to create a European union based on Theosophy and Gnosticism. Called the *Hieron du Val d'Or,* this society's objectives were much the same as the CFR or Trilateral Commission's—to create a global God-ordained system "wherein nations would be no more than provinces, their leaders but proconsuls in the service of a world occult government consisting of an elite." To most researchers, this sounds like an early-day New World Order.

As Baigent, Leigh, and Lincoln saw it, "During the 19th century the *Prieure de Sion,* working through Freemasonry and the *Hieron du Val d'Or,* attempted to establish a revived and 'updated' Holy Roman Empire—a kind of theocratic United States of Europe, ruled simultaneously by the Habsburgs and by a radically reformed Church." Apparently this effort was frustrated by events early in the twentieth century.

The Habsburgs' power gradually was restricted to the Austrian Empire, which collapsed following the assassination of Habsburg Archduke Francis Ferdinand and the end of World War I. Today, the Habsburgs appear to be making a comeback with Karl Habsburg-Lothringen representing Austria in the European Parliament, his sisters politically active in both Spain and Sweden and Gyorgy von Habsburg an influential executive with the largest film producer and distributor in central Europe.

Evidence that Priory members may still have direct connections to Freemasons seeking political change was developed when Baigent, Leigh, and Lincoln studied privately published tracts dealing with the Priory in the French National Library. One of these was supposedly written by one Madeleine Blancassal, a phony name concocted from the Priory's interest in the Magdalene and two Languedoc rivers. Of particular interest was that this work, according to its title page, was published by the Grand Alpine Lodge of Switzerland—a Masonic lodge comparable to Britain's Grand Lodge or France's Grand Orient Lodge and connected to the P2 Lodge scandal.

Although Alpine Lodge officials denied any knowledge of the tract, at least two other works bore the Alpine imprint and French journalist Mathieu Paolio claimed to have seen these publications in the Alpine Lodge library. Shortly after Paolio published a book in France exposing the Priory's interest in the Merovingian bloodline, he accepted an assignment to Israel where he was executed as a spy.

A FAR-REACHING WEB

Icke claimed that Henry Kissinger is a member of the Grand Alpine Lodge and that "it is involved at a very high level in the global manipulation."

Recall that Kissinger's name cropped up in the official investigation of the P2 Lodge scandal in Italy in the 1980s. Icke's allegation obliquely connects Kissinger to the Priory, which Baigent, Leigh, and Lincoln discovered has an "American Contingent."

This author trio worked to trace the missing parchments said to have been found by the priest Sauniere at Rennes-le-Chateau in the late nineteenth century. Piecing together confusing, sometimes deceitful, information, they concluded that at least three of Sauniere's documents had been purchased from the priest's niece and taken to England in the mid-1950s by three men, at least one of whom was a member of British Intelligence. According to official papers authorizing the transfer, "These genealogies contain proof of the direct descent, through the male line of [Merovingian] Sigibert IV, son of Dagobert II . . . through the House of Plantard, Counts of Rhedae [an older name for Rennes-le-Chateau]. . . . "

The papers were held by Lloyds International of London until 1979, when they apparently were returned to a Paris bank after Lloyds discontinued the use of deposit boxes.

In checking on the English connections to the Priory papers, Baigent, Leigh, and Lincoln found all the names traced back to a large insurance company named Guardian Assurance, today called Guardian Royal Exchange Assurance. They also found that all of the men named were prominent figures with aristocratic titles or standing in the banking and business community. Some had connections with Winston Churchill and intelligence services.

In January 1984 the plot thickened when the authors received a two-page letter from Plantard under the *Prieure de Sion* logo and a crest containing the letter R and C, thought to refer to the Order of the Rosy Cross. This *Mise en Garde* or Cautionary Notice warned of legal action against anyone suspected of taking or faking Priory documents. The letter carried four signatures—Pierre Plantard, John E. Drick, Gaylord Freeman, and A. Robert Abboud. Freeman has been previously mentioned in Priory documents.

Significantly, all the names on the *Mise* document, with the exception of Plantard, were connected to First National Bank of Chicago. Freeman became the bank's president in 1960, eventually becoming board chairman. He sat on the board of the Atlantic Richfield oil company and was associated with the MacArthur Foundation and the Aspen Institute. Abboud succeeded Freeman as the bank's board chairman and also served as president of Occidental Petroleum Corporation. Drick, beginning in 1969, became president and a board member of the bank and sat on the board of other large American firms.

According to Professor Donald Gibson, "The First National Bank of Chicago was interconnected with Rockefeller financial interests." Furthermore, prior to 1983, the London branch of First National Bank of Chicago had shared office space with none other than Guardian Royal Exchange Assurance.

Buoyed by this seemingly strong connection between the Priory and an "American Contingent," Baigent, Leigh, and Lincoln were chagrined to discover that Drick had died in 1982, two years before the Priory documents were produced. To compound this mystery, it was determined that the three American signatures on the *Mise* letter were exact copies—even to the order presented—as their signatures on the 1974 annual report of the First National Bank of Chicago. Furthermore, Freeman denied any knowledge of the Priory. Confronted with deceit and falsified documents emanating from England, the trio wrote, "One thing seemed evident— someone with an interest in the [Priory of Sion] was active in London."

In an interview with the trio, Plantard explained everything away— he said Drick's name was still being used on Priory documents even after his death with the use of a stamp, like that carrying the other two signatures. Asked why such men as Freeman, Abboud, and Drick would concern themselves with a society whose aim was the restoration of the Merovingian royalty, Plantard told the authors that these men's primary objective was a united Europe.

Another fascinating tidbit concerning these authors' work gave an indication of the intricate interconnectedness of today's secret societies. In their book *Holy Blood, Holy Grail*, several times the authors cite Sir Steven Runciman as an expert historian with particular knowledge of the Crusaders, the Knights Templar, and even the Priory of Sion. Runciman's name was one of those listed in the personal address book of Clay Shaw, the New Orleans Trade Mart director put on trial for complicity in the Kennedy assassination. Along with Sir Steven, other prominent European names in Shaw's book included the Marquesse Giuseppe Rey of Italy, Baron Rafaelo de Banfield of Italy, Princess Jacqueline Chimay of France, and Lady Margaret D'Arcy, Lady Hulce, and Sir Michael Duff of England.

Plantard also sent the trio of authors a copy of his letter to the Priory resigning his position as grand master, which became effective in mid-1984. This communication also announced the reinstitution of a Priory statute which prohibited members from revealing anything about the order, including their membership. Plantard said he was resigning for reasons of health, "personal and family independence" and due to his disapproval of "certain maneuvers" of "our English and American brethren." "Following M. Plantard's resignation, the *Prieure de Sion* became, in effect, invisible," commented the authors.

A short time later, Baigent, Leigh, and Lincoln received an anonymous tract accusing the Priory of involvement with Lucio Gelli and his Italian P2 Lodge and Vatican activities concerning *Banco Ambrosiano*. Author Vankin also raised the possibility that the Priory was the mysterious power behind the fascist P2 Lodge. In their search for confirmation of this allegation, the authors discovered tenuous connections between the Priory and other largely unknown European secret societies.

One of these was Alpha Galates, whose members were interested in the chivalry of medieval knights. Members of this group apparently were connected to a wartime French publication entitled *Vaincre*, which has been accused of both supporting and working against the collaborationist Vichy government. This publication was edited by Plantard, and contributors included men linked to both the Priory and the Swiss Alpine Masonic Lodge.

Another secret society was known as the Kreisau Circle, formed in 1933 by a small group of career military officers and professionals who opposed Hitler. The circle met at the Kreisau estate of its leader Helmut James Graft von Moltke and plotted to overthrow the Nazi regime. Many circle members, including Count Claus von Stauffenberg who planted a bomb near Hitler in July 1944, were arrested and executed for their role in the failed plot.

It was Hans Adolf von Moltke who offered praise to Plantard upon his becoming grand master of Alpha Galates. Toward the end of the war, members of the Kreisau Circle were sending peace feelers to members of both British and American Intelligence, including Allen Dulles, then with the OSS in Switzerland. The von Moltkes were also heavily involved in the European unity movement, one facet of which was Retinger's American Committee on a United Europe. Recall that Retinger, "father of the Bilderbergers," was connected to Dulles and other CIA officials, CFR officials, Averell Harriman, and David and Nelson Rockefeller. A close working relationship was developed between the CIA and the Vatican, chiefly through the Knights of Malta and Cardinal Francis Spellman of New York, spiritual adviser to the Knights and the man who first brought Vatican attention to banker Bishop Paul Marcinkus of P2 scandal notoriety.

As previously mentioned, in the 1950s Plantard helped create the *Comites de Salut Public* or Public Safety Committees which were instrumental in returning De Gaulle to power in France.

Obviously, this cloudy mixture of conspiracies pointed to some level of a reality not addressed by the daily media. Baigent, Leigh, and Lincoln stated, "We found indisputable evidence attesting to the involvement of an organized and coherent cadre working in concert behind the scenes, sometimes using other institutions as a facade. This cadre was not named specifically, but everything indicated that it was indeed the *Prieure de Sion*."

They pondered over the Priory's activities in the "shadowy underworld of European affairs—where the Mafia overlaps with secret societies and intelligence agencies, where big business clasps hands with the Vatican, where immense sums of money are deployed for clandestine purposes, where the demarcation lines between politics, religion, espionage, high finance and organized crime begin to dissolve . . . [into] a somewhat murky sphere . . . where Christian Democratic parties of Europe, various movements dedicated to European unity, royalist cliques, neo-chivalric orders, Freemason sects, the CIA, the Knights of Malta and the Vatican swirled together, pooled themselves temporarily for one purpose or another. . . ."

But no one—least of all those hardworking researchers Baigent, Leigh, and Lincoln—has been able to get a firm handle on the Priory and its surrounding secret groups with their phony documents, contradictory statements, and obscure backgrounds.

"The *Prieure de Sion* had begun to seem to us like a holographic image, shifting prismatically according to the light and the angle from which it was viewed," they wrote in 1986. "From one perspective, it appeared to be an influential, powerful and wealthy international secret society whose members included eminent figures in the arts, in politics, in high finance. From another perspective, it seemed a dazzlingly ingenious hoax devised by a small group of individuals for obscure purposes of their own. Perhaps, in some fashion, it was both."

Lincoln eventually gave up on trying to sort out the tangled mess. In the mid-1990s when asked for an update on the Priory, he replied disheateningly, "In my old age, I've decided to stick to that which can be verified." Lack of absolute proof and documentation, of course, is the hallmark of any good secret society.

Some researchers believe the Priory of Sion represents the pinnacle of today's power pyramid, that the Priory recruits receptive Freemasons through Rosicrucianism on into the Priory. Whether planned that way or not, the new European Union appears to be a close copy of the united Europe envisioned by New World Order leaders and the Priory of Sion.

COMMENTARY

It would appear that the links to conspiratorial secret societies have come full circle—from the CIA, CFR, and Bilderbergers back through the Round Tables and Freemasonry, on back through the Illuminati and the Knights Templar to the Knights of Malta and the Priory of Sion and their recent connections to the CIA, CFR, and Bilderbergers.

And always there has been an agenda of discrediting both national and church authorities as well as an attempt to unify first Europe, then the rest of the world.

This assault has been particularly aimed at the Roman Catholic church, which has stood as the predominate religion of the Western world since the time of the Roman Empire. Every Protestant denomination—whether Baptist, Methodist, Presbyterian, Episcopalian, fundamentalist, Unitarian, etc.—has drawn its traditions from the Catholic church.

Yet many people—formally declared heretics by the church in the past—believe that early on church leaders got the stories of Jesus' immaculate conception, spiritual leadership, and resurrection all wrong. Even today there are alternative traditions concerning Jesus, Mary Magdalene, and John the Baptist which conflict with official church dogma.

Rather than participating in ecumenical studies to determine which traditions have the more factual basis, the church instead attempted to eradicate any challenge to its authority by the most violent and murderous means.

One of the most prominent and powerful threats to church dogma came through the Knights Templar. Originally a small and secretive group of knights formed to protect pilgrims after the First Crusade's success in capturing the city of Jerusalem, the order actually spent little time patrolling the highways.

Instead, this group of knights—well-connected to powerful European families—excavated deep under the site of Solomon's Temple in Jerusalem. Whatever they found there was transported back to Europe and apparently hidden in the south of France near a small village named Rennes-le-Chateau.

While no one seems to have absolute proof of the specifics of this Templar "treasure," most researchers have concluded that in addition to a literal treasure of gold and silver, they found ancient scrolls and artifacts which could have been used to destroy church traditions at the very time they were being established.

One group which may have had their religious beliefs strengthened by the Templar find was the Cathars, located primarily in the Languedoc region of what was to become southern France. This group of highly spiritual people already had a tradition concerning the arrival at Marseilles of Mary Magdalene with the children of Jesus and their subsequent intermarriage with Frankish Jews resulting in a line of priest-kings called the Merovingians.

Threatened by the power of the Merovingian lineage, church officials arranged the assassination of King Dagobert and, through their control over the Merovingian "mayors" or court officials, set up their own royalty. When the peace-loving Cathars preached against such abuses by the church, Pope Innocent III in 1209 began to move against them militarily.

In a campaign known as the Albigensian Crusade, a large papal army swept through southwestern France and exterminated anyone believed tainted by the Cathar heresy. The Cathars were virtually wiped out, with only a few escaping to other countries or into the protective ranks of the Knights Templar.

The Templars were conspicuous by their absence in the Albigensian Crusade, lending much credence to the claim that the "treasure" recovered in Jerusalem supported the Cathar beliefs. In fact, the Templars—many of whom were from Cathar families—hid many Cathars from the pope's army.

Meanwhile, the Knights Templar apparently were able to intimidate the church into granting exceptional rights and favors to the order, which quickly became one of the most powerful multinational organizations in the world.

While fighting in the Crusades, the Templars had gained much esoteric knowledge dealing with architecture, construction, metallurgy, astronomy, and geography. Much of this knowledge came from their association with an Ismaili sect called the Assassins, headed by a ruthless tyrant known as the Old Man of the Mountain. The Assassins and their leader claimed to possess ancient knowledge dating back to the time of Noah and beyond.

In 1307 it was the Templars' turn to feel the wrath of the Vatican and King Philip IV of France, who had been turned down as a member and was heavily in debt to the order. In that year, Philip had all Templars in France arrested and tortured. Most fled the country by means of a large Templar fleet of ships headquartered at La Rochelle on the Atlantic coast. It was believed that they took a "treasure" with them which consisted not only of valuables but also papers containing the "secrets" discovered in Jerusalem.

Some Templars were thought to have crossed the Atlantic, arriving in what was later to be called New England 185 years before Christopher Columbus set sail.

Other Templars fled to Scotland where they were welcomed by King Robert the Bruce, who was fighting both neighboring England and the Vatican at the time. This Templar contingent may have contributed to the independence of Scotland by participating in the defeat of the English at the Battle of Bannockburn in 1314. It was in Scotland that the Templar traditions survived and became interwoven with the Scottish Rite ritual of Freemasonry.

In other nations, the Templars were simply absorbed into other secret societies and orders such as the Knights of Christ, the Knights Hospitaller, and the Teutonic Knights. In this manner, their unorthodox ideas were spread throughout Europe and became centered in the Strict Observance lodges of Freemasonry, that birthplace of "Illuminized" Freemasonry.

In recent years, several authors have discovered that a previously unknown French secret society may have been the masterminds behind the Knights Templar. This group, known as the Priory of Sion, is now viewed by many as the apex of a pyramidal power structure exerting disproportionate control over even the most powerful modern societies.

Although it only became known to the public in the past thirty years, existent documents reveal that the Priory was in existence no later than 1178 and, according to questionable Priory documents, the order was formed about the time knights of the First Crusade took Jerusalem. There the Knights of the Order of Notre Dame de Sion was formed. They also state that the Priory and the Templars were the same organization, even with the same grand master.

A schism came about in 1188 and the Templars went their own way while the Priory became dedicated to restoring the Merovingian royal dynasty and largely dropped from sight.

Recent Priory notoriety came about as the result of publicity over a "mystery" tied to the Languedoc village of Rennes-le-Chateau, where a priest named Francois Berenger Sauniere discovered hidden documents in the late nineteenth century. After taking his find to church authorities, Sauniere came into sudden wealth and received several high-ranking visitors.

It is believed that his discovery involved buried treasure and/or documents detailing a genealogy linking the descendants of Jesus through the Merovingian royalty to persons living today. It may be these displaced royals who have been behind a movement to create a unified Europe and restore the old Holy Roman Empire. This group is thought to involve members of the Habsburg dynasty as well as individuals connected to intelligence services both in Britain and America.

Investigation into the European unity movement as well as the Priory of Sion discerns clandestine connections between many of the modern secret societies, Freemasonry, intelligence agencies, and the Vatican. This underworld of intrigue became briefly public when the P2 Lodge scandal broke in Italy during the 1980s. Even then, the news media of the United States failed to take much notice of this startling, if complex, plot to subvert a modern nation.

While controversy continued over the legitimacy of the modern Priory, evidence grew indicating a certainly conspiratorial reality behind the shifting pronouncements and papers of the group.

It is clear that secret societies—both then and now—were concerned not only with political issues but with matters pertaining to royal bloodlines, religion, and spiritualism.

Yet individuals within these societies both supported and bankrolled "Godless" Communism. While this support could be simply another application of the Hegelian dialectic process of backing both sides of a conflict, it also points to members' knowledge of and intense interest in the elder secret society traditions studied so closely by Marx, Trotsky, and Lenin.

This hidden knowledge involved secrets from the distant past which have provided a basis for secret society theologies. These secrets continue to attract the attention of high-level society members and even intelligence agencies.

It is these secrets which connect modern conspiratorial societies to the Ancient Mysteries.

PART V

ANCIENT MYSTERIES

Nothing is truly new; it has all been done or said before. What can you point to that is new? How do you know it didn't exist long ages ago? We don't remember what happened in those former times, and in the future generations no one will remember what we have done back here.

—Ecclesiastes 1:9–11, Living Bible

The Bible—without question the most influential book ever produced—was written by men with secrets to conceal both from the Roman and Jewish authorities and from other competing sects.

Until archeological advances beginning in the nineteenth century, virtually everything humans knew about their origins came from the Bible filtered through the church priesthood. Individuals were both canonized and executed, cultures built and destroyed, and wars fought—all based on this one book.

Today it is clear that the Bible—inspired as it may be—is a hodgepodge of myths, legends, and parables from various cultures cobbled together with bits of history and philosophy.

Many passages were originally written using code words whose meanings were lost over time, causing misinterpretations. In other instances there was just plain tampering to advance some then-current dogma or political agenda.

Bible scholar and former intelligence analyst Pat Eddy wrote, "One of the most important purposes [of this tampering] was to support the aims of those who sought to make Christianity more attractive to potential Jewish converts by proving that the events of Jesus' life fulfill prophecy from the Old Testament. . . . Christians have all been told, from their earliest trips to Sunday School, that the birth, death, and important events in the life of Jesus were all foretold in the Old Testament. Few have ever questioned this assertion."

What Bible scholars euphemistically term "redactions" are nothing less than editing. Such editing of the Bible has contributed to misunderstandings and erroneous translations, keeping many of its messages a secret from the uninitiated. Often such secrets were suppressed by the Roman church because they contradicted its dogma.

Within the New Testament, there are tantalizing hints that even Jesus kept some secrets. Matthew 13:10 (Revised Standard) states, "Then the disciples came to him [Jesus] and said to him, 'Why do you speak to them [the public] in parables?' And he answered them, 'To you it has been given to know the secrets of the kingdom of heaven, but to them it has not been given. For to him who has [knowledge] will more be given, and he will have abundance; but from him who has not, even what he has will be taken away. This is why I speak to them in parables, because seeing they do not see, and hearing, they do not hear, nor do they understand."

Mark 4:33 added, "With many such parables he spoke the word to them, as they were able to hear it; he did not speak to them without a parable, but privately to his own disciples he explained everything." Explained everything? What did Jesus explain? Since only the parables are presented in the New Testament, it is clear that not all his secrets were given to the public.

Many secret societies and sects existed in biblical times that claimed to possess ancient knowledge. Like the religions of today, these groups vied with one another for control over these ancient secrets. Much like the later "Invisible College," these societies collectively were known as Mystery Schools, reservoirs of esoteric knowledge that was largely incomprehensible and thus fear-inspiring to the general public. Their literature was carefully constructed to both conceal and reveal some of their knowledge.

"In the ancient world, nearly all the secret societies were philosophic and religious. During the medieval centuries, they were chiefly religious and political, although a few philosophic schools remained. In modern times, secret societies, in the Occidental countries, are largely political or fraternal, although in a few of them, as in Masonry, the ancient religious and philosophic principles still survive," explained Hall.

Eddy wrote, "In order to completely understand the dynamic of tampering with Jesus' pronouncements, the reader must understand how the minds of the first-century religious protagonists worked. The tamperings were not random events like some form of intellectual graffiti. There was a pattern, and therein lies the story."

THE ROAD TO ROME

The road leading back from the fully established Roman church of the second millennium to the time of Jesus was a rocky one, filled with controversies, schisms, and contentiousness.

Even before the crucifixion there was an intense rivalry between the followers of Jesus and those of John the Baptist. The end result was the

Johannite heresy—the idea that John was the true messiah rather than Jesus. Although largely exterminated by the early church, this concept continued up to modern times within certain elements of Freemasonry as well as the Mandaeans of Iraq.

Following the crucifixion, the rivalries between the Jewish community and the early Christians—and even within Jesus' own followers—intensified.

There was a growing schism between the fundamentalist Jewish Christians belonging to the Essene sect and the Greek or Hellenized Christians in first century Jerusalem. Sounding much like the fundamentalists in America today, pious Jews attacked these foreigners for abandoning religious services for a Greek-style sports arena filled with wrestlers and discus throwers.

James and Mary Magdalene, as leaders of the Jerusalem church, were even at odds with Paul, who was bringing his Christian message to the gentiles to the north. There were immense squabbles over the most minute issues. In Galatians 5:12, Paul had become so exasperated with a continuing argument over circumcision that he expressed the hope that those initiating the controversy would emasculate themselves!

"The first Jewish Christians believed that obeying all of the stringent Jewish religious laws, including circumcision and eating only Kosher food, were necessary for salvation," noted Eddy. "Paul preached that salvation could be attained through faith and that the Jewish religious laws should not be allowed to impede people from becoming Christians. Paul's view eventually won out, as more and more gentiles converted to Christianity. By the third century they outnumbered the Jewish Christians by a large margin, defined Christianity according to Paul's theology, and began castigating the original Jewish Christians as heretics."

Irenaeus, the Bishop of Lyon, by the middle of the second century condemned as heretics the followers of Jesus and James known as Nazarenes or the "poor." "They, like Jesus himself, as well as the Essenes and Zadokites [followers of King Solomon's chief priest Zadok] of two centuries before, expound upon the prophetic books of the Old Testament," Irenaeus complained. "They reject the Pauline epistles and they reject the apostle Paul, calling him an apostate [rejecter] of the Law." Gardner noted, "The Nazarenes . . . denounced Paul as a 'renegade' and a 'false apostle,' claiming that his 'idolatrous writings' should be 'rejected altogether.'"

Dr. Elaine Pagels, who chaired the Department of Religion of Barnard College at Colombia University, reported, "Diverse forms of Christianity flourished in the early years of the Christian movement. Hundreds of rival teachers all claimed to teach the 'true doctrine of Christ' and denounced one another as frauds. Christians in churches scattered from Asia Minor to Greece, Jerusalem, and Rome split into factions, arguing over church leadership. All claimed to represent 'the authentic tradition.'"

"Far above the wrangling in the local churches sat the Roman church, unconcerned, untroubled, and probably, uncomprehending," Eddy wrote, adding that the church at this time was primarily concentrating on missionary work in Europe, an activity which paid unexpected benefits. "Unwittingly, the Christianization of these heathen ultimately saved the Roman church because the barbarians and their priests regarded the Roman church as the authority for their religious beliefs. When the barbarians overran Rome, the Roman Church was spared."

Though spared by the barbarians, the church still had to contend with a variety of sects, each with its own version of Christianity.

One such group was the Gnostics, who claimed to have an intuitive understanding of the mysteries of God and Earth. It was an understanding that resulted from rigorous training, initiation, and intuitive experiences, not simply intellectual study. The church found Gnostics particularly dangerous, for they disdained the need for a hierarchy of priestly officials to interpret the word of God.

Far from dangerous heretics, these passive Christians claimed to be the keepers of secret knowledge as indicated by the Gnostic papyrus books discovered at Nag Hammadi in 1945. It was this discovery which first afforded any view of Gnosticism other than the damning rhetoric of the church.

Gnosticism, derived from the Greek word *gnosis* or knowledge, reportedly was founded in the first century by Simon the Magician, a contemporary of Jesus later known as the "Father of All Heretics." He advanced the ideas of the Greek philosophers, such as Socrates, who taught that the human soul exists outside the physical body and therefore has access to universal knowledge and that wisdom (*Gnosis*) was brought down to Earth from the heavens.

Another important Gnostic was Basilides, an early Egyptian Christian who through his Alexandrian cult sought to blend into Christianity the ancient mysteries of Mesopotamia. These Alexandrians believed that strange extraterrestrial beings called "aeons" acted as messengers between the heavens and Earth. The Persian Zoroaster began his own form of Gnosticism about five hundred years before the time of Jesus. Known as Zoroastrianism, this movement spread widely until pushed out by invading Muslims in the seventh century.

Occult author Andre Nataf stated that Gnosticism originated in Mesopotamia, first in the area of Iran then spreading into Asia Minor, Syria, and Babylon, where it was picked up by the Israelite captives and carried back to Palestine and Egypt. "Certain details prove that the Gnostic holy books [from Qumran and Nag Hammadi] must be assigned such an early date that Christianity itself may be seen as no more than a 'branch of Gnosticism,'" wrote Nataf. "But Gnosticism could equally be compared to any religion at all. All religious knowledge develops, after all, from an ancient primitive origin, lost in the 'mists of time.'"

According to the Hebrew Cabala, Gnostics seek to know the "secrets" of God, looking for answers within the sacred texts of whatever religion they accept. They seek the understanding of existence through interpretation of what they perceive as deeper meaning within the symbology of religious literature. "Gnosticism is religious existentialism," commented Nataf. Gnosticism flourished until declared a heresy by a council of bishops of the Roman church in A.D. 325.

Gnosticism was an integral part of the Ancient Mysteries since both involved the belief that only personal inner enlightenment could bring understanding. According to the Masonic philosopher Manly P. Hall, "This knowledge of how man's manifold constitution could be most quickly and most completely regenerated to the point of spiritual illumination constituted the secret, or esoteric, doctrine of antiquity."

Hall said such enlightenment and awareness had to be jealously guarded from "profane" persons who might abuse or misuse such knowledge. So lengthy periods of initiation were instituted and the most sensitive ancient knowledge was shrouded in symbols and allegory. "Christianity itself may be cited as an example," he wrote. "The entire New Testament is in fact an ingeniously concealed exposition of the secret processes of human regeneration."

Gardner wrote that such regeneration, specifically of the human spirit or energy, involved elevated consciousness which took place by degrees through the thirty-three vertebra of the spinal column. "The science of this regeneration is one of the 'Lost Keys' of Freemasonry," he explained, "and it is the reason why ancient Freemasonry was founded upon 33 degrees."

In the process of knowing, the Gnostic felt a sense of superiority and self-satisfaction. "This meant that they could subscribe to the outward doctrines of any religion, and could continue to operate under many different politico-religious systems," explained Daraul. "Gnosticism profoundly influenced men's minds even in Europe up to and after the Middle Ages, and its basic way of thinking is probably an underlying factor in other secret societies whose members would be surprised to know it."

Gnosticism also played an important role in an early Jewish ascetic sect known as the Essenes. The Essenes provoked such conflict with religious leaders of the other major Jewish sects, the Pharisees and Sadducees—they even argued that the established Hebrew lunar year was inaccurate—that the sect finally moved out of Jerusalem and established a monastery at Qumran on the north end of the Dead Sea which they called "the Wilderness." The Essene community was divided into two parts—married and unmarried members. All property was communal. In fact, the animosity of many modern Christians toward the Essenes largely came as a reaction to their overtly communistic lifestyle. These critics apparently forgot that all early Christians lived in much the same manner.

Members spent their days working and their nights in prayer. They taught the immortality of the soul and also tended toward a dualist outlook, believing in a spirit of goodness or light and one of evil or darkness.

The Essenes may have carried on the hermetic traditions of the Greeks. In the early twentieth century, a Russian-born train engineer named Georgi Ivanovich Gurdjieff claimed to have found the intact manuscript of an Essene master in an Indian monastery which explained the relationship of musical rhythms to the human body as taught by the sixth-century B.C. Greek philosopher Pythagoras. A great influence on the later Plato—that guiding light of Freemasonry, the Illuminati, John Ruskin, and Cecil Rhodes—Pythagoras offered the prescient idea that the Earth travels around the sun and was noted for his concept concerning the vibrations within celestial mechanics which he called the "harmony of the spheres."

Interestingly enough, it was Pythagoras, well known for his accurate prophecies, who may have been the first to predict a "New World Order." Some researchers interpreted this to mean the arrival of the messiah.

The word Essenes was derived from the Greek words *essaios,* meaning secret or mystic, and *essenoi*, indicating healing or physician. According to Gardner, the Essenes were connected to esoteric healing traditions as a later branch of an Egyptian mystery school called the Great White Brotherhood of the Therapeutate. "It was into this White Brotherhood of wise therapeutics and healers—the original Rosicrucians—that Jesus was later initiated to progress through the degrees and it was his high standing in this regard which gained him the so often used designation of 'Master,'" added Gardner. Other authors also state that Jesus was an Essene and Hall added that so were his parents, Mary and Joseph, along with his brother James. Most modern fundamentalists tend to dismiss this connection because tying Jesus to Gnosticism and the Essenes disturbs their rigid dogma.

It would further disturb them to hear Gardner's claim that, despite the interpretation of Bible translators, Jesus did not come from Nazareth. He said the word "Nazarene" and its variants came from the Hebrew word *Nozrim*, "a plural noun stemming from the term *Nazrie ha-Brit* 'Keepers of the Covenant,' a designation of the Essene Community at Qumran on the Dead Sea. It is actually a point of contention whether the town of Nazareth existed at all during Jesus' lifetime, for it does not appear on contemporary maps, nor in any books, documents, chronicles or military records of the period."

"It is generally supposed that the Essenes were the custodians of [esoteric] knowledge and also the initiators and educators of Jesus," wrote Hall. "If so, Jesus was undoubtedly initiated in the same temple of Melchizedek where Pythagoras had studied six centuries before." The Bible tends to confirm this in Hebrews 6:20 stating, ". . . where Jesus has gone as a forerunner on our behalf, having become a high priest forever after the order of Melchizedek."

Gardner claimed the name Melchizedek—acknowledged as one of the most mysterious persons in the Bible—is an Essene composite of the archangel Michael and the Hebrew high priest or Zadok, hence Michael-Zadok. At least one author on this subject believed Melchizedek actually was the Sumerian deity Enki.

"The Essenes were regarded as among the better educated class of Jews," said Hall. "The fact that so many artificers [craftsmen] were listed among their number is responsible for the order's being considered as a progenitor of modern Freemasonry."

As with both Freemasons and the followers of Pythagoras, a prominent Essene symbol was the mason's trowel. And like the Freemasons, the Essenes produced literature involving intricate codes and allegories to protect their knowledge from the uninitiated as well as from the Roman authorities.

For example, when writing about the Romans, they used the term *Kittim,* thought to refer to the ancient Chaldeans of Mesopotamia. "The Essenes resurrected the old word for use in their own time and enlightened readers knew that *Kittim* always stood for 'Romans,'" explained Gardner, adding, "Study of the Scrolls . . . reveals a number of such coded definitions and pseudonyms that were previously misunderstood or considered of no particular importance." Another example was the use of the term "the poor," which most people conclude meant people of few resources. The Scrolls make it clear that the early Christian church in Jerusalem referred to their members as "the poor," indicating their humble lives.

According to Gardner and others, the terms "leper" and the "blind" were used to signify persons not initiated into the Essene traditions or "Way." "Texts mentioning 'healing the blind' or 'healing a leper' refer more specifically to the process of conversion to the Way," Gardner explained. "Release from excommunication [by the community] was described as being *'raised from the dead.'* The definition 'unclean' related mostly to uncircumcized Gentiles, and the description 'sick' denoted those in public or clerical disgrace." (emphasis in the original)

Several modern researchers, following in the steps of the Essenes and Cabalists, agree the Bible is a coded message. Michael Drosnin, formerly a reporter with the *Washington Post* and the *Wall Street Journal,* caused a stir in 1997 with the publication of his book *The Bible Code.* Drosnin wrote that Israeli mathematician Dr. Eliyahu Rips believed he had found a hidden crosswordlike code within the Bible, which accurately foretold of both Kennedy assassinations, World War II, the moon landing, the bombings of Hiroshima and the Oklahoma City federal building, and the election of President Bill Clinton. He wrote that a skeptical senior code breaker for the U.S. National Security Agency, Harold Gans, was shocked when he verified this Bible code using his own computer program.

C. L. Turnage, a diligent student of this concept, wrote, "Whether it be the obvious prosaic literal interpretation, gematria, symbolic, or a hidden computer code, the Bible appears to be a book unlike any other. People down through the ages have interpreted its pages according to their degree of technological advancement and their limited understanding of the Mesopotamian origin of the Hebrew religion." According to Turnage, the Bible's code involved symbolic references to multiple deities. "These coded references pointed the way toward an understanding that such beings were the gods, or Elohim, of the Bible, whose worship began in Sumer," she noted, "and who ultimately originated on another world."

It is easy to see how the many translators and interpreters of the Bible went astray. Down through the years, interpretations of the Bible were made by men and women unfamiliar with either modern technology such as flight or with the allegories and codes employed by the original authors.

The Essenes also were one of the most effective of the ancient secret societies. Although undoubtedly known to their neighbors, their presence was either not recorded in the New Testament or later excised. Some researchers have referred to the Essenes as the protectors of "Mystic Christianity," the earliest form of Christianity which was based on the Ancient Mysteries.

Little to nothing was known regarding the Essenes until the discovery of the Dead Sea Scrolls in 1947, just two years after a Gnostic library was found in mountain caves near the upper Egyptian town of Nag Hammadi. Between 1947 and 1960, eleven caves eventually yielded about 800 manuscripts, 170 of them fragments of Old Testament works.

Apparently, as the Roman armies advanced during the Jewish Revolt of A.D. 70, the Essenes fled from Qumran after hiding their sacred texts in earthen jars buried in nearby caves. This literary treasure was discovered by two Bedouin shepherds who sold a few parchments to an antique dealer.

Eventually word of the discovery reached the ears of Hebrew University archeologist Yigael Yadin, who mortgaged his home and traveled into dangerous Arab areas seeking the scrolls. He managed to secure seven of them for his university, which promptly published them.

"Not so for the remaining scrolls," reported Eddy. "The Rockefeller Archaeological Museum in Palestine soon became involved and managed to acquire the rest of the scrolls from the government of Jordan . . . who stipulated that no Jewish scholars be allowed access to the ancient Jewish texts. Today, Israel controls the scrolls as a result of overrunning the place where they were stored during the Six Day War of 1967. . . . These scrolls are largely unpublished today [and] no one knows if all of them have been obtained. There is the possibility that others are in the possession of, or have been destroyed by, the Bedouins."

The Essene authors of the Dead Sea Scrolls had a profound effect on the first Christians in Jerusalem, who soon were differing in theology from Paul and his followers outside Palestine. This is evidenced by the fact that the interpretations of the Old Testament found in the scrolls are similar to the interpretations of James and the Jerusalem Christians.

The conflicts both within and without Christianity were settled by the Roman emperor Constantine in what Gardner described as "a strategic buy-out by the enemy." "Apart from various cultic beliefs, the Romans had worshipped the Emperors in their capacity as gods descended from others like Neptune and Jupiter," he explained. "At the Council of Arles in 314, Constantine retained his own divine status by introducing the omnipotent God of the Christians as his personal sponsor. He then dealt with the anomalies of doctrine by replacing certain aspects of Christian ritual with the familiar pagan traditions of sun worship, together with other teachings of Syrian and Persian origin. In short, the new religion of the Roman church was constructed as a 'hybrid' to appease all influential factions. By this means, Constantine looked towards a common and unified 'world' religion—Catholic meaning *universal*—with himself at its head."

This attempt to co-opt Christianity was sealed at the Council of Nicaea in A.D. 325, the same council where Arias was punched and tossed out. It was here that the Arians were banished and the Nicene Creed established, which formally defined God as a deity of three equal and coexisting parts—the Father, Son, and Holy Spirit or Ghost.

One year later, Constantine ordered the confiscation and destruction of all works which questioned the newly constructed orthodoxy and opened the Lateran Palace to the bishop of Rome creating an early Vatican of sorts. In A.D. 331 the emperor ordered new copies made of Christian texts, most of which had been lost or destroyed during the previous persecutions. "It was at this point that most of the crucial alterations in the New Testament were probably made and Jesus assumed the unique status he has enjoyed ever since," noted Baigent, Leigh, and Lincoln.

Based on the recent discoveries which made available such ancient texts as the Gospel of Truth, the Gospel of Thomas, the Testimony of Truth, the Gospel of Mary, and the Interpretation of Knowledge, researchers today have a much broader and more complete knowledge of biblical times than ever before in history, despite the fact that much of this new information has still not reached a general audience.

Author Nesta Webster, a passionate Christian writing in 1924, long before the recent finds, deplored the connection between Jesus and the Essenes as well as their source of knowledge. "The Essenes were therefore not Christians, but a secret society . . . bound by terrible oaths not to divulge the sacred mysteries confided to them," she declared. "And what were those mysteries but those of the Jewish secret tradition which we now know as the Cabala? . . . The truth is clearly that the Essenes were Cabalists, though doubtless Cabalists of a superior kind. . . . The Essenes are of importance . . . as the first of the secret societies from which a direct line of tradition can be traced up to the present day."

Some of today's recently acquired knowledge in astronomy and philosophy may have been commonplace to the Gnostic Essenes of Jesus' time. Furthermore, Gardner observed, "Entirely divorced from the fabricated Christianity of the Roman Empire, their faith was closer to the original teachings of Jesus than any other. . . ."

Of all the Christian factions, the Essenes may indeed have had the purest of the ancient traditions at that time, thanks to the ancient Hebrew writings known as the Cabala.

THE CABALA

Predominately of Jewish origins, the Cabala, also written as Kabbalah or Qabbalah, means "tradition" and, like recent claims about the Bible, was supposed to contain hidden meanings. Such cleverly coded knowledge was thought to be found within the Torah and other old Hebraic texts such as the *Sefer Yezirah* (Book of Creation) and the *Sefer HaZohar* (Book of Light).

These books, which predate the Talmud, a compilation of elder Jewish laws and traditions first written in the fifth century A.D., were produced centuries before the time of Jesus. According to the Book of Light, "mysteries of wisdom" were given to Adam by God while still in the fabled Garden of Eden. These elder secrets were then passed on through Adam's sons to Noah on to Abraham long before the Hebrews existed as a distinct people.

According to Nataf, "The mysterious Cabala is a form of Gnosticism [in which] man seeks to find divinity within himself."

The author of the *HaZohar* wrote that "the human dimension contains all things, and all that exists in accordance with that. . . . Man contains all that is in heaven above and on earth below. . . ." Here the Cabala exhibits an obvious connection to the celebrated proclamation of Hermes Trismegistus, also known as the Egyptian god Thoth, who proclaimed, "As above, so below."

The connection between Hebrew traditions and Egyptian mysticism may be even stronger than previously believed, as many authors, including Jewish scholars, now believe the Cabala was an oral tradition concerning ancient Egyptian "mysteries" handed down from Moses through the leadership level of the Israelites.

The idea of ancient secrets being passed down to Moses from the earliest times was strongly supported by Eliphas Levi, a pen name of the nineteenth century French Bible scholar Alphonse Louis Constant. "There is a tremendous secret which has already turned the world upside down, as shown by the religious traditions of Egypt, which were symbolically resumed by Moses in the early chapters of Genesis," wrote Levi, who claimed that the Cabala contained knowledge carried out of Sumer by Abraham, "the inheritor of the secrets of Enoch and the father of initiation in Israel."

The biblical patriarch Abraham, a native of Sumer known early on as Abram, by some traditions was said to possess a tablet of symbols representing all of the knowledge of humankind handed down from the time of Noah. Known to the Sumerians as the "Table of Destiny," it was this table of knowledge—known to the early Jews as the Book of Raziel—which reportedly provided King Solomon with his vast wisdom. "The philosophical cipher of the Table became known as *Ha Qabala* [light and knowledge]," reported Gardner, "and it was said that he who possessed *Qabala* also possessed *Ram,* the highest expression of cosmic knowingness. The very name Ab-ram—or Av-ram—means '[He] who possesses *Ram,*' and the expression was used in India, Tibet, Egypt and in the Celtic world of the Druids to denote a high degree of universal aptitude."

The Sumerian "Table of Destiny" is thought to be the same as the "Tables of Testimony" mentioned in Exodus 31:18. Other Bible verses—Exodus 24:12 and 25:16—make it clear that these tables are not the Ten Commandments. "This ancient archive is directly associated with the Emerald Table of Thoth-Hermes and, as detailed in alchemical records of Egypt, the author of the preserved writings was the biblical Ham. . . . He was the essential founder of the esoteric and arcane 'underground stream' which flowed through the ages and his Greek name, Hermes, was directly related to the science of pyramid construction, deriving from the word *herma*, which relates to a 'pile of stones'. . . . Outside Egypt and Mesopotamia, the Table was known to Greek and Roman masters such as Homer, Virgil, Pythagoras, Plato, and Ovid, while in much later times the 17th century Stuart Royal Society of Britain was deeply concerned with the analysis and application of the sacred knowledge [in] conjunction with the Knights Templar and the Rosicrucian movement," explained Gardner.

Much like our understanding of history and religion today, the information within the Cabala became garbled over the centuries through both misinterpretations as well as foreign influences. "The speculative side of the Jewish Cabala borrowed from the philosophy of the Persian Magi [magicians in the occult sense], of the neo-Platonists, and of the neo-Pythagoreans," noted Webster. "There is, then, some justification for the anti-Cabalists' contention that what we know today as the Cabala is not of purely Jewish origin."

Pure or tainted, the mystical knowledge of the Cabala passed from Mesopotamia through Palestine into medieval Europe where it first appeared in writing at the end of the thirteenth century. It was scribed by a Spanish Jew named Moses de Leon, who may have devised the title *HaZohar,* a literary creation which caused critics to accuse him of fabricating the entire work. Today, most scholars—both Jewish and gentile—agree that the content of the Cabala legitimately predates the Christian era.

"We are looking at a point in history which was to define and control the world from then until now," wrote Icke. "The knowledge the [Hebrew] Levites stole from Egypt and expanded as a result of their stay in Babylon, became known as the Cabala. . . . The Cabala is the secret knowledge hidden in codes within the Old Testament and other texts. Judaism is the literal interpretation of it."

It has been stated how the Knights Templar brought Cabalistic knowledge back to Europe from the Holy Land at the time of the Crusades and that this knowledge was passed along through the alliance of the order and mason guilds. Masonic historians have acknowledged that the first evidence of "Judeo-Christian mysteries" introduced into Freemasonry came during this very time. It has also been documented that the hidden knowledge within the Cabala has been utilized through the centuries by nearly all secret societies, including Freemasonry, the Rosicrucians, and through the Illuminati on into modern groups.

Masonic historian Wilmshurst confirmed this, stating, "Since the suppression of the Mysteries . . . their tradition and teachings have been continued in secret and under various concealments, and to that continuation our present Masonic system is due."

According to Picknett and Prince, Cabalistic thought was also introduced to Europe within the banker/ruler court of the de Medicis in Florence, Italy, in the fourteenth and fifteenth centuries, notably through a Cabalist named Pico della Mirandola.

Author Webster cites nineteenth-century literature claiming that Moses Mendelssohn, the noted Jewish philosopher and Bible translator who did so much to liberate Jews from repressive German laws, not only was a Jewish Cabalist but one of those men who inspired and mentored Illuminati leader Adam Weishaupt. Mendelssohn, who came to be known as "the German Socrates" after being favorably portrayed in a drama by his Masonic friend Gotthold Lessing, may have also been a link between Weishaupt and banker Mayer Rothschild. Another may have been Michael Hess, the tutor of Rothschild's children and a "follower of Moses Mendelssohn," who later headed the Philanthropin School for needy Jewish children established by Rothschild.

This blending of Cabalistic teachings with later secret societies was further confirmed in 1984 when more than five hundred papers of a John Byrom were discovered in England. Byrom, who lived from 1691 to 1763, was a Freemason, a fellow of the Royal Society, and a leader of the Jacobite movement to restore the Stuart monarchy. He was a member of a group called the "Sun Club," also known as the "Cabala Club." His papers, according to Picknett and Prince, were "chiefly concerned with sacred geometry and architecture, and cabalistic, Masonic, hermetic and alchemical symbols."

All of the early societies—including the Mystery Schools of Greece and Egypt—sought to penetrate the secrets of the past.

The industrial revolution as well as the evolution theories of Charles

Darwin have led most people to believe in the "progress of man"—that humankind evolved from tree-climbing primates to moderns with high technology. Today, recent discoveries and new interpretations of ancient literature and artifacts are leading many to believe the opposite—that humankind "fell" from a golden age into barbarity and is only now regaining lost knowledge.

Even world population figures suggest an early decline rather than growth in the human species. "Global population figures between 6000 B.C. and the beginning of our era are extremely significant," wrote Tomas. "There were about 250 million people on earth 2,000 years ago. The population of the planet in 4800 B.C. was 20 million. In the year 5000 B.C. there were 10 million on all the continents. One thousand years earlier—in 6000 B.C.—only 5 million people inhabited the earth. On the basis of these figures, the population of the globe was well under 1 million about 10,000 B.C.—an astonishingly low figure. Why was man such a rare creature if he has had a continuous existence as a primate and then as a rational being for at least 2 million years?"

According to the records of the ancient Sumerians and Egyptians, civilized humankind has been on Earth for more than 500,000 years. Yet the archeological record indicates that man may have actually regressed in knowledge and abilities until beginning a slow advancement some 13,000 years ago. Obviously, a new model of history is necessary.

Masonic philosopher Hall wrote that the Mystery Schools were created as secret societies to prevent outside interference as initiates attempted to bridge the gap between the material and spiritual worlds.

He explained that "when our solar system began its labors, spirits of wise beings from other solar systems came to us and taught us ways of wisdom that we might have the birthright of knowledge which God gives to all His creations. It was these minds which are said to have founded the Mystery Schools of the Ancient Wisdom. . . . Gradually a separation took place among the schools of the Mysteries. The zeal of the priests to spread their doctrines in many cases apparently exceeded their intelligence. . . . The result was that these untutored minds, slowly gaining positions of authority, became at last incapable of maintaining the institution. . . . So the Mystery Schools vanished . . . while the colossal material organizations, having no longer any contact with their divine source, wandered in circles, daily becoming more involved in the rituals and symbols which they had lost the power of interpreting."

If the religious institutions could not correctly interpret their own theology, the same could be said of their scientific counterparts, who even today cannot explain artifacts still in existence. Recently, open-minded members of both the public and the sciences are taking a second look at some of this planet's most intriguing anomalies and mysteries.

ANCIENT SECRETS AND MYSTERIES

The world's first secrets dealt with the true origins of mankind. Neither of the two most prevalent theories of today—Darwinism and Creationism—can fully account for human origins and development.

Darwin's theory of survival of the fittest fails to explain how humans overcame the thousands of deficiencies within the human DNA structure, while Creationism overlooks an impressive fossil record. Clearly a new model is required.

Recently, the theories regarding the origin of modern humans were further confused by the discovery of fossils indicating that Neanderthal, a primitive man, lived side-by-side with Cro-Magnon, modern man, in what is now Israel. Yet mysteriously, these two races apparently did not interbreed. "Only one solution to the mystery is left," reported James Shreeve, author of *The Neanderthal Enigma: Solving the Mystery of Modern Human Origins*. "Neanderthals and moderns did not interbreed in the Levant because they *could* not. They were reproductively incompatible, separate species...." (emphasis in the original)

Furthermore, scientific testing showed that modern human remains in prehistoric Israel predated Neanderthal remains by as much as forty thousand years, presenting a severe blow to the theory of continuous evolution.

These findings also may have resolved the question of the infamous "missing link" between primitives and modern mankind—namely, that there is no such link. There appear to have been two separate species. Again, this requires a new model for human origins.

New models are today being expounded by a growing number of archeological, theological, and historical revisionists who are contesting the pat answers offered by conventional science over the past several decades.

Human nature being what it is, mainstream scientists and theologians are circling the wagons to defend their long-cherished theories. With the same intransigence of those who once proclaimed the Earth was flat, they are determined to defend their positions to the end despite a growing body of evidence to the contrary.

Such evidence is not a recent phenomenon. Many of this planet's deepest mysteries involve artifacts dating back thousands of years. They include:

—A number of unusually small ancient Chinese porcelain "seals" discovered all over Ireland in the eighteenth and nineteenth centuries, a time when there was no known commerce between the Emerald Isle and China.

—Mysterious life-size crystal skulls dated to at least 3,600 years ago found in South America. According to the staff of the British Museum Laboratory, the skulls give indications of being made with some sort of powered cutter.

—Numerous giant stone balls found in Costa Rica in the 1930s were from granite not found in the area, and their symmetry was so perfect as to defy explanation of who made them or how.

—Throughout England, France, and Germany today stand many ancient stone forts—there are at least sixty in Scotland alone—built with large rocks which at some point were "vitrified," melted from such heat as to become fused and glassy. The heat necessary to produce such an effect—up to 1,100 degrees Celsius—ruled out the possibility that the stones were melted by conventional fires.

—What for all purposes appeared to be a computer dated almost one hundred years before Jesus discovered in 1900 off the island of Antikythera near Crete. Known as the "Antikythera Mechanism," the device contained a system of differential gears not known to have been used until the sixteenth century.

—A small vessel containing a copper cylinder with an iron rod inside, discovered in an Iraqi village and dated from at least 220 years B.C., turned out to be nothing less than a battery. When alkaline grape juice was added to the strange object, it produced a half volt of electricity.

—Unexplained manufactured sites such as Stonehenge and Silbury

Hill in Britain, the huge heads of Easter Island, the Peruvian Nazca lines, the Great Serpent Mound of Ohio, and the controversial prehistoric "Rock Wall" east of Dallas, Texas, seem to indicate a technology lost in prehistory.

—Former NASA official Maurice Chatelain wrote of thirteen mystical sites within a 450-mile radius of the long-venerated Greek island of Delos which, connected by straight lines, produce a perfect Maltese cross, emblem of the Crusader knights. Chatelain said such a gigantic pattern could only have been created from a vantage point in space.

—According to Chatelain, coins of exactly the same weight have been found in geographic locations thousands of miles apart and in different cultures separated by thousands of years.

—In 1996 Han Ping Chen, an authority on the ancient Chinese Shang dynasty, confirmed that markings found on Central American Olmec figures dated to more than three thousand years ago were clearly archaic Chinese characters. Puzzled archeologists admitted that identical writing systems cannot be independently invented.

—Carvings located twenty-five feet above the floor in the ancient Temple of Seti I in Abydos, Egypt, resemble nothing less than two jet airplanes and an Apache attack helicopter. Their presence has been noted by recent travelers and reportedly were mentioned in an 1842 report, yet no one knows what they truly represent.

—Cuneiform Babylonian tablets in the British Museum described the phases of Venus, the four moons of Jupiter, and the seven satellites of Saturn, none of which could have been seen in ancient Babylon without the aid of modern telescopes.

—The maps of Turkish admiral Piri Reis, dated from the early sixteenth century and said to be based on earlier maps predating Alexander the Great, accurately depict the Amazon basin of South America and the northern coastline of Antarctica, neither of which was surveyed until after the advent of aircraft in the twentieth century. The accurateness of these maps regarding Antarctica are especially puzzling since it has been under an ice cap for at least four thousand years.

—A rectangular ziggurat built before 8,000 B.C. recently found near

Okinawa, points to people with advanced technologies living long before the generally accepted date of the first civilizations.

Why don't we know more about our past and such artifacts as those few mentioned above? The answer lies in the destructive nature of humans. Only a few of Homer's poems survived the destruction of his works by the Greek tyrant Peisistratus in Athens. Nothing survived the destruction of the Egyptian library in the Temple of Ptah in Memphis. Likewise, an estimated two hundred thousand volumes of priceless works disappeared with the destruction of the library of Pergamus in Asia Minor. When the Romans leveled the city of Carthage, they destroyed a library said to have contained more than five hundred thousand volumes. Then came Julius Caesar, whose war against Egypt resulted in the loss of the great library at Alexandria, considered the greatest collection of books in antiquity. With the loss of the *Serapeum* and the *Bruchion* branches of that library, a total of some seven hundred thousand volumes of accumulated knowledge went up in flames. What little survived was destroyed by Christians in A.D. 391. European libraries also suffered under the Romans and later from zealous Christians. Between the sacking of Constantinople and the Catholic Inquisition, an inestimable number of ancient works were irretrievably lost. Collections in Asia fared little better, as Chinese emperor Tsin Shi Hwang-ti ordered wholesale book burning in 213 B.C.

"Because of these tragedies we have to depend on disconnected fragments, casual passages and meager accounts," lamented Australian author Andrew Tomas. "Our distant past is a vacuum filled at random with tablets, parchments, statues, paintings, and various artifacts. The history of science would appear totally different were the book collection of Alexandria intact today."

The mystery of humankind's past can be symbolized by two of the planet's oldest edifices.

Conventional wisdom tells us that Egypt's Great Pyramid and Sphinx were built by the Egyptians some 4,500 years ago. However, the recent discovery on both of erosion from heavy rainfall—an event which could only have occurred more than 10,000 years ago prior to the Giza Plateau becoming a desert—is evidence that these famous structures were built thousands of years before the ancient Egyptian civilization came on the scene. Maverick Egyptologist John Anthony West, who two decades ago took the lead in publicizing the prehistoric origin of the Sphinx, has been supported in recent years by the work of Boston University geologist Dr. Robert Schoch. Following scientific study in the early 1990s, West, Schoch, and other experts concluded that the Sphinx was constructed no more recently than 7,000 to 5,000 years ago—and this was considered by some a very conservative figure. "I remain convinced that the Sphinx must pre-date the breakup of the last Ice Age. . . . If technology of that order had been available in Egypt, I think we'd see evidence of it elsewhere in the ancient world," wrote West.

Despite recent scientific work on the Sphinx that supports West's theories and the popularity of a 1993 NBC special on the subject, Egyptian authorities—apparently at the behest of traditional Egyptologists if not more secret groups—continue to deny researchers like West access to the antiquities they study.

The famous psychic Edgar Cayce in 1934 stated that the ancient Egyptians were the descendants of a previous civilization who constructed the Great Pyramid and Sphinx as a "Hall of Records"—their version of a time capsule—for the purpose of imparting scientific knowledge to future generations. Cayce even said that this library of knowledge would be found beneath the paws of the Sphinx. In the early 1990s, ground-penetrating radar confirmed what Cayce and some modern remote viewers have stated—that a chamber exists beneath the paws of the Sphinx. Oddly enough, no one has been authorized to excavate the site.

If the Sphinx was built before the end of the last Ice Age, it would date completion of the structure to some time prior to 15,000 years ago, which certainly excludes the Egyptians as its creators. Others are now admitting that a much older and even more sophisticated civilization predated the Egyptians.

"The workmanship level of jewelry as well as architecture in ancient Egypt was higher in the earlier periods," noted Tomas. Clearly, the Egyptian civilization did not spontaneously appear. It was the legacy of a predecessor.

The famous Egyptian Book of the Dead, in a passage containing a confession to the "Lord of Righteousness," reveals a remarkable correlation to the Ten Commandments of the Old Testament:

BIBLE	BOOK OF THE DEAD
Have no other gods before me	I do not tamper with divine balance
Make no idols	I stop not a god when he comes forth
Do not misuse the name of God	I do not offend the god who is at the helm
Keep the Sabbath holy	(Egyptians had no Sabbath)
Honor your mother and father	I do not harm my kinsmen
Do not kill	I do not kill
Do not commit adultery	I am not an adulterer
Do not steal	I do not rob
Do not lie	I do not tell lies instead of truth
Do not covet another's property	I do no wrong or mischief to others

This comparison provided compelling support for those who claim that the biblical Israelites drew heavily from the ancient Egyptian texts. The Egyptians, in turn, gained their knowledge and beliefs from the older cultures of Babylon and Sumer.

Many authors in recent years have detailed a widely disparate number of archeological anomalies reaching from Tibet and India to South and Central America on into the Middle East. A reconstructed human called "Kennewick Man," whose remains were found in Washington State in 1996, more resembles *Star Trek*'s Captain Picard than he does an Indian. An archeological dig in 1977 found that Monte Verde, Chile, was inhabited at least 12,500 years ago—1,000 years prior to when the original Americans were supposed to have crossed the Bering Strait ice bridge.

"The emerging answer suggests that [prehistoric Americans] were not Asians or Mongoloid stock who crossed a land bridge into Alaska 11,500 years ago, as the textbooks say," reported *Newsweek*, "but different ethnic groups, from places very different from what scientists thought even a few years ago." So far, conventional science is at a loss to explain where these people came from or how they got to the Americas in prehistoric times.

The signs of advanced prehistoric civilizations are worldwide and unmistakable, yet do not easily fit in the conventional view of history. Recent discoveries and new interpretations of available data both add to a growing body of evidence indicating that civilizations with advanced technology existed long before written history.

In a book little known in America, *Gods of the New Millennium: Scientific Proof of Flesh and Blood Gods*, British author Alan F. Alford wrote, "A shadowy pre-history seems to exist as a legacy in the form of stone, maps and mythology, which our 20th century technology has only just allowed us to recognize."

Who were these people and where did they get their technology? Could such a prehistorical advanced civilization be the basis for the legends of Atlantis and Mu?

Many blame the fact that these issues have been ignored for far too long on the specialization of fields of study. Both science and religion rarely give any serious consideration to each other. Archeologists rarely mix with linguists or geologists with historians. Hence much of mankind's history has been left to those who present it from their own limited perspective. The more suspicious see it as a conspiracy by the wealthy elite to maintain power and control by keeping the public ignorant of their true origins and potential.

The idea that the origins of man are still largely hidden from us by both time and design is naturally quite disturbing to those who have spent lifelong careers presenting mankind's history as one long evolution from savage to civilized man. Yet it is apparent from the available evidence that modern man may just now be regaining knowledge lost millennia ago.

It appears that bits and pieces of prehistoric knowledge survived in various esoteric forms through secret societies such as the Mystery Schools of Egypt and the schools of Pythagoras. These little-understood groups passed along not only religious concepts such as reincarnation or the transmigration of souls, but also real knowledge in architectural design, construction, astronomy, agronomy, and history. One of the underlying and unifying concepts of these early groups was monotheism, the belief in only one universal creative god.

The Hebrews are among the most well-documented peoples of the ancient world, yet there is no mention of working on the Great Pyramid in the otherwise detailed records of their time as Egyptian slaves. By all traditions, Hebraic knowledge stemmed from their patriarchs Abraham and Moses. The latter not only led them from Egyptian bondage but presented them with a lengthy list of laws and social customs.

WAS THERE MORE TO MOSES?

Considering the material covered thus far, it is clear that the knowledge hidden within the secret societies, both ancient and modern, can be traced back to ancient Egypt.

According to the Bible, it was Moses and his exodus from Egypt with the Hebrews that set world history on the course that we all know. According to Webster, Moses gained the oral tradition of knowledge from the Egyptian Mystery Schools, which he handed down through subsequent Hebrew leaders. Many researchers believe pieces of this knowledge were passed along to the Western world through cryptic passages in the Talmud, the Jewish Cabala, and the Old Testament along with an oral tradition handed down through the secret societies.

Many thoughtful people have questioned both the origins and accounts of Moses. Sigmund Freud, in his 1939 book *Moses and Monotheism,* proposed that Moses was not a Jew but a ranking Egyptian connected to the reign of Pharaoh Akhenaten. One argument used by Freud was that many of the laws Moses presented to his Jewish following were of Egyptian origin. The similarity between the Ten Commandments and the Egyptian Book of the Dead has already been noted. Freud also questioned why any Jew would have wanted to retain any Egyptian customs once free of slavery.

Freud was not the first to question Moses' Hebraic lineage. The author of the Old Testament book of Exodus (2:19) describes Moses as an Egyptian. Manetho, a priest and adviser to Pharaoh Ptolemy I some three hundred years before the birth of Jesus, wrote in the *Aegyptiaca* or *History of Egypt,* that Moses was a ranking Egyptian priest educated in the Ancient Mysteries at the lower Egyptian city of Heliopolis.

Gardner offered an even more startling supposition. He was puzzled that, considering Moses' high position in Egypt as stated in the Old Testament, there appears to be no mention of him in the vast quantity of Egyptian literature now available. After careful study, he made a compelling argument that Moses and the Egyptian pharaoh Akhenaten, or Amenhotep IV as he was officially known, were the same person. This was not an entirely new concept, as it was advanced by the Rosicrucians as far back as the eighteenth century.

Akhenaten, the most mysterious and little-known of the pharaohs, incurred the wrath of the Egyptian religious authorities when he closed the various Egyptian temples and built new ones to the vague and faceless god Aten. The omniscient Aten appears very close to the Mystery Schools' view of one universal god. Furthermore, according to Gardner, Aten is the equivalent of the Hebrew *Adon*. Aten may have transliterated into the Hebrew *Amen,* meaning "so be it," a term still used in churches today, which evolved from the name of the supreme Sumerian god Anu.

Akhenaten's childhood parallels that of Moses. When Pharaoh Amenhotep III's second wife Tiye became pregnant, it was decreed that if the child was a son and hence a pretender to the throne, he should be killed. Her first child was indeed a son, Tuthmosis, who died prematurely. Gardner said a second son was saved when "the royal midwives conspired with Tiye to float the child downstream in a reed basket to the house of her father's half-brother Levi." Here the child was nursed by Tey, of the house of Levi. This youngster, named Aminadab, then was reared by these Hebrews. He received a religious education at Heliopolis and later married his half sister Nefertiti, which placed him in line for the throne.

The story of a child being saved by a basket of bull rushes in fact can be traced back to the Sumerian Sargon the Great who claimed, "My changling mother . . . set me in a basket of rushes, and with pitch she sealed my lid. She cast me into the river, which . . . carried me to Akki, the drawer of water."

When the old Pharaoh Amenhotep III died, he was succeeded by his son Aminadab, now proclaimed Amenhotep IV. Amenhotep meant "Amen is pleased" and Aminadab, who had been taught of the Hebrew's one god, soon changed his name to Akhenaten, meaning "Glorious Spirit of the Aten."

Akhenaten's support of Aten was unpopular with the people, particularly the powerful priesthood, and he was forced to abdicate the throne, which passed to his cousin Smenkhkare. Banished from Egypt about 1361 B.C., Pharaoh Akhenaten gathered his friends and relatives—mostly the Hebrew relatives of Tey—and fled. The worship of Aten was eventually suppressed and any mention of Akhenaten's name was forbidden, adding to the enigma concerning his life. According to Gardner, Akhenaten's son by a deputy wife named Kiya later became the famous boy pharaoh Tutankhaten, who was forced to change his name to Tutankhamen to reflect the return to the worship of *Amen* rather than *Aten.*

Linking Akhenaten to the biblical account, he and a "brother," Aaron the Levite, returned to Egypt on orders of the "God of Abraham" to retrieve the Hebrews. After a duel in magic with Egyptian sorcerers, they departed with the remaining Hebrews.

"Evidence from Egypt indicates that Moses/Akhenaten led his people from Pi-Rameses—near modern Kantra—southward, through Sinai, to Lake Timash. This was extremely marshy territory and, although manageable on foot with some difficulty, any pursuing horses and chariots would have foundered disastrously," Gardner observed. He also noted that Akhenaten's supporters still believed him the rightful heir to the throne and called him *Mose, Meses,* or *Mosis,* meaning "heir or born of." Thus, Moses might denote a title rather than a name.

Even in the Middle Ages, scholars pondered over the similarities of Moses, Hermes, and Thoth, all of whom were great leaders who obtained their knowledge directly from God. Tile work in the Sienna Cathedral in Italy bears an inscription reading, "Hermes Mercury Trismegistus, Contemporary Moses."

Further support for the Moses/Akhenaten theory may be found in Miriam, the woman most closely associated with the prophet and who was so instrumental in the Exodus from Egypt and subsequent events. In her we may find further support for the "Moses as Pharaoh" theory. "All records indicate that toward the end of Akhenaten's reign, Merykiya—Beloved of Khiba—had become the dominant queen [under the name] Mery-amon—Beloved of Amon—carrying a dual legacy from the kings of Egypt and Mesopotamia," stated Gardner. "It was she who moved into exile with Akhenaten/Moses to become known to the Israelites as Miriam . . . and it was her royal blood which, through her daughter—the sister of Tutankhamen—cemented the succession for the eventual Royal House of Judah."

If Moses was Akhenaten, this makes the connection between the ancient Egyptians and Hebrews much stronger than previously suspected, and it goes far in explaining the obvious blending of Egyptian beliefs into Hebrew theology. Even if Moses and Akhenaten were not the same person, it is documented that Moses was well schooled in ancient knowledge and gained high status while living in Egypt. The New Testament book of Acts (7:22) stated, "And Moses was learned in all of the wisdom of the Egyptians, and he was mighty in words and in deeds."

Moses, by the biblical account, became the patriarch of the Hebrews after receiving messages and commandments from God while visiting Mount Sinai. While he met with Jehovah, his followers watched from a safe distance. What they saw was described in Exodus 19:18 (New International), "Mount Sinai was covered with smoke, because the Lord descended on it in fire. The smoke billowed up from it like smoke from a furnace, the whole mountain trembled violently."

This description is quite compatible with the prophet Elijah's later account of a meeting with Yahweh in 1 Kings 19:9–13. Elijah recounted that as he stood on the holy mountain, the Lord passed by him with a great wind, flying dust and rocks and trembling earth. "There was a fire, but the Lord was not in the fire," said Elijah, "And after the fire, there was the sound of a gentle whisper." The prophet proceeded to hold a conversation with his god.

When Moses returned from his mountaintop experience, he carried with him tablets of stone. Once again there is a question of translation. Since all this occurred prior to the advent of the written Hebrew language, authors Knight and Lomas explained, "These tablets could only have been written in Egyptian hieroglyphics as Moses would not have understood any other script [as Hebrew did not become a written language for another 1,000 years]. The idea of messages materializing out of marks on stone amazed ordinary people and the scribes who could make 'stone talk' were considered to be holders of great magic. This is easily appreciated when one realizes that the Egyptians called hieroglyphics 'the Words of the God,' a term that would often be repeated throughout the Bible."

Jehovah is an English transliteration of the Hebrew Yahweh or Lord, a word which itself was early on expressed only by the consonants YHWH to prevent verbal misuse of the name. YHWH is an acronym of the famous Hebrew words in response to Moses' question regarding how he was supposed to name his Lord: "I am that I am." (Exodus 3:14) The Canaanite term for Yahweh was *Elohim*, a plural noun derived from *El* or *Eloh*, meaning "Lofty One." Yet the Bible continued to used the plural Elohim for the one God. Another Hebrew word for "Lord," meaning the one true God, was *Adon* or *Adonai*. In the earliest texts, the term "El" or "El-Shaddai (Lord of the Mountain) is used 238 times. El, used biblically as a synonym for Elohim, derives from the ancient Sumerian Enlil or Great Mountain Lord. It is clear that the original biblical authors were referring to a definitive single male personality rather than some vague and hypothetical god.

"From the dawn of the subsequent Hebrew culture, however, everything changed as Jehovah became ever more rationalized as an individual 'absolute'—a unilateral overlord of all things," noted Gardner. "The Hebrew perception of Jehovah also became totally abstract, so that all physical connection with humankind was lost."

"In Hebrew religion—and in Hebrew religion alone—the ancient bond between man and nature was destroyed," explained Middle East expert Henri Frankfort. "Those who served Jehovah must forego the richness, the fulfillment, and the consolation of a life which moves in tune with the great rhythms of the earth and sky."

Moses displayed to his people stone tablets containing a set of laws given by Jehovah, many of which were promptly broken on orders of this same Lord. After admonishing Moses and his people not to kill, steal, or covet another's property, Jehovah ordered them to the lands of the Amorites, Hittites, Canaanites, and others to kill men, women, and children and take their lands and possessions. This harsh order seems unworthy of a loving and merciful god and may be explained by the Egyptian priest Manetho, who wrote, "The wonders which Moses narrates as having taken place upon the Mountain of Sinai, are in part, a veiled account of the Egyptian initiation which [Moses] transmitted to his people when he established a branch of the Egyptian Brotherhood. . . ." In order words, these orders came from a physical person rather than from some spirit.

An even more controversial interpretation was made by author Dr. Joe Lewels, former chairman of the Department of Journalism at the University of Texas at El Paso, who opined in his 1997 book *The God Hypothesis* that Jehovah was indeed a being of flesh and blood who flew in a craft that created fire, wind, and noise. This vehicle was used to transport Moses to the summit of Mount Sinai as stated in Exodus 19:4, "You have seen what I did to the Egyptians, and how I bore you [as] on eagle's wings and brought you to myself."

Lewels also noted that Moses and the Israelites were never allowed to see Jehovah's face and wondered if his countenance was so nonhuman as to provoke fear and loathing. "It should be pointed out that this is not in the least an original idea," wrote Lewels, who mentioned the Mandaeans, an early Jewish sect who believed in a dualistic universe, divided equally into the worlds of light and darkness. "To them, the physical world, including the Earth, was created and ruled over by the Lord of Darkness, a reptilian being ... variously called Snake, Dragon, Monster and Gian ... thought to be the true creator of humanity," noted Lewels.

This same concept was also advanced by researcher and author R. A. Boulay, who noted that from all cultures of the world have come stories of dragons or reptilians who coexisted with man—even created man—and were associated with powerful gems or crystals, walked on legs, flew in the air, fought each other over territory, and were revered by humans as "gods." "The world-wide depiction of flying reptiles makes it abundantly clear that our creators and ancestors were not of mammal origin but were an alien saurian breed," concluded Boulay in his 1997 book *Flying Serpents and Dragons: The Story of Mankind's Reptilian Past.*

Recent writers such as Lewels and Boulay concluded that the biblical Jehovah was actually one of the ancient Sumerian "gods" who took a special interest in the descendants of the Mesopotamian patriarch Abraham.

"From the beginning of his relationship with the Hebrew people, Jehovah used every means at his command to exert authority and control over his flock," said Lewels. In referring to the Genesis 17 covenant between Jehovah and Abraham, Lewels saw the command that all males be circumcised as a marking system, much as ranchers today notch the ears of their cattle.

Needless to say, it is extremely difficult to attempt to interpret concepts dating back thousands of years. One of the biggest problems in trying to sort out the truth behind the old stories and legends is the fact that many different names were used by different people at different times for the same person, place, or concept in symbolic stories called allegories or parables.

Such allegories, usually passing as myths, are the backbone of the Western world's early religious and philosophical beliefs. Popularly thought to be separate pantheons of mythical characters, a close study of the ancient "sky gods" of major cultures clearly indicates that all stem from a common source. Indeed, when the earliest text from the Minoan culture was translated, it was found to contain a Semite dialect from Mesopotamia. It has been established that the Greek culture—the foundation of Western civilizations—stemmed from the early Minoans on Crete.

No one will agree on these specific connections between the "gods" because of the large amount of incidental material that grew up around them. But a general comparison of mythologies indicates common features which appear to go beyond coincidence and reveal the striking similarities between the ancient "gods":

	SUMERIAN	EGYPTIAN	GREEK	ROMAN
Heavenly Father	Anu	Amen-Ra	Cronos	Saturn
Heavenly Mother	Antu	Mut	Hera	Juno
Earth Lord	Enlil	Set	Zeus	Jupiter
Earth Mother	Ninhursag	Isis	Athena	Minerva
Earth Brother/Builder	Enki	Osiris	Apollo	Vulcan
Warrior Rival	Marduk	Horus	Ares	Mars
Underworld Lord	Nergal	Anubis	Hades	Pluto
Provider of Love	Asherah	Hathor	Aphrodite	Venus
Facilitator of the Gods	Ninurta	Thoth	Hermes	Mercury

The real question is how did Moses, and hence the Egyptians obtain knowledge of the Ancient Mysteries? Much of it apparently was passed down from the biblical patriarchs Isaac and Abraham.

In a family intrigue worthy of a soap opera, Abraham's first son, Ishmael, was born to an Egyptian servant named Hagar because Abraham's wife, Sarai, was barren. Even though it was her own scheme, Sarai mistreated Hagar, who fled.

According to Genesis 17, it was about this time we are told that Jehovah changed his follower's name from Abram (Exalted Father) to Abraham (Father of Nations) and ordered all male children circumcised. Abraham was promised a lineage that would rule over many nations, including Egypt and those of Mesopotamia. Sarai's name was changed to Sarah (Princess), who soon gave birth to Isaac, the second son born to Abraham, who was one hundred years old at the time, according to Genesis 17:17. In Genesis 17:19, Abraham is told that Jehovah's covenant will be established through Isaac. Apparently Isaac carried genetic traits gained through Sarah that were thought superior to those of Ishmael.

Abraham's ancestors are all named in the Bible and, through his father Terah, can be traced back almost two thousand years to Noah's son, Shem, and thus on back to Adam.

It is significant that Abraham came from Ur of the Chaldees near the northern end of the Persian Gulf, a principal Sumerian city. In early

Genesis, Abraham is only described as a Hebrew with a 318-man army of trained troops who was blessed by the mysterious Melchizedek. Later, in Genesis 24, Abraham has become "great," with many flocks and herds, silver and gold, camels and a large household filled with servants. He obviously was no small-time nomad but a wealthy and powerful citizen of Sumeria.

Following the destruction of Ur during a war about 2000 B.C., Abraham's family moved northward to the city of Haran, named for Abraham's brother, who was the father of Lot of Sodom and Gomorrah fame. Early in the twentieth century, archeologists discovered several northern Mesopotamian cities named after relatives of Abraham, including Haran, Terah, Nahor, Serug, and Peleg. "Clearly, the patriarchs represented no ordinary family, but constituted a very powerful dynasty," commented Gardner. It was this dynasty that passed the ancient traditions of the Sumerians from Abraham to Moses.

ALL ROADS LEAD TO SUMER

The world's deepest secrets all lead back to Sumer in Mesopotamia, the first known great civilization, located between the Tigris and Euphrates Rivers at the headwaters of the Persian Gulf. In biblical times, it was called Chaldea or Shinar. Today, it is known as Iraq.

The Sumerian culture seemed to appear from nowhere more than six thousand years ago, and, before it strangely vanished, it had greatly influenced life as far east as the Indus River, which flows from the Himalayas through Pakistan to the Arabian Sea, and as far west as the Nile of the later Egyptian kingdoms.

About 2400 B.C. Sumer was invaded from the west and north by Semitic tribes and by about 2350 B.C. was captive to the warrior leader Sargon the Great, who founded the Semite Akkadian dynasty which stretched from the Persian Gulf to the Mediterranean. After years of further wars and population displacements, the lands of Sumer were united under Hammurabi of Babylon, whose famous "Code" of laws may have been instituted to discipline the mass migrations of people in the wake of catastrophes at the time.

Alan Alford noted that the devastating eruption of the Greek island of Santorin and mysterious destruction on Crete as well as at Mohenjo-

Daro, capital of an Indus Valley culture, took place about the time of Hammurabi's rule. Alford saw a connection between these events and the removal of the Easter Island population, the emergence of Andean civilizations, and the arrival of the Mayas in Central America—all of which occurred about the same time. It is also now clear that the Code of Hammurabi was drawn from laws set down by the Sumerians centuries earlier, particularly the earliest law code yet discovered, issued by the Sumerian king Ur-Nammu.

Virtually nothing was known about the Sumerians until about 150 years ago when archeologists, spurred on by the writings of Italian traveler Pietro della Valle in the early seventeenth century, began to dig into the strange mounds dotting the countryside in southern Iraq. Beginning with the discovery of Sargon II's palace near modern-day Khorsabad by the Frenchman Paul Emile Botta in 1843, archeologists found buried cities, broken palaces, artifacts, and thousands of clay tablets detailing every facet of Sumerian life. By the late nineteenth century, Sumerian had been recognized as an original language and was being translated. Despite today's knowledge, the general public still has been taught little about this first great human civilization that suddenly materialized in Mesopotamia.

It is fascinating to realize that it may be possible to know more about this six-thousand-year-old civilization than we may ever know about the more recent Egyptians, Greeks, and Romans. The explanation lies in the Sumerian cuneiform writing. Whereas the papyrus of other elder empires disintegrated over time or were destroyed by the fires of war, cuneiform was etched onto wet clay tablets with a stylus, creating a wedge-shaped script. These tablets were then dried, baked, and kept in large libraries. About five hundred thousand of these clay tablets have now been found and have provided modern researchers with invaluable knowledge of the Sumerians.

The Sumerian tablets went largely undeciphered until a German high school teacher named Georg Grotefend began the systematic translation of cuneiform in 1802. Today many tablets still have not yet been translated into English because the sheer quantity has overwhelmed the world's handful of translators.

It must be understood that the Sumerian alphabet was essentially shorthand for a much older original language made up of logograms (symbols representing concepts rather than words) resembling nothing less than antique Chinese characters. Since it was not a detailed language like English, there has been wide latitude in its translation. When these translations began in the nineteenth century, the symbol for the Sumerian's creators was simply thought to mean mythical "gods" and everything proceeded from that point.

Archeological studies have shown that shortly after 4000 B.C. within the Tigris-Euphrates Valley, marshes had been drained, canals dug, dams and dikes constructed, a large-scale irrigation system initiated, and large, gleaming cities built.

The first twelve major city-states—with exotic names like Ur, Nippur, Uruk, Lagash, Akkad, and Kish—were all centered around towering, stair-stepped temples called ziggurats (Holy Mountains) and each was ruled by its own "god," called an *ensi*. Spiraling outward from the ziggurat were public buildings, markets, and homes. Surrounding each city were large tracts of land also controlled by the local *ensi*. As these city-states developed, they came under the leadership of a king, called a *lugal*, who answered to the local "god."

Despite our superficial knowledge of the Sumerians, we have already been able to credit them with many world "firsts." Professor Samuel Noah Kramer, author of *History Begins at Sumer* and *The Sumerians*, noted that these people developed the first writing system (cuneiform), the wheel, schools, medical science, the first written proverbs, history, the first bicameral congress, taxation, laws, social reforms, the first cosmogony and cosmology, and the first coined money (a weighed silver shekel).

Many of the records left to us are of mundane daily affairs such as tax records, court hearings, and market quotations. In fact, these ancient people were little different than today's societies. They laughed, loved and hated, squabbled and conspired, plotted against one another and eventually fought each other.

Author Tomas described the bust of the Sumerian queen Shub-ad, on display in the British Museum: "The lovely young lady wears an amazingly modern wig, large earrings, and necklace. The sophisticated girl, who used cosmetics, a wig, and expensive jewelry, died in a ritual suicide in 2900 B.C.—2,150 years before the foundation of Rome and 2,000 years before Moses started his writings."

Sumerians traveled frequently and widely and are thought to have brought their advanced technology of shipbuilding and mapping to the early Phoenicians, who settled along the eastern Mediterranean coast in what is now Lebanon.

Their knowledge of the heavens was both amazing and puzzling. "The whole concept of spherical astronomy, including the 360-degree circle, the zenith, the horizon, the celestial axis, the poles, the ecliptic, the equinoxes, etc., all arose suddenly in Sumer," noted Alford. Sumerian knowledge of the movements of the sun and moon resulted in the world's first calendar, used for centuries afterward by the Semites, Egyptians, and Greeks.

As Alford pointed out, few people realize that we owe not only our geometry but also our modern timekeeping systems to the Sumerian base-sixty mathematical system. "The origin of 60 minutes in an hour and 60 seconds in a minute is not arbitrary, but designed around a sexagesimal [based on the number 60] system," Alford reported, adding that the modern zodiac was a Sumerian creation based on their twelve gods. They used it to chart a great precessional cycle, dividing the 360-degree view from the Earth's North Pole during its twelve-month orbit around the sun into twelve equal parts—or houses—of 30 degrees each. Taking into account the slight wobble in Earth's orbit, movement through this complete cycle takes 25,920 years, an event known as the Platonian Year, named for the Greek scholar Plato who inspired the Knights Templar, Illuminati, and Rhodes's Round Tables.

"The uncomfortable question which the scientists have avoided is this: how could the Sumerians, whose civilization only lasted 2,000 years, possibly have observed and recorded a celestial cycle that took 25,920 years to complete? And why did their civilization begin in the middle of a zodiac period? Is this a clue that their astronomy was a legacy from the gods?" asked Alford.

His question could be enlarged to ask how did the early primitive humans of almost six thousand years ago suddenly transform from small packs of hunter-gatherers into a full-blown—advanced even by today's standards—civilization? Even the writers of *The New Encyclopaedia Britannica* acknowledged that serious questions remain concerning the Sumerian histories and cautiously explained that such queries "are posed from the standpoint of 20th century civilization and are in part colored by ethical overtones, so that answers can only be relative."

Since we now have thousands of translated Sumerian tablets along with their inscribed cylinder seals, perhaps we should allow the Sumerians themselves to explain.

The answer is that they claimed everything they achieved came from their gods.

"All the ancient peoples believed in gods who had descended to Earth from the heavens and who could at will soar heavenwards," explained Middle Eastern scholar Zecharia Sitchin in the prologue to the first book of a series detailing his translations and interpretations of Sumerian accounts of their origin and history. "But these tales were never given credibility, having been branded by scholars from the very beginning as myths."

Recognizing that even the most learned researcher before the turn of the twentieth century could not possibly have begun to think in terms of concepts we accept as commonplace today, Sitchin reasoned, "Now that astronauts have landed on the Moon, and unmanned spacecraft explore other planets, it is no longer impossible to believe that a civilization on another planet more advanced than ours was capable of landing its astronauts on the planet Earth some time in the past."

It is significant to learn that the Sumerians never considered, or referred to, the beings who brought them knowledge as "gods." This was a later interpretation by the Romans and Greeks, who fashioned their own "gods" after the earlier oral traditions.

The Sumerians called them the Anunnaki or Those Who Came to Earth from Heaven.

THE ANUNNAKI

To understand the Sumerian version of the origin of humanity requires only a slight shift in mindset.

Sitchin, who has done so much to synthesize the vast amount of Sumerian knowledge into a consistent—if extraordinary—hypothesis, often has told how his shift of mindset occurred. As a schoolboy studying Hebrew in Palestine, Sitchin had the audacity to question why the Old Testament term *Nefilim* was translated as "giants" when the original word meant "Those Who Were Cast Down." Predictably, instead of being praised for his initiative and attention to accuracy, young Sitchin was chastised for questioning the Bible. But the incident set him on a lifetime quest for the truth behind the inconsistencies and puzzles of the ancient texts.

Sitchen's question was well founded. Rather than simply "giants," the *Holman Bible Dictionary* defines the Old Testament Nefilim as "ancient heroes who, according to most interpreters, are the products of sexual union of heavenly beings and human women" as stated in Genesis 6:4 (New International): "The Nefilim were on the earth in those days—and also afterward—when the sons of God went to the daughters of men and had children by them. They were the heroes of old, men of renown."

A native of Russia, Sitchin was educated in Palestine and London, where he graduated with a degree in economic history from the University of London following studies at the London School of Economics and Political Science. After a stint as a writer and editor for economic and historical journals, Sitchin relocated to New York City in 1948 and soon became a U.S. citizen. During his years of study, Sitchin became fluent in a number of languages, including ancient Egyptian, Hebrew, and Akkadian, a later form of Sumerian.

Sitchin and others have simply taken the attitude that perhaps the ancient Sumerians were putting down on their clay tablets history as they understood it rather than mere myths. After all, the Sumerian descriptions of many ancient cities were believed fanciful stories until their ruins were discovered and excavated. Why not also consider their written history as reality?

After years of dedicated translation and study, Sitchin realized that the biblical Nefilim and the Sumerian Anunnaki represented the same concept—that in the Earth's most distant past, beings came down from the stars and founded the earliest civilizations, a theme which has run through nearly all secret societies, from Freemasonry to the Thule Society, as previously reported.

Using Sitchin's translations as a springboard, many authors in recent years have contributed to a more detailed understanding of the Anunnaki story. Based on Sitchin's work, as well as others including Alan F. Alford, R. A. Boulay, Neil Freer, Dr. Arthur David Horn, Dr. Joe Lewels, C. L. Turnage, Lloyd Pye, Laurence Gardner, and William Bramley, the account of the Anunnaki went something like this:

About 450,000 years ago, a group of spacefaring humanoid extraterrestrials arrived at planet Earth. They came from a planet about three times the size of Earth, which the Sumerians called Nibiru. Nibiru was depicted in the ancient Sumerian literature as the twelfth planet of our solar system.

As early as 1981 American scientists were theorizing the existence of a tenth planet in our system based on sightings by an orbiting telescope and studies of irregularities in the orbit of Pluto indicating an additional solar body. "If new evidence from the U.S. Naval Observatory of a 10th planet in the solar system is correct, it could prove that the Sumerians . . . were far ahead of modern man in astronomy," commented a writer for the *Detroit News*. There is no inconsistency here, as the Sumerians counted the moon and the sun as planetary bodies, thus arriving at the number twelve, the same number as their pantheon of Anunnaki overlords.

Truly amazing is the fact that these ancient Sumerians, whom we are told were just developing writing, accurately described and diagrammed the planets Uranus, Neptune, and Pluto, even though these three worlds cannot be seen without the aid of a telescope. Uranus was not known to modern man until discovered in 1781, Neptune in 1846, and Pluto in 1930.

Long considered fanciful myths, recent interpretations of Sumerian texts, particularly one entitled *Enuma Elish* now known as the Creation Epic, provided a most plausible explanation for the present composition of our solar system. "Why not take the epic at face value, as nothing more nor less than the statement of cosmological facts as known to the Sumerians, as told them by the Nefilim?" Sitchin concluded.

The texts described how more than four billion years ago, Nibiru, a rogue planet, entered our system, narrowly missing a large planet called Tiamat, which cracked due to the gravitational stresses. In a subsequent pass by Nibiru—in Sitchin's early works he refers to this orb by its Babylonian name Marduk—Tiamat was actually struck and then bombarded by Nibiru's attendant moons. Various sized fragments of Tiamat remained in its original orbit, becoming the asteroid belt, while the other half of the planet was knocked into a new orbit closer to the sun. This fragment over time coalesced into Earth. It was accompanied by one of Nibiru's moons (Kingu) which became our own satellite.

Interestingly enough, this theory could explain why the Earth is missing much of its crust, particularly on the half encompassing the Pacific Ocean, as well as the origin of the asteroid belt. This theory also offered an explanation for comets, which have caused so much speculation among scientists. The idea is that when Nibiru and Tiamat collided, many tons of seawater from both worlds were thrown into space—termed "mingling of the waters" by the Sumerian scribes—along with dirt and debris which became erratic flying balls of "dirty" ice.

This concept was strengthened by the recent discovery of meteorites in Antarctica containing the same gases known to compose the atmosphere of Mars, as well as by the discovery by NASA scientists in 1996 of what appeared to be the remains of microorganisms in a Martian meteorite thought to be four billion years old.

Nibiru, called the "Planet of the Crossing" because its orbit crossed the solar system between Mars and Jupiter, proceeded on its elliptical orbit, which took it far outside the solar system before being pulled back by gravitational force. Nibiru has been symbolized in numerous societies—particularly Egyptian—as a "winged disc," a circle with wings stretching to either side.

Life on Earth evolved based on its one-year orbit around the sun, the solar year. Life on Nibiru developed based on its one-year orbit around the sun—3,600 years to Earthlings. It then stands to reason that life on Nibiru would have evolved somewhat sooner than on Earth. This disparity of time may also be illustrated as how an insect with a weeks-long life might perceive a human with a normal lifespan as immortal.

About 450,000 years ago, during Earth's second ice age, the highly developed inhabitants of Nibiru—the Anunnaki of the Sumerian texts—journeyed to Earth as the two planets came into proximity. According to the Sumerians, their initial landings were made in water, just as our own astronauts at first splashed down in the ocean.

Logically, these ancient astronauts would have sought a base camp which provided moderate weather and a good source of water and fuel. Only one location met all these criteria—Mesopotamia. The Indus River valley and the Nile were two other good choices but did not offer easy access to fossil fuel, which is still plentiful in southern Iraq.

Some researchers view with suspicion the fact that the sites of these first Anunnaki settlements in the southern part of present day Iraq remain one of the few locations in the world where First World visitors cannot easily visit, thanks to the continued confrontation with Saddam Hussein with its attendant boycott and bombardments.

With the supreme Nibirian ruler, Anu—or An or El, depending on the source—supervising their effort from the home planet, the Anunnaki began a systematic colonization of Earth under the leadership of Anu's two sons, Enlil and Enki. All of the Anunnaki leaders were later to assume the role of "gods," or Nefilim, to their human subjects. Amazingly enough, one of these Nefilim was named Nazi. One must wonder if the twentieth century German occultists knew of this connection.

Enlil was the mission commander, while Enki served as executive and science officer. There was immediate and long-standing antagonism between the two half brothers due to Nibirian protocol. As in later Earth dynasties, the firstborn Enki was relegated to secondary status because his mother was not the official wife of Anu. This removed him from the royal line of succession. Yet it was Enki who led the first expedition to Earth.

In one well-preserved text, Enki described his splashdown in the Persian Gulf, "When I approached Earth, there was much flooding. When I approached its green meadows, heaps and mounds [dams and dikes] were piled up at my command. I built my house in a pure place. . . ."

Enki was both scientist and engineer. Under his leadership, the marshes on the northern shore of the Persian Gulf were drained, dikes along with irrigation systems were built as well as canals connecting the Tigris with the Euphrates. Reinforcements arrived under the leadership of Enki's first-born son, Marduk. Over thousands of years Earth time—but only a few years to the Anunnaki—a thriving colony of these visitors was put in place and their attention turned to their primary objective—gold.

Several researchers have composed elaborate metaphysical explanations for Anunnaki activities on Earth, many having to do with energy fields and spiritual planes disrupted by the passing of Nibiru and the creation of Earth. One theory was that the higher-evolved Anunnaki were attempting to rescue "lost souls" left behind after the planetary collision.

But more documented and acceptable is the idea suggested by Sitchin and others that these colonists were after Earth's mineral wealth—particularly gold—for use on their home planet. "The Anunnaki sought gold to save their atmosphere, which had apparently sprung leaks similar to those we have created in ours by damaging the Earth's ozone layer with hydroflourocarbons," explained author Lloyd Pye. "The Anunnaki solution was to disperse extremely tiny flakes of gold into their upper atmosphere to patch holes. . . . Ironically, modern scientists contend that if we are ever forced to repair our own damaged ozone layer, tiny particulates of gold shot into the upper atmosphere would be the best way to go about it."

Apparently an initial effort to retrieve gold from the Persian Gulf by a water-treatment system proved inadequate for their needs. Anu, along with his heir Enlil, visited the colony and assigned Enki to find more gold. Enlil was placed in overall command of the Earth colony while Enki led a foray to Africa and, eventually, to South America, where gold mining operations were set up. Proof of such early gold mining has come from scientific studies conducted for the Anglo-American Corporation, a leading South African mining corporation, in the 1970s. Company scientists discovered evidence of ancient mining operations which were dated as far back as 100,000 B.C. Similar ancient mine excavations have been found in Central and South America. This indicated the Anunnaki mining efforts were worldwide and may go far in explaining the early diffusion of humans.

Further substantiation of such wide-ranging travel may be found by comparing the names of ancient Mesopotamian cities as recorded by the second century A.D. geographer Ptolemy to counterparts in Central America:

MESOPOTAMIAN NAME	CENTRAL AMERICAN LOCALITIES
Chol	Chol-ula
Colua	Colua-can
Zuivana	Zuivan
Cholima	Colima
Zalissa	Xalisco

The raw mined ore was then carried from the far-flung mines by cargo craft back to Mesopotamia for smelting and processing into hourglass-shaped ingots called ZAG or "purified precious." Engravings of such ingots are numerous and some of the actual ingots have been found in archeological excavations.

In an effort to ease the increasing rivalry between the half brothers Enlil and Enki, their father Anu placed Enlil in charge of the Mesopotamian colony E.DIN—perhaps the basis for the biblical Eden—while assigning Enki to AB.ZU or Africa, the "land of the mines."

Further problems for these extraterrestrial colonists arose due to climate changes, which caused hardships among the Anunnaki, and the unrelenting drudgery of the mining operations. One Sumerian text reported, "When the gods [Anunnaki], like men, bore the work and suffered the toil—the toil of the gods was great, the work was heavy, the distress was much."

Obviously, such revisionism of ancient history has—and will continue to—have profound impact on conventional science. Dr. Arthur David Horn resigned as a professor of biological anthropology at Colorado State University in 1990 after he concluded that the conventional explanations for man's origins he taught were "nonsense." After much study, he too came to believe that extraterrestrials were intricately involved in the origin and development of humans.

"The Anunnaki had been mining gold on Earth for more than 100,000 years when the rank-and-file Anunnaki, who were doing the back-breaking work in the mines, mutinied about 300,000 years ago," Horn explained, elaborating on Sitchin's work. "Enlil, their commander-in-chief, wanted to punish them severely and he called an Assembly of the Great Anunnaki, which included his father Anu. Anu was more sympathetic to the plight of the Anunnaki miners. He saw that the work of the mutineers was very hard and that their distress was considerable. He wondered out loud . . . if there wasn't another way to obtain gold. At this point, Enki suggested that a Primitive Worker, an *Adamu*, be created that could take over the difficult work. Enki pointed out that a primitive humanoid—what we call *Homo erectus* or a closely related humanoid—was quite prevalent in *Abzu* [Africa] where he worked."

Enki's plan to create a worker race was approved by the Assembly, and was the starting point for humankind's origin, based on the Sumerian accounts. This explanation also clarifies one of the most puzzling verses in the Bible. After being assured in the Bible that there is only one true God, Genesis 1:26 quoted the singular God as saying, "Let us make man in our image, after our likeness. . . ."

This verse may carry two explanations—first, that the plural *Elohim* of the Old Testament, interpreted as "God" by the monotheists who wrote Genesis, indeed may have referred to the Anunnaki Assembly which approved the creation of man and, second, the idea of creating man "in our image" meant simply genetic manipulation of an existing species, not the creation of a new race. As Sitchin explained, "As both Orientalists and Bible scholars now know . . . the editing and summarizing by the compilers of the Book of Genesis [was] of much earlier and considerably more detailed texts first written down in Sumer."

The Anunnaki Earth mission's medical officer was a female named Ninharsag, also known as Ninti, who had already been working with Enki in genetic experimentation. On at least one Sumerian cylinder seal an illustration of Enki and Ninharsag depicted them surrounded by vials or vessels, a table, shelves, a plant, and a helper, the scene looking very much like a laboratory. According to the Sumerian accounts, they produced many mutated creatures including animals such as bulls and lions with human heads, winged animals, and apes and humanoids with the head and feet of goats. If true, it is obvious such experiments may have been the source for the many legends of "mythological" creatures and superhumans, such as Atlas, Goliath, Gargantua, Polyphemus, and Typhon.

In the nineteenth century, huge sphinxlike statues were excavated in what once was the palace of the Assyrian King Sargon II, who ruled Mesopotamia from 721 to 705 B.C. These statues included a winged bull and a lion with human heads. Much of this art was purchased by John D. Rockefeller and transported to New York.

The Sumerian account of the creation of the first man—written as LU.LU in the Sumerian or in Hebrew, *Adama*, literally translated as Man of Earth or simply Earthling—is quite clear in light of today's knowledge concerning cloning. But up to within twenty-five years ago or so, the whole concept would have been incomprehensible to even the most learned scholar. Enki and Ninharsag took the reproductive cell or egg from a primitive African female hominoid and fertilized it with the sperm of a young Anunnaki male. The fertilized ovum was then placed inside an Anunnaki woman—reportedly Enki's own wife Ninki—who carried the child to term.

Although a cesarean section was required at birth, a healthy young male *Adama* hybrid was produced for the first time on Earth, bypassing natural evolution by millions of years. According to the ancient Sumerian reporters, "When Mankind was first created, they knew not the eating of bread, knew not the dressing with garments, ate plants with their mouth like sheep, drank water from the ditch. . . ."

Afterward, Enki and Ninharsag went on to produce a number of *Adamas,* both male and female, although at this time they were incapable of reproduction and lived very short lives compared to the Anunnaki. This was apparently done in a conscious effort to prevent any competition from the new human race. It is interesting to note that, according to the Genesis 3:5, the very first order of the *Elohim* was that man—in the allegorical form of Adam and Eve—was to remain ignorant less "ye shall be as gods" (King James).

Several connections between the Sumerian version of man's creation and the Bible are apparent. The Bible speaks of woman being created from Adam's rib. "The great Sumerologist, Samuel N. Kramer, pointed out near the middle of this century that the tale of Eve's origin from Adam's rib probably stemmed from the double meaning of the Sumerian word TI, which means both 'rib' and 'life,'" explained Horn. So, Eve may have received her "life" from Adam without any bone being involved, or genetic material may have been extracted from bone marrow.

The laboratory which produced the first *Adamas* was called SHI.IM.TI or "the house where the wind of life is breathed in" by the Sumerians. Compare this phrase with Genesis 2:7 in which God, after forming man from "the dust of the ground" or *Adamu* meaning earth, "breathed into his nostrils the breath of life."

"Adam was the first test-tube baby," proclaimed Sitchin after the birth of the first modern test-tube baby in 1978. He saw this modern birth as support for his Sumerian translations, especially in light of the fact that modern science only began to conceptualize manipulating our genetic makeup within the twentieth century.

That the ancient Sumerians passed along symbols representing the long-forgotten science of cloning is suggested by the caduceus, the logo of physicians even today. This ancient symbol of life-giving medical treatment represented by entwined snakes along a winged staff bears a striking resemblance to the double spiral strings of DNA molecules. DNA (deoxyribonucleic acid), only discovered in 1946, is composed of the amino acids within the human cell that store that individual's genetic blueprint. It is the manipulation of DNA which can produce a clone (duplicate) or a hybrid.

Evidence that the first primitive humans originated in Africa has grown since the 1970s when some of the oldest prehuman remains were found there. The bones of "Lucy" and other australopithecines clearly indicated that early primates lived in that area of Earth more than three million years ago but were not as evolved as even the Neanderthal. Contrary to popular belief, scholars C. P. Groves, Charles E. Oxnard, and Louis Leakey have agreed that *Australopithecus* was totally different in morphology from humans. Groves commented that "non-Darwinian" principles would be required to explain any connection between "Lucy" and modern humans.

But woe to those who attempt to argue against conventional thinking. According to many independent researchers, there appears to be a conspiracy against any discovery which conflicts with prevailing wisdom. One example was the fate of Thomas E. Lee of the National Museum of Canada, who in the early 1950s discovered advanced stone tools in ice on Manitoulin Island in Lake Huron. These tools were shown to be at least 65,000 years old and perhaps as old as 125,000 years, totally contradicting conventional theories. Lee claimed he was "hounded" from his position, his work was misrepresented, and no one would publish his findings. Most of the artifacts "vanished" into storage bins, and the museum director was fired for refusing to discharge Lee.

"The treatment of Lee was not an isolated case," noted the authors of *Forbidden Archeology*. "There exists in the scientific community a knowledge filter that screens out unwelcome evidence. This process of knowledge filtration has been going on for well over a century and continues right up to the present day." One particularly exasperated researcher recently wrote, "Realize, that scientific institutions, such as the Smithsonian and the National Geographic Society, are set up by the world's elite factions in the first place to either debunk, distort or simply ignore any scientific data that tends to enlighten people about their true origins."

As bluntly stated in the Bible, Adam and his progeny were not destined for a life of ease, but one of hard work and survival at the hands of their "Lords." "The term that is commonly translated as 'worship' was in fact *avod*—'work,'" stated Sitchin. "Ancient and biblical man did not 'worship' his god; he worked for him."

Horn stated that study of the Sumerian texts made it clear that "the Anunnaki treated their created slaves poorly, much like we treat domestic animals we are simply exploiting—like cattle. Slavery in human societies was common from the first known civilizations until quite recently. Perhaps it shouldn't surprise us to learn that the Anunnaki were vain, petty, cruel, incestuous, hateful—almost any negative adjective one can think of. The evidence indicates that they worked their slaves very hard and had little compassion for the plight of humans. Yet, the Anunnaki eventually decided to grant humankind their first civilization, the Sumerian civilization."

But such civilization did not come before further tweaking of the human genetic code and finally an attempt to exterminate all human life.

Since the first human workers were like mules and could not procreate, the Anunnaki had to constantly create new batches, a time-consuming procedure considering the span of time between in vitro fertilization and birth. So Enki and Ninharsag set about to create an *Adama* race which could reproduce itself.

Genesis 2:8–15 makes it clear that the *Adama* was created elsewhere and then placed in the Garden of Eden or that area of the original Anunnaki colony called E.DIN, accurately described as the plain between the Tigris and Euphrates Rivers. The Sumerian texts related how an envious Enlil forcibly took humans from Enki's African lab and returned with them to E.DIN where they were put to work producing food and serving the Anunnaki. But Enlil needed even more workers and turned to his brother Enki for help.

Alford theorized that in retaliation for Enlil's raid on his African lab, Enki traveled to Eden, where he created a human reproduction lab for Enlil but secretly manipulated the genetic code to allow sexual reproduction.

Although the Sumerian texts describing the details of this process have been either lost or undiscovered as yet, researchers have assumed that the procedure again involved obtaining life-producing *Adama* DNA, possibly by extracting a rib while the subject was under anesthetics. This time the male *Adama*'s DNA was combined with a female *Adama* rather than an Anunnaki, with possibly some accompanying DNA sequence cutting and splicing, a procedure within our technology today.

The result was a male *Adama* with the ability to reproduce through sex with an *Adama* female, or to "know" a woman as the Bible euphemistically puts it. The man Adam had gained the "knowledge" of reproduction, a feat that many *Elohim*/Anunnaki, including Enlil, deplored. They complained that next the humans would want to live as long as themselves. "The man has now become like one of us, knowing good and evil," reported Genesis 3:22 (New International), "He must not be allowed to reach out his hand and take also from the tree of life and eat, and live forever." Therefore, DNA manipulation drastically reduced the human life span along with the ability to make full use of human brain capacity.

As the human population grew, both in the far-flung Anunnaki mining operations and in Mesopotamia, many *Adamas* were taken to work in the other cities that were growing up along the Tigris and Euphrates rivers. Some were returned to mining chores, and others may have escaped into the wilds or were sent away for population control. In any case, the *Adama* were sent out of Eden.

The result of this human population growth and their increasingly close contact with the Anunnaki was predictable. Genesis 6:1–4 related, "When men began to increase in number on the earth and daughters were born to them, the sons of God [the *Nefilim*/Anunnaki] saw that the daughters of men were beautiful, and they married any of them they chose. . . . The *Nefilim* were on the earth in those days—and also afterward—when the sons of God went to the daughters of men and had children by them. . . ."

Over the centuries, the *Adama* race, in addition to such interbreeding, was the object of continued experimentation which eventually resulted in changing Neanderthal to Cro-Magnon.

But some specific deficiencies remained, including a progressive decline in the human life span. Descendants of the early *Adamas* lived for thousands of Earth years thanks to their Anunnaki genes. This time frame slowly declined as interbreeding continued and the effects of life on Earth took their toll. But the extreme life spans of the pure Anunnaki rulers made them appear as immortal. The Epic of Gilgamesh stated, "Only the gods live forever under the sun, as for mankind, numbered are their days, whatever they achieve is but wind."

Authors Gardner and Alford and others believed that the longevity of the Anunnaki was further increased by chemicals and/or enzymes which retarded the aging process. Gardner stated the oft-mentioned "Star Fire" of the ancient gods may have been an antiaging compound of the enzymes melatonin and serotonin found in menstrual blood.

Longevity is well reported in the Bible, which describes life spans ranging into the hundreds of years for pre-Noah humans like Adam, Seth, Enosh, Kenan, Enoch, and Methuselah. Pointing out that every early civilization sought the "Fountain of Youth" or some form of immortality, Alford saw the obvious concern over age by the ancient scribes, but argued that their dating system was deficient.

Since both the fossil record and the Sumerian texts place the advent of humans at more than 450,000 years ago, some adjustment must be made with the biblical numbers, Alford reasoned. He found that by multiplying the biblical ages by 100, he arrived at 165,000 years between the birth of Adam's son Seth and Noah at the time of the Flood. This number is more consistent with the Sumerian accounts.

"The Jewish people spent an extremely long exile in Egypt for 400 years prior to the Exodus. Later they spent around 60 years exiled in Babylon," explained Alford. "The Jews were thus a long way from the Sumerian origin of their patriarch Abraham, and had lost the knowledge of the sexagesimal system in which their ancestry through to Abraham was recorded."

According to Sitchin's time line, the first human—the *Adama*—was produced about three hundred thousand years ago. After further genetic manipulation, Anunnaki males began interbreeding with human women about one hundred thousand years ago. Not long after this, a new ice age began decimating the human population outside Anunnaki control. Neanderthal disappeared while Cro-Magnon survived only in the Middle East. By fifty thousand years ago, humans fathered by Anunnaki were permitted to rule in selected cities, further angering Enlil, already incensed that some Anunnaki would mate with human women. He even complained that the sound of mating humans kept him awake at night. Enlil became determined to do something about the irritating humans.

FLOODS AND WARS

Accordingly, about twelve thousand years ago, when the Anunnaki leadership realized that severe climatic changes would occur with the imminent return of the planet Nibiru, Enlil made his move. In their Great Assembly, Enlil convinced the majority to allow nature to take its course—to wipe out the humans while the Anunnaki waited events out in evacuation ships orbiting the Earth.

Although Enlil's plan was accepted, brother Enki had a plan of his own. Whether out of some affection for humans or simply to thwart Enlil's plan, he passed along the murderous "secret of the gods" to one of his most prized human assistants, identified as the Sumerian Ziusudra or Utnapishtim.

"The Akkadian version of the Flood refers to Noah as Utnapishtim, the son of Ubar-Tutu, and locates both of them in Shuruppak [the seventh city built by the Anunnaki]," Alford reported. "Shuruppak has been firmly identified as the medical center of the gods. It was also referred to as the city of Sud, who has been identified as Ninharsag—the same goddess who had assisted Enki with the genetic creation of the LU.LU." The same Flood story was repeated in a Babylonian legend featuring Atra-Hasis as Noah.

Utnapishtim has been called the "Sumerian Noah" and the parallels between the biblical account of Noah and the Gilgamesh account of the Great Flood are both striking and obvious. Referring to the story of Noah, Sitchin stated, "The biblical account is an edited version of the original Sumerian account. As in the other instances, the monotheistic Bible has compressed into one Deity the roles played by several gods who were not always in accord."

According to the Sumerian texts, it was Enlil's rival brother Enki who instructed Utnapishtim/Noah how to construct an ark, including the use of readily available bitumen to make it waterproof. The Gilgamesh version gave some interesting details deleted from the biblical account. Enki provided Utnapishtim with an excuse to explain to his neighbors why he was building a boat—he told them that as a follower of Enki he was forced to leave the Enlil-controlled area and needed the boat to journey to Enki's territory in Africa.

Enki instructed Utnapishtim/Noah, "Aboard ship take thou the seed of all living things. . . ." This instruction is most fascinating because, since Enki had been the science officer involved in the genetic engineering of humans, it would seem plausible that Utnapishtim/Noah took DNA samples of all living things rather than a boatload of animals, insects, and plants. A ship's cabin full of sample vials would be much more reasonable than a floating zoological park.

Alford advanced the theory that Enki, genetically working through Utnapishtim/Noah and three ethnically different surrogate wives, produced three sons who represented the three races of the world. Thus, after the Flood, the races of humankind were represented. Other writers theorized that the different races of humankind represent genetic experiments by extraterrestrial races other than the Anunnaki.

The Akkadian account also made it clear the Great Flood was not the result of heavy rains. It described a darkness accompanied by colossal winds which increased in intensity, destroying buildings and rupturing dikes. Such conditions would be expected by the near passage of a large planetary body. Scattered archeological excavations over many years indicate that what is regarded as the Great Flood was a planetwide catastrophe, though not every portion of the world was under water. One theory of the Flood was that the gravitational forces caused by the passing of Nibiru caused the Antarctic ice sheet, already unstable due to the end of the last ice age, to slip into the ocean, raising sea levels all over the planet. Even today, most of the original Anunnaki cities in Mesopotamia remain deep under water and silt near the mouths of the Tigris and Euphrates rivers.

After six days and nights, according to the Akkadian version, the elements went calm but no land was seen. Finally, as in the biblical account, the ark came to rest on a mountaintop, identified as Mount Ararat. After sending a dove, a swallow, and a raven from the ark, only the raven stayed gone, indicating that more dry land was nearby. Utnapishtim/Noah and his family then left the ark and offered a burnt sacrifice, which drew the attention of the returning Anunnaki. An ancient text stated the "gods crowded like flies" around the cooking flesh. Apparently, they had developed a hunger for fresh food during their long confinement in the orbiting ships.

Confronted by the fact of human survival, and perhaps accompanied by some remorse over his actions, Enlil had little choice but to relent and permit further cohabitation by the humans.

This scenario could certainly explain the sudden absence of a sizable portion of the human population about ten thousand years ago—most were lost in the Great Flood.

With flood waters subsiding and Nibiru moving out of the solar system, the Anunnaki and the handful of surviving humans set about reconstructing the world. But this post-Flood world was to prove less peaceful than the previous one.

Prior to the Flood, any humans not working directly for the Anunnaki were roaming hunter-gatherers. Virtually overnight they suddenly became farmers. "Farming may be more work than hunting, judging by the available ethnographic data, and [results] in an unstable man-modified ecosystem with low diversity index results," noted archeologist Kent Flannery. "Since early farming represents a decision to work harder and eat more 'third-choice' food, I suspect that people did it because they felt they had to, not because they wanted to farm. Why they felt they had to, we may never know, in spite of the fact that their decision reshaped all the rest of human history."

The Sumerian tablets explained why humans began to cultivate the land and domesticate animals—because their gods ordered them to do so. And with farming came the concentration of people in cities, larger and grander than before the Flood. Each was ruled by one of the Anunnaki rulers, now beginning to be considered "gods" by the humans. As further evidence of the Flood, the earliest efforts at agriculture were found not in the rich soil of the river valleys but in the mountain highlands of Mesopotamia and Palestine.

Again, this is explained in a Sumerian text fragment, which stated, "Enlil went up to the peak and lifted his eyes; He looked down; there the waters filled as a sea. He looked up: there was the mountain of the aromatic cedars. He hauled up the barley, terraced it on the mountain. That which vegetates he hauled up, terraced the grain cereals on the mountain."

Like humans, certain food crops appeared to have no antecedent in the Earth's evolutionary chain. They just suddenly appeared—fully cultured—about thirteen thousand years ago according to archeological finds. "There is no explanation for this botanogenetic miracle, unless the process was not one of natural selection but of artificial manipulation," commented Sitchin, noting that three critical phases of human development—farming (circa 11,000 B.C.), prehistoric culture (circa 7500 B.C.), and civilization (circa 3800 B.C.)—occurred at intervals of 3,600 years, the same period of time for a complete orbit by Nibiru.

In addition to "kingship" over crops and animals, the Anunnaki began to bestow leadership on selected humans. As humans grew ever more populous, the Anunnaki/Nefilim realized they had to take steps to maintain control over their creation. They also desired intermediaries between themselves and the humans, whom they still considered little better than animals.

During a post-Flood assembly of the Anunnaki/Nefilim, it was decided to divide the Earth into four regions, with the human population split up within three of these areas—lower Mesopotamia, the Nile Valley, and the Indus Valley. The Anunnaki reserved the Sinai Peninsula—their new spaceflight center following the Flood—as their private, or "holy," sanctuary.

Obviously, this divide-and-rule strategy for the scattered human communities required separate leaders. Thus was born the concept of "kingship"—human rulers especially chosen by the Anunnaki or "gods" to represent them. The practice of dynastic kingship based on a royal lineage traceable to the gods is one that has impacted countries and governments up to the present day.

This practice began in the Sumerian city of Kish, which Sitchin equates with the biblical Cush. Garner agreed, locating the biblical Cush east of Babylon, not in Egypt. Genesis 10:8–12 relates that Cush was a grandson of Noah and father of the legendary Nimrod, who ruled and built such cities as Babylon, Erech, and Akkad from his base in Sumer, before constructing cities in Assyria, including Nineveh.

It may have been Nimrod's attempt to thwart Enlil's dispersion plan that led to the Old Testament story of the Tower of Babel. This narrative began at Baalbek, believed a post-Flood center for Anunnaki space shuttle operations located in what is now Lebanon. Massive granite blocks there, called "the Trilithon" and weighing more than three hundred tons each, buttress the idea that this may have once been a landing or launch pad. "The textual evidence, the geographical evidence and the physical evidence all support each other to confirm that Baalbek was designed as a landing platform of the rockets of the gods," offered Alford.

An Arabic text found at Baalbek stated it was there that Nimrod and his followers tried to construct a *shem*, translated in Genesis 11:4 as, ". . . let us make a *name* for ourselves." "*Shem*, inadvertently misunderstood, was rendered by most translators as a sign for the word 'name.' However, it originally signified 'that which goes up,'" explained author Turnage. "Sitchin designates the origin of *shem* as Mesopotamian, originating from the word *mu* or the Semitic derivative *shu-mu*, or *sham* . . . 'that by which one is remembered,' evolving into 'name.' The original meaning of the words however, was originally connected with the concept of something that flies."

"The realization that *mu* or *shem* in many Mesopotamian texts should be read not as 'name' but as 'sky vehicle' opens the way to the understanding of the true meaning of many ancient tales, including the biblical story of the Tower of Babel," wrote Sitchin.

His explanation for the trouble at Babel was that the humans there attempted to construct their own launch tower, apparently hoping to produce their own *shem* or flying vehicle with a view toward arguing against the breakup of humanity with the off-world ruler An. "Come, let us build ourselves a city with a tower that reaches to the heavens," they were quoted in Genesis 11:4 (New International), "so that we may make a [*shem*] for ourselves and not be scattered over the face of the whole earth."

This activity only added to Enlil's fear of human competition and made him even more determined to break up the humans. His reaction may have been reflected in Genesis 11:5–8 (Revised Standard), "And the Lord came down to see the city and the tower, which the sons of men had built. And the Lord said, 'Behold, they are one people and they have all one language; and this is only the beginning of what they will do; and nothing that they propose to do will now be impossible for them. Come, let us go down, and confuse their language, that they may not understand one another's speech.' So the Lord scattered them abroad from there over the face of all the earth, and they left off building the city."

Soon the three branches of humankind—all descendants of Shem, Ham, and Japheth, the three sons of Utnapishtim/Noah—were transported to the preordained locations, where different languages indeed developed over time.

Alford theorized that Utnapishtim/Noah may have had wives representing separate racial groups. The offspring of these wives would have been of different races, offering an explanation for the presence of the Negroid race in Africa, Mongoloid in Asia, and Caucasoid in the Near East.

Both the Sumerian texts and the Bible agree that Shem and his descendants remained in the area encompassing Mesopotamia, Ham and his kin were taken to Africa—to include parts of Arabia—while Japheth's people were transported to the Indus Valley, possibly becoming the mysterious "Aryans" who suddenly appeared there in prehistoric times.

A congenial peace should have come with this dispersion, accompanied by the growth of new cities with their newly installed kings and increased food production. But, unfortunately, it appeared that the ancient "gods" were no more able to produce lasting peace than were humans.

Trouble began even as the Anunnaki began to relocate their spaceflight facilities from Sumer—now mostly underwater—to the Sinai peninsula at a place which came to be called El Paran (God's Glorious Place). As before the Flood, Mount Ararat—in what is now eastern Turkey and reportedly where the ark finally grounded—provided the northernmost landmark for a glide path to the Sinai landing facility. This base was located on the Thirtieth Parallel in the geographic center of Sinai, while the southern landmark was the two highest peaks of Mount Sinai, known respectively as Mount Catherine (8,652 feet above sea level) and the lower Mount Moses (7,500 feet). What was lacking for this glide path was a matching landmark to the west.

"There the terrain is too flat to offer natural landmarks," explained Sitchin, "and it was thus, we are certain, that the Anunnaki proceeded to build the artificial twin peaks of the two great pyramids of Giza."

"The Great Pyramid of Cheops was also a space beacon," agreed NASA scientist Maurice Chatelain, who developed the Apollo space missions communication and data-processing systems. "From high above, the pyramid is visible at a very great distance to the naked eye, and in space it shows on the radar screen much farther out because of its slanted sides that reflect radar beams perpendicularly if the approach angle is 38 degrees above the horizon. It is easy to calculate that the polished stone surface . . . is a radar reflector. . . . Such a powerful reflector could have served as a beacon for the approach of a space ship and possibly has been serving for this purpose for a long time. We know that the pyramid had been painted in various colors, which could have been metalized to increase the reflectivity to laser or radar beams."

The editors of the *Holman Bible Dictionary* reported that "Sinai" probably came from the word meaning "shining" and was likely derived from the Babylonian god Sin. Sin was simply the Semitic name for Nannar, the firstborn son of the Anunnaki leader Enlil and sovereign of Ur, the home city of Abraham. Some researchers theorize that perhaps at some distant time the peaks of Mount Sinai also may have supported giant reflectors to aid the triangulation of landing pilots.

Sin also was the Chaldean name for the moon, where the Sumerians claimed Enki first obtained living organisms or "seed" for his human hybrid experiments from that left over from the clash between Nibiru and the planet Tiamat. "The enormity of this single name change on human history is beyond comprehension," declared Henry. "When the Christian interpreters came along, they repeated the story that we were born in sin. They were entirely accurate in their statement. However, they omitted the fact that Sin referred to the Moon, the source of our genetic material!"

Due to the destruction of the Anunnaki Mission Control Center at the Sumerian city of Nippur during the Flood and the need for a location equidistant from the glide path lines, a new control center was built at

Mount Moriah, translated as "Mount of Directing." It was the site of the future holy city of Jerusalem, long considered a most sacred place by all major Western religions.

By the time their space-related work was completed, new generations of the Anunnaki had been born on Earth. Appearing like a script from some ancient soap opera—one that would be replayed down through recorded history—there are accounts of intrigues, conspiracies, and outright wars pitting brother against brother and sister against sister. These conflicts, rebellions, and wars would eventually involve humankind, providing their first exposure to armed combat, which continues even today.

According to the Sumerian texts, Enki's firstborn son, Marduk, gained sovereignty over the lands of Egypt and became known as Ra. It was his children, Shu and Tefnut, who set an example for future pharaohs by wedding each other. Their offspring, Geb and Nut, also married and were the next royal couple as well as the parents of some of Egypt's most famous god/rulers—Osiris, his sister/wife Isis, Seth, and Nephtys, sister of Isis. All this interfamily marriage led to a succession problem solved by dividing the country. Osiris was given Lower Egypt and Seth the mountainous Upper Egypt. Unsatisfied with his apportionment, Seth began to maneuver against Osiris and thus began the legendary wars of ancient Egypt.

Following the death of Osiris, his son Horus sought revenge on Seth, who moved eastward, capturing the Sinai spaceport. Enraged that the descendants of Enki had control of the space facilities, the followers of Enlil attacked Seth's forces. This family rivalry had been passed down since the earliest times.

Led by Ninurta, a son of Enlil, the Sinai facility was retaken. Rulership fell to the new kings of Babylon, Assyria, and Caanan, who themselves were engaged in near ceaseless wars. Many of these conflicts were faithfully recorded in the Old Testament, complete with obscure names and unpronounceable places which have proved difficult for historians to fully understand due to the ever-changing names from one language to another.

Armed conflict, which had begun with rivalries and intrigues between the Anunnaki overlords, now was being carried on by their human followers and had turned into a conscious control mechanism along with the religious veneration of the Anunnaki, already proven to be successful in keeping the unsophisticated humans in line.

But, as is usually the case in so many wars, things got out of hand for the Anunnaki.

In a story reminiscent of Romeo and Juliet, a granddaughter of Enlil named Inanna married the youngest son of Enki, Dumuzi, with the wary blessing of both feuding families. But when Dumuzi was killed after being taken into custody by Marduk/Ra for violating the Anunnaki moral code, Inanna attacked Marduk/Ra.

To stop this conflict, Marduk/Ra was tried for Dumuzi's death. As it could not be proven whether the death had been deliberate or accidental, it was decided to sentence Marduk/Ra to life imprisonment in a huge, impenetrable place whose walls reached the skies. Sitchin identified Marduk's prison as none other than the Great Pyramid.

He wrote that his translations of the Sumerian texts explained that the curious well shaft within the Great Pyramid—a puzzling hand-hewed tunnel connecting the pyramid's descending passage to its ascending passage—was dug to bypass the large granite stone which plugs the ascending passage in order to rescue Marduk/Ra after he was granted a reprieve but ordered into exile. This capture, imprisonment, and supposed death of an Egyptian god is well recounted in ancient Egyptian hieroglyphics.

Inanna, far from satisfied with this turn of events and desirous of power for herself, could only be sidetracked by being given control over another area, possibly the population in the Indus Valley. Mounded ruins representing Mohenjo-Daro, the largest city of a civilization dated back to before 2500 B.C., were first recognized on the Indus River in southern Pakistan in 1922. Although thoroughly—and strangely—devastated in some prehistoric time, the baked-brick construction of buildings and the preplanned layout of the city indicated to some researchers an obvious connection with Sumer. Alford said the city was inhabited by a people called the Harappans, who "worshipped a sole female deity, whose depiction bore an amazing similarity to other images of the goddess Inanna."

Whether this Indus goddess was Inanna or not, she continued her quest for power, according to the Sumerian texts, eventually replacing Ninharsag among the major Anunnaki leaders. She also found a human hybrid that she used to carve out a new empire. This man was Sharru-Kin, better known as Sargon the Great. Believed to be the offspring of a human mother and an Anunnaki father, Sargon founded the Semite Akkadian dynasty about 2200 B.C., which finally encompassed all of Mesopotamia. Recall that Sargon claimed that he, like the later Moses, was placed in a sealed basket of reeds by his mother and floated down a river to safety.

"Sargon's records of his conquests describe Inanna as actively present on the battlefields but attribute to Enlil the overall decision regarding the scope of the victories and the extent of the territories," noted Sitchin.

With the fall of Sargon and the Akkadian empire, Marduk/Ra slipped from exile and attempted to regain his sovereignty over Babylon. This led to changing alliances as the forces of Enlil and Inanna lined up against those of Marduk and his father Enki. Even a son of Marduk named Nergal or Erra, joined the forces of Enlil arrayed against him, making the conflict a true civil war.

Fearing Marduk's ambitions, the Anunnaki persuaded Anu to allow the use of seven mighty weapons, now believed by many to have been tactical nuclear missiles, against Marduk/Ra. This all occurred some time before the year 2000 B.C.

It is at this point that the biblical patriarch Abraham joined the narrative. According to Sitchin, Abraham was far from just a wandering Hebrew as often popularly believed. He said that careful study of a variety of texts clearly indicated that Abraham of Ur was a ranking Sumerian. "Coming to Egypt, Abraham and Sarah were taken to the Pharaoh's court; in Canaan, Abraham made treaties with the local rulers," he noted. "This is not the image of a nomad pillaging others' settlements; it is the image of a personage of high standing skilled in negotiation and diplomacy."

Abraham also commanded armed troops, as evidenced by Genesis 14:14–16, which recorded how he took 318 "trained men" to rescue his nephew Lot and family from an invading coalition of armies following the orders of Marduk.

Moving with the apparent intention of retaking the Sinai spaceport, these armies from the north had been turned back before reaching the Sinai and had stopped to sack the cities of Sodom and Gomorrah in the Siddim Valley on the southern edge of the Dead Sea after defeating the kings of the cities. It was here they had taken Lot prisoner before moving back north and here that Lot was returned after his rescue by Abraham.

And it was also here that the world may well have felt the first blast of a nuclear explosion.

Sitchin posited that it was in fact Abraham and his warriors who stopped Marduk's marauders from reaching the Sinai space facilities at

El Paran. This feat brought praise and blessing from Melchizedek as well as a covenant with Yahweh, identified as Enlil. Alford argued that Abraham's god Yahweh, originally *El Shaddai* or God of the Mountains, may have been a son of Enlil named Ishku, also known as Adad. According to Alford, it was this Anunnaki who later kept in communication with his chosen people through a radio transmitter-receiver named in the Bible as the Ark of the Covenant.

Boulay also saw the ark as a radio device and thought it significant that the ark had to be completed according to very precise instructions before the tablets containing the Ten Commandments were placed inside. "The tablets presumably contained the power source necessary to activate the receiver-transmitter," he wrote.

A verse in the Old Testament (Numbers 7:89) may even have described the location of the device's speaker: "When Moses entered the Tent of Meeting to speak with the Lord, he heard the voice speaking to him from between the two cherubim above the atonement cover on the ark of the Testimony. And he spoke with him." (New International)

Since their Enlilite "gods" had failed to protect them from the invading coalition army, the kings of Sodom and Gomorrah may have switched their allegiances to Marduk. Whatever the reasons, Enlil and his sons, Ninurta and Adad, years later prepared to launch the nuclear missiles as an act of revenge.

But in honor of Abraham's past service, they decided to give him warning. As also described in Genesis 18, Yahweh came to Abraham and warned him that the cities would be destroyed because they had turned away from him. Evidence that the destruction of Sodom and Gomorrah was a planned event can be found in this warning coupled with Abraham's bargaining with Yahweh, reducing the number of righteous persons for which the cities might be spared down from fifty to ten.

This foreknowledge is also evidenced by the warning of Lot in Sodom by two "angels," although the original Hebrew word *Mal'akhim* actually only meant "emissaries." Following some trouble with the neighbors over the visitors, as quoted in Genesis 19:12–13, the pair told Lot, "Have you anyone else here? Sons-in-laws, sons, daughters, or any one you have in the city, bring them out of the place; for we are about to destroy this place, because the outcry against its people has become great before the Lord, and the Lord has sent us to destroy it." (Revised Standard)

Lot and his kindred fled to the mountains as instructed, but the fiery cataclysm reached out to his own family. According to Genesis 19:26, Lot's wife, who had lagged behind, was turned to "a pillar of salt." Sitchin noted that the original Sumerian word interpreted by Hebrew scribes as "salt" also meant "vapor." Lot's wife then was vaporized by the explosion which consumed Sodom and Gomorrah. Lot and the rest of his family may have been shielded by the crest of a hill or the like. The Sumerian text *Erra Epos* quoted one of those behind the destruction as vowing, "The people I will make vanish, their souls shall turn to vapor." In the atomic bombings of Hiroshima and Nagasaki, it was common for some victims shielded from the initial blast to survive while unprotected people standing next to them were vaporized.

In the meantime, Abraham, standing miles away in the mountains, looked down and saw a column of dense smoke rising as if from a furnace.

Another result of the attack may have been a breach in the south end of the Dead Sea, which not only covered the bombed cities with salt-water but created the shallow southern section of the sea below the Lisan peninsula.

Ironically, it may have been Marduk's own son who triggered the nuclear attack as one Babylonian text stated, "But when the son of Marduk in the land of the coast was, He-of-the-Evil-Wind [Nergal] with heat the plain-land burnt."

Evidence for the nuclear aspect of this destruction came from archeological reports that surrounding settlements were suddenly abandoned for several centuries about 2040 B.C. and that spring water near the Dead Sea has been found to still contain harmful amounts of radioactivity.

Concurrent with the devastation of Sodom and Gomorrah, the Sinai spaceport also was targeted for nuclear destruction, apparently to prevent it from falling into Marduk's hands. Other targets, unrecorded and as yet undiscovered, may also have experienced nuclear detonations.

According to Sitchin, Alford, and others, the Sinai detonation produced an unnatural scarring of the peninsula, which can still be seen from space, as well as a multitude of scorched rocks in the area.

"In the eastern Sinai, millions of blackened stones are found strewn for tens of miles. These stones are, without any doubt, unnatural," reported Alford. "Photographs clearly demonstrate that the rocks are blackened only on the surface."

The nuclear blasts also created an unexpected and tragic aftermath. A radioactive cyclone was created, which moved northeastward through Mesopotamia, obliterating all life and ending the Sumerian civilization.

Conventional history states that mighty Sumer, which suddenly appeared about six thousand years ago, simply vanished just as suddenly, absorbed by the new empires of Babylon and Assyria. The Sumerian texts tell a much more horrible story.

According to various "lamentations" translated by the Sumerian scholar Kramer, they reported, "On the land [Sumer] fell a calamity, one unknown to man; one that had never been seen before, one which could not be withstood. A great storm from heaven . . . A land-annihilating storm . . . An evil wind, like a rushing torrent . . . A battling storm joined by scorching heat . . . By day it deprived the land of the bright sun, in the evening the stars did not shine. . . . The people, terrified, could hardly breathe; the evil wind clutched them, does not grant them another day. . . . Mouths were drenched with blood, heads wallowed in blood. . . . The face was made pale by the Evil Wind. It caused cities to be desolated, houses to become desolate; stalls to become desolate, the sheepfolds to be emptied. . . . Sumer's rivers it made flow with water that is bitter; its cultivated fields grow weeds, its pastures grow withered plants. . . . Thus all its gods evacuated Uruk; they kept away from it; they hid in the mountains, they escaped to the distant plains." This one great storm of radioactive fallout annihilated the world's first great civilization, leaving the bodies of the population "stacked up in heaps."

It was at this time that the detailed narratives of Sumer and its gods ceased. It would be centuries before civilization and writing once more flourished in Mesopotamia as memory of the great cataclysm faded into vague stories of the nightmare.

"What actually transpired," explained Gardner, "was that the original Mesopotamian writings were recorded as history. This history was later rewritten to form a base for foreign religious cults—first Judaism and then Christianity. The corrupted dogma—the new approved history—was so different from the original writings, the early firsthand reports were labeled 'mythology.'"

It was the Anunnaki's nuclear Armageddon, with their millennia-old colony of Eden blown away. One theory was that the Anunnaki, shocked by what they had wrought, retreated to an enclave in the Sinai where most of them made the decision to return home, perhaps leaving behind only a caretaker force.

To humans, all this occurred in ancient times, more than four thousand years ago. To the Anunnaki, this would be just a little over a year of their time. Some researchers feel an Anunnaki rescue mission may still be on the way to Earth. Only time will tell.

Survivors of this early holocaust faced a period of regression and barbarism. The remaining humans made the best of things and began rebuilding their civilizations, a slow process without the aid of their "gods."

Abraham and his people moved away from the devastation to the south, where he fathered Isaac at the age of one hundred years, thanks to his hybrid genes. Isaac's son, Jacob, became known as Israel, a name soon applied to his entire people. Some believe that the name Israel is nothing less than a combination of the Egyptian gods OsirIS and RA and the Mesopotamian god EL.

After about thirty-five generations of Israelites had passed along oral accounts of the events above, it was finally written down in Hebrew. What happened next, as they say, is history.

COMMENTARY

It must be stressed that the preceding only begins to scratch the surface of the wealth of data now available—both archeological and in the cuneiform tablets—that supports this incredible narrative with its far-reaching implications. And none of the authors and researchers studying this subject feel they have all the facts.

Dr. Horn may have spoken for most when he wrote, "Let us make clear, once again, that we do not believe the ancient Sumerian and other Mesopotamian stories are 'absolutely true' history. These stories that have come to us through thousands of years of oral tradition and writing are bound to be somewhat distorted—probably in some cases deliberately distorted by the Anunnaki. But, I feel these ancient stories are probably as close as we'll come to the truth today. . . ."

Also understand that all of the above narrative is recounted, in one form or another, in the Sumerian texts uncovered only in the last 150 years, all of which predate the Bible by at least two thousand years.

Just consider what current events will sound like two thousand years from now—the greatest nation on Earth bombing some of the smallest and weakest for no clear reasons, people starving in parts of the world while farmers are paid not to plant crops in others, technophiles sitting at home playing electronic golf rather than the real thing, and police forces ordered to arrest people who simply desire to ingest a psychoactive weed. People of that future era will also likely laugh it all off as fantastic myths.

Yet searchers for truth cannot afford to laugh off the accounts of the Sumerian reporters who have been proven so accurate in much of their records. Just as the overwhelming evidence of conspiratorial control in government, business, and the media cannot be ignored.

It is amazing that we have as much information today as we do. Sitchen expressed admiration for the countless unsung persons who, wittingly or unwittingly, preserved the elder knowledge as well as they did. "Bearing in mind that these ancient texts come to us across a bridge of time extending back for millennia, one must admire the ancient scribes who recorded, copied, and translated the earliest texts—as often as not, probably, without really knowing what this or that expression or technical term originally meant but always adhering tenaciously to the traditions that required a most meticulous and precise rendition of the copied texts," he acknowledged.

He also pointed to the internal consistency of their accounts, stating, "The statement that the first to establish settlements on Earth were astronauts from another planet was not lightly made by the Sumerians. In text after text, whenever the starting point was recalled, it was always this: 432,000 years before the Deluge [the Great Flood], the DIN.GIR—"Righteous Ones of the Rocketships"—came down to Earth from their own planet."

Outlandish as these concepts may appear to some, many people today believe strongly that in the near future this version of history will become both popular and widespread, eventually studied and taught in seminaries, universities, and science centers. Already, breakthroughs in astronomy, anthropology, archeology, and Egyptology have only tended to support the theses of Sitchin and others.

None of this is meant to deny the existence of a universal creative force—God—the absolute All or Oneness of all energy and matter. The modern UFO contactees and abductees uniformly tell us that even the "aliens" they have experienced claim awareness of a Supreme Being.

The knowledge of this one God, who must have created the Anunnaki creators, plus the awareness that there is more to life than this material plane of existence, has been secretly nurtured within all of the secret societies. Beyond any question, there are metaphysical—spiritual—aspects of this whole issue, but that is not within the purview of this work.

The Sumerian explanation for creation and the origin of man is most compelling. It is not only internally consistent but well supported by evidence from all around the world. Likewise it provides feasible explanations for some of Earth's most puzzling anomalies and mysteries. It just makes more sense than many of the reaches of rationalization by past science.

So we have arrived at the Secret of Secrets, the hidden knowledge passed down through the ages by the Mystery Schools and secret societies—not only is humankind not alone in the universe but nonhuman intelligences most probably had a hand in our creation. See *Alien Agenda* (HarperCollins, 1997) for an overview of the UFO phenomenon and its connection to both modern governments and secret societies.

The idea of ancient advanced civilizations is really not a new one. In 1882, during a time of ignorance and total disbelief in things extraterrestrial, scholar Ignatus Donnelly in *Atlantis: The Antediluvian World* wrote that the gods and goddesses of ancient mythologies were actually the kings and queens of Atlantis, a pre-Flood high-tech civilization from which sprang all subsequent human societies.

Frederick Soddy, the British Nobel Prize–winning chemist who established isotopes as a geologic age determinate, in 1909 wrote, "I believe that there have been civilizations in the past that were familiar with atomic energy, and that by misusing it they were totally destroyed."

Swiss author Erich von Daniken, though harshly criticized by mainstream scientists and theologians, wrote immensely popular books on early extraterrestrial visitors, or Ancient Astronauts, beginning in 1970. Subsequent discoveries in archeology and anthropology have only reinforced von Daniken's theories. As recently as 1998 he wrote, "As the giant mother-spaceship of the extraterrestrials cruised into our solar system, the ETs aboard . . . discovered a wealth of all forms of life, amongst which were our primitive ancestors. . . . The aliens therefore took one of the creatures and altered it genetically—no longer, these days, such an unthinkable idea."

Some authors, such as Charles Fort, William Bramley, David Icke, and R. A. Boulay see humanity as little more than a herd of animals under the control of alien masters.

"Human beings appear to be a slave race languishing on an isolated planet in a small galaxy," resolved Bramley in 1989. "As such, the human race was once a source of labor for an extraterrestrial civilization and still remains a possession today. To keep control over its possession and to maintain Earth as something of a prison, that other civilization ("Custodians") has bred never-ending conflict between human beings, has promoted human spiritual decay, and has erected on Earth conditions of unremitting physical hardship. This situation has lasted for thousands of years and it continues today."

"In summary," wrote Icke in 1999, "a race of interbreeding ['royal' reptile-human hybrid] bloodlines . . . were centered in the Middle East and Near East in the ancient world and, over the thousands of years since, have expanded their power across the globe . . . creating institutions like religions to mentally and emotionally imprison the masses and set them at war with each other."

Author Boulay opined, "Man has been conditioned for millennia to deny the truth of his ancestry and as a palliative we have developed a convenient form of amnesia. We have accepted the interpretation of history propagated by a self-perpetuating priesthood and academia."

Journalist Charles Fort in 1941 concluded, "I think we are property. I should say we belong to something: that once upon a time, this Earth was No-Man's Land, that other worlds explored and colonized here, and fought amongst themselves for possession, but that now it's owned by something. . . ."

Alan F. Alford mused over how the elder gods might try to maintain control today. "Anyone could turn up claiming to be Jesus or Yahweh," he wrote. "On the contrary, there might be little advantage to the gods immediately announcing themselves to the masses. News of their return might be disseminated on a need-to-know basis, with only a few of the world leaders permitted to approach them. Life might appear to carry on as normal, but with a new political agenda. We might detect their presence in inexplicable events, changes in government policy or acts of war that don't quite make sense, and perhaps an increase in government secrecy."

Other authors, such as Masons Hall and Mackey along with the Christian Webster, also traced the secret knowledge back to Mesopotamia, but they saw the division between humans and nonhumans as a metaphysical struggle between light and darkness.

In the 1920s Webster asked, "How is it possible to ignore the existence of an Occult Power at work in the world? Individuals, sects or races fired with the desire of world domination, have provided the fighting forces of destruction, but behind them are the veritable powers of darkness in eternal conflict with the powers of light."

Mackey stated ancient knowledge was composed of "two great religious truths"—the unity of God and the immortality of the soul. He noted that elder Masonic "Constitutions" traced this hidden knowledge or "science, as it is always called, from [the pre-Flood father of Noah] Lamech to [the legendary Sumerian leader] Nimrod, who 'found' or invented the Craft of Masonry at the building of the Tower of Babel, and then to [Greek geometrist] Euclid, who established it in Egypt, whence it was brought by the Israelites into Judea, and there again established by David and Solomon, at the building of the Temple . . . it was brought into France. . . . From France it was carried to England. . . ."

Hall said this knowledge can be used to "step across the line which divides the true from the false, the spiritual from the material, the eternal from the temporal." He said the ancient knowledge was given to early man by "their progenitors, the Serpent Kings, who reigned over the Earth. It was these Serpent Kings who founded the Mystery Schools . . . and other forms of ancient occultism."

It is the immense and ancient power of the knowing elite—traceable through both blood and philosophy—that has sought to usurp and control virtually every major movement toward the development of full human potential, from long before early Christianity to the New Age. Since it has been clearly demonstrated that this knowledge—or view of the world—is still tightly held within the inner sanctums of the secret societies, there appear to be but three possibilities: the small inner elite continues to accumulate wealth and power in the hope of contacting our ancient creators (nonhuman intelligences); or they have already achieved such contact and are being guided or controlled; or they *are* the ancient creators, the Anunnaki, the Serpent Kings.

If the Sumerian version of our history is correct, then the Anunnaki may still be here, under a variety of guises based on advanced technology. After all, while the destruction of Sodom and Gomorrah would be more than four thousand years ago to us, it would only be just a little more than a year to the Anunnaki.

Whatever the truth may be, we must be wary of leaders who attempt—whether by force, manipulation, or deceit—to move whole populations in directions they may not wish to go and might not be beneficial to all.

We must acknowledge that while many "leaders" are not in government, they may control our lives far more than any petty bureaucrat because of the inordinate power they have over what we see and hear.

In the past, wars and religion were successfully used as control mechanisms. Today, with nuclear weapons making large-scale wars unthinkable and organized religion on the wane, economics—the power of money—has become the method of choice for control of the masses by the inner elite of the secret societies.

The bad news is that most of what has been presented in this book is true. The good news is that you are reading this, which means the centuries-old plot to control human destiny has not yet achieved total success, though the warning signs are everywhere. From the viewpoint of 1948, author George Orwell described a picture of the future as "a boot stamping on a human face—forever." Is this to be our future?

As we enter the third millennium, new thoughts, new ideas and new knowledge seem to be pushing us forward at an ever-increasing pace. We find our worldview and mindset constantly evolving into whole new patterns of understanding in what are obviously extraordinary times.

In just the first few months of 1999, a national television audience was presented a variety of programming devoted to government conspiracies, UFOs, alien contact, new rooms and tunnels discovered within the Great Pyramid, and the distinct possibility of a prehistorical highly advanced civilization on Earth, with the promise of more revelations to come.

Many of us look the other way, hoping we won't have to deal with the mind-expanding questions that new knowledge brings. We avoid those TV shows and books which are liable to upset our traditional mindset.

But it's no use. We hear about them in office conversations, radio talk shows, and even occasionally as brief pieces in the mainstream media. The discussion of topics which once were prohibited are now commonplace.

So what's to be done in this era of spiritual poverty in the midst of material wealth?

Knowledge is indeed power. It is time for those who desire true free-dom to exert themselves—to fight back against the forces who desire domination through fear and disunity.

This does not have to involve violence. It can be done in small, sim-ple ways, like not financing that new Sport Utility Vehicle, cutting up all but one credit card, not opting for a second mortgage, turning off that TV sitcom for a good book, asking questions and speaking out in church or synagogue, attending school board and city council meetings, voting for the candidate who has the least money, learning about the Fully Informed Jury movement and using it when called—in general, taking responsibility for one's own actions. Despite the omnipresent advertising for the Lotto—legalized government gambling—there is no free lunch. Giving up one's individual power for the hope of comfort and security has proven to lead only to tyranny.

It is a time for truth—about our past and present, about who really rules and about what's being done to this planet in the name of progress and profit. Love your country so much that you will look past the jingo-ism and sound bites to starkly view the fear-inspiring depravations and corruption within the national government and oligarchy. Such truth must be made available to everyone, not just to the manipulative elitists of the secret societies.

The time for secrecy is at an end.

Don't wait for the corporate controlled media to inform and explain. Read and listen to everything within reach and search for sources of alter-native information—on the Internet, in documentaries, in old library books and unconventional bookstores. Read and watch things you nor-mally wouldn't. Then quietly contemplate. Use that God-given supercom-puter called your "brain." Perhaps more important, feel what's right within your heart, your soul, your innermost being.

And remember there remains one last great secret. This one is within the hands of the general public. Namely, that there are more of us than there are of them. And we keep gaining knowledge daily.

This knowledge comes from individual initiative, not from govern-ment committees or the so-called "experts." If one truly desires to be free, there must first be a search for truth, without the aid of paid experts, academic snobs, media pundits, clerics, gurus, or government leaders—all of whom have their own agendas to press.

True innovators like Thomas Edison, Alexander Graham Bell, and

Bill Gates did not conform their thinking to conventional wisdom. Like these men, and many more like them, each individual makes his or her own destiny. We are creative beings and would like to create the best possible world for ourselves. But this is impossible when the creative process is based on incomplete or erroneous information designed to instill fear and dissension.

There are more people today who sincerely desire peace and brotherly love than ever before. Unfortunately, those who strive for power and control usually achieve it. And they want to keep it. But the time for brute force has past. Today, they can control the six billion members of the human community only through deceit and secrecy.

Once you have found your own heartfelt truth, that truth must be shared, so as to lift the curtain of secrecy which contributes to the ignorance, fear, and confusion of our time and create a new spirit of human tolerance and togetherness.

As recorded in John 8:32, "You will know the truth and the truth will make you free."

SOURCES

If there is no citation, the information may be found in conventional histories and encyclopedias.

INTRODUCTION: A QUESTION OF CONSPIRACY

6   "product of chaos": Hedrick P. Smith, "Brzezinski Says Critics are Irked by his Accuracy," *The New York Times*, (January 18, 1981), p. L3.

6   pushed by right-wing extremists: George Johnson, *Architects of Fear: Conspiracy Theories and Paranoia in American Politics* (Los Angeles: Jeremy P. Tarcher, Inc., 1983), pp. 21–22.

6   "Disney" version of history: Jonathan Vankin and John Whalen, *Fifty Greatest Conspiracies of All Time* (New York: Citadel Press, 1995), p. xii.

6   outside history pattern attacked or rejected: Anthony C. Sutton, *America's Secret Establishment: An Introduction to the Order of Skull & Bones* (Billings, MN: Liberty House Press, 1986), p. 1.

7   *Tragedy and Hope* suppressed: G. Edward Griffin, *The Creature from Jekyll Island* (Westlake Village, CA: American Media, 1994), p. 269.

7   French publisher quotes: Paul Manning, *Martin Bormann: Nazi In Exile* (Secaucus, NJ: Lyle Stuart Inc., 1981), p. 271.

8   Webb Hubbell, *Friends in High Places* (New York: William Morrow and Company, Inc., 1997), p. 282.

8   Dr. Steven Greer: The Art Bell Coast-to-Coast Radio Show, January 5–6, 1998.

8   conspiracy poll: "Conspiracy Theory Poll," *Nexus*, (October–November, 1998), pp. 7–8.

9   "power is a fact of life": Jonathan Vankin, *Conspiracies, Crimes and Cover-ups: Political Manipulation and Mind Control in America* (New York: Paragon House Publishers, 1992), p. 252.

9   no "coincidence or stupidity": Gary Allen, *None Dare Call It Conspiracy* (Seal Beach, CA: Concord Press, 1971), p. 8.

10 "pluralistic" view: Johnson, p. 12.
10 to rationalize fear and hatred: Ibid.
10 "strikingly similar world views": Johnson, p. 23.

RULE BY THE FEW

10 elites govern America: Thomas R. Dye and L. Harmon Zeigler, *The Irony of Democracy: An Uncommon Introduction to American Politics* (Belmont, CA: Duxbury Press, 1975), p. 1.
10 2 percent ownership: William Greider, *Secrets of the Temple: How the Federal Reserve Runs the Country* (New York: Simon & Schuster, 1987), p. 39.
11 Census Bureau statistics: Editors, "Inequality: Still on the Rise," *U.S. News & World Report* (July 6, 1996), p. 15.
11 "two-tier society": Mortimer B. Zuckerman, "Voting pocketbook issues," *U.S. News & World Report* (November 9, 1998), p. 84.
12 Walter Rathenau: A. Ralph Epperson, *The Unseen Hand: An Introduction to the Conspiratorial View of History* (Tucson, AZ: Publius Press, 1985), p. 8.
12 "fifty men": Richard J. Whalen, *The Founding Father* (New York: New American Library, 1964), p. 182.
12 "military-industrial complex": David Wallechinsky and Irving Wallace, editors, *The People's Almanac* (New York: Doubleday & Company, Inc., 1975), p. 464.

A VIEW FROM THE FEW

13 Benjamin Disraeli: Nesta H. Webster, *Secret Societies and Subversive Movements* (Palmdale, CA: Omni Publications, reprint of the original 1924 edition), p. iv.
13 power . . . so subtle: Woodrow Wilson, *The New Freedom* (New York: Doubleday, 1914), pp. 13–14.
13 Justice Frankfurter: James Perloff, *The Shadows of Power: The Council on Foreign Relations and the American Decline* (Appleton, WS: Western Islands, 1988), p. 3.
13 Roosevelt's letter to House: Elliot Roosevelt, ed., *F.D.R. His Personal Letters 1928–1945*, Vol. I (New York: Duell, Sloan & Pearce, 1950), pp. 371–73.
13 "a dozen organizations": Elliot Roosevelt, *The Conservators* (New York: Arbor House, 1983), p. 320.
13 Mayor John F. Hylan: "Hylan Takes Stand on National Issues," *The New York Times* (March 27, 1922), p. 3.
14 The Secret Team: L. Fletcher Prouty, Col, USAF, (Ret.), *The Secret Team: The CIA and Its Allies in Control of the United States and the World* (Englewood Cliffs, NJ: Prentice-Hall, Inc., 1973), pp. 2–3.
14 "This great machine": Ibid., p. 424.
14 USA not run by "democratic" government: R. Buckminster Fuller, *Critical Path* (New York: St. Martin's Press, 1981), p. 117.

14 Franklin D. Roosevelt: Epperson (1985), p. 7.

15 James Forrestal: Epperson (1985), p. 305.

15 Forrestal's statement on Korea: Cornell Simpson, *The Death of James Forrestal* (Los Angeles: Western Islands, 1966), p. 5.

16 "death warrant": Epperson (1985), p. 311.

16 danger has not diminished: David Wise and Thomas B. Ross, *The Invisible Government* (New York: Vintage Books, 1974), p. ix.

PART I: MODERN SECRET SOCIETIES

21 Clinton administration members: Membership roster of the Trilateral Commission (March 1, 1998); Robert Gaylon Ross, Sr., *Who's Who of the Elite* (San Marcos, TX: RIE, 1995), pp. 19–97.

21 Clinton hurried to CFR: John F. McManus, "Insiders Call the Shots," *The New American* (October 12, 1998), p. 44.

THE TRILATERAL COMMISSION

22 "a council . . . would be a good start": Zbigniew Brzezinski, "America and Europe," *Foreign Affairs* (October, 1970), p. 29.

22 "impact of technology": Zbigniew Brzezinski, *Between Two Ages: America's Role in The Technetronic Era*, (New York: Viking Press, 1970), p. 9.

23 "limitations on national sovereignty": Ibid., p. 296.

23 "more attainable": Ibid., p. 308.

23 "victory of reason over belief": Ibid., p. 72.

23 Bilderbergers at Knokke: Robert Eringer, *The Global Manipulators* (Bristol, England: Pentacle Books, 1980), p. 56.

23 founding members: Ibid.

24 "foster closer cooperation": *Trialogue: A Bulletin of North American, European, Japanese Affairs*, No. 16 (Winter, 1977–78), p. 12.

24 $120,000: Annual Report of Rockefeller Brothers Fund, Inc., 1977, p. 36.

24 "secrets" obtained from commission: Eringer, p. 60.

25 leaders needed: David Wallechinsky and Irving Wallace, editors, *The People's Almanac #3* (New York: Bantam Books, 1981), p. 93.

25 Huntington and FEMA: Epperson (1985), pp. 411–12.

25 Cooper, Sawhill, and Bergsten: Eringer, p. 61.

25 "Shadow Government": Ibid.

25 "tentacles have reached": Wallechinsky and Wallace (1981), p. 92.

26 "Trilateralists make no bones": Editors, "We've Been Asked, Trilateral Commission: How Influential?" *U.S. News & World Report* (May 22, 1978), pp. 74–75.

26 persistent maneuvering: Anthony C. Sutton and Patrick M. Wood, *Trilaterals Over Washington* (Scottsdale, AZ: The August Corp., 1979), p. 1.

26 unsettling thing: William Greider, "The Trilateralists are coming! The Trilateralists are coming!" *Dallas Times Herald* (February 3, 1977).

26 calculations meaningless: Sutton and Wood, pp. 2–3.

27 "most logical catalyst": Ibid, Preface.

28 world economic power: Barry M. Goldwater, *With No Apologies* (New York: William Morrow, 1979), p. 280.

28 "concerned citizens": David Rockefeller, "Foolish Attacks on False Issues," *Wall Street Journal* (April 30, 1980).

28 Brzezinski makes his own policy: Nicholas von Hoffman, "Who's running foreign policy, anyhow?" *Fort Worth Star-Telegram* (October 21, 1980).

28 "a worrisome conspiracy": Ibid.

29 Reagan accepts George Bush: Ronald Reagan's remarks to the Republican National Convention, *Congressional Quarterly Weekly Reports, July-September, 1980*, Vol. 38, No. 29 (July 19, 1980), p. 2062.

29 Reagan's transition team: Epperson (1985), p. 247.

30 Trilateral "task force": Sutton and Wood, p. 2.

30 controlled by "Secret Brotherhood": Texe Marrs, *Dark Majesty* (Austin, TX: Living Truth Publishers, 1992), p. 28.

30 Rockefeller's newest cabal: Goldwater, p. 280.

31 "Guess who's coming to the White House": Washington Post Wire, "Trilateralists get invited to White House," *Dallas Times Herald* (March 18, 1981).

COUNCIL ON FOREIGN RELATIONS

31 "the Inquiry": Perloff, p. 32.

32 Article II: Epperson (1985), p. 196.

32 Council in Soviet press: J. Anthony Lucas, "The Council on Foreign Relations—Is It a Club? Seminar? Presidium? 'Invisible Government'?" *The New York Times Magazine* (November 21, 1971), p. 123.

33 "New York liberal elite": Peter G. Peterson, "Letter from the Chairman," *Council on Foreign Relations 1997 Annual Report*, p. 6.

33 early CFR officers: Perloff, p. 38.

33 funding for CFR: Epperson (1985), p. 196–97.

34 Lucas on "globalist activism": Lucas, p. 125.

34 "mission statement": *Council on Foreign Relations 1997 Annual Report*, p. 5.

34 Admiral Chester Ward: Barry Goldwater, *With No Apologies* (New York: William Morrow and Company, 1979), p. 278.

35 "intricate channels": Lucas, p. 34.

35 "want world banking monopoly": Epperson (1985), p. 197.

35 "CFR . . . put to work": Phyllis Schlafly and Chester Ward, *Kissinger on the Couch* (New Rochelle, NY: Arlington House, 1975), p. 151.

35 *Foreign Affairs'* voice becomes policy: *The New Encyclopaedia Britannica*, Vol. 4, p. 877.

35 "it *is* the eastern Establishment": Alvin Moscow, *The Rockefeller Inheritance* (Garden City, New York: Doubleday & Company, Inc., 1977), p. 225.

36 John Kenneth Galbraith: Lucas, p. 129.

36 Morgan control moves to Rockefellers: Griffin, p. 302.

36 "historical records speaks . . . loudly": Perloff, p. 7.

36 "it is their property": Wallechinsky and Wallace (1981), p. 87.

37 CIA's principal constituency: Victor Marchetti and John D. Marks, *The CIA and the Cult of Intelligence* (New York: Dell Publishing Co., 1974), p. 267.

37 "put through a call to New York": Ibid.

37 Kissinger and Nelson: Moscow, 172–73.

37 $50,000 gift: Ibid., p. 371.

37 aid in writing book: Ibid., p. 226; Wallenchinsky and Wallace (1981), p. 87.

38 "CFR only has 3,200 members": Robert Anton Wilson, *Everything Is Under Control: Conspiracies, Cults and Cover-ups* (New York: Harper-Perennial, 1998), p. 129.

38 "not a dime's worth of difference": Allen, p. 123.

38 "break the insider control": Ibid., p. 130.

38 move toward "apocalyptic events": Perloff, p. 220.

BILDERBERGERS

39 Harold Wilson: David Icke, *. . . and the truth shall set you free* (Cambridge, England: Bridge of Love Publications, 1995), p. 369.

39 first American meeting: Neal Wilgus, *The Illuminoids* (New York: Pocket Books, 1978), p. 126.

39 Clinton at Bilderberg: "Clinton to Attend Meeting in Germany," *Arkansas Democrat Gazette* (June 4, 1991).

40 Hillary Clinton at Bilderberg: James P. Tucker Jr., "Bilderberg Tracked to Scotland," *The Spotlight* (May 18, 1998), p. 4.

40 Retinger and friends: Eringer, p. 16–22.

40 Donovan as "Anglophile": John Ranelagh, *The Agency: The Rise and Decline of the CIA* (New York: Simon & Schuster, 1987), p. 231.

40 "special consultant" Jackson as Bilderberger: Vankin and Whalen, p. 254

41 "unofficial CFR": Wilgus, p. 127.

41 MI6 creation: Dr. John Coleman, *Conspirators' Hierarchy: The Story of the Committee of 300* (Carson City, NV: America West Publishers, 1992), p. 207.

41 "evolving an international order": Ibid., p. 22.

41 "The Bilderberg agenda . . ." James P. Tucker Jr., "TC, Bilderberg Set to Meet," *The Spotlight*, (April 30, 1990), p. 7.

42 Common Market nurtured at Bilderberg: Eringer, p. 26.

42 Jack Sheinkman: Trisha Katson, "Some U.S. Bilderbergers Break Silence," *The Spotlight*, (June 24, 1996), p. 1.

42 "The Bildergerg Elite": Icke (1995), p. 167.

42 Prince Bernhard: Epperson (1985), p. 206.

42 Turnberry Hotel report: Jim McBeth, "Whole world in their hands," *The Scotsman* (May 15, 1998), reprinted in *The Spotlight* (June 1, 1998), p. 12.

43 William F. Buckley and Paul Gigot: Katson, p. 4.

43 C. Gordon Tether: Eringer, p. 33.

ROCKEFELLERS

44 rural Texas newspaper: "Rockefeller's Enormous Income," *The Wise County Messenger* (May 26, 1897).

45 "never trust anyone completely": Moscow, p. 64.

45 Rothschilds financed Rockefeller monopoly: "Central Banking and the Private Control of Money," revised and update excerpts from the book of the video *The Money Masters: How International Banker Gained Control of America, Nexus* (February-March, 1999), p. 12.

45 "competition is a sin": Epperson (1985), p. 73.

45 "moral criminality": Wallechinsky and Wallace, p. 211.

46 "this dangerous conspiracy": Moscow, p. 81.

46 interlocking directors: John M. Blair, *The Control of Oil* (New York: Pantheon Books, 1976), pp. 144–46.

46 Rockefeller family control: Ibid., p. 149.

47 "Rockefeller's revenge": Phillip J. Longman and Jack Egan, "Why Big Oil is getting a lot bigger," *U.S. News & World Report* (December 14, 1998), p. 26.

47 eugenics and sterilizations: Vankin and Whalen, p. 22.

47 Eugenics Records Office: Ibid., pp. 23–24; Icke (1995), p. 140.

48 Dr. Ernst Rudin: Tarpley and Chaitkin: p. 49.

48 Gen. William Draper: Ibid., p. 54–56.

49 "protect their racial superiority": Icke (1995), p. 141.

49 "no strings attached": Moscow, p. 95.

50 Nelson behind the scenes: Ibid., p. 171.

51 London School of Economics supporters: Epperson (1985), p. 195.

51 stand by British Empire: Moscow, p. 132.

51 waste as abhorrent: Ibid., p. 130.

51 Rockefeller and Dr. Bronk: Linda Moulton Howe, *Glimpses of Other Realities—Volume II: High Strangeness* (New Orleans, LA: Paper Chase Press, 1998), p. 408.

52 undisputed protégé: Ibid., p. 228.

52 "David's fascination . . . dovetailed": Ibid., p. 227.

53 Rockefeller met 27 heads of state: Gary Allen, *The Rockefeller File* (Seal Beach, CA: '76 Press, 1976), p. 28.

53 $461 million: *Rockefeller Brothers Fund Annual Report,* 1997, p. 20.

53 Korean unification: Ibid., p. 43.

54 "One World" strategy: Ibid., p. 5.

54 "unlikely partners": Ibid., p. 11.

54 HEW pioneered: Moscow, p. 93.

54 Rockefeller project expected to succeed: Ibid., p. 420.

MORGANS

55 "alliance with the House of Rothschild": Gabriel Kolko, *The Triumph of Conservatism* (New York: MacMillan and Co., 1963), p. 142.

55 Rothschilds operate anonymously: Eustace Mullins, *The Secrets of the Federal Reserve* (Staunton, VA: Bankers Research Institute, 1983), p. 53.

55 "who better than J. Pierpont Morgan": Griffin, p. 415.

55 "possibilities are obvious": Ibid., p. 419.
56 "Rothschild financial agent": Griffin, p. 209.
56 Morgan and rifle swindle: Litchfield, pp. 163–64.
56 "predominant source": *The New Encyclopaedia Britannica,* Vol. 8, p. 320.
57 "capital from British bankers": Ibid.
57 interlocking directorships: Ibid.
57 Morgan and Rockefeller created Fed: Griffin, p. 209.

ROTHSCHILDS

59 von Thurn and Taxis "prospered": Derek Wilson, *Rothschild: The Wealth and Power of a Dynasty* (New York: Charles Schribner's Sons, 1988), p. 11.
59 "Mayer set the pattern": *The New Encyclopaedia Britannica*, Vol. 10, p. 201.
59 Nathan manipulated the situation": Icke (1995), p. 42.
59 money provided liquidity and prestige: Wilson, p. 39.
59 importance of proximity to politicians and royalty: Niall Ferguson, *The House of Rothschild* (New York: Viking, 1998), p. 9.
61 "mutual-aid society": W. Cleon Skousen, *The Naked Capitalist* (Salt Lake City, UT: self published, 1970), p. 8.
62 "Morgan's apparent anti-Semitism": Griffin, p. 419.
62 Morgan and Rockefeller as "gofers": David Icke, *The Biggest Secret* (Scottsdale, AZ: Bridge of Love Publications, 1999), p. 219.
62 Warburgs lobby for Rothschilds: Ferguson, p. 285.
62 Jacob Henry Schiff: *Nexus* (February-March, 1999), p. 11.
63 Harrimans and Bushs: Sutton, pp. 21–22.
63 intermarriages: Howard M. Sachar, *A History of the Jews in America* (New York: Alfred A. Knopf, 1992), p. 92.
63 Pamela Churchill Harriman: Sally Bedell Smith, "Empire of the Sons," *Vanity Fair* (January, 1997), p. 113.
63 Nathan's 20,000 pound stake: *Nexus,* p. 11.
64 "remarkable coup": Wilson, p. 38.
64 Rothschilds took control of Bank of England: Icke (1999), p. 212.
64 "cool pragmatists": Griffin, P. 228.

SECRETS OF MONEY AND THE FEDERAL RESERVE SYSTEM

64 "the crucial anomaly": Grieder, p. 12.
65 Marco Polo and fiat money: Griffin, p. 156.
66 "Colonial Script": *Nexus* (February-March, 1999), p. 13.
67 rich and state unite: Griffin, p. 329.
67 "every path of force or folly": Martin A. Larson, *"The Essence of Jefferson"* (New York: Joseph J. Binns, Publisher, 1977), p. 192.
67 banks and standing armies: Ibid., 196.
67 bank unconstitutional: Ibid., p. 185–86.
68 "I continue to abhor . . . ": Wilson, p. 32.

68 Rothschilds and Bank of the United States: Griffin, p. 331.
68 "a curse to a republic": Epperson (1985), p. 134.
68 "powers in Europe": Ibid., p. 137.
68 Biddle, a Rothschild agent: Mullins, p. 5.
69 "premonitions of the fate": Ibid.
69 "furtive as any conspirator": Mullins, p. 8.
70 Morgan starts 1907 panic: Epperson (1985), p. 169.
70 panics due to London operations: Mullins, p. 5.
70 Woodrow Wilson's solution: Epperson (1985), p. 169.
70 "That solution was a central bank": Ibid.
70 "commission was a sham": Griffin, p. 437.
71 "union of all banks": Ibid., p. 440.
71 "Aldrich Plan is Wall St. plan": Mullins, p. 11.
71 "poetically accurate": Greider, p. 276.
72 guidance of Warburg: Griffin, p. 445.
72 function of the organization: Ibid.
72 Wilson in shadow of Wall Street: Ferdinand Lundberg, *America's Sixty Families* (New York: Vanguard Press, 1937), p. 114.
72 Bankers faith in House: Skousen, p. 21
72 William McAdoo: Ibid.
73 "psycho-political attack": Griffin, p. 469.
73 "attention is warranted": Kim Clark, "Demystifying Alan," *U.S. News & World Report* (May 17, 1999), p. 64.
73 "an exact science": Allen, p. 53.
73 "most gigantic money trust on earth": Mullins, p. 28.
74 a few families own bank stock: Mullins, p. 179.
74 1997 Eric Samuelson report: "Central Banking and the Private Control of Money," *Nexus* (December 1998-January, 1999), p. 12.
74 Federal Reserve note: Griffin, pp. 466–67.
75 Fed publication quote: Epperson (1985), p. 173.
75 "negative trade balance": *The New Encyclopaedia Britannica*, Vol. 29, p. 194.
75 Epperson's comment: Epperson (1985), p. 173.
76 "The . . . mechanism": Griffin, p. 207.
76 "too esoteric for ordinary citizens": Greider, p. 12.
76 Henry Ford, Sr.: Ibid., p. 55.
77 bankers don't want understanding: Goldwater, p. 281.
77 the Fed as religious institution: Greider, p. 53.
77 more money, more debt: Phillip J. Longman and Jack Egan, "Will the Bears eat Goldilocks?," *U.S. News & World Report* (January 11, 1999), p. 43.
78 gold standard abandoned: Greider, p. 228.
78 "familiar clichés": Ibid., p. 55.
78 massive debt: William Bramley, *The Gods of Eden* (San Jose, CA: Dahlin Family Press, 1990), p. 432.

EMPIRE BUILDING

79 "moved beyond the confines of Frankfurt": Griffin, p. 219.

79 "best business I have ever done": Frederic Morton, *The Rothschilds: A Family Portrait* (New York: Atheneum, 1962), p. 45.

80 bankers to crowned heads of Europe: Griffin, p. 219.

80 "remaining behind the scenes": Ibid.

80 Lionel de Rothschild: Wilson. P. 454.

80 gaps, omissions and no information predating 1915: Ferguson, p. xvii and 28.

81 "mysterious suicide": Smith, p. 96.

81 1996 death of Amshel Rothschild: *Facts on File,* Vol. 56, No. 2906 (August 15, 1996), p. 588; "Who Killed Amshel Rothschild?," *The Spotlight* (August 19, 1996), p. 6; 1997 *Britannica Book of the Year* (Chicago: Encyclopaedia Britiannica, Inc., 1997), p. 200.

81 $9 million in losses: Smith, p. 116.

81 hanging could not have been easy: Smith, p. 108.

82 "primogenitude": Ibid., p. 455.

82 "out of the loop": Ibid., p. 111.

82 "permit me to control": Epperson (1985), p. 140.

82 Edmund Rothschild and Japan: Albert J. Alletzhauser, *The House of Nomura: The Inside Story of the Legendary Japanese Financial Dynasty* (New York: Arcade Publishing, 1990), pp. 177–78.

82 Rothschild and Balfour: *The New Encyclopaedia Britannica,* Vol. 10, p. 202.

83 "father of modern Israel": Wilson, p. 71.

83 "Rothschilds financed John D. Rockefeller": William T. Still, *New World Order: The Ancient Plan of Secret Societies* (Lafayette, LA: Huntington House Publishers, 1990), p. 136.

THE ROYAL INSTITUTE FOR INTERNATIONAL AFFAIRS—ROUND TABLES

84 "perpetuate British power": Donald Gibson, *Battling Wall Street: The Kennedy Presidency* (New York: Sheridan Square Press, 1994), p. 82.

84 "special relationship": Icke (1995), pp. 150–51.

84 Curtis and Commonwealth: *The New Encyclopaedia Britannica* (Chicago: Encyclopaedia Britannica, Inc., 1991), Vol. 3, p. 805.

84 "secret society": Carroll Quigley, *The Anglo-American Establishment: From Rhodes to Cliveden* (New York: Book in Focus, 1981), p. ix.

RHODES AND RUSKIN

85 "struck at by madness": *The New Encyclopaedia Britannica,* Vol. 10, p. 248.

85 Ruskin, Blavatsky and Plato: Icke (1995), p. 233.

86 "my continual aim": Kenneth Clark, *Ruskin Today* (New York: Reinhart & Winston, 1964), p. 267.

86 "Rhodes copies lecture": Carroll Quigley, *Tragedy and Hope: A History of the World in Our Time* (New York: MacMillan, 1966), p. 130.

86 Rhodes as Freemason: Michael Baigent and Richard Leigh, *The Temple and the Lodge* (New York: Arcade Publishing, 1989), p. 265.

86 "financiers to Cecil Rhodes": Griffin, p. 219.

86 Edmond Rothschild's de Beers holdings: *Facts on File*, Vol. 57, No. 2970 (November 6, 1997), p. 824.

87 Rhodes as Rothschild agent: Dr. John Coleman, *Conspirators' Hierarchy: The Story of the Committee of 300* (Carson City, NV: America West Publishers, 1992), p. 150.

87 Boers dispossessed: Coleman, p. 151.

87 Frank Aydelotte quote: Gary Allen with Larry Abraham: p. 80.

87 "Round Tablers fanned out": Coleman, p. 153.

87 Round Table "maze": Ibid.

87 "international Anglophile network": Carroll Quigley, *The World Since 1939: A History* (New York: Collier Books, 1968), p. 290.

88 recovery of USA: Wallechinsky and Wallace (1975), p. 1331.

88 equal rights for white men: *The New Encyclopaedia Britannica*, Vol. 10, p. 27.

88 "substantial contributions": Quigley (1968), p. 291.

89 system to be greatly extended: Ibid., pp. 291–92.

89 chief aims commendable: Ibid., p. 294.

89 Institute for Advanced Study: Ibid., pp. 190 and 225.

89 "gracious and cultured gentlemen": Ibid., p. 294.

89 "centuries-old plan": Still, p. 191.

89 "Rhodes committed the same error": Bramley, p. 361.

SKULL AND BONES

90 "group within CFR": Sutton, pp. 3–4.

90 "man at the heart of the heart": Ron Rosenbaum, "The Last Secrets of Skull and Bones," *Esquire* (September, 1977) p. 85.

91 Russell in Germany: Sutton, p. 223.

91 Connection to Illuminati: Rosenbaum, p. 87–88.

91 "Illuminati in disguise": Ecke, p. 214.

91 "story of opium and Empire": Webster Griffin Tarpley and Anton Chaitkin, *George Bush: The Unauthorized Biography* (Washington, D.C.: Executive Intelligence Review, 1992), p. 119.

91 other clubs: Ibid., p. 121.

92 "gentiles and vandals": Sutton, p. 7.

92 "core group": Ibid., p. 8.

92 quest for genetic dominance: Ecke, p. 215.

92 intermarriage: Rosenbaum, p. 149.

92 John B. Madden: Tarpley and Chaitkin, p. 117.

93 Jack Blum: Jonathan Beaty and S. C. Gwynne, *The Outlaw Bank: A Wild Ride Into the Secret Heart of BCCI* (New York: Random House, 1993), p. 7.

93 wealth of Carnegie controlled: Sutton, p. 24.

94 "political recruiting agency": Tarpley and Chaitkin, p. 124.

94 "great and present danger": Texe Marrs, *Dark Majesty* (Austin, TX: Living Truth Publishers, 1992), p. 187.

94 "recruiting center": Rosenbaum, p. 88.

94 "headlong decline": Rosenbaum, p.150.

95 Lyndon LaRouche: Tarpley and Chaitkin, p. 341.

95 "Order set up or penetrated": Sutton, p. 25.

95 "dense network of relationships": Gibson, p. 131.

95 top six stockholders: Ibid., p. 132.

96 "a class reunion": quoted at www.geocities.com/. . . 1Hill/8425/BONES.HTM.

TAX-EXEMPT FOUNDATIONS AND ALPHABET AGENCIES

96 merge with Soviet Union: Epperson (1985), p. 209; Perloff, p. 205.

97 Aspen Institute an "engima": Paul Anderson, "The Aspen Institute: A 'private university' running the world from high in the Rockies?" *Aspen Times Weekly* (July 25–26, 1998), p. 13-A.

98 IPS, Raskin and Barnett: Coleman, pp. 235–36.

98 IPS goals served Soviet Union: S. Steven Powell, *Covert Cadre: Inside the Institute for Policy Studies* (Ottawa, IL: Green Hill Publishers, Inc., 1987), pp. 360–64.

98 McGeorge Bundy: Perloff, p. 129.

99 H. G. Wells: Per Fagereng, "H. G. Wells: I Told You So . . . ," *Portland Free Press* (November/December, 1996), p. 7.

100 NSC principals and power: John Prados, *Keepers of the Keys: A History of the National Security Council from Truman to Bush* (New York: William Morrow and Company, 1991), p. 31.

101 "torch has been passed from century to century": Still, p. 191.

101 Gore and Wall Street: Ianthe Jeanne Dugan, "Al Gore's Wooing Wall Street," *The Washington Post-National Weekly Edition* (January 18, 1999), p. 12.

101 Karl Marx for free trade: Editorial, *The Spotlight*, (December 13, 1999), p. 2.

IT'S NEWS TO US

102 "what to think about": Michael Parenti, *Inventing Reality: The Politics of the Mass Media* (New York: St. Martin"s Press, 1986), p. 23.

102 Pew Research Center poll and *Editor & Publisher*: John Leo, "Elephant in the living room," *U.S. News & World Report* (April 20, 1998), p. 18.

102 media's major role: Parenti, p. 10.

103 "uncritical transmission": Ibid., p. 51.

103 Britt Hume: Ibid., p. 52

103 twenty-three corporations: Martin A. Lee and Norman Solomon, *Unreliable Sources* (New York: Carol Publishing Group), pp. 70–71.

103 top ten media companies: Editors, *Standard & Poor's Industry Surveys—Publishing* (New York: McGraw-Hill, 1998), p. 6.

104 like railroad and oil trusts of 1890s: William Greider, *One World, Ready or Not* (New York: Simon & Schuster, 1997), p. 182.

104 Bertelsmann A.G.: *Standard & Poor's Industry Surveys—Publishing*, p. 5.

104 "policy-shaping groups": Lee and Solomon, p. 82.

104 CFR media members: *CFR/Trilateral Influence on the Carter/Reagan/Bush/Clinton Administration*, non-copyrighted material from the Fund to Restore an Educated Electorate, Kerrville, TX; obtained from *The United States Government Manual 1991/92*, Office of the Federal Register—National Archives and Records Administration; Standard & Poor's *Register of Corporations, Directors and Executives*, 1991; *Annual Report 1991/92*, Council on Foreign Relations, New York City.

105 Reed Irvine and AIM: Michael Collins Piper, "'Watchdog' Won't Bite," *The Spotlight* (May 7, 1990), p. 25.

106 Walter Cronkite, Daniel Schorr and Morley Safer: Bill Kirtz, "Disgust with the ranks," *Quill* (a publication of the Society of Professional Journalists) (May, 1998), p. 8.

107 top ten censored stories: Editors, "Unfit to Print," *Utne Reader* (July-August), 1996), p. 22.

107 "harshly disciplined": Greider (1997), p. 472.

107 Todd Putnam's NBC story: Michael Litchfield, *It's A Conspiracy* (Berkeley, CA: Earth Works Press, 1992), p. 13.

PART II: THE FINGERPRINTS OF CONSPIRACY

113 "artificial community of interest": Howard Zinn, *A People's History of the United States* (New York: Harper Colophon Books, 1980), p. 354.

REPORT FROM IRON MOUNTAIN

114 "clear and predictable danger": *Report from Iron Mountain on the Possibility and Desirability of Peace* (New York: The Dial Press, Inc., 1967), p. 4.

114 "the basic social system": Ibid., p. 29.

115 "principal organizing force" and "economic stabilizer": Ibid., pp. 33 and 38.

115 disestablishment catastrophic: Ibid., pp. 91–92.

115 not be allowed to disappear: Ibid., p. 88.

115 "elimination of national sovereignty": Ibid., p. 39.

115 necessary social classes: Ibid., p. 40.

115 control by Selective Service System, p. 42.

115 reintroduction of slavery: Ibid., p. 70.

116 war substitutes: Ibid., p. 84.

116 threat will have to be invented: Ibid., p. 67.

116 War/Peace Research Agency: Ibid., pp. 95–96.

117 "outrageous document": Ibid., p. xv.

PERSIAN GULF

118 "battle of the New World Order": Vankin and Whalen, p. 43.

119 Glaspie and Saddam's conversation: Russell S. Bowen, *The Immaculate Deception* (Carson City, NV: America West Publishers, 1991), pp. 145–46; Tarpley and Chaitkin, pp. 562–63; Vankin and Whalen, p. 45.

119 Glaspie's summer vacation: Tarpley and Chaitkin, p. 563.

119 Paul Adler: Warren Hough and Lawrence Wilmot, "Saddam: Bush-Whacked?" *The Spotlight* (April 8, 1991), p. 3.

120 Bobby Lee Cook: Warren Hough, "Iraq Policy No Accident," *The Spotlight* (October 5, 1992), p. 3.

120 Kinssinger Associates, Ibid.

120 Barr's impeachment: Mike Blair, "Gonzalez: Impeach Top Cop," *The Spotlight* (September 28, 1992), p. 1.

WHO PAYS THE TAB?

121 Bush administration repayments: Mike Blair, "You Pay for Bad Loans to Iraq," *The Spotlight* (April 27, 1992), p. 3.

121 loan guarantees enabled arms buildup: Bowen, pp. 150–51.

121 Bush quote: Tarpley and Chaitkin, p. 564.

122 $4 billion secret payoff: Warren Hough, "Did George Bush Get a Big Payoff?" *The Spotlight* (August 30, 1993), p. 22.

122 1990 Bahrain agreement for bases: Bowen, p. 171.

122 Harken stock sale: Ibid., 172.

123 doubtful the "real" reason will emerge: Vankin and Whaley, p. 50.

123 "weapons of mass destruction": Jay Higgnbotham, "Letters," *U.S. News & World Report* (January 18, 1999), p. 4.

123 Scott Ritter and Auster quote: Bruce B. Auster, "Inspecting the Inspectors," *U.S. News & World Report* (January 18, 1999), p. 30.

124 inspection account: Ibid.

VIETNAM

125 Ho Chi Minh as agent: Lloyd Shearer, "When Ho Chi Minh was an Intelligence Agent for the U.S.," *Parade* (March 18, 1973), p. 15; *The New Encyclopaedia Britannica*, Vol. 5, p. 954.

126 U.S. conspired against Geneva: Michael McClear, *The Ten Thousand Day War-Vietnam:1945–1975* (New York: Avon Books, 1981), p. 49.

126 Kennedy quote: McClear, pp. 43–44.

JFK OPPOSED GLOBALISTS

127 Galbraith comment on CFR: David Halberstam, *The Best and the Brightest* (New York: Random House, 1972), p. 60.

127 Kennedy on same old faces: Lukas, p. 126.

127 1951 CFR study group: Gibson, p. 82.

127 Dulles and SEATO: *The New Encyclopaedia Britannica*, Vol. 4, p. 265.

127 Sulzberger quote: Perloff, p. 121.

128 "rejection of Kennedy . . . became intense": Gibson, pp. 4–5.
128 "most knowledgeable president": Theodore Sorensen, *Kennedy* (New York: Bantam Books, 1965), p. 444.
128 JFK "reshaped laws and policies": Gibson, p. 24.
128 attack on economic program: Ibid., p. 14.
128 James J. Saxon: Jim Marrs, *Crossfire: The Plot That Killed Kennedy* (New York: Carroll & Graf, 1989), p. 275.
129 "Kennedy apparently reasoned": Ibid.
129 JFK's tax and investment policies: Gibson, p. 33.
129 "conflicts between Kennedy and elites": Ibid., p. 41.
130 JFK consistently rejects ground forces: Ibid. p. 49.
130 "green light" cable: H. R. McMaster, *Dereliction of Duty* (New York: HarperPerennial, 1997), p. 67.
130 Ambassador Nolting: Ibid., p. 68.
130 Senator Mike Mansfield: Marrs, p. 307.
131 Oswald's wife on Federal Reserve Bank: Wilson, p. 333.

ALL THE WAY WITH LBJ

131 December 2, 1963, memo: copy in author's files.
131 destroyer patrols resumed: H. R. McMaster, *Dereliction of Duty* (New York: HarperPerennial, 1997), p. 213.
132 Commander Wesley McDonald: Editors, "The 'Phantom Battle' That Led To War," *U.S. News & World Report* (July 23, 1984), p. 62.
132 "we are not going to take it lying down" and "Our boys": Ibid., p. 64.
132 Gruening and Morse: Ibid., p. 66.
132 McNamara and Bundy urge military force: McMaster, p. 213.
133 "seeds were sown": Editors, "The 'Phantom Battle' That Led To War," *U.S. News & World Report* (July 23, 1984), p. 56.
133 CFR Board of Directors: Gibson, p. 83.
133 Donovan as Morgan agent; CFR and intelligence "inbred": Ibid. p. 72.
133 Rostow failed security checks: Perloff, p. 127.
134 "an end to nationhood": Walt Rostow, *The United States in the World Arena* (New York: Harper & Brothers, 1960), p. 549.
134 McNamara created DIA: Stewart Alsop, "CIA: The battle for secret power," *The Saturday Evening Post* (July 27, 1963), p. 20.
134 McNamara and World Bank: Perloff, p. 128.
134 Bundy and OPLAN 34-A: McClear, pp. 94–95.
134 Bundy brothers control: Sutton, p. 52.
135 Advisory system built around Rusk: McClear, p. 95.
135 Acheson and Lovett recommended Rusk: McMaster, p. 3.
135 LBJ's "wise men": Walter Isaacson and Evan Thomas, *The Wise Men* (New York: Simon and Schuster, 1986), pp. 700–701.
135 Maxwell Taylor: Perloff, p. 133
135 Kissinger influenced Nixon: McMaster, p. 289.
136 Kissinger's "pretty high diplomacy": Ibid., p. 356.
136 Rep. John Rarick: Ibid., p. 134.
137 "we must be prepared to lose": James E. King, Jr., "Nuclear Plenty and Limited War," *Foreign Affairs* (January, 1957), p. 256.

TRADING WITH THE ENEMY

137 David Rockefeller's trip: Perloff, p. 123.

138 LBJ removes restrictions and North Vietnamese assistance: Ibid., p. 124.

138 Cyrus Eaton: Sutton (1985), p. 324.

138 Kama River factory: Perloff, p. 43.

138 George Pratt Shultz: Ibid., p. 169.

138 offered Rockefeller money: James Simon Kunen, *The Strawberry Statement: Notes of a College Revolutionary* (New York: Avon Books, 1970), pp. 130–31.

138 Kunen's quote: Ibid., p.2.

139 costs of the war: *The New Encyclopaedia Britannica*, Vol. 12, pp. 362–63.

139 "deliberate mismanagement": Perloff, p. 135.

KOREA

140 "trusteeship for Korea": A. J. Grajdanzev, "Korea in the Postwar World," *Foreign Affairs* (April, 1944), p. 482.

140 1944 CFR memo: Epperson (1985), p. 316.

141 "American negotiations and lend-lease shipments": Perloff, p. 89.

141 fourty-seven CFR members: Epperson (1985), p. 316.

141 "mandate to originate foreign policy": *The New Encyclopaedia Britannica*, Vol. 4, p. 265.

141 General Albert Wedemeyer and his report: Perloff, p. 89.

142 "a clear signal": Ibid., p. 90.

143 General Lin Piao: Ibid., p. 92.

143 Truman's orders: Ibid., p. 91.

144 Soviet generals and UN Undersecretary: Epperson(1985), pp. 319–120.

144 Griffin quote: G. Edward Griffin, *The Fearful Master* (Los Angeles: Western Islands, 1964), p. 177.

144 MacArthur quote: Ibid., p. 322.

144 "historic progress": Adlai Stevenson, "Korea in Perspective," *Foreign Affairs* (April, 1952), p. 360.

145 Dean Acheson: Perloff, pp. 92–93.

RISE OF THE NAZI CULT

145 Churchill wants no occultism revealed: Trevor Ravenscroft, *The Spear of Destiny* (York Beach, MA: Samuel Weiser, Inc., 1973), p. xiii.

145 Airey Neave: Michael Baigent, Richard Leigh and Henry Lincoln, *The Messianic Legacy* (New York: Dell Publishing, 1986), p. 161.

146 "they were a cult": Peter Levenda, *Unholy Alliance* (New York: Avon Books, 1995), pp. 133–34.

146 "more than religion": Joachim C. Fest, *Hitler* (New York: Harcourt Brace Jovanovich, Inc., 1974), p. 555.

146 Joly and Hugo as Rosicrucians: Michael Baigent, Richard Leigh and Henry Lincoln, *Holy Blood, Holy Grail* (New York: Dell Publishing, 1983), p. 192.

147 *Protocols* quotes: Ravenscroft, pp. 109–110, 113.

147 *Protocols* summaries: *Protocols of the Learned Elders of Zion,* translated from the Sergei Nilus edition of 1905 by Victor E. Marsden, former Russian correspondent for the London *Morning Post,* 1934, pp. 142–226.

151 "best criticism . . . is reality": Adolf Hitler, *Mein Kampf* (New York: Houghton Mifflin Company, 1940), p. 424.

151 *Protocols* as historic truth: Konrad Heiden, *Der Fuehrer* (Boston: Houghton Mifflin Company, 1944), pp. 11–13.

152 "Illuminati Protocols": Icke (1995), p. 57.

152 "Scion of the 33rd degree": Baigent, Leigh, and Lincoln, p. 193.

152 "radically altered text": Ibid., p. 194.

152 Eckart as "Christian mystic" and Indian lore: Levenda, pp. 69–70.

THEOSOPHISTS, THULISTS, AND OTHER CULTISTS

153 Blavatsky and Theosophical Society: *The New Encyclopaedia Britannica,* Vol. 11, pp. 696–97.

153 "a propagandist society": Webster, p. 309.

154 Germans as keepers of secret science: William Henry, *One Foot in Atlantis* (Anchorage, AK: Earthpulse Press, 1998), p. 45.

154 Nazi projects traced to theosophy: Levenda, p. 15.

154 "incestuous embrace": Ibid., p. 18.

154 "international network of secret connections": Heiden, p. 20.

155 Thule as Atlantis: Ravenscroft, pp. 160–61.

155 Eckart as Master-Adept: Ibid., p. 161.

155 Thule as "Society of Assassins": Ibid., pp. 169–70.

156 "knew nothing about workers: Editors, "The Twisted Dream," *The Third Reich* (New York: Time-Life Books, Inc., 1990), p. 148.

156 modern Thulists crude: Ravenscroft, p. 159.

156 Haushofer in Vril Society: Bramley, p. 409.

157 General Karl Haushofer: Levenda, pp. 87–88.

157 "We need a fellow at the head": William L. Shirer, *The Rise and Fall of the Third Reich* (New York: Simon and Schuster, 1960), p.39.

THE LEADER ARRIVES

158 Hitler and peyotl: Ravenscroft, P. 77.

158 Stein's meeting with Hitler: Ibid., pp. 60–65.

158 "spoke and spoke": Toland, p. 209.

158 "inner voice" and sleepwalker: Walter C. Langer, *The Mind of Adolf Hitler: The Secret Wartime Report* (New York, London: Basic Books Inc., 1972), pp. 42 and 31.

159 "List and Liebenfels": Levenda, p. 32.

159 Hitler and Lucifer: A. Ralph Epperson, *The New World Order* (Tucson, AZ: Publius Press, 1990), p. 132.

159 Hitler's poem: John Toland, *Adolf Hitler* (New York: Doubleday & Company, Inc., 1976), p. 64.

159 "supernatural vision": Toland, pp. xix-xx.

160 "mystical enlightenment": Levenda, p. 66.

160 Captain Karl Mayr: Toland, p. 83.

160 "orders from headquarters": Hitler, p. 291.

160 Hitler wants party of his own: Ibid., p. 296–97.

161 Eckart as "spiritual founder": Shirer, p. 38.

161 *Mein Kampf* dedicated to Eckart: Hitler, p. 993.

161 Eckart called the tune: James Herbert, *Spear* (New York: Signet Books, 1980), p. 126.

161 "Secret Doctrine": Ravenscroft, pp. 235–36; Levenda, pp. 13–15; Colin Wilson, *The Mammoth Book of the Supernatural* (New York: Carroll & Graf, Publishers, Inc., 1991), pp. 389–90.

161 seven races: Ravenscroft, p. 237.

162 loss of magical powers: Ibid., p. 241.

162 "protect the purity of their blood": Ibid., p. 242.

162 "Aryan tribes subjugate foreign peoples": Hitler, p. 400.

163 *Voelkischer Beobachter*: Shirer, p. 46.

163 twenty-five points: Louis L. Snyder, *Encyclopaedia of the Third Reich* (New York: McGraw-Hill Book Company, 1976), pp. 63–64.

HITLER'S SUPPORT GROUP

163 petition from business leaders: Toland, p. 277.

163 Dulles brother at Schroeders: Mullins, p. 75.

164 Schroeder bank as Germany's agent: Ibid., p. 77.

164 "no foolish economic experiments": Heiden, p. 643.

165 Ford as "one great man": Hitler, p. 930.

165 Ford's medal: James Pool, *Who Financed Hitler: The Secret Funding of Hitler's Rise to Power, 1919–1933* (New York: Pocket Books, 1997), p. 95.

165 Edwin Pipp quote: Ibid., p. 67.

165 Ford chartered ship: Ibid.

165 Hitler condemns Rothschild: Ferguson, p. 23.

165 Schacht and Bank of England: Toland, pp. 185–86.

166 interlocking directorships with I.G. Farben: Bramley, p. 415.

166 Farben's Schmitz on board of National City Bank: Manning, p. 159.

166 Schmitz's Standard oil stock: Charles Higham, *Trading with the Enemy: An Expose of the Nazi-American Money Plot—1933–1949* (New York: Delacorte Press, 1983), p. 292.

166 American I.G. Chemical Company as source of information: Manning, p. 57.

166 Joseph Kennedy in Hoover note: Higham, p. 181.

167 Montague Norman and Bank of England: Howard S. Katz, *The Warmongers* (New York: Books In Focus, Inc., 1979), pp. 78–79.

167 Sir Henri Deterding: Pool, p. 228–30.

167 Hitler as relative to Rothschild: Langer, p. 112.

167 William Patrick Hitler and Frankenberger confusion: Toland, pp. 245–47.

168 "enthusiasm for young girls": Ferguson, p. 186.
168 "riding my grandmother's chambermaids": Sally Bedell Smith, "Empire of the Sons," *Vanity Fair* (January, 1997), p. 102.
168 "explain the enormous support": Epperson (1985), p. 266.
169 "weather great misfortunes": *The New Encyclopaedia Britannica*, Vol. 10, p. 202.
169 Rothschild arranges Paris meeting: Wilson, p. 377.
169 Lord Victor Rothschild: Ibid., p. 386 and 423.
169 Robert Rothschild gassed: Ibid., Vol. 7, p. 15.
169 German bank support: Shirer, p. 144.
169 loans to BMW and Mercedes: Manning, p. 67.

HITLER'S FORTUNE TURNS

170 "dream by supernatural forces": Albert Speer, *Inside the Third Reich*, (New York: The Macmillan Company, 1970), p. 211.
170 Hess and horoscopes: Schellenberg, p. 194.
171 cult in-fighting: Levenda, pp. 90–91.
171 secretly solicited advice: Ibid., p. 84.

JAPAN AGAINST THE WALL

172 CFR in "cozy relationship": Lucas, p. 125.
173 ads calling for war: Perloff, p. 66.
173 "justification for world government": Ibid., pp. 65–66.
173 loans and "Flying Tigers": Litchfield, p. 12.
174 Roosevelt "prototypic Wall Steeeter": Ibid., p. 53.
174 "CFR-One World Money group": Curtis B. Dall, *FDR: My Exploited Father-in-Law* (Washington, D.C.: Action Associates, 1970), p. 185.
174 Admiral James O. Richardson: Wilson, p. 337.
174 Japanese war preparations known: Quigley, p. 81.
174 Marshall's message: Litchfield, p. 10.
175 Australian intelligence and Popov reports: Vankin and Whaley, p. 261.
175 Toland's names: Perloff, pp. 67–68.
175 Marshall and Knox in White House: Ibid.
175 Stimson's diary entry: Wilson, p. 338.
176 Germans intercept Roosevelt-Churchill conversation: Gregory Douglas, *Gestapo Chief: The 1948 Interrogation of Heinrich Muller* (San Jose, CA: R. James Bender Publishing, 1995), pp. 46–50.
176 warning came on parallel level: Douglas, p. 51.

WORLD WAR II

177 Jeannette Rankin: *Encyclopaedia Britannica*, Vol. 9, pp. 938–39.
177 courtmartial findings: Vankin and Whaley, p. 260.
177 forty-volume report: Perloff, p. 68.

BUSINESS AS USUAL

178 Walter Teagle and tetraethyl: Higham, pp. 34–35.

178 Schroeder, Rockefeller and Company: Ibid., p. 22.

179 Thurman Arnold: Ibid., p. 46.

179 gasoline to Germany via Spain: Ibid., p. 59.

179 "The Fraternity": Ibid., pp. xiv-xvi.

179 Roosevelt's amendment: Ibid., p. xxi.

180 Morgenthau's CFR father: Perloff, p. 58.

180 worldwide control system: Quigley (1966), p. 50.

180 Bank for International Settlements as money funnel: Higham, p. 2.

180 Gates McGarrah and Helms: Gibson, p. 71.

180 Switzerland: Manning, p. 119.

180 steel connections: Ibid., p. 25.

181 ITT deal: Higham, p. 99.

181 General Motors: Ibid., p. 162.

181 tank manufacturers: Epperson (1985), p. 273.

181 Nuremberg Trials bury truth: Higham, p. 210.

181 James Steward Martin quote: Ibid., p. 217.

182 *Allianz* insures *Auschwitz*: Editors with Jack Egan, "Insuring Nazi Death Camps," *U.S. News & World Report* (February 22, 1999), p. 52.

182 *Deutsche Bank* financed *Auschwitz*: John Marks, "Loans for Auschwitz," *U.S. News & World Report* (February 15, 1999), p. 41.

WORLD WAR I

183 "the Rothschild Formula": Griffin, p. 235.

183 "Black Hand": Still, p. 154.

183 Daniel Coit Gilman: Sutton, p. 27.

183 "altering the life": Epperson (1985), p. 257.

184 "we were in it . . . ": Allen, p. 62.

184 $100,000,000 loan: Epperson (1985), p. 258.

184 Morgan's billion dollar loans: *The New Encyclopaedia Britannica,* Vol. 8, p. 320.

184 Barruch's $200 million profit: Allen., p. 64.

184 war profits, mosquito nets and buckboards: Smedley D. Butler, *War is a Racket* (New York: Round Table Press, Inc., 1935), reprinted in *Portland Free Press* (November/December, 1996), pp. 31–32.

185 Page's telegram: Griffin, p. 239.

185 "agreement leaked out": George Sylvester Viereck, *The Strangest Friendship in History: Woodrow Wilson and Colonel House* (New York: Liveright Publishers, 1932), p. 108.

186 control of daily press: *Congressional Record,* Vol. 54 (February 9, 1917), p. 2947.

186 Rockefeller advertising: Griffin, p. 245.

186 Polls show opposition to war: Barbara W. Tuchman, *The Zimmermann Telegram* (New York: Dell Publishing Co., 1958), p. 170.

A STIMULUS FOR WAR

187 "The maneuver": Winston Churchill, *The World Crisis* (New York: Scribner's Sons, 1949), p. 300.

187 "embroiling Germany with other Great Powers": Ibid., p. 275.

187 "floating ammunition dump": Griffin, p. 261.

187 Wilson orders manifest hidden: Colin Simpson, *The Lusitania* (Boston: Little, Brown & Co., 1972), pp. 264–65.

187 attempted 1902 take over: Griffin, p. 246.

188 German warning notice: Ibid., actual ad from the *Des Moines Register* reproduced, p. 262.

188 Wilson's sleepless hours: Simpson, p. 97.

188 plot by Winston Churchill: Ibid., p. i.

189 American not convinced: Tuchman, p. 170.

190 "note was a forgery": Ibid., p. 167.

190 German agent newsman: Ibid., pp. 168–69.

191 Warburg marriages: Neal Wilgus, *The Illuminoids* (New York: Pocket Books, 1978), pp. 121–22.

THE RUSSIAN REVOLUTION

192 "greatest myth of contemporary history": Griffin, p. 263.

192 Trotsky and Wall Street: Still, p. 139.

192 Jacob Schiff's $20 million: Allen, p. 69.

192 Elihu Root's $20 million: Icke (1995), p. 78.

192 Arsene de Goulevitch: Allen, p. 72.

192 American International Corporation: Icke (1995), pp. 77–78.

193 rich back Bolshevik Revolution: Allen, p. 73.

193 Churchill on worldwide conspiracy: A. Ralph Epperson, *The New World Order* (Tucson, AZ: Publius Press, 1990), pp. 104–105.

194 Fichte and Hegel as Illuminati: Sutton, p. 34.

195 "key to understanding world history": Texe Marrs (1995), p. 114.

195 "stop the war with Germany": Griffin, p. 265.

195 Trotsky's release: Ibid., p. 266; Icke (1995), p. 76; Still, 140.

196 Lenin and "sealed train": Still, p. 140.

196 Max Warburg and German High Command: Allen, p. 68.

196 Russian Revolution "multidimensional": Icke (1995), p. 77.

196 "moves as another force wishes": Still, p. 142.

THE RISE OF COMMUNISM

197 Carbonari or charcoal-burners: Arkon Daraul, *A History of Secret Societies* (New York: Carol Publishing Group, 1995), pp. 100–101.

197 Bolsheviks traced to Charcoal-burners: Ibid., p. 110.

197 "Communism, just like Carbonism": Still, p. 129.

198 Marx in Hegelian Doctor Club: *The New Encyclopaedia Britannica*, Vol. 23, p. 573.

198 "bring the world to ruins": Still, p. 129.

198 Moses Hess and Robert Owen: *The New Encyclopaedia Britannica*, Vol. 23, p. 574.
199 Internationale is Illuminated Freemasonry: Still, p. 137.
200 Oswald Spengler: Epperson (1985), p. 145.

COMMENTARY

200 Maxwell Taylor quote: Editors, "Maxwell Taylor: 'Write Off A Billion,' *Executive Intelligence Review* (September 22, 1981), p. 56.

PART III: REBELLION AND REVOLUTION

205 Schoenberg becomes Belmont: Griffin, p. 414.
205 Belmont as Rothschild agent: *Encyclopaedia Britannica*, Vol. 2, p. 81.
205 Belmont rumored as illegitimate Rothschild and daily correspondence: Wilson, p. 179.
206 Alphonse Rothschild: Ibid., p. 181.
206 "difficult to understand": Ibid., p. 182.

WAR BETWEEN THE STATES

207 "International Banking Syndicate": Epperson (1985), p. 152.
207 Otto von Bismarck: Griffin, p. 374.
207 Nathan Rothschild official European banker: Wilson, p. 178.
207 Rothschilds financed cotton imports: Smith, p. 101.
208 European rulers well pleased: Bruce Catton, narrative; Richard M. Ketchum, ed., *The American Heritage Picture History of the Civil War* (New York: American Heritage Publishing Co., Inc., 1960), p. 249.
208 gap and destruction of Rothschild letters: Ferguson, p. 28.
208 Lincoln's comment on race: ed. R. W. Johannsen, *The Lincoln-Douglas Debates of 1858* (New York: Oxford University Press, 1965), pp. 162–63.
208 "my paramount object": Dye and Zeigler, p. 83.

SECRET SOCIETY AGITATION

209 "branch of the Illuminati": Griffin., p. 392.
209 bloodcurdling oath: Fletcher Pratt, *A Short History of the Civil War* (New York: Pocket Book, Inc., 1948), p. 218.
209 slave empire with monopolies: Editors, *The New Handbook of Texas*, Vol. 3 (Austin, TX: Texas State Historical Society, 1996), p. 1145.
210 "financial nucleus": Ibid. p. 37.
210 Bickley at University of London and correspondent: Ollinger Crenshaw, "The Knights of the Golden Circle," *The American Historical Review*, Vol. XLVII, No. 1 (October, 1941), pp. 24 and 43.
210 Bickley lectured in England: Ibid. p. 47.

210 end of slavery predicted: Ibid., p. 26.

210 "Texasizing" Mexicans: Ibid., pp. 30–31.

210 Washington the target: Ibid., p. 32.

210 invasions of Mexico and San Houston: *The New Handbook of Texas,* p. 1145.

210 South's military organization: Crenshaw, pp. 33–34.

211 "the fact is, we want a fight": Ibid., p. 38.

211 "disunion triumphed": William W. Freehling, *The Road to Disunion* (New York: Oxford University Press, 1990), p. viii.

211 Edmund Wright: Pratt, p. 219.

211 conspiracy cases weak: Donald Dale Jackson, *The Civil War—Twenty Million Yankees* (Alexandria, VA: Time-Life Books, 1985), p. 29.

211 "enemy behind us": Catton, p. 497.

211 "the loyal opposition": Larry Starkey, *Wilkes Booth Came to Washington* (New York: Random House, 1976), p. 23.

211 Knights' other names: Ibid.

212 income tax and Karl Marx: Epperson (1985), p. 155.

212 "Greenbacks": Catton, p. 395.

212 "government's greatest creative opportunity": Griffin, p. 384.

212 Booth and James as Knights: Pratt, p. 223; Epperson (1985), p. 154.

212 Judah Benjamin and Rothschilds: Epperson (1985), p. 160.

212 "sinister power behind the throne": Howard M. Sachar, *A History of the Jews in America* (New York: Alfred A. Knopf, 1992), p. 77.

213 "Confederate cabal in Canada": Starkey, p. 187.

213 Jefferson Davis: ed. Ronald Gibson, *Jefferson Davis and the Confederacy* (Dobbs Ferry, NY: Oceana Publications, Inc., 1977), p. 10.

213 what the Jacobins called it: Shelby Foote, *The Civil War, A Narrative-Fort Sumter to Perryville* (New York: Vintage Books, 1986), p. 539.

213 11,000 British troops and *Dixie*: Catton, p. 255.

PREEMPTIVE STRIKES

214 Lincoln quote: Foote, p. 538.

214 easy to forget Northern insurrection: Griffin, pp. 381–382.

215 Russian fleets in America: Catton, p. 253.

215 "the inhibiting effect": Griffin, p. 378.

215 "one of the strongest powers on the globe": Catton, p. 397.

216 Belmont influences European bankers: *Encyclopaedia Britannica,* Vol. 2, p. 81.

216 Belmont buys Southern bonds: Griffin, p. 383.

216 Chicago *Tribune* assails Belmont: Sachar, p. 78.

216 Salomon Rothschild is pro-South: Wilson, p. 185.

216 "even to blood-letting": D. P. Crook, *The North, the South, and the Powers* (New York: John Wiley & Sons, 1974), p. 198.

216 boot print of Rothschilds: Griffin, p. 395.

216 K.G.C. tract: Jackson, p. 28.

THE ANTI-MASONIC MOVEMENT

217 50,000 Masonis in 1826: Still, p. 107.

217 Captain William Morgan plans: *The New Encyclopaedia Britannica*, Vol. 1, p. 448.

218 Morgan quote: Epperson (1990), p. 162.

218 Henry L. Valance: Still, p. 107.

218 Reverend Charles G. Finney: Ibid.

218 Masons burned aprons: William J. Whaley, *Christianity and American Freemasonry* (Milwaukee, WI: Bruce Publishing Company, 1958), p. 9.

218 "Blood Oaths": Still, p. 102.

218 New York investigation: Ibid., p. 108.

219 news media "silent as the grave": Ibid.

219 Shay's Rebellion: Zinn, pp. 92–94.

219 "the tree of liberty": Ibid., p. 94.

220 "French Jacobin conspiracy": Ibid., p. 95.

220 John Quincy Adams and George Washington: Still, p. 94.

220 why did Hamilton and Washington bother: Bramley, p. 320.

THE FRENCH REVOLUTION

221 Freemasonry and Illuminati: *The New Encyclopaedia Britannica*, Vol. 26, p. 891.

222 Masons originated Revolution: Webster, p. 165n.

222 "key rebel leader": Bramley, p. 326.

222 Duke of Orleans buys grain: Still, p. 85; Epperson (1985), p. 87.

222 "invisible hand": Webster, p. 244.

222 Illuminized Freemasonry: Webster, p. 238.

222 Cagliostro: Still, p. 84; Webster, p.174.

JACOBINS AND JACOBITES

223 James establishes his own Masonry: Albert Gallatin Mackey, *The History of Freemasonry* (New York: Gramercy Books, 1996), p. 270.

223 Stuart—Freemason theory repugnant: Ibid., p. 267.

223 Charter creates chapters: Ibid., p. 281.

224 Jacobite character indisputable: Webster, p. 134.

224 first time politics introduced: Mackey, p. 285.

224 Revolutionary leaders in third degree: Webster, pp. 244–45.

224 Count Mirabeau: Ibid., pp. 241–42.

225 Brigands hired to storm Bastille: Ibid., p. 86.

225 first time grievances exploited: Still, p. 83.

225 Grand Orient Lodges: Webster, p. 244; Epperson (1985), p. 88.

226 "invaded by intriguers": Webster, p. 149.

226 Grand Orient formed and victory of revolutionary party: Ibid., pp. 149–50.

227 secret convention directed everything: Ibid., p. 245.

227 "the invisible hand": Epperson (1985), p. 88.

227 "shipwreck of civilization": Webster, p. 246.

SIR FRANCIS BACON AND THE NEW ATLANTIS

228 "founder of Freemasonry": Still, p. 47.

228 Bacon and Knights Templar: Icke (1995), p. 33.

228 gave birth to Freemasons: Mackey, p. 307.

228 "In Stuart England"; Laurence Gardner, *Bloodline of the Holy Grail* (Rockport, MA: Element Books, Inc., 1996), p. 322.

229 "indistinguishable from one another": Michael Baigent and Richard Leigh, *The Temple and the Lodge* (New York: Arcade Publishing, 1989), p. 145.

229 Sir Robert Moray: Ibid., p. 154.

229 famous believers: Wallechinsky and Wallace (1975), p. 87.

229 no evidence of Shakespeare: Ibid., p. 531.

229 Latin anagram: *The New Encyclopaedia Britannica,* Vol. 27, p. 266.

230 Bacon described utopia: Andre Nataf, *The Wordsworth Dictionary of the Occult* (Hertfordshire: Wordsworth Reference, 1994), p. 16.

230 Manly P. Hall: Still, p. 49.

230 America known before Christian era: Manly P. Hall, *America's Assignment with Destiny* (Los Angeles: The Philosophical Research Society, 1951), pp. 49–50.

230 "School of Atheism": *The New Encyclopaedia Britannica,* Vol. 9, p. 914.

231 Bradford and two rival systems: Still, p. 58.

231 Nathaniel Bacon as relative: Ibid., p. 50.

232 Col. LaVon P. Linn: Bramley, p. 305.

232 Freemasons on both sides: Baigent and Leigh, p. 216.

THE AMERICAN REVOLUTION

232 "Boston Tea Party": Arthur Edward Waite, *A New Encyclopaedia of Freemasonry* (New York: Wings Books, 1996), p. xxxiv.

232 only one non-Mason signed declaration: Hall (1951), p. 96.

232 mysterious stranger: Manly P. Hall, *The Secret Teachings of All Ages* (Los Angeles: The Philosophical Research Society, Inc., 1988), p. 200.

233 Franklin quote and comment: Epperson (1975), p. 129.

233 "deficit spending": Griffin, p. 162.

234 Loyal Nine: Zinn, p. 66.

234 "no divinity in it": ed. Moncure Daniel Conway, *Thomas Paine: Political Writings* (Franklin Mint Corp., Franklin Center, PA, 1978), p. 19.

234 "new social order": Bramley, p. 305.

234 only leaders aware of "plan": Still, pp. 61–62.

235 images related to alchemical tradition: Gardner, p. 347.

235 bald eagle substituted for phoenix: Bramley, p. 311.

THE ILLUMINATI

236 Seligmann Geisenheimer: Ferguson, p. 75.

236 Kolmer as Altotas: Webster, p. 200.

236 Casanova's involvement and quote: Waite, Vol. I, p. 101.

236 Persian calendar adopted: Ibid., p. 201.

236 Alumbrados: *The New Encyclopaedia Britannica,* Vol. 1, p. 303.

237 "enmity of the Jesuits": Webster, p. 197.

237 code name Spartacus: Ibid., p. 200.

237 "Eternal Flower Power": Sandra Glass, "The Conspiracy," *Teenset* (March, 1969), pp. 34–40.

237 "Man is not bad": Epperson (1975), p. 79.

237 "behold our secret": Ibid., p. 81.

238 strength in concealment: Still, p. 73.

238 real purpose remains impenetrable: Webster, p. 197.

238 honest and dishonest secret societies: Ibid., p. 198.

238 every member a ruler: Epperson (1975), p. 81.

238 Mirabeau memoirs: Webster, P. 205.

239 "the express purpose": Epperson (1975), p. 83.

239 "what it means to rule": Webster, p. 221.

239 "two immediately below me": Ibid., p. 223.

240 "extravagance of the scheme": Epperson (1975), p. 83.

240 adopted "Institution" degrees: Waite, Vol. I, p. 386.

240 Jefferson in defense of Weishaupt: Ibid., p. 84.

240 "Strict Observance Order": Webster, p. 233.

240 Baron von Knigge: Waite, Vol. I, pp, 433–34.

240 Knigge with authority from Weishaupt: Webster, p. 234.

241 Freemasons move to Frankfurt and admit Jews: Still, p. 82.

241 Rothschild members: Jacob Katz, *Jews and Freemasonry in Europe* (Boston: Harvard Press, 1970),

241 Strict Observance under a different name: Lynn Picknett and Clive Prince, *The Templar Revelation* (New York: Touchstone, 1997), p. 142.

241 "active and influential" Duke of Brunswick in Order: Baigent and Leigh, p. 218.

241 "every important personality": Waite, Vol. I, p. 11.

241 Strict Observance "transformed": Ibid., p. 173.

241 Count de Virieu: Still, p. 82.

241 "secret society within a secret society": Still, Ibid.

242 Weishaupt knew how to draw from each association: Webster, p. 231.

242 existence of name Illuminati irrelevant: Still, p. 81.

FREEMASONRY

243 Masonry in China: Waite, pp. 104–107.

243 knowledge of Greek geometers: Johnson, pp. 36–37.

243 G is for Geometry: Mackey, p. 41.

244 square and compass as Star of David: Christopher Knight and Robert Lomas, *The Hiram Key* (New York: Barnes & Noble Books, 1998), p. 240.

244 Abraham to Hermes to Euclid: Mackey, p. 70.

244 Freemason name from Lombardy: Ibid., p. 42.

245 *Collegium Fabrorum*: Mackey, p. x.

245 Godfrey de Bouillon as founder: Webster, p. 139.

245 "true, inner history": W. L. Wilmshurst, *The Meaning of Masonry* (New

York: Bell Publishing Company, 1980), a reprint of the fifth edition published in March, 1927, in London, p. 26.

245 organization that forgot original meaning: Picknett and Prince, p. 126.

245 "substituted secrets": Knight and Lomas, p. 4.

245 Freemasonry started at Rosslyn Chapel: Ibid., p. 313.

246 a combination of traditions with the Cabala: Webster, pp. 123–24.

246 "intimate union with Knights of St. John of Jerusalem": Ibid., p. 137.

246 connection to Diana and Isis: Picknett and Prince, p. 131.

247 "unknown superiors" and Templar list: Michael Baigent, Richard Leight and Henry Lincoln, *Holy Blood, Holy Grail* (New York: Dell Publishing Co., 1983), p. 149.

248 "interior, advanced knowledge": Wilmshurst., p. 64.

248 "a sacred secret": A. Ralph Epperson, *Masonry: Conspiracy Against Christianity* (Tucson, AZ: Publius Press, 1997), pp. 18–19.

248 Albert Pike quote: Epperson (1990), p. 33.

248 most Masons never pass first stage: Wilmshurst, p. 56.

248 Casanova's memoirs: Waite, Vol. I, p. 101.

248 "obligated by oath": Epperson (1990), p. 17.

249 pyramid structure manipulates majority: Icke (1995), pp. 199 and 201.

249 inaccuracies, anachronisms, and absurdities: Mackey, p. 16.

249 defection from orthodox religion: Wilmshurst, p. 15.

249 divest all past preconceptions: Ibid., p. 12.

249 "private study": Ibid., p. 5.

249 "guided by the 'gods'": Ibid., p. 173.

250 scientific assistance from 'gods': Ibid., pp. 174–75.

250 founded the Great Mysteries: Manly P. Hall, *What the Ancient Wisdom Expects of its Disciples* (Los Angeles, CA: Philosophical Research Society, 1982), p. 27.

250 reincarnation: Wilmshurst, p.195.

250 accusations have pursued order: Mackey, p. ix.

COUNT SAINT-GERMAIN AND OTHER MAGICIANS

251 Leopold-George, son of Francis II: Bramley, pp. 285–86.

251 son of a Jew or Wolf: Webster, pp. 172–73.

251 Arabian princess and reptile: Richard Cavendish, *The Black Arts* (New York: Perigee Books, 1967), p. 176.

252 Voltaire's quote: Andrew Tomas, *We Are Not the First* (New York: Bantam Books, 1973), p. 145.

252 Valet's confirmation: Cavendish, p. 176.

252 "studied in the pyramids": Ibid., p. 155.

252 "a major coup": Bramley, p. 295.

252 Saint-Germain initiates Cagliostro: *The New Encyclopaedia Britannica,* Vol. 10, p. 318.

252 Karl "head of all German Freemasons": Bramley, p. 284.

253 Karl praises Saint-Germain as philosopher: Tomas, p. 145.

253 "Egyptian masonry": Webster, p. 174.

253 Saint-Germain and William of Hesse: *The New Encyclopaedia Britannica,* Vol. 10, p. 318; Bramley, p. 293.
253 "a fascinating link": Bramley, p. 285.
253 Jean-Baptiste Willermoz: Nataf, p. 191; Waite, Vol. II, p. 91.
253 Saint-Germain at Wilhelmsbad: Tomas, p. 153.
254 "any reference to Falk": Webster, p. 188.
254 Gotthold Lessing: Ibid., p. 191.
254 Falk and the Duke of Orleans: Ibid., p. 194.
254 "applied for guidance": Ibid., p. 189.
254 "real initiates . . . carefully kept dark": Ibid., p. 190–91.

MASONIC PLOTS

255 famous Masons: Still, p. 115; Mackey, p. ix; Baigent and Leigh, pp. 264–66.
255 no political orientation or consistency: Baigent and Leigh, p. 265.
255 Lucifer's order over God's chaos: Epperson (1997), p. 150.
255 "they work to invent chaos": Texe Marrs, p. 101.
255 "mechanism in operation": Bramley, p. 259.
256 Raskob and Roosevelt plot: Vankin and Whalen, p. 237.
256 "worldwide fascist conspiracy": Vankin, p. 175.
256 Mino Pecorelli: Ibid., p. 176.
256 other P2 ties: Icke (1995), p. 205.
256 Richard Brenneke: Ibid., p. 206.
256 Gelli description: Vankin and Whalen, p. 115.
257 "a state-within-a-state": Vankin, p. 175.
257 Gelli friends with Bush: Icke (1995), p. 204.
257 Operation Gladio: Wilson, p. 200.
257 "Gnomes of Zurich": Ibid., p. 201.
257 Pan Am 103 and CIA: Vankin and Whalen, pp. 282–84.
258 Panamanian Company: Ibid.
258 testimony on Kissinger: Icke (1995), p. 206.
258 Moro's death tied to CIA: Vankin, p. 189.
258 Sindona using Vatican money: Richard Hammer, *The Vatican Connection* (Neew York: Charter Books, 1982), p. 265.
259 "reveal some very delicate information": *The New Encyclopaedia Britannica,* Vol. 10, p. 831.
259 Saint Ambrose: Wilson, p. 39.
259 Marcinkus prosecution blocked by White House: Wilson, p. 293.
259 "largest bank frauds": Vankin and Whalen, p. 116.
259 "something similar happening": Icke (1995), p. 205.

FREEMASONRY VS. CHRISTIANITY

260 perpetuation of mysteries and initiations: Epperson (1997), p. 88.
260 "when Christianity became state religion": Wilmshurst, pp. 211–12.
260 *In Eminenti: The New Encyclopaedia Britannica,* Vol. 3, p. 374.

260 purpose is to destroy Christianity: Epperson (1997), p. 350.
260 good side and bad side: Still, p. 27.
261 Freemasonry like algebra: Webster, p. 271.
261 "Divine Wisdom": Still, p. 27.
261 "a world-wide university": Hall (1988), p. 176.
261 "a doctrine of the universe": Wilmshurst, p. 74.
261 "positive energy": Ibid., p. 111.
261 "regeneration": Ibid., p. 42.
261 "aura": Ibid., p. 99.
261 "celestial beings": Ibid., p. 83.
261 inexpedient to say more: Ibid., pp. 133–34.
262 transition from Deist to Satanist: Still, p. 75.
262 Satanists vs. Luciferians: Ibid., p. 31.
262 secret is Luciferian doctrine: A. Ralph Epperson, *The New World Order* (Tucson, AZ: Publius Press, 1990), pp. 27 and 63.
262 "*Via Lucis*": Wilmshurst, pp. 209–10.
262 Lucis Trust and Lucifer Publishing: Constance Cumby, *The Hidden Dangers of the Rainbow* (Lafayette, LA: Huntington House, Inc., 1983), p. 193.
262 Lucifer explanation: Epperson (1990), p. 80.
262 Pike on Osiris and Typhon: Epperson (1997), pp. 274–75.
263 God has dual nature: Still, p. 31.
263 Adonai rival to Osiris: Epperson (1997), p. 110.
263 "worship of the Sun": Ibid., p. 113.
263 "the Sun God . . . created nothing": Ibid., p. 116.
264 "a repetitive geometric law prevails": Gardner, p. 247.
264 "the measure of the universe": Wilmshurst, p. 155.
264 "more than science": Picknett and Prince, p. 113.
264 "Hermetic element": Mackey, p. 329.

ROSICRUCIANS

265 Rosicrucian element in High Degrees: Ibid., p. 351.
265 Count Mirabeau's claim: Webster, p. 90.
265 Andrea connections to Duke of Brunswick: Mackey, p. 330.
266 "more . . . humanizing system": Ibid.
266 Order of the Gold and Rosy Cross: Picknett and Prince, p. 141.
266 da Vinci created Shroud of Turin: Ibid., pp. 24 and 33.
266 "Rosicrucianism was the Renaissance": Ibid., p. 135.
266 "spiritually aware environment": Gardner, p. 308.
267 "pernicious Protestant establishment": Ibid., p. 313.
267 Ashmole as Rosicrucian: Webster, p. 122.
267 J. M Ragon: Ibid.
267 "virtually one and the same": Picknett and Prince, p. 141.
267 Pharaoh Tuthmosis III: Gardner, p. 310.
267 "combination of ancient secret tradition": Webster, p. 89.

PART IV: ELDER SECRET SOCIETIES

KNIGHTS TEMPLAR

275 Payens as cousin to Count Champagne: Graham Hancock *The Sign and the Seal* (New York: Touchstone Books, 1993), p. 93.
275 all came from Champagne or Languedoc: Picknett and Prince, p. 100.
275 Payens and Champagne together in Holy Land: Hancock, p. 95.
276 "Great House": Trent C. Butler, ed., *Holman Bible Dictionary* (Nashville, TN: Holman Bible Publishers, 1991), p. 1325.
276 carbon copy of Sumerian temple: Knight and Lomas, p. 23.
277 Royal Engineers find Templar artifacts: Ibid., p. 267.
277 Templars acquired scrolls of knowledge: Knight and Lomas, pp. 267–69; Picknett and Prince, pp. 110–11; Gardner, pp. 257–58.
277 Templars did not find Ark: Hancock, p. 96.
277 insight into Church misinterpretation: Gardner, p. 265.
278 "Templars possessed purest 'Christian' documents": Knight and Lomas, p. 58.
279 "inner circle was different": Picknett and Prince, p. 106.
279 Payens and Montbard returned with Rule and wealth: Knight and Lomas, p. 31.
279 "most wealthy and powerful institution in Christendom": Baigent and Leigh, p. 43.
279 first preceptory on Saint-Clair Land: Ibid., p. 295.
280 "law unto themselves": Ibid., p. 46.
280 Count Fulk of Anjou: Zoe Oldenbourg, *The Crusades* (New York: Random House, 1966), pp. 264–65.
280 Assasins with Templars at Damascas: Daraul, p. 42.

ASSASSINS

281 "Assasseen": Daraul, p. 28.
281 Hasan's schoolmates: Ibid., p. 19.
281 Cairo Lodge perfected techniques: Webster, p. 38.
281 Abdullah ibn Maymun's plans: Webster, p. 38.
282 "wholesale assassination": Ibid., p. 46.
283 recruitment "Paradise": Daraul, pp. 21–22; Webster, pp. 46–47.
283 Thug sign similar to Assassins: Daraul, P. 37.
283 molding Templar dogmas and ceremonies: Mackey, p. 236.
283 S. Ameer Ali quote: Ibid., p. 38.
284 "bad as anyone else who did not accept Assassin doctrine": Daraul, p. 43.
284 Damascus attack: Oldenbourg, p. 262.
284 Templar arrangements with Assassins: Mackey, p. 238.

TEMPLAR BANKERS AND BUILDERS

285 "all the functions of a 20th century merchant bank": Baigent and Leigh, pp. 47–48.

286 sixty percent interest per year: Ibid.

286 Templars as tax collectors: Ibid., p. 49.

287 "Mother Goddess" site: Gardner, p. 264.

287 Bernard's daily conferences: Hancock, p. 102.

287 Templars pass knowledge to Bernard: Ibid.

287 Greek *goetik* as magical: Ibid., p. 263.

287 Templars formed stonemasons: Picknett and Prince, p. 110.

288 magical stained glass: Gardner, p. 264.

288 Bernard's definition of God: Hancock, p. 306.

288 Ark transported: Gardner, p. 263.

288 *Arcis foederis*: Picknett and Prince, p. 113.

289 "a strange combination": Gardner, p. 294.

289 uncertainty about consecrated status and description: Knight and Lomas, p. 305.

289 Rosslyn not a simple chapel: Ibid., p. 306.

290 Wolframs's *Templeis* or Templars: Hancock, p. 91.

290 *Munsalvaesche* connected to *Montsegur*: Gardner, p. 239.

291 Arabic manuscript housed by Anjou: Ibid., p. 240.

291 true church being suppressed by dark power: David Hatcher Childress, Introduction to Charles G. Addison's *The History of the Knights Templar* (Kempton, IL: Adventures Unlimited Press, 1997), p. 18.

CATHARS

292 prejudice against Jews: Michael Costen, *The Cathars and the Albigensian Crusade* (Manchester: Manchester University Press, 1997), p. 38.

292 "complex series of connections": Picknett and Prince, p. 185.

292 "most serious and widespread" heresy: Costen, p. 52.

293 Cathars as Buddhists: Arthur Guirdham, *The Cathars and Reincarnation* (Essex: The C. W. Daniel Company Ltd., 1970), p. 25.

293 "their way of life . . . no threat": Picknett and Prince, p. 89.

293 unusual opportunity to choose for themselves: Costen, pp. 200–201.

293 Jesus as spirit: Guirdham, p. 27.

293 Old Testament God as Satan: Costen, p. 63.

294 "this reincarnation business": Guirdham, p. 29.

294 "the overriding reason": Picknett and Prince, p. 90.

294 Cathars not heretics: Gardner, p. 269.

294 expertise in Cabala: Ibid., p. 270.

294 Saint Bernard's report: Ibid., p. 269.

295 quote from *Gospel of Philip:* James M. Robinson, general editor, *The Nag Hammadi Library* (New York: Harper & Row Publishers, 1981), pp. 138–39.

295 Sister Catherine: Picknett and Prince, p. 95.

295 Jesus' bloodline and the Merovingians: Baigent, Leigh, and Lincoln, p. 399.

296 James as Joseph of Arimathea: Gardner, p. 167.

296 "Never any secret . . . ": Laurence Gardner, "The Hidden History of Jesus and the Holy Grail," *Nexus* (February-March, 1998), p. 21.

297 movements with women judged heretical: Cullen Murphy, "The Bible According to Eve," *U.S. News & World Report* (August 10, 1998), p. 52.
297 Mary as *almah*: Gardner (1996), p. 119.
297 Jane Schaberg: Murphy, p. 50.
297 *Golden Legend*: Gardner (1996), p. 117.
297 Mary and children: Ibid., p. 115.
297 de Joinville quote: Ibid., p. 129.
297 "greatest of all threats": Ibid., p. 123.
298 Rennes le Chateau: Ibid., p. 117.
298 "the body of Our Lord": Baigent, Leigh, and Lincoln, p. 58.
298 Bogomilism beliefs: Costen, p. 58.
298 Yuri Stoyanov: Picknett and Prince, p. 94.

THE ALBIGENSIAN CRUSADE

299 "Peace of God": Costen, pp.23–24.
299 Order of the Temple ineffectual: Ibid., p. 101.
300 "motivated by religious zeal" and biggest army: Ibid., p. 121.
300 "inhabitants massacred": Ibid., p. 123.
301 "curious phenomenon": Picknett and Prince, p. 91.
301 Montsegur "mysteries": Ibid., p. 92.
301 no resistance: Costen, p. 160.
301 pecuniary treasure taken three months earlier: Baigent, Leigh, and Lincoln, p. 62.
302 Templars hungry for knowledge: Picknett and Prince, p. 220.
302 Templars' "warm rapport" with Cathars: Baigent, Leigh, and Lincoln, pp. 73–74.
302 Bertrand de Blanchefort: Ibid., p. 93.
302 "new weapon, the Inquisition": Costen, p. 179.
303 Inquisition created for Cathars: Picknett and Prince, p. 85.

THE TEMPLARS' DEMISE

303 King Henry III threatened: Baigent, Leigh, and Lincoln, p. 71.
303 King John in Knights' Temple: Baigent and Leigh, p. 45.
304 Cyprus bought from Richard the Lion Heart: Oldenbourg, p. 456.
304 Teutonic Knights' *Ordenstaat*: Baigent, Leigh, and Lincoln, p. 73.
304 King Philip turned down: Ibid., p. 74.
304 Philip engineered Pope's death: Ibid., p. 75.
304 Philip's agreement to support Clement: Mackey, p. 256.
305 plot to restore Merovingians: Addison, p. 15.
305 captured knights and paid witnesses: Gardner (1996), p. 271.
306 Templars betrayed by Church: Knight and Lomas, p. 282.
306 Jacques de Molay ordered books burned: Baigent, Leigh, and Lincoln, p. 75.
306 hidden in Paris Treasury vaults: Gardner, p. 271.
306 eighteen galleys transported treasure: Ibid., p. 272.

306 five years of legal wrangling: Baigent and Leigh, p. 65.
307 Knight engraving and Newport Tower: Knight and Lomas, p. 289.
307 Templar cross in Patagonia: Scott Corrales, "Bright Lights, Lost Cities" *Fate* (September, 1999), p. 23.
307 corn cobs and aloe: Knight and Lomas, p. 290.
307 "certain evidence": Ibid.
307 Waldseemueller: Ibid., p. 292.
308 "silly misunderstanding": Knight and Lomas, p. 290.
308 Knights of Christ: Baigent, Leigh, and Lincoln, p. 78.
309 fled across the sea: Baigent and Leigh, p. 64.
309 one route open: Ibid., p. 69–73.
310 "full-scale rout": Ibid., p. 36.
310 Templars commanded by Henry Saint-Clair: Gardner, p. 294.
310 "body of Templars" Mackey, p. 259.
310 Johannite sect and *Christos*: Picknett and Prince, p. 146.
311 Payens initiated into Johannite beliefs: Webster, p. 68.
311 Hiram Abif symbolizes Molay: Mackey, p. 265.
312 Molay's face on Shroud of Turin: Knight and Lomas, p. 286–87.
312 Hospitallers became Knights of Malta: Gardner, p. 261.
312 Catholic and Protestant wings: Icke (1999), p. 133.
312 "both were same force": Ibid., p. 157.
312 Knights of Malta between Vatican and CIA: Baigent, Leigh, and Lincoln (1986), p. 359.
313 five organizations claiming Templar origins: Baigent and Leigh, p. 41.
313 Templars and Hospitallers merged: Baigent and Leigh, p. 97.
314 business conducted in secrecy: Gardner, p. 305.
314 "last vestige of free thinking": Ibid., p. 265.
314 Order still flourishing: Ibid., p. 272.
314 Templars existed as Rosicrusians and Freemasons: Picknett and Prince, p. 221.

THE PRIORY OF SION

315 Sauniere's activities: Baigent, Leigh, and Lincoln, p. 32.
316 "defying even a computer": Ibid., p. 33.
316 Saint Sulpice as Priory front: Picknett and Prince, p. 186.
316 Sauniere and Emma Calve: Vankin and Whalen, p. 217.
316 "To Dagobert II King . . . ": Baigent, Leigh, and Lincoln, p. 34.
317 "builder of Solomon's temple": Ibid., p. 36.
317 authors suspect body being taken out: Ibid.
317 Latin words: Ibid.
317 "consecutive accounts": Ibid., p. 37.
317 "visibly shaken": Ibid., p. 38.
317 speculation over Sauniere's discovery: Picknett and Prince, p. 182.
318 Antonie Gelis: Ibid., p. 193.
318 Balncheforts as Cathars: Baigent, Leigh, and Lincoln, p. 73.
319 Templars remained free: Ibid., p. 94.
319 "curious feature" of dossiers, Picknett and Prince, p. 45.

319 Royalists with delusions: Ibid., p. 41.
319 names connected to Templars, Priory: Baigent, Leigh, and Lincoln, pp. 415–38.
319 Priory Grand Masters: Ibid., p. 131.
320 orchestrated critical events: Ibid., p. 107.
320 "avowed and declared objective": Ibid.
321 "meandering history of Europe": Vankin and Whalen, p. 221–22.
321 Jesus' story holds "many dangerous secrets": Vankin, p. 227.
321 protocols program for infiltrating and control: Baigent, Leigh, and Lincoln, p. 194.
322 Order charter with Hugh de Payens name: Ibid., p. 113.
322 Templars and Priory schism: Picknett and Prince, p. 40.
323 Priest wrote Gisors founded Rosy Cross: Baigent, Leigh, and Lincoln, p. 124.
323 *Ordre de Sion* charter at Orlean: Ibid., p. 119.
323 "studies and mutual aid to members": Ibid., p. 201.
323 not for financial gain: Ibid., p. 205.
323 press article regarding Pierre Plantard: Ibid., p. 214.
324 "Gray Eminence": Speer, p. 452.
324 return treasure to Israel: Baigent, Leigh, and Lincoln, p. 225.
324 dismiss the Priory as "lunatic fringe": Ibid., p. 226.
324 fragile at best, fictitious at worst: Picknett and Prince, p. 44.
324 Priory a "fraud": Robert Richardson, "The History of Sion Hoax," *Gnosis Magazine* (Spring, 1999), p. 54.
325 concocted story plagiarized from Order of Rose-Croix: Ibid., p. 53.
325 Monti's group "highly likely" as guise: Ibid.
325 Blanchfort not a Templar Grand Master: Ibid.
325 Blanchfort as Templar Grand Master: Childress, pp. 46–53; Baigent, Leigh, and Lincoln, p. 32.
325 "single-minded intent": Picknett and Prince, p. 44.

MEROVINGIANS

326 Francio descended from Noah: Gardner, p. 164.
326 Meroveus traced to Jesus: Ibid., pp. 166 and 140.
326 sea beast: Ibid., p. 166.
326 Merovingians as extraterrestrials: Baigent, Leigh, and Lincoln: p. 459, n8.
326 David Wood: Baigent, Leigh, and Lincoln (1986), p. 232.
326 lost tribe of Benjamin: Picknett and Prince, p. 49.
327 "seed of the royal house of David": Baigent, Leigh, and Lincoln, p. 393.
327 Guillem de Gellone as king of the Jews: Ibid., p. 395.
328 two official objects of worship: Gardner, p. 160.
328 Arian Christianity of neighbors: Baigent, Leigh, and Lincoln, p. 386.
328 "ultimate Christian religion": Ibid., p. 173.
329 Siegebert and Bouillon: Ibid., p. 224.
329 Jesus bloodline "not explicitly stated": Baigent, Leigh, and Lincoln, p. 387.
329 Bouillon's dynasty and "royal tradition": Ibid., pp.107 and 396.

330 church's ideal came to fruition: Gardner, p. 223.

330 church proclaimed Merovingians "irreligious": Ibid., p. 167.

330 Hitler dismantled plan for Merovingian throne: Henry, p. 193.

331 Marie Antoinette and Hapsburgs: Baigent, Leigh, and Lincoln, p. 404.

331 *Hieron du Val d'Or*: Ibid., p. 197–200.

332 "theocratic United States of Europe": Ibid., p. 410.

332 Grand Alpine Lodge: Ibid., p. 99.

332 journalist Mathieu Paolio: Ibid. and Wilson, p. 117.

A FAR-REACHING WEB

332 Henry Kissinger as member: Icke (1999), p. 149.

333 "these genealogies contain proof": Baigent, Leigh, and Lincoln (1986), p. 248.

333 "Rhedae" older name for Rennes-le-Chateau: Ibid., p. 295.

333 three names on *Mise* document connected to First National Bank of Chicago: Ibid., p. 285.

334 Chicago bank connected to Rockefellers: Gibson, p. 62n.

334 "active in London": Baigent, Leigh, and Lincoln (1986), p. 289.

334 prominent Europeans in Shaw's book: Jim Garrison, *On the Trail of the Assassins* (New York: Sheridan Square Press, 1988), p. 146.

335 reasons for resignation: Baigent, Leigh, and Lincoln (1986), pp. 303–304.

335 Priory became invisible: Ibid., p. 310.

336 "indisputable evidence": Ibid., pp. 313–14.

336 "shadowy underworld" and "murky sphere": Ibid., pp. 309–11.

336 "a holographic image": Ibid., p. 294.

336 Lincoln's disheartened comment: Vankin and Whalen, p. 223.

PART V: ANCIENT MYSTERIES

345 "one of the most important purposes": Patricia G. Eddy, *Who Tampered with the Bible* (Nashville, TN: Winston-Derek Publishers, Inc., 1993), p. 81.

346 descriptions of secret societies: Hall (1988), p. 22.

346 tampering not random: Ibid., p. x.

THE ROAD TO ROME

347 Paul's view won out: Ibid., p. 202.

347 Irenaeus, Bishop of Lyon: Gardner (1996), p. 154.

348 "diverse forms of Christianity": Elaine Pagels, *The Gnostic Gospels* (New York: Vintage Books, 1981), pp. 7–8.

348 the Roman Church: Eddy, pp. 219–20.

348 Simon the Magician: Nataf, p. 182.

348 Basilides the Egyptian: Hall (1988), p. 25.

349 Christianity "branch of Gnosticism": Nataf, p. 37.

349   "religious existentialism": Ibid., p. 35.
349   "doctrine of antiquity": Hall (1988), p. 76.
349   New Testament as example: Ibid.
349   "Lost Keys" of Freemasonry: Laurence Gardner, *Genesis of the Grail Kings* (London: Bantam Press, 1999), pp. 128–29.
350   "Gnosticism profoundly influenced men's minds": Daraul, p. 84.
350   monastery called "the Wilderness": Gardner (1996), p. 63.
350   Georgi Ivanovich Gurdjieff: Nataf, p. 141.
350   Pythagoras's "New World Order": Gardner (1996), p. 63.
351   Great White Brotherhood: Gardner (1999), p. 127.
351   Mary and Joseph as Essenes: Hall (1988), p. 179.
351   Nazarene as Essene term: Gardner (1996), pp. 36–37.
351   Jesus in Melchizedek's temple: Hall (1988), p. 178.
351   "Michael-Zadok": Gardner (1996), p. 38.
351   progenitors of Freemasonry: Hall (1988), p. 178.
352   Essene use of codes and allegory: Gardner (1996), p. 27.
352   *leper, blind* and the *Way*: Ibid., p. 28.
352   NSA code breaker shocked by Bible code: Michael Drosnin, *The Bible Code* (New York: Simon & Schuster, 1997), p. 23.
352   "a book unlike any other": C. L. Turnage, *New Evidence the Holy Bible Is an Extraterrestrial Transmission* (Santa Barbara, CA: Timeless Voyager Press, 1998), p. 104.
353   references to gods, or Elohim: Ibid., p. 105.
353   fate of the Dead Sea Scrolls: Eddy, pp. 222–23.
354   Constantine's "strategic buy-out": Gardner (1996), pp. 157–58.
354   "crucial alterations": Baigent, Leigh, and Lincoln, p. 368.
355   Essenes not Christians: Webster, p. 27.
355   "their faith was closer to original teachings": Gardner (1996), p. 161.

THE CABALA

355   "mysteries of wisdom": Webster, p. 8.
356   Cabala as form of Gnosticism: Nataf, pp. 20–21.
356   Moses' oral tradition: Webster, p. 6.
356   "a tremendous secret": Nataf, p. 152; Webster, pp. 10–11.
356   Ab-ram who possesses *Ram*: Gardner (1999), p. 100.
356   Table of Destiny tied to Emerald Table of Thoth/Hermes: Ibid., pp. 219–20.
357   borrowed philosophies: Webster, p. 11.
357   Moses de Leon: Ibid., p. 9.
357   "a point in history": Icke (1999), p. 82.
358   Masonic system due to Mysteries: Wilmshurst, p. 212.
358   Pico della Mirandola: Picknett and Prince, p. 135.
358   Mendelssohn as Cabalist: Webster, pp. 228–29.
358   Moses Mendelssohn as Rothshild partner: Ferguson, pp. 113 and 285.
358   Follower of Moses Mendelssohn: Ferguson, p. 75.
358   John Byrom: Picknett and Prince, pp. 139–40.
359   Global population figures: Tomas, p. 163.

359 "birthright of knowledge founded Mystery Schools": Hall (1982), pp. 25–28.

ANCIENT SECRETS AND MYSTERIES

360 Neanderthals and Cro-Magnons together: James Shreeve, "The Neanderthal Peace," *Discover* (September, 1995), p. 77.

360 "incompatible, separate species": Ibid., p. 79.

361 unusual Chinese seals in Ireland: Simon Welfare and John Fairley, *Arthur C. Clarke's Mysterious World* (New York: A&W Visual Library, 1980), pp. 43–44.

361 crystal skulls: Ibid., pp. 51–55.

361 giant round stones: Ibid., pp.55–58.

361 "vitrified" stone forts: Ibid., pp. 58–60.

361 "Antikythera Mechanism": Marrs (1997), pp. 61–62.

361 Baghdad battery: Ibid., pp. 63–64.

362 gigantic Maltese Cross: Maurice Chatelain, *Our Ancestors Came from Outer Space* (Garden City, NY: Doubleday & Company, Inc., 1978), pp. 71–74.

362 identical weight coins: Ibid., p. 130.

362 Chinese characters in Central America: Charles Fenyvesi, "A Tale of Two Cultures," *U.S. News & World Report* (November 4, 1996), pp. 46–48.

362 helicopter and jets in Seti's Temple: Terry O'Neill, "Helicopter Hoax?" *Fate* (June, 1999), pp. 27–29.

362 Babylonian cuneiform: Tomas, p. 65.

362 Piri Reis maps: Marrs (1997), pp. 68–69.

363 "our distant past is a vacuum": Ibid., pp. 8–9.

364 Sphinx predates Ice Age: John Anthony West, *Serpent in the Sky* (Wheston, IL: Quest Books, 1993), p. 229.

364 "Hall of Records": Edgar Evans Cayce, Gail Cayce Schwartzer, and Douglas Richards, *Mysteries of Atlantis Revisited* (New York: St. Martin's Press, 1997), p. 129.

364 Earlier jewelry better: Tomas, p. 17.

365 Bible commandments: Exodus 20:1–17.

365 Egyptian "Protestation of Innocence": *The Book of the Dead: Papyri of Ani, Hunefer, Anhai* (Geneva: Productions Liber SA, 1979), pp. 91–93.

365 Monte Verde, Chile: Sharon Begley and Andrew Murr, "The First Americans," *Newsweek* (April 26, 1999), p. 56.

365 "different ethnic groups": Ibid., p. 52.

366 "a shadowy prehistory": Alan F. Alford, *Gods of the New Millennium: Scientific Proof of Flesh & Blood Gods* (Walsall, England: Eridu Books, 1996), p. I.

WAS THERE MORE TO MOSES?

367 Sigmund Freud and Moses: Don Ecker, "One God Or One Overseer?" *UFO Magazine* (June, 1999), pp. 56–58.

367 Manetho the adviser: Gardner (1999), p. 185.

368 Aten as *Adon* and *Amen*: Ibid., p. 216.
368 Akhenaten floated downstream: Gardner (1996), p. 12.
368 Sargon the Great: Gardner (1999), p. 186.
369 "marshy territory": Gardner (1996), p. 13.
369 "contemporary Moses": Henry, p. 81.
369 Miriam: Gardner (1999), p. 208.
370 "the Words of the God": Knight and Lomas, p. 157.
370 El-Shaddai or El for God: Butler: pp. 404 and 416.
371 "individual absolute": Gardner (1999), p. 108.
371 Bond between man and nature destroyed: Henri Frankfort, *Kingship and the Gods* (Chicago: University of Chicago Press, 1948), p. 343.
371 Moses establishes branch: Gardner (1996), p. 267.
372 Jehovah as reptile being: Joe Lewels, *The God Hypothesis* (Mill Spring, NC: Wild Flower Press, 1997), p. 242.
372 "not of mammal origin": R. A. Boulay, *Flying Serpents and Dragons: The Story of Mankind's Reptilian Past* (Escondido, CA: The Book Tree, 1997), p. 55.
372 "circumcision as form of branding": Lewels, p. 243.
374 "very powerful dynasty": Gardner (1999), p. 16.

ALL ROADS LEAD TO SUMER

374 Events occurred during Hammurabi's rule: Alford, p. 358.
375 Hammurabi Code drawn from Sumerians: Zecharia Sitchin, *The 12th Planet* (New York: Avon Books, 1976), pp. 42–43.
375 Sumerian "firsts": Ibid., pp. 120–21.
376 Queen Shub-ad's description: Tomas, p. 17.
377 Geometry and time system: Alford, p. 124.
377 "uncomfortable question": Ibid.
377 "answers are relative": *The New Encyclopaedia Britannica,* Vol. 21, p. 907.
378 Tales branded as myths: Sitchin (1976), p. viii.
378 "now that astronauts have landed on the Moon": Ibid.

THE ANUNNAKI

379 Nefilim as ancient heroes: Butler, p. 1017.
380 Sumerians ahead of modern man in astronomy: Hugh McCann, "10th Planet? Pluto's Orbit Says 'Yes,'" *Detroit News* (January 16, 1981), p. 1.
380 take epic at face value: Sitchin (1976), p. 211.
382 Nefilim named Nazi: Zechariah Sitchin, *The Wars of Gods and Men* (New York: Avon Books, 1985), p. 155.
382 Enki's approach to Earth: Sitchin (1976), p. 291.
382 gold to repair upper atmosphere: Lloyd Pye, *Everything You Know Is Wrong* (Madeira Beach, FL: Adamu Press, 1997), pp. 231–32.
383 Comparison of names: Ignatius Donnelly, *Atlantis: The Antediluvian World* (New York: Gramercy Publishing Co., 1949), p. 138.

383 ancient South African mines: Zecharia Sitchin, *Genesis Revisited* (New York: Avon Books, 1990), p. 22.
383 "purified precious": Sitchin (1976), p. 319.
384 "distress was much": Ibid., p. 331.
384 "Assembly of the Great Anunnaki": Dr. Arthur David Horn, *Humanity's Extraterrestrial Origins* (Mount Shasta, CA: A & L Horn, 1994), p. 62.
384 Genesis based on earlier texts from Sumer: Sitchen (1990), p. 159.
385 Mutants created: Ibid., pp. 164–65.
385 Statues bought by Rockefeller: Henry, p. 21.
385 "drank water from the ditch . . . ": Sitchin (1976), p. 107.
386 Kramer's comment on TI: Horn, p. 64.
386 "Adam was the first test-tube baby": Sitchin (1990), p. 162.
387 "non-Darwinian" principles required: Michael A. Cremo and Richard L. Thompson, *Forbidden Archeology* (Los Angeles: Bhaktivedanta Book Publishing, 1998), pp. 711 and 722.
387 Thomas E. Lee: Ibid., p. xxix.
387 "knowledge filter": Ibid., pp. xxx and xxxi.
387 scientific institutions set up by elite: Personal correspondence from Jonathan Starbright, 1999.
387 not "worship" but "work": Sitchin (1976), p. 337.
387 Anunnaki treated slaves poorly: Horn, p. 65.
388 Enki retaliates against Enlil: Ibid., pp. 288–89.
389 *Epic of Gilgamesh* quote: Alford, p. 277.
389 "Star Fire": Gardner (1999), pp. 126 and 129.
390 Jews lost knowledge: Alford, p. 297.

FLOODS AND WARS

390 Utnapishtim and father in Shuruppak: Ibid., p. 306.
391 "biblical account is an edited version": Sitchin (1976), p. 380.
391 "the seed of all living things": Ibid., p. 381.
391 three races saved: Alford, p. 305.
392 "crowded like flies": Sitchen (1976), p. 384.
392 Kent Flannery: Horn, p. 101.
393 agriculture began in highlands: Ibid., p. 102.
393 Enlil institutes mountain farming: Zecharia Sitchin, *The Wars of Gods and Men* (New York: Avon Books, 1985), p. 121.
393 no explanation for botanogenetic miracle and three phases: Sitchen (1976), pp. 414–15.
393 Earth divided into four regions: Horn, p. 119; Alford, pp. 229–30; Sitchin (1976), p. 415.
394 Kish as Cush: Sitchen (1976), p. 20.
394 "the Trilithon": Alford, p. 52.
394 "rockets of the gods": Ibid., p. 175.
394 Arabic text found at Baalbek: Ibid., p. 53.
394 Shem as something that flies: Turnage, p. 12.
394 not "name" but "sky vehicle": Sitchin (1976), p. 148.
395 different racial groups: Alford, pp. 303–6.

396 Anunnaki built two great pyramids of Giza: Sitchin (1985), p. 135.
396 Great Pyramid as space beacon: Chatelain, pp. 60–61.
396 Mount Sinai as "shining": Butler, ed., p. 991.
396 enormity of name change: Henry, p. 113.
397 Marduk's Egyptian progeny: Sitchin (1985), p. 39.
398 Marduk held in Great Pyramid: Ibid., p. 222.
398 rescue of Marduk: Ibid., 226–28.
398 "worshipped a sole female deity": Alford, p. 135.
399 Inanna and Enlil with Sargon: Sitchin (1985), p. 249.
399 Abraham as personage of high standing: Ibid., p. 292.
400 Yahweh as Iskur or Adad: Alford, p. 362.
400 Ark as radio transmitter: Ibid., p. 363.
400 Tablets activated ark: Bouley, p. 292.
401 "vapor" not "salt": Sitchen (1985), pp. 313–14n.
401 son of Marduk launched nukes: Ibid., p. 324.
401 settlements abandoned and radioactivity: Ibid., p. 315.
401 blackened stones: Alford, p. 227.
402 Kramer's translated "Lamentations": Ibid., pp. 220–21.
402 "stacked up in heaps": Sitchin (1985), p. 340.
402 "what actually transpired": Gardner, p. 60.

COMMENTARY

403 "as close as we'll come to the truth": Horn, p. 104.
404 "admire the ancient scribes": Sitchin (1990), p. 171.
404 "Righteous Ones of the Rocketships": Sitchin (1985), pp. 76–77.
405 altered primitive genetically: Erich von Daniken, *The Return of the Gods* (Boston: Element Books, 1998), p. 40.
406 "slave race languishing on an isolated planet": Bramley, p. 37.
406 "race of interbreeding bloodlines": Icke (1999), p. 1.
406 Man conditioned to deny truth of ancestry: Boulay, p. 337.
406 "I think we're property": Charles Fort, *The Books of Charles Fort* (New York: Henry Holt, 1941), p. 163.
406 a few world leaders permitted to approach them: Alford, p. 407.
407 eternal conflict between powers of darkness and light: Webster, pp. 405–6.
407 "two great religious truths": Mackey, p. 181.
407 "science, as it is always called": Mackey, p. 33.
407 knowledge to cross the line: Hall (1982), p. 37.
407 "Serpent Kings": Ibid., p. 29.

INDEX

BOOKS BY JIM MARRS

THE TRILLION-DOLLAR CONSPIRACY

How the New World Order, Man-Made Diseases, and Zombie Banks Are Destroying America

ISBN 978-0-06-197069-6 (paperback)

Bestselling author Jim Marrs offers a terrifying proposition: the current economic collapse has been engineered by a tyrannous New World Order led by the Obama administration and multinational corporations.

RULE BY SECRECY

The Hidden History That Connects the Trilateral Commission, the Freemasons, and the Great Pyramids

ISBN 978-0-06-093184-1 (paperback)

Jim Marrs reveals the secrets that connect Egypt's Great Pyramids, the Freemasons, and the Council on Foreign Relations in this astonishing book.

THE RISE OF THE FOURTH REICH

The Secret Societies That Threaten to Take Over America

ISBN 978-0-06-124559-6 (paperback)

Jim Marrs gives startling new evidence that the Nazis have been secretly planning a return to power—in the United States.

ALIEN AGENDA

Investigating the Extraterrestrial Presence Among Us

ISBN 978-0-06-095536-6 (paperback)

Jim Marrs presents an impressive array of facts to confirm the reality of UFOs, as well as the depth of the government campaign to keep America in the dark.